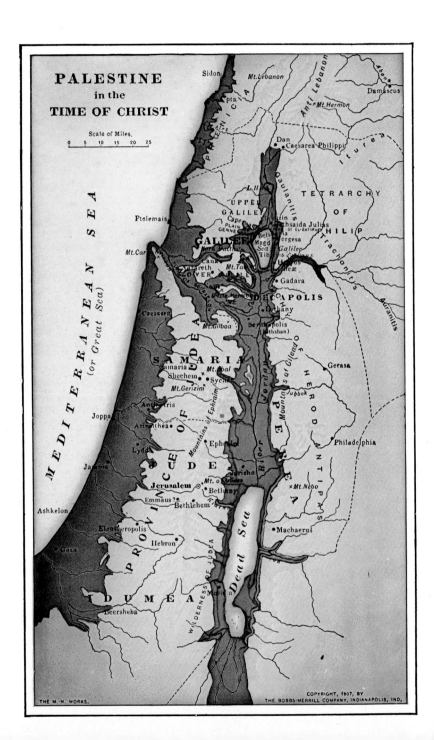

PALESTINE
in the
TIME OF CHRIST

Scale of Miles.
0   5   10   15   20   25

MEDITERRANEAN SEA
(or Great Sea)

Sidon

Mt. Lebanon

Abana

Damascus

Mt. Hermon

Anti Lebanon

PHŒNICIA

Dan

Caesarea Philippi

Iturea

L. II

TETRARCHY

UPPER
GALILEE

OF

Ptolemais

Cana

PHILIP

Gaulanitis

Chorazin

Bethsaida Julias

PLAIN OF EL-BATIHAH

PLAIN OF
GENNESARET

Bethsaida

Gergesa

Trachonitis

GALILEE

Magdala

Sea

Galilee

Capernaum

of

Mt. Carmel

Cana

Nazareth

LOWER GALILEE

Tiberias

Hippos

Auranitis

Mt. Tabor

Endor

Caesarea

Little Hermon

DECAPOLIS

Gadara

Dibany

Mt. Gilboa

Scythopolis
(Bethshan)

Gerasa

SAMARIA

Samaria

Mt. Ebal

Shechem

Sychar

HEROD

Mt. Gerizim

Antipatris

Mountains of Gilead

Arimathea

Joppa

Mountains of Ephraim

Jabbok

Lydda

Ephraim

ANTIPAS

Philadelphia

Jamnia

JUDEA

Jericho

River Jordan

Jerusalem

Mt. of Olives

PEREA

Mt. Nebo

Emmaus?

Bethany

Bethlehem

Ashkelon

Eleutheropolis

Hebron

WILDERNESS OF JUDEA

Dead Sea

Machaerus

Gaza

IDUMEA

Beersheba

PROVINCE OF

A HARMONY OF THE GOSPELS
FOR STUDENTS OF THE LIFE OF CHRIST

A. T. ROBERTSON, M.A., D.D., LL.D., Litt. D.

BY PROFESSOR A. T. ROBERTSON

A HARMONY OF THE GOSPELS FOR STUDENTS OF THE LIFE OF CHRIST. Based on the BROADUS HARMONY.

A GRAMMAR OF THE GREEK NEW TESTAMENT IN THE LIGHT OF HISTORICAL RESEARCH. Third Edition. Pages 1538.

A SHORT GRAMMAR OF THE GREEK NEW TESTAMENT. Fifth Edition. Pages 284. Translation in Dutch, French, German and Italian.

PRACTICAL AND SOCIAL ASPECTS OF CHRISTIANITY. The Wisdom of James. Second Edition. Pages 271.

PAUL THE INTERPRETER OF CHRIST. Second Edition. Pages 155.

TYPES OF PREACHERS IN THE NEW TESTAMENT. Pages 238.

EPOCHS IN THE LIFE OF JESUS. Pages 212. Numerous Editions.

EPOCHS IN THE LIFE OF PAUL. Numerous Editions. Pages 337.

JOHN THE LOYAL: Studies in the Ministry of the Baptist. Pages 327. Several editions.

THE PHARISEES AND JESUS. The Stone (Princeton) Lectures. The Studies in Theology Series. Pages 201.

LUKE THE HISTORIAN IN THE LIGHT OF RESEARCH. Pages 267.

THE NEW CITIZENSHIP. Pages 157. Second Edition.

THE GLORY OF THE MINISTRY. Pages 243. Second Edition.

MAKING GOOD IN THE MINISTRY. A sketch of John Mark. Pages 174. Second Edition.

PAUL'S JOY IN CHRIST. Studies in Philippians. Pages 267. Second Edition.

THE DIVINITY OF CHRIST IN THE GOSPEL OF JOHN. Pages 173. Second Edition.

THE STUDENT'S CHRONOLOGICAL NEW TESTAMENT. Second Edition.

COMMENTARY ON THE GOSPEL ACCORDING TO MATTHEW. The Bible for Home and School. Pages 308.

STUDIES IN MARK'S GOSPEL. Pages 158.

STUDIES IN THE NEW TESTAMENT. Many editions. Pages 284.

THE TEACHING OF JESUS CONCERNING GOD THE FATHER. The Teaching of Jesus Series. Pages 190.

KEYWORDS IN THE TEACHING OF JESUS. Pages 127. Several Editions.

LIFE AND LETTERS OF JOHN A. BROADUS. Pages 476. Numerous Editions.

SYLLABUS FOR NEW TESTAMENT STUDY. Pages 207. Fourth Edition.

A HARMONY OF THE GOSPELS FOR STUDENTS OF THE LIFE OF CHRIST

Based on the Broadus Harmony in the Revised Version

BY

A. T. ROBERTSON, M.A., D.D., LL.D., Litt.D.

CHAIR OF NEW TESTAMENT INTERPRETATION
SOUTHERN BAPTIST THEOLOGICAL SEMINARY
LOUISVILLE, KENTUCKY

"Take my yoke upon you, and learn of me."

HarperSanFrancisco

A Division of HarperCollins*Publishers*

ISBN: 0-06-066890-3

00 HAD 80 79 78 77

TO

ELIZA S. BROADUS

ELDEST DAUGHTER OF JOHN A. BROADUS

AN ELECT LADY BELOVED IN MANY LANDS

PREFACE

It is now just thirty years since one day his young assistant suggested to Dr. John A. Broadus that he prepare a harmony of the Gospels that should depart from the old plan of following the feasts as the turning points in the life of Jesus. He acted on the hint and led the way that all modern harmonies have followed. The book has gone through a dozen large editions and has become the standard harmony for many thousands of students all over the world. Broadus was concerned to bring out "the inner movements of the history, towards that long-delayed, but foreseen and inevitable collision, in which, beyond all other instances, the wrath of man was made to praise God." This he succeeded in doing with marvelous power.

A generation has passed by and it is meet that the work of Broadus should be reviewed in the light of modern synoptic criticism and research into every phase of the life of Christ. So I have made a new analysis that preserves Broadus's real purpose, but with new sections and new notes. The notes at the end of the old volume, written by me for the first edition, have been thoroughly revised and brought up to date. The Old Testament passages referred to in the Gospels are given in the text. The Gospel of Mark appears in the first column, then Matthew, Luke, and John. It is now known that Matthew and Luke made use of Mark for the framework of their Gospels. This change simplifies amazingly the unfolding of the narrative.

There is still dispute concerning the historical worth of the Gospel of John, but the Johannine authorship is not disproved. It still holds the field in my opinion. Dr. C. F. Burney's theory of an Aramaic original is already giving a new turn to Johannine criticism.

A harmony of the Gospels cannot meet every phase of modern criticism. The data are given, as free from bias as circumstances allow, so that all students can use the book and interpret the facts according to their various theories. Numerous historical items call for notes of various kinds that throw light on the passage in question. No effort is made to reconcile all the divergent statements of various details in the different Gospels. The differences challenge the student's interest as much as the correspondences and are natural marks of individual work. The notes and appendices at the end of the volume are meant for students who wish help for historical study of the life of Christ. A harmony cannot give all the aid that one needs, but it is the one essential book for the serious study of the life of Jesus. Students in colleges, theological seminaries, Young Men's Christian Association and Young Women's Christian Association classes, Sunday School teachers and pupils, preachers, all who read the Gospels intelligently must have a modern harmony of the Gospels. One who has never read a harmony will be amazed at the flood of light that flashes from the parallel and progressive records of the life of Jesus Christ.

Broadus began teaching the life of Jesus in 1859 and kept it up till his death in 1895. I began like work in 1888 and have kept on without a break till now. I count it one of the crowning mercies of my life that I have led so many successive classes of young ministers and young women (some five thousand in all) through the study of Christ's life. If only one can pass on to others in all their freshness and power the teachings of Jesus, he cannot fail. There was a time when men hung in wonder upon the words of Jesus, listening with awe and rapture as he spoke. The Figure of Christ fills the world today as never before. Back to Christ the world has come, the Christ of Faith and of Experience, the Jesus of History, the Man of Galilee, the Hope of Today, the Jesus Christ of the Four Gospels in the full blaze of modern critical and historical study.

A. T. ROBERTSON.

Louisville,
Kentucky

CONTENTS

	PAGE
PREFACE	vii
CHIEF DIVISIONS OF THE HARMONY	xi
ANALYTICAL OUTLINE OF THE HARMONY	xiii
TABLE FOR FINDING ANY PASSAGE IN THE HARMONY	xxxiii
THE HARMONY OF THE GOSPELS	1
EXPLANATORY NOTES ON POINTS OF SPECIAL DIFFICULTY IN THE HARMONY	253
1. About Harmonies of the Gospels	253
2. Synoptic Criticism	255
3. The Authorship of the Fourth Gospel	256
4. The Jesus of History	258
5. The Two Genealogies of Christ	259
6. The Probable Time of the Saviour's Birth	262
7. The Feast of John 5:1, and the Duration of Our Lord's Ministry	267
8. The Four Lists of the Twelve Apostles	271
9. The Sermon on the Mount	273
10. The Combination of Luke and John	276
11. Did Christ Eat the Passover?	279
12. The Hour of the Crucifixion	284
13. The Time of the Resurrection of Christ	287
14. The Length of Our Lord's Stay in the Tomb	289
A LIST OF THE PARABLES OF JESUS	292
A LIST OF THE MIRACLES OF JESUS	294
LIST OF OLD TESTAMENT QUOTATIONS IN THE GOSPELS	295
A LIST OF SOME UNCANONICAL SAYINGS OF JESUS	302
SIMILAR INCIDENTS AND CHIEF REPEATED SAYINGS	304

CHIEF DIVISIONS OF THE HARMONY

PAGE

PART I: THE SOURCES OF THE GOSPELS . . .   **1**
§ 1

PART II: THE PRE-EXISTENT STATE OF CHRIST AND HIS INCARNATION **2**
§ 2

PART III: THE TWO GENEALOGIES IN MATTHEW AND LUKE **3**
§ 3

PART IV: THE BIRTH AND CHILDHOOD OF THE BAPTIST AND OF JESUS **5**
§§ 4–19. (Probably B.C. 7 to A.D. 7)

PART V: THE BEGINNING OF THE BAPTIST'S MINISTRY **15**
§§ 20–23. (Probably A.D. 25)

PART VI: THE BEGINNING OF CHRIST'S PUBLIC MINISTRY **19**
§§ 24–36. (In all parts of Palestine. Probably A.D. 26 and 27)

PART VII: THE GREAT GALILEAN MINISTRY . . .   **30**
§§ 37–71. (Probably A.D. 27 to 29)

PART VIII: THE SPECIAL TRAINING OF THE TWELVE IN DISTRICTS AROUND GALILEE . .   **85**
§§ 72–95. (Probably Passover in A.D. 29 to Tabernacles in A.D. 29)

PART IX: THE LATER JUDEAN MINISTRY **114**
§§ 96–111. (Probably Tabernacles to Dedication in A.D. 29)

PART X: THE LATER PEREAN MINISTRY **131**
§§ 112–127. (Probably Dedication in A.D. 29 to Last Journey in A.D. 30)

PAGE

**PART XI: THE LAST PUBLIC MINISTRY IN JERUSA-
LEM** 152
§§ 128 a–138. (Friday before the Passover to Tuesday of
Passion Week, A.D. 30 or 29)

PART XII: IN THE SHADOW WITH JESUS 173
§§ 139–152. (Tuesday afternoon to Thursday night of
Passion Week, A.D. 30 or 29)

**PART XIII: THE ARREST, TRIAL, CRUCIFIXION, AND
BURIAL OF JESUS** 205
§§ 153–168. (Early Friday morning to Saturday of Passion
Week, A.D. 30 or 29)

**PART XIV: THE RESURRECTION, APPEARANCES, AND
ASCENSION OF CHRIST** 239
§§ 169–184. (Forty days from Sunday of Passion Week,
A.D. 30 or 29)

ANALYTICAL OUTLINE OF THE HARMONY

PART I: THE SOURCES OF THE GOSPELS

SECTION   PAGE

1: IN THE DEDICATION LUKE EXPLAINS HIS METHOD OF RE-
SEARCH   1
Luke 1: 1–4.

PART II: THE PRE-EXISTENT STATE OF CHRIST AND HIS INCARNATION

SECTION

2: IN HIS INTRODUCTION JOHN PICTURES CHRIST AS THE
WORD (LOGOS)   2
John 1: 1–18.

PART III: THE TWO GENEALOGIES IN MATTHEW AND LUKE

SECTION

3: APPARENTLY JOSEPH'S GENEALOGY IN MATTHEW AND
MARY'S IN LUKE   3
Matt. 1:1–17; Luke 3:23–38.

PART IV: THE BIRTH AND CHILDHOOD OF THE BAPTIST AND OF JESUS

SECTIONS 4–19
SECTION

4: THE ANNUNCIATION OF THE BIRTH OF THE BAPTIST TO
ZACHARIAS   5
Luke 1: 5–25.

5: THE ANNUNCIATION TO THE VIRGIN MARY OF THE BIRTH
OF JESUS   6
Luke 1: 26–38.

6: THE SONG OF ELIZABETH TO MARY UPON HER VISIT .   7
Luke 1: 39–45.

SECTION   PAGE

7: THE MAGNIFICAT OF MARY 7
Luke 1: 46–56.

8: THE BIRTH AND CHILDHOOD OF THE BAPTIST AND HIS
DESERT LIFE 8
Luke 1: 57–80.

9: THE ANNUNCIATION TO JOSEPH OF THE BIRTH OF JESUS 9
Matt. 1: 18–25.

10: THE BIRTH OF JESUS 9
Luke 2: 1–7.

11: THE PRAISE OF THE ANGELS AND THE HOMAGE OF THE
SHEPHERDS 10
Luke 2: 8–20.

12: THE CIRCUMCISION OF JESUS 10
Luke 2: 21.

13: THE PRESENTATION IN THE TEMPLE WITH THE HOMAGE
OF SIMEON AND ANNA 10
Luke 2: 22–38.

14: MAGI VISIT THE NEW-BORN KING OF THE JEWS . . . 11
Matt. 2: 1–12.

15: THE CHILD JESUS CARRIED TO EGYPT, AND THE CHIL-
DREN AT BETHLEHEM SLAIN 12
Matt. 2: 13–18.

16: THE CHILD BROUGHT FROM EGYPT TO NAZARETH . . . 13
Matt. 2: 19–23; Luke 2: 39.

17: THE CHILDHOOD OF JESUS AT NAZARETH 13
Luke 2: 40.

18: THE VISIT OF THE BOY JESUS TO JERUSALEM WHEN
TWELVE YEARS OLD 13
Luke 2: 41–50.

19: THE EIGHTEEN YEARS AT NAZARETH 14
Luke 2: 51–52.

PART V: THE BEGINNING OF THE BAPTIST'S MINISTRY

SECTIONS 20–23

SECTION

20: THE TIME OF THE BEGINNING 15
Mark 1: 1; Luke 2: 1–2.

21: THE MESSAGE AND THE MESSENGER 15
Mark 1: 2–6; Matt. 3: 1–6; Luke 3: 3–6.

SECTION   PAGE

22: A SPECIMEN OF JOHN'S PREACHING   16
    Matt. 3: 7–10; Luke 3: 7–14.

23: THE FORERUNNER'S PICTURE OF THE MESSIAH BEFORE
    SEEING HIM   17
    Mark 1: 7–8; Matt. 3: 11–12; Luke 3: 15–18.

PART VI: THE BEGINNING OF CHRIST'S PUBLIC MINISTRY

SECTIONS 24–36

SECTION

24: JESUS BAPTIZED BY JOHN IN THE JORDAN   19
    Mark 1: 9–11; Matt. 3: 13–17; Luke 3: 21–23.

25: THE THREE TEMPTATIONS OF JESUS   20
    Mark 1: 12–13; Matt. 4: 1–11; Luke 4: 1–13.

26: THE TESTIMONY OF THE BAPTIST TO THE COMMITTEE OF
    THE SANHEDRIN   22
    John 1: 19–28.

27: JOHN'S IDENTIFICATION OF JESUS AS THE MESSIAH . .   22
    John 1: 29–34.

28: JESUS MAKES HIS FIRST DISCIPLES   23
    John 1: 35–51.

29: JESUS WORKS HIS FIRST MIRACLE   24
    John 2: 1–11.

30: JESUS MAKES A FIRST SOJOURN AT CAPERNAUM, ACCOM-
    PANIED BY HIS KINDRED AND HIS EARLY DISCIPLES .   24
    John 2: 12.

31: THE FIRST CLEANSING OF THE TEMPLE AT THE PASSOVER   25
    John 2: 13–22.

32: THE INTERVIEW OF NICODEMUS WITH JESUS   25
    John 2: 23; 3: 21.

33: THE PARALLEL MINISTRY OF JESUS AND JOHN WITH
    JOHN'S LOYALTY TO JESUS   26
    John 3: 22–36.

34: CHRIST'S REASONS FOR LEAVING JUDEA   27
    Mark 1: 14; Matt. 4: 12; Luke 3: 19–20; 4: 14; John
    4: 1–4.

35: JESUS IN SAMARIA AT JACOB'S WELL AND IN SYCHAR .   27
    John 4: 5–42.

36: THE ARRIVAL OF JESUS IN GALILEE   29
    John 4: 43–45.

PART VII: THE GREAT GALILEAN MINISTRY

SECTIONS 37–71

Eight Groups in the Period

SECTION   PAGE

(1) The Rejection at Nazareth and the New Home in
    Capernaum. . . . . 31ff.
    Sections 37–43.

(2) The First Tour of Galilee with the Four Fisher-
    men and the Call of Matthew (Levi) on the
    return with the Growing Fame of Jesus. . . 35ff.
    Sections 44–48.

(3) The Sabbath Controversy in Jerusalem and in
    Galilee. . . . . 42ff.
    Sections 49–51.

(4) The Choice of the Twelve and the Sermon on
    the Mount. . . . . 46ff.
    Sections 52–54.

(5) The Spread of Christ's Influence and the Inquiry
    from John in Prison. . . . . . . 55ff.
    Sections 55–59.

(6) The Second Tour of Galilee (now with the
    Twelve) and the Intense Hostility of the Phari-
    sees. . . . . 61ff.
    Sections 60–63.

(7) The First Great Group of Parables with the Visit
    to Gerasa (Khersa) and to Nazareth (final one). 64ff.
    Sections 64–69.

(8) The Third Tour of Galilee (following the Twelve)
    and the Effect on Herod Antipas. . . . 78ff.
    Sections 70–71.

37: GENERAL ACCOUNT OF HIS TEACHING IN GALILEE . . 31
    Mark 1: 14–15; Matt. 4: 17; Luke 4: 14–15.

38: THE HEALING AT CANA OF THE SON OF A COURTIER OF
    CAPERNAUM. 31
    John 4: 46–54.

39: THE FIRST REJECTION AT NAZARETH 31
    Luke 4: 16–31.

40: THE NEW HOME IN CAPERNAUM 32
    Matt. 4: 13–16.

SECTION   PAGE

41: JESUS FINDS FOUR FISHERS OF MEN IN FOUR FISHERMEN   33
Mark 1: 16–20; Matt. 4: 18–22; Luke 5: 1–11.

42: THE EXCITEMENT IN THE SYNAGOGUE BECAUSE OF THE TEACHING OF JESUS AND THE HEALING OF A DEMONIAC ON THE SABBATH   34
Mark 1: 21–28; Luke 4: 31–37.

43: HE HEALS PETER'S MOTHER-IN-LAW AND MANY OTHERS .   34
Mark 1: 29–34; Matt. 8: 14–17; Luke 4: 38–41

44: THE FIRST TOUR OF GALILEE WITH THE FOUR FISHERMEN   35
Mark 1: 35–39; Matt. 4: 23–25; Luke 4: 42–44.

45: A LEPER HEALED AND MUCH POPULAR EXCITEMENT . .   36
Mark 1: 40–45; Matt. 8: 2–4; Luke 5: 12–16.

46: THRONGED IN CAPERNAUM, HE HEALS A PARALYTIC LOWERED THROUGH THE ROOF OF PETER'S HOUSE . . .   37
Mark 2: 1–12; Matt. 9: 1–8; Luke 5: 17–26.

47: THE CALL OF MATTHEW (LEVI) AND HIS RECEPTION IN HONOR OF JESUS   39
Mark 2: 13–17; Matt. 9: 9–13; Luke 5: 27–32.

48: JESUS IN THREE PARABLES DEFENDS HIS DISCIPLES FOR FEASTING INSTEAD OF FASTING   40
Mark 2: 18–22; Matt. 9: 14–17; Luke 5: 33–39.

49: AT A FEAST IN JERUSALEM (POSSIBLY THE PASSOVER) JESUS HEALS A LAME MAN ON THE SABBATH AND DEFENDS THIS ACTION TO THE PHARISEES IN A GREAT DISCOURSE   42
John 5: 1–47.

50: ANOTHER SABBATH CONTROVERSY WITH THE PHARISEES WHEN THE DISCIPLES PLUCK EARS OF GRAIN IN THE FIELDS   44
Mark 2: 23–28; Matt. 12: 1–8; Luke 6: 1–5.

51: A THIRD SABBATH CONTROVERSY WITH THE PHARISEES OVER THE HEALING OF A MAN WITH A WITHERED HAND IN A SYNAGOGUE   45
Mark 3: 1–6; Matt. 12: 9–14; Luke 6: 6–11.

52: JESUS TEACHES AND HEALS GREAT MULTITUDES BY THE SEA OF GALILEE   46
Mark 3: 7–12; Matt. 12: 15–21.

53: AFTER A NIGHT OF PRAYER JESUS SELECTS TWELVE APOSTLES   47
Mark 3: 13–19; Luke 6: 12–16.

SECTION   PAGE

54: THE SERMON ON THE MOUNT. PRIVILEGES AND RE-
QUIREMENTS OF THE MESSIANIC REIGN, CHRIST'S
STANDARD OF RIGHTEOUSNESS   48
Matt. 5–7; Luke 6: 17–49.

The Place and the Audience   48
Matt. 5: 1–2; Luke 6: 17–19.

(1) The Introduction: The Beatitudes and the Woes.
Privileges of the Messiah's Subjects   48
Matt. 5: 3–12; Luke 6: 20–26.

(2) The Theme of the Sermon: Christ's Standard of
Righteousness in Contrast with that of the
Scribes and Pharisees   49
Matt. 5: 13–20.

(3) Christ's Ethical Teaching Superior to that of the
Scribes (both the Old Testament and the Oral
Law) in Six Items or Illustrations (Murder,
Adultery, Divorce, Oaths, Retaliations, Love
of Enemies)   50
Matt. 5: 21–48; Luke 6: 27–30, 32–36.

(4) The Practice of Real Righteousness Unlike the
Ostentatious Hypocrisy of the Pharisees as in
Almsgiving, Prayer, Fasting   51
Matt. 6: 1–18.

(5) Single-hearted Devotion to God as Opposed to
Worldly Aims and Anxieties   52
Matt. 6: 19–34.

(6) Captious Criticism, or Judging Others . . .   53
Matt. 7: 1–6; Luke 6: 37–42.

(7) Prayer and The Golden Rule   54
Matt. 7: 7–12.

(8) The Conclusion of the Sermon. The Lesson of
Personal Righteousness Driven Home by Pow-
erful Parables   54
Matt. 7: 13–8: 1; Luke 6: 43–49.

55: JESUS HEALS A CENTURION'S SERVANT AT CAPERNAUM .   55
Matt. 8: 5–13; Luke 7: 1–10.

56: HE RAISES A WIDOW'S SON AT NAIN   56
Luke 7: 11–17.

57: THE MESSAGE FROM THE BAPTIST AND THE EULOGY OF
JESUS   57
Matt. 11: 2–19; Luke 7: 18–35.

SECTION   PAGE

58: WOES UPON THE CITIES OF OPPORTUNITY. THE CLAIMS
OF CHRIST AS THE TEACHER ABOUT THE FATHER . .   59
Matt. 11: 20–30.

59: THE ANOINTING OF CHRIST'S FEET BY A SINFUL WOMAN
IN THE HOUSE OF SIMON A PHARISEE. THE PARABLE
OF THE TWO DEBTORS   60
Luke 7: 36–50.

60: THE SECOND TOUR OF GALILEE   61
Luke 8: 1–3.

61: BLASPHEMOUS ACCUSATION OF LEAGUE WITH BEELZEBUB   61
Mark 3: 19–30; Matt. 12: 22–37.

62: SCRIBES AND PHARISEES DEMAND A SIGN   62
Matt. 12: 38–45.

63: CHRIST'S MOTHER AND BRETHREN SEEK TO TAKE HIM
HOME   63
Mark 3: 31–35; Matt. 12: 46–50; Luke 8: 19–21.

64: THE FIRST GREAT GROUP OF PARABLES   64
Mark 4: 1–34; Matt. 13: 1–53; Luke 8: 4–18.

Introduction to the Group

Mark 4: 1–2; Matt. 13: 1–3; Luke 8: 4.

1: *To the Crowds by the Sea*

(a) Parable of the Sower   64
Mark 4: 3–25; Matt. 13: 3–23; Luke 8: 5-18.

(b) Parable of the Seed Growing of Itself . .   67
Mark 4: 26–29.

(c) Parable of the Tares   68
Matt. 13: 24–30.

(d) Parable of the Mustard Seed   68
Mark 4: 30–32; Matt. 13: 31–32.

(e) Parable of the Leaven and Many Such Parables   68
Mark 4: 33–34; Matt. 13: 33–35.

2. *To the Disciples in the House*

(a) Explanation of the Parables of the Tares .   69
Matt. 13: 36–43.

(b) The Parable of the Hid Treasure   69
Matt. 13: 44.

(c) The Parable of the Pearl of Great Price . .   69
Matt. 13: 45–46.

SECTION   PAGE

     (d) The Parable of the Net. 70
          Matt. 13: 47–50.

     (e) The Parable of the Householder. 70
          Matt. 13: 51–53.

65: IN CROSSING THE LAKE, JESUS STILLS THE TEMPEST . 70
    Mark 4: 35–41; Matt. 8: 18, 23–27; Luke 8: 22–25.

66: BEYOND THE LAKE JESUS HEALS THE GERASENE DEMONIAC 71
    Mark 5: 1–20; Matt. 8: 28–34; Luke 8: 26–39.

67: THE RETURN AND THE HEALING OF JAIRUS' DAUGHTER
    AND OF THE WOMAN WHO ONLY TOUCHED CHRIST'S
    GARMENT 74
    Mark 5: 21–43; Matt. 9: 18–26; Luke 8: 40–56.

68: HE HEALS TWO BLIND MEN AND A DUMB DEMONIAC, A
    BLASPHEMOUS ACCUSATION 77
    Matt. 9: 27–34.

69: THE LAST VISIT TO NAZARETH 77
    Mark 6: 1–6; Matt. 13: 54–58.

70: THE THIRD TOUR OF GALILEE AFTER INSTRUCTING THE
    TWELVE AND SENDING THEM FORTH BY TWOS . . . 78
    Mark 6:6–13; Matt. 9:35–11:1; Luke 9:1–6.

71: THE GUILTY FEARS OF HEROD ANTIPAS IN TIBERIAS
    ABOUT JESUS BECAUSE HE HAD BEHEADED THE BAP-
    TIST IN MACHÆRUS 82
    Mark 6: 14–29; Matt. 14: 1–12; Luke 9: 7–9.

PART VIII: THE SPECIAL TRAINING OF THE TWELVE IN DISTRICTS AROUND GALILEE

SECTIONS 72–95

SECTION

72: THE FIRST RETIREMENT. THE TWELVE RETURN, AND
    JESUS RETIRES WITH THEM BEYOND THE LAKE TO
    REST. FEEDING OF THE FIVE THOUSAND 85
    Mark 6: 30–44; Matt. 14: 13–21; Luke 9: 10–17; John
    6: 1–14.

73: THE PREVENTION OF THE REVOLUTIONARY PURPOSE TO
    PROCLAIM JESUS KING (A POLITICAL MESSIAH) . . . 88
    Mark 6: 45–46; Matt. 14: 22–23; John 6: 14–15.

74: THE PERIL TO THE TWELVE IN THE STORM AT SEA AND
    CHRIST'S COMING TO THEM ON THE WATER IN THE
    DARKNESS 89
    Mark 6: 47–52; Matt. 14: 24–33; John 6: 16–21.

SECTION   PAGE

75: THE RECEPTION AT GENNESARET 90
Mark 6: 53–56; Matt. 14: 34–36.

76: THE COLLAPSE OF THE GALILEAN CAMPAIGN BECAUSE
JESUS WILL NOT CONFORM TO POPULAR MESSIANIC EX-
PECTATIONS 90
John 6: 22–71.

77: PHARISEES FROM JERUSALEM REPROACH JESUS FOR AL-
LOWING HIS DISCIPLES TO DISREGARD THEIR TRA-
DITIONS ABOUT CEREMONIAL DEFILEMENT OF THE
HANDS. A PUZZLING PARABLE IN REPLY 92
Mark 7: 1–23; Matt. 15: 1–20; John 7: 1.

78: THE SECOND WITHDRAWAL TO THE REGION OF TYRE
AND SIDON AND THE HEALING OF THE DAUGHTER OF
A SYRO-PHŒNICIAN WOMAN 94
Mark 7: 24–30; Matt. 15: 21–28.

79: THE THIRD WITHDRAWAL NORTH THROUGH PHŒNICIA
AND EAST TOWARDS HERMON AND SOUTH INTO DE-
CAPOLIS (KEEPING OUT OF THE TERRITORY OF HEROD
ANTIPAS) WITH THE HEALING OF THE DEAF AND DUMB
MAN AND THE FEEDING OF THE FOUR THOUSAND . . 95
Mark 7: 31–8: 9; Matt. 15: 29–38.

80: THE BRIEF VISIT TO MAGADAN (DALMANUTHA) IN GALI-
LEE AND THE SHARP ATTACK BY THE PHARISEES AND
SADDUCEES. (NOTE THEIR APPEARANCE NOW AGAINST
JESUS) 97
Mark 8: 10–12; Matt. 15: 39–16: 4.

81: THE FOURTH RETIREMENT TO BETHSAIDA JULIAS IN THE
TETRARCHY OF HEROD PHILIP WITH SHARP REBUKE OF
THE DULNESS OF THE DISCIPLES ON THE WAY ACROSS
AND THE HEALING OF A BLIND MAN IN BETHSAIDA . 98
Mark 8: 13–26; Matt. 16: 5–12.

82: NEAR CÆSAREA PHILIPPI JESUS TESTS THE FAITH OF
THE TWELVE IN HIS MESSIAHSHIP 99
Mark 8: 27–30; Matt. 16: 13–20; Luke 9: 18–21.

83: JESUS DISTINCTLY FORETELLS THAT HE, THE MESSIAH,
WILL BE REJECTED AND KILLED AND WILL RISE THE
THIRD DAY 100
Mark 8: 31–37; Matt. 16: 21–26; Luke 9: 22–25.

84: THE COMING OF THE SON OF MAN IN THAT GENERA-
TION 101
Mark 8: 38–9: 1; Matt. 16: 27–28; Luke 9: 26–27.

SECTION   PAGE

85: THE TRANSFIGURATION OF JESUS ON A MOUNTAIN (PROB-
ABLY HERMON) NEAR CÆSAREA PHILIPPI 102
Mark 9: 2–8; Matt. 17: 1–8; Luke 9: 28–36.

86: THE PUZZLE OF THE THREE DISCIPLES ABOUT THE RESUR-
RECTION AND ABOUT ELIJAH ON THEIR WAY DOWN THE
MOUNTAIN 103
Mark 9: 9–13; Matt. 17: 9–13; Luke 9: 36.

87: THE DEMONIAC BOY, WHOM THE DISCIPLES COULD NOT
HEAL 104
Mark 9: 14–29; Matt. 17: 14–20; Luke 9: 37–43.

88: RETURNING PRIVATELY THROUGH GALILEE, HE AGAIN
FORETELLS HIS DEATH AND RESURRECTION 107
Mark 9: 30–32; Matt. 17: 22–23; Luke 9: 43–45.

89: JESUS, THE MESSIAH, PAYS THE HALF-SHEKEL FOR THE
TEMPLE 107
Matt. 17: 24–27.

90: THE TWELVE CONTEND AS TO WHO SHALL BE THE GREAT-
EST UNDER THE MESSIAH'S REIGN. HIS SUBJECTS
MUST BE CHILDLIKE 108
Mark 9: 33–37; Matt. 18: 1–5; Luke 9: 46–48.

91: THE MISTAKEN ZEAL OF THE APOSTLE JOHN REBUKED BY
JESUS IN PERTINENT PARABLES 109
Mark 9: 38–50; Matt. 18: 6–14; Luke 9: 49–50.

92: RIGHT TREATMENT OF A BROTHER WHO HAS SINNED
AGAINST ONE, AND DUTY OF PATIENTLY FORGIVING A
BROTHER (PARABLE OF THE UNMERCIFUL SERVANT) . 111
Matt. 18: 15–35.

93: THE MESSIAH'S FOLLOWERS MUST GIVE UP EVERYTHING
FOR HIS SERVICE 112
Matt. 8: 19–22; Luke 9: 57–62.

94: THE UNBELIEVING BROTHERS OF JESUS COUNSEL HIM TO
EXHIBIT HIMSELF IN JUDEA, AND HE REJECTS THE
ADVICE 112
John 7: 2–9.

95: HE GOES PRIVATELY TO JERUSALEM THROUGH SAMARIA 113
Luke 9: 51–56; John 7: 10.

PART IX: THE LATER JUDEAN MINISTRY

SECTIONS 96–111

SECTION   **PAGE**

96: THE COMING OF JESUS TO THE FEAST OF TABERNACLES
CREATES INTENSE EXCITEMENT CONCERNING THE MES-
SIAHSHIP 114
John 7: 11–52.

97: STORY OF AN ADULTEROUS WOMAN BROUGHT TO JESUS
FOR JUDGMENT 115
John 7: 53–8: 11.

98: AFTER THE FEAST OF TABERNACLES IN THE TEMPLE
JESUS ANGERS THE PHARISEES BY CLAIMING TO BE
THE LIGHT OF THE WORLD 116
John 8: 12–20.

99: THE PHARISEES ATTEMPT TO STONE JESUS WHEN HE
EXPOSES THEIR SINFULNESS 116
John 8: 21–59.

100: JESUS HEALS A MAN BORN BLIND WHO OUTWITS THE
PHARISEES. THE RULERS FORBID THE RECOGNITION
OF JESUS AS THE MESSIAH. THE CONVERSION OF THE
HEALED MAN 118
John 9: 1–41.

101: IN THE PARABLE (ALLEGORY) OF THE GOOD SHEPHERD
JESUS DRAWS THE PICTURE OF THE HOSTILE PHARI-
SEES AND INTIMATES THAT HE IS GOING TO DIE FOR
HIS FLOCK AND COME TO LIFE AGAIN 119
John 10: 1–21.

102: THE MISSION OF THE SEVENTY. CHRIST'S JOY IN THEIR
WORK ON THEIR RETURN 120
Luke 10: 1–24.

103: JESUS ANSWERS A LAWYER'S QUESTION AS TO ETERNAL
LIFE, GIVING THE PARABLE OF THE GOOD SAMARITAN 122
Luke 10: 25–37.

104: JESUS THE GUEST OF MARTHA AND MARY 122
Luke 10: 38–42.

105: JESUS AGAIN GIVES A MODEL OF PRAYER (COMP. § 54)
AND ENCOURAGES HIS DISCIPLES TO PRAY. PARABLE
OF THE IMPORTUNATE FRIEND 123
Luke 11: 1–13.

106: BLASPHEMOUS ACCUSATION OF LEAGUE WITH BEELZEBUB 123
Luke 11: 14–36.

SECTION   PAGE

107: WHILE BREAKFASTING WITH A PHARISEE, JESUS SE-
     VERELY DENOUNCES THE PHARISEES AND LAWYERS
     AND EXCITES THEIR ENMITY   125
     Luke 11: 37–54.

108: HE SPEAKS TO HIS DISCIPLES AND A VAST THRONG ABOUT
     HYPOCRISY, COVETOUSNESS (PARABLE OF THE RICH
     FOOL), WORLDLY ANXIETIES, WATCHFULNESS (PARA-
     BLE OF THE WAITING SERVANTS AND OF THE WISE
     STEWARD), AND HIS OWN APPROACHING PASSION . .   126
     Luke 12.

109: ALL MUST REPENT OR PERISH. (TWO CURRENT TRAG-
     EDIES): PARABLE OF THE BARREN FIG TREE . . .   128
     Luke 13: 1–9.

110: JESUS HEALS A CRIPPLED WOMAN ON THE SABBATH AND
     DEFENDS HIMSELF AGAINST THE RULER OF THE SYNA-
     GOGUE. (CF. §§ 49–51 AND 114.) REPETITION OF THE
     PARABLES OF THE MUSTARD SEED AND OF THE LEAVEN   129
     Luke 13: 10–21.

111: AT THE FEAST OF DEDICATION JESUS WILL NOT YET
     OPENLY SAY THAT HE IS THE MESSIAH. THE JEWS
     TRY TO STONE HIM . . . . . . -   129
     John 10: 22–39.

PART X: THE LATER PEREAN MINISTRY

SECTIONS 112–127
SECTION

112: THE WITHDRAWAL FROM JERUSALEM TO BETHANY BE-
     YOND JORDAN   131
     John 10: 40–42.

113: TEACHING IN PEREA, ON A JOURNEY TOWARD JERUSA-
     LEM, WARNED AGAINST HEROD ANTIPAS   131
     Luke 13: 22–35.

114: WHILE DINING (BREAKFASTING) WITH A CHIEF PHARI-
     SEE, HE AGAIN HEALS ON THE SABBATH AND DEFENDS
     HIMSELF (COMP. §§ 49 TO 51 AND 110) THREE PARA-
     BLES SUGGESTED BY THE OCCASION   132
     Luke 14: 1–24.

115: GREAT CROWDS FOLLOW HIM, AND HE WARNS THEM TO
     COUNT THE COST OF DISCIPLESHIP TO HIM (COMP. §§ 70
     AND 83)   133
     Luke 14: 25–35

SECTION   PAGE

116: THE PHARISEES AND THE SCRIBES MURMUR AGAINST
     JESUS FOR RECEIVING SINNERS. HE DEFENDS HIM-
     SELF BY THREE GREAT PARABLES (THE LOST SHEEP,
     THE LOST COIN, THE LOST SON) 134
     Luke 15: 1-32.

117: THREE PARABLES ON STEWARDSHIP (TO THE DISCIPLES,
     THE PARABLE OF THE UNJUST STEWARD; TO THE
     PHARISEES, THE PARABLE OF THE RICH MAN AND
     LAZARUS; TO THE DISCIPLES, THE PARABLE OF THE
     UNPROFITABLE SERVANTS) 135
     Luke 16: 1, 17: 10.

118: JESUS RAISES LAZARUS FROM THE DEAD 137
     John 11: 1-44.

119: THE EFFECT OF THE RAISING OF LAZARUS (ON THE
     PEOPLE, ON THE SANHEDRIN, ON THE MOVEMENTS OF
     JESUS) 139
     John 11: 45-54.

120: JESUS STARTS ON THE LAST JOURNEY TO JERUSALEM BY
     WAY OF SAMARIA AND GALILEE 139
     Luke 17: 11-37

121: TWO PARABLES ON PRAYER (THE IMPORTUNATE WIDOW,
     THE PHARISEE AND THE PUBLICAN) 140
     Luke 18: 1-14.

122: GOING FROM GALILEE THROUGH PEREA, HE TEACHES
     CONCERNING DIVORCE 141
     Mark 10: 1-12; Matt. 19: 1-12.

123: CHRIST AND CHILDREN AND THE FAILURE OF THE DIS-
     CIPLES TO UNDERSTAND THE ATTITUDE OF JESUS . . 143
     Mark 10: 13-16; Matt. 19: 13-15; Luke 18: 15-17.

124: THE RICH YOUNG RULER, THE PERILS OF RICHES, AND
     AMAZEMENT OF THE DISCIPLES. THE REWARDS OF
     FORSAKING ALL TO FOLLOW THE MESSIAH WILL BE
     GREAT, BUT WILL BE SOVEREIGN (PARABLE OF THE
     LABORERS IN THE VINEYARD) 143
     Mark 10: 17-31; Matt. 19: 16-20: 16; Luke 18: 18-30.

125: JESUS AGAIN FORETELLS TO THE DISCIPLES HIS DEATH
     AND RESURRECTION (COMP. §§ 83, 85, 86, 88), AND
     REBUKES THE SELFISH AMBITION OF JAMES AND JOHN 146
     Mark 10: 32-45; Matt. 20: 17-28; Luke 18: 31-34.

126: BLIND BARTIMÆUS AND HIS COMPANION HEALED . . . 148
     Mark 10: 46-52; Matt. 20: 29-34; Luke 18: 35-43.

SECTION   PAGE

127: JESUS VISITS ZACCHÆUS, AND SPEAKS THE PARABLE OF
THE POUNDS, AND SETS OUT FOR JERUSALEM . . .   **150**
Luke 19: 1–28.

PART XI: THE LAST PUBLIC MINISTRY IN JERUSALEM

SECTIONS 128–139

SECTION

128 a: JESUS ARRIVES AT BETHANY NEAR JERUSALEM . . .   **152**
John 11: 55–12: 1; 9–11.

128 b: HIS TRIUMPHAL ENTRY INTO JERUSALEM AS THE MESSIAH
Mark 11: 1–11; Matt. 21: 1–11, 14–17; Luke 19: 29–44;
John 12: 12–19.

129: THE BARREN FIG TREE CURSED, AND THE SECOND
CLEANSING OF THE TEMPLE (COMP. § 31) . . .   **156**
Mark 11: 12–18; Matt. 21: 18–19, 12–13; Luke 19:
45–48.

130: THE DESIRE OF SOME GREEKS TO SEE JESUS PUZZLES
THE DISCIPLES AND LEADS JESUS IN AGITATION OF
SOUL TO INTERPRET LIFE AND DEATH AS SACRIFICE
AND TO SHOW HOW BY BEING "LIFTED UP" HE WILL
DRAW ALL MEN TO HIM **157**
John 12: 20–50.

131: THE BARREN FIG TREE FOUND TO HAVE WITHERED .   **159**
Mark 11: 19–25; Matt. 21: 19–22; Luke 21: 37–38.

132: THE RULERS (SANHEDRIN) FORMALLY CHALLENGE THE
AUTHORITY OF JESUS AS AN ACCREDITED TEACHER
(RABBI) **160**
Mark 11: 27–12: 12; Matt. 21: 23–22: 14; Luke 20:
1–19.

133: THE PHARISEES AND THE HERODIANS TRY TO ENSNARE
JESUS ABOUT PAYING TRIBUTE TO CÆSAR **164**
Mark 12: 13–17; Matt. 22: 15–22; Luke 20: 20–26.

134: THE SADDUCEES ASK HIM A PUZZLING QUESTION ABOUT
THE RESURRECTION **165**
Mark 12: 18–27; Matt. 22: 23–33; Luke 20: 27–40.

135: THE PHARISEES REJOICE OVER THE ROUT OF THE SAD-
DUCEES AND A PHARISAIC LAWYER ASKS JESUS A
LEGAL QUESTION **167**
Mark 12: 28–34; Matt. 22: 34–40.

SECTION   PAGE

136: JESUS, TO THE JOY OF THE MULTITUDE, SILENCES HIS ENEMIES BY THE PERTINENT QUESTION OF THE MESSIAH'S DESCENT FROM DAVID AND LORDSHIP OVER DAVID 168
Mark 12: 35–37; Matt. 22: 41–46; Luke 20: 41–44.

137: IN HIS LAST PUBLIC DISCOURSE, JESUS SOLEMNLY DENOUNCES THE SCRIBES AND PHARISEES (COMP. § 107) 169
Mark 12: 38–40; Matt. 23: 1–39; Luke 20: 45–47.

138: JESUS CLOSELY OBSERVES THE CONTRIBUTIONS IN THE TEMPLE, AND COMMENDS THE POOR WIDOW'S GIFT . 172
Mark 12: 41–44; Luke 21: 1–4.

PART XII: IN THE SHADOW WITH JESUS

SECTIONS 139–152

SECTION

139: SITTING ON THE MOUNT OF OLIVES, JESUS SPEAKS TO HIS DISCIPLES ABOUT THE DESTRUCTION OF JERUSALEM, AND HIS OWN SECOND COMING IN APOCALYPTIC LANGUAGE. THE GREAT ESCHATOLOGICAL DISCOURSE 173
Mark 13: 1–37; Matt. 24: 25; Luke 21: 5–36.

140: JESUS PREDICTS HIS CRUCIFIXION TWO DAYS HENCE (JEWISH FRIDAY) 186
Mark 14: 1–2; Matt. 26: 1–5; Luke 22: 1–2.

141: AT THE FEAST IN THE HOUSE OF SIMON THE LEPER MARY OF BETHANY ANOINTS JESUS FOR HIS BURIAL . . . 187
Mark 14: 3–9; Matt. 26: 6–13; John 12: 2–8.

142: JUDAS, STUNG BY THE REBUKE OF JESUS AT THE FEAST, BARGAINS WITH THE RULERS TO BETRAY JESUS . . 188
Mark 14: 10–11; Matt. 26: 14–16; Luke 22: 3–6.

143: THE PREPARATION FOR THE PASCHAL MEAL AT THE HOME OF A FRIEND (POSSIBLY THAT OF JOHN MARK'S FATHER AND MOTHER) 189
Mark 14: 12–16; Matt. 26: 17–19; Luke 22: 7–13.

144: JESUS PARTAKES OF THE PASCHAL MEAL WITH THE TWELVE APOSTLES AND REBUKES THEIR JEALOUSY . 190
Mark 14: 17; Matt. 26: 20; Luke 22: 14–16, 24–30.

145: DURING THE PASCHAL MEAL, JESUS WASHES THE FEET OF HIS DISCIPLES 190
John 13: 1–20.

SECTION   PAGE

146: AT THE PASCHAL MEAL JESUS POINTS OUT JUDAS AS THE
     BETRAYER 191
     Mark 14: 18–21; Matt. 26: 21–25; Luke 22: 21–23;
     John 13: 21–30.

147: AFTER THE DEPARTURE OF JUDAS JESUS WARNS THE
     DISCIPLES (PETER IN PARTICULAR) AGAINST DESER-
     TION, WHILE ALL PROTEST THEIR LOYALTY 193
     Mark 14: 27–31; Matt. 26: 31–35; Luke 22: 31–38;
     John 13: 31–38.

148: JESUS INSTITUTES THE MEMORIAL OF EATING BREAD AND
     DRINKING WINE 195
     Mark 14: 22–25; Matt. 26: 26–29; Luke 22: 17–20;
     1 Cor. 11: 23–26.

149: THE FAREWELL DISCOURSE TO HIS DISCIPLES IN THE
     UPPER ROOM 197
     John 14.

150: THE DISCOURSE ON THE WAY TO GETHSEMANE . . . 198
     John 15: 16.

151: CHRIST'S INTERCESSORY PRAYER 200
     John 17.

152: GOING FORTH TO GETHSEMANE, JESUS SUFFERS LONG IN
     AGONY 201
     Mark 14: 26, 32–42; Matt. 26: 30, 36–46; Luke 22:
     39–46; John 18: 1.

PART XIII: THE ARREST, TRIAL, CRUCIFIXION, AND BURIAL OF JESUS

SECTIONS 153–168
SECTION

153: JESUS IS BETRAYED, ARRESTED, AND FORSAKEN . . . 205
     Mark 14: 43–52; Matt. 26: 47–56; Luke 22: 47–53;
     John 18: 2–12.

154: JESUS FIRST EXAMINED BY ANNAS, THE EX-HIGH PRIEST 209
     John 18: 12–14, 19–23.

155: JESUS HURRIEDLY TRIED AND CONDEMNED BY CAIAPHAS
     AND THE SANHEDRIN, WHO MOCK AND BUFFET HIM . 209
     Mark 14: 53, 55–65; Matt. 26: 57, 59–68; Luke 22: 54,
     63–65; John 18: 24.

156: PETER THRICE DENIES HIS LORD 212
     Mark 14: 54, 66–72; Matt. 26: 58, 69–75; Luke 22:
     54–62; John 18: 15–18, 25–27.

SECTION   PAGE

157: AFTER DAWN, JESUS IS FORMALLY CONDEMNED BY THE
      SANHEDRIN   215
      Mark 15: 1; Matt. 27: 1; Luke 22: 66–71.

158: REMORSE AND SUICIDE OF JUDAS THE BETRAYER   . .   215
      Matt. 27: 3–10; Acts 1: 18–19.

159: JESUS BEFORE PILATE THE FIRST TIME   216
      Mark 15: 1–5; Matt. 27: 2, 11–14; Luke 23: 1–5; John
      18: 28–38.

160: JESUS BEFORE HEROD ANTIPAS THE TETRARCH   . . .   220
      Luke 23: 6–12.

161: JESUS THE SECOND TIME BEFORE PILATE   220
      Mark 15: 6–15; Matt. 27: 15–26; Luke 23: 13–25;
      John 18: 39–19: 16.

162: THE ROMAN SOLDIERS MOCK JESUS   226
      Mark 15: 16–19; Matt. 27: 27–30.

163: JESUS ON THE WAY TO THE CROSS (VIA DOLOROSA) ON
      GOLGOTHA   226
      Mark 15: 20–23; Matt. 27: 31–34; Luke 23: 26–33;
      John 19: 16–17.

164: THE FIRST THREE HOURS ON THE CROSS   228
      Mark 15: 24–32; Matt. 27: 35–44; Luke 23: 33–43;
      John 19: 18–27.

165: THE THREE HOURS OF DARKNESS FROM NOON TO THREE P.M.   232
      Mark 15: 33–37; Matt. 27: 45–50; Luke 23: 44–46;
      John 19: 28–30.

166: THE PHENOMENA ACCOMPANYING THE DEATH OF CHRIST   234
      Mark 15: 38–41; Matt. 27: 51–56; Luke 23: 45, 47–49.

167: THE BURIAL OF THE BODY OF JESUS IN THE TOMB OF
      JOSEPH OF ARIMATHEA AFTER PROOF OF HIS DEATH .   235
      Mark 15: 42–46; Matt. 27: 57–60; Luke 23: 50–54;
      John 19: 31–42.

168: THE WATCH OF THE WOMEN BY THE TOMB OF JESUS .   237
      Mark 15: 47; Matt. 27: 61–66; Luke 23: 55–56.

PART XIV: THE RESURRECTION, APPEARANCES, AND ASCENSION OF CHRIST

SECTIONS 169–184

SECTION

169: THE VISIT OF THE WOMEN TO THE TOMB OF JESUS . .   239
      Mark 16: 1; Matt. 28: 1.

SECTION   PAGE

170: THE EARTHQUAKE, THE ROLLING AWAY OF TE   ONE
BY AN ANGEL, AND THE FRIGHT OF THE   MAN
WATCHERS 240
Matt. 28: 2–4.

171: THE VISIT OF THE WOMEN TO THE TOMB OF JESUS ABOUT
SUNRISE SUNDAY MORNING AND THE MESSAGE OF THE
ANGELS ABOUT THE EMPTY TOMB 240
Mark 16: 2–8; Matt. 28: 5–8; Luke 24: 1–8; John 20: 1.

172: MARY MAGDALENE AND THE OTHER WOMEN REPORT TO
THE APOSTLES, AND PETER AND JOHN VISIT THE
EMPTY TOMB 242
Luke 24: 9–12; John 20: 2–10.

173: THE APPEARANCE OF JESUS TO MARY MAGDALENE AND
THE MESSAGE TO THE DISCIPLES 242
Mark 16: 9–11; John 20: 11–18.

174: THE APPEARANCE OF JESUS TO THE OTHER WOMEN . . 243
Matt. 28: 9–10.

175: SOME OF THE GUARD REPORT TO THE JEWISH RULERS . 244
Matt. 28: 11–15.

176: THE APPEARANCE TO TWO DISCIPLES (CLEOPHAS AND
ANOTHER) ON THE WAY TO EMMAUS 244
Mark 16: 12–13; Luke 24: 13–32.

177: THE REPORT OF THE TWO DISCIPLES AND THE NEWS OF
THE APPEARANCE TO SIMON PETER 245
Luke 24: 33–35; 1 Cor. 15: 5.

178: THE APPEARANCE TO THE ASTONISHED DISCIPLES
(THOMAS ABSENT) WITH A COMMISSION AND THEIR
FAILURE TO CONVINCE THOMAS 245
Mark 16: 14; Luke 24: 36–43; John 20: 19–25.

179: THE APPEARANCE TO THE DISCIPLES THE NEXT SUNDAY
NIGHT AND THE CONVINCING OF THOMAS 247
John 20: 26–31; 1 Cor. 15: 5.

180: THE APPEARANCE TO SEVEN DISCIPLES BESIDE THE SEA
OF GALILEE. THE MIRACULOUS DRAUGHT OF FISHES 247
John 21.

181: THE APPEARANCE TO ABOUT FIVE HUNDRED ON AN AP-
POINTED MOUNTAIN IN GALILEE, AND A COMMISSION
GIVEN 249
Mark 16: 15–18; Matt. 28: 16–20; 1 Cor. 15: 6.

182: THE APPEARANCE TO JAMES THE BROTHER OF JESUS . 250
1 Cor. 15: 7.

SECTION   PAGE

183: THE APPEARANCE TO THE DISCIPLES WITH ANOTHER
       COMMISSION 250
      Luke 24: 44–49; Acts 1: 3–8.

184: THE LAST APPEARANCE AND THE ASCENSION 251
      Mark 16: 19–20; Luke 24: 50–53; Acts 1: 9–12.

TABLE FOR FINDING ANY PASSAGE IN THE HARMONY

MARK

Chap.	Verse	Section	Page	Chap.	Verse	Section	Page
1	1	20	15	8	13–26	81	98
1	2–6	21	15	8	27–30	82	99
1	7–8	23	17	8	31–37	83	100
1	9–11	24	19	8	38–9: 1	84	101
1	12–13	25	20	9	2–8	85	102
1	14	34	27	9	9–13	86	103
1	14–15	37	31	9	14–29	87	104
1	16–20	41	33	9	30–32	88	107
1	21–28	42	34	9	33–37	90	108
1	29–34	43	34	9	38–50	91	109
1	35–39	44	35	10	1–12	122	141
1	40–45	45	36	10	13–16	123	143
2	1–12	46	37	10	17–31	124	143
2	13–17	47	39	10	32–45	125	146
2	18–22	48	40	10	46–52	126	148
2	23–28	50	44	11	1–11	128b	152
3	1–6	51	45	11	12–18	129	156
3	7–12	52	46	11	19–25	131	159
3	13–19	53	47	11	27–12:12	132	160
3	19–30	61	61	12	13–17	133	164
3	31–35	63	63	12	18–27	134	165
4	1–2	64	64	12	28–34	135	167
4	3–25	64	64	12	35–37	136	168
4	26–29	64	67	12	38–40	137	169
4	30–32	64	68	12	41–44	138	172
4	33–34	64	68	13	1–37	139	173
4	35–41	65	70	14	1–2	140	186
5	1–20	66	71	14	3–9	141	187
5	21–43	67	74	14	10–11	142	188
6	1–6	69	77	14	12–16	143	189
6	6–13	70	78	14	17	144	190
6	14–29	71	82	14	18–21	146	191
6	30–44	72	85	14	27–31	147	194
6	45–46	73	88	14	22–25	148	196
6	47–52	74	89	14	26, 32–42	152	201
6	53–56	75	90	14	43–52	153	205
7	1–23	77	92	14	53, 55–65	155	209
7	24–30	78	94	14	54, 66–72	156	212
7	31–8: 9	79	95	15	1	157	215
8	10–12	80	97	15	1–5	159	216

MARK—Continued

Chap.	Verse	Section	Page	Chap.	Verse	Section	Page
15	6–15	161	220	16	1	169	239
15	16–19	162	226	16	2–8	171	240
15	20–23	163	226	16	9–11	173	243
15	24–32	164	228	16	12–13	176	244
15	33–37	165	232	16	14	178	245
15	38–41	166	234	16	15–18	181	249
15	42–46	167	235	16	19–20	184	251
15	47	168	237				

MATTHEW

Chap.	Verse	Section	Page	Chap.	Verse	Section	Page
1	1–17	3	3	9	35–11:1	70	78
1	18–25	9	9	11	2–19	57	57
2	1–12	14	11	11	20–30	58	59
2	13–18	15	12	12	1–8	50	44
2	19–23	16	13	12	9–14	51	45
3	1–6	21	15	12	15–21	52	46
3	7–10	22	16	12	22–37	61	61
3	11–12	23	17	12	38–45	62	62
3	13–17	24	19	12	46–50	63	63
4	1–11	25	20	13	1–3	64	64
4	12	34	27	13	3–23	64	64
4	13–16	40	32	13	24–30	64	68
4	17	37	31	13	31–32	64	68
4	18–22	41	33	13	33–35	64	68
4	23–25	44	35	13	36–43	64	69
5	1–2	54	48	13	44	64	69
5	3–12	54	48	13	45–46	64	69
5	13–20	54	49	13	47–50	64	70
5	21–48	54	50	13	51–53	64	70
6	1–18	54	51	13	54–58	69	77
6	19–34	54	52	14	1–12	71	82
7	1–6	54	53	14	13–21	72	85
7	7–12	54	54	14	22–23	73	88
7	13–8: 1	54	54	14	24–33	74	89
8	2–4	45	36	14	34–36	75	90
8	5–13	55	55	15	1–20	77	92
8	14–17	43	34	15	21–28	78	94
8	18, 23–27	65	70	15	29–38	79	95
8	19–22	93	112	15	39–16:4	80	97
8	28–34	66	71	16	5–12	81	98
9	1–8	46	37	16	13–20	82	99
9	9–13	47	39	16	21–26	83	100
9	14–17	48	40	16	27–28	84	101
9	18–26	67	74	17	1–8	85	102
9	27–34	68	77	17	9–13	86	103

MATTHEW—Continued

Chap.	Verse	Section	Page	Chap.	Verse	Section	Page
17	14–20	87	104	26	17–19	143	189
17	22–23	88	107	26	20	144	190
17	24–27	89	107	26	21–25	146	191
18	1–5	90	108	26	31–35	147	194
18	6–14	91	109	26	26–29	148	196
18	15–35	92	111	26	30, 36–46	152	201
19	1–12	122	141	26	47–56	153	205
19	13–15	123	143	26	57, 59–68	155	209
19	16–20:16	124	143	26	58, 69–75	156	212
20	17–28	125	146	27	1	157	215
20	29–34	126	148	27	3–10	158	215
21	1–11, 14–17	128 b	152	27	2, 11–14	159	216
21	{ 18–19	129	156	27	15–26	161	220
	12–13, }			27	27–30	162	226
21	19–22	131	159	27	31–34	163	226
21	23–22:14	132	160	27	35–44	164	228
22	15–22	133	164	27	45–50	165	232
22	23–33	134	165	27	51–56	166	234
22	34–40	135	167	27	57–60	167	235
22	41–46	136	168	27	61–66	168	237
23	1–39	137	169	28	1	169	239
24 and 25 }	......	139	173	28	2–4	170	240
				28	5–8	171	241
26	1–5	140	186	28	9–10	174	243
26	6–13	141	187	28	11–15	175	244
26	14–16	142	188	28	16–20	811	249

LUKE

Chap.	Verse	Section	Page	Chap.	Verse	Section	Page
1	1–4	1	1	3	15–18	23	17
1	5–25	4	5	3	19–20	34	27
1	26–38	5	6	3	21–23	24	20
1	39–45	6	7	3	23–38	3	3
1	46–56	7	7	4	1–13	25	20
1	57–80	8	8	4	14	34	27
2	1–7	10	9	4	14–15	37	31
2	8–20	11	10	4	16–31	39	31
2	21	12	10	4	31–37	42	34
2	22–38	13	10	4	38–41	43	34
2	39	16	13	4	42–44	44	35
2	40	17	13	5	1–11	41	33
2	41–50	18	13	5	12–16	45	36
2	51	19	14	5	17–26	46	37
3	1–2	20	15	5	27–32	47	39
3	3–6	21	15	5	33–39	48	40
3	7–14	22	16	6	1–5	50	44

LUKE—Continued

Chap.	Verse	Section	Page	Chap.	Verse	Section	Page
6	6–11	51	45	17	11–37	120	139
6	12–16	53	47	18	1–14	121	140
6	17–19	54	48	18	15–17	123	143
6	20–26	54	48	18	18–30	124	143
6	27–36	54	51	18	31–34	125	146
6	37–42	54	53	18	35–43	126	148
6	43–49	54	54	19	1–28	127	150
7	1–10	55	55	19	29–44	128b	152
7	11–17	56	56	19	45–48	129	156
7	18–35	57	57	21	37–38	131	159
7	36–50	59	60	20	1–19	132	160
8	1–3	60	61	20	20–26	133	164
8	4	64	64	20	27–40	134	165
8	5–18	64	64	20	41–44	136	168
8	19–21	63	63	20	45–47	137	169
8	22–25	65	70	21	1–4	138	172
8	26–39	66	71	21	5–36	139	173
8	40–56	67	74	22	1–2	140	186
9	1–6	70	78	22	3–6	142	188
9	7–9	71	82	22	7–13	143	189
9	10–17	72	85	22	14–16, 24–30	144	190
9	18–21	82	99				
9	22–25	83	100	22	21–23	146	191
9	26–27	84	101	22	31–38	147	194
9	28–36	85	102	22	17–20	148	195
9	36	86	103	22	39–46	152	201
9	37–43	87	104	22	47–53	153	205
9	43–45	88	107	22	54, 63–65	155	209
9	46–48	90	108	22	54–62	156	212
9	49–50	91	109	22	66–71	157	215
9	51–56	95	113	23	1–5	159	216
9	57–62	93	112	23	6–12	160	220
10	1–24	102	120	23	13–25	161	221
10	25–37	103	122	23	26–33	163	226
10	38–42	104	122	23	33–43	164	228
11	1–13	105	123	23	44–46	165	232
11	14–36	106	123	23	45, 47–49	166	234
11	37–54	107	125	23	50–54	167	235
12	1–59	108	126	23	55–56	168	237
13	1–9	109	128	24	1–8	171	240
13	10–21	110	129	24	9–12	172	242
13	22–35	113	131	24	13–32	176	244
14	1–24	114	132	24	33–35	177	245
14	25–35	115	133	24	36–43	178	245
15	1–32	116	134	24	44–49	183	250
16	1–17:10	117	135	24	50–53	184	251

JOHN

Chap.	Verse	Section	Page	Chap.	Verse	Section	Page
1	1–18	2	2	11	55–12:1, 9–11	128 a	152
1	19–28	26	22	12	12–19	128 b	152
1	29–34	27	22	12	20–50	130	157
1	35–51	28	23	12	2–8	141	187
2	1–11	29	24	13	1–20	145	190
2	12	30	24	13	21–30	146	191
2	13–22	31	25	13	31–38	147	193
2	23–3:21	32	25	14	......	149	197
3	22–36	33	26	15 and 16	......	150	198
4	1–4	34	27	17	......	151	200
4	5–42	35	27	18	1	152	201
4	43–45	36	29	18	2–12	153	205
4	46–54	38	31	18	12–14, 19–23	154	209
5	1–47	49	42	18	24	155	209
6	1–14	72	85	18	15–18, 25–27	156	212
6	14–15	73	88	18	28–38	159	216
6	16–21	74	89	18	39–19:16	161	221
6	22–71	76	90	19	16–17	163	226
7	1	77	92	19	18–27	164	228
7	2–9	94	112	19	28–30	165	232
7	10	95	113	19	31–42	167	235
7	11–52	96	114	20	1	171	240
7	53–8:11	97	115	20	2–10	172	242
8	12–20	98	116	20	11–18	173	242
8	21–59	99	116	20	19–25	178	245
9	1–41	100	118	20	26–31	179	247
10	1–21	101	119	21	......	180	247
10	22–39	111	129				
10	40–42	112	131				
11	1–44	118	137				
11	45–54	119	139				

NOTE:—The verses that are omitted in the Canterbury Revision do not appear in this Harmony. They are Mark 7:16; 9:44, 46; 11:26; 15:28; Matthew 17:21; 18:11; 23:14; Luke 17:36; 23:17; John 5:4.

In addition to the Gospels use is made of
Acts 1:3–8 in § 183, page 250.
Acts 1:9–12 in § 184, page 251.
Acts 1:18–19 in § 153, page 215.
1 Cor. 11:23–26 in § 148, page 195.
1 Cor. 15:5 in § 177, page 245.
1 Cor. 15:5 in § 179, page 247.
1 Cor. 15:6 in § 181, page 249.
1 Cor. 15:7 in § 182, page 250.

A HARMONY OF THE GOSPELS
FOR STUDENTS OF THE LIFE OF CHRIST

PART I

THE SOURCES OF THE GOSPELS

§ 1. IN THE DEDICATION LUKE EXPLAINS HIS METHOD OF RESEARCH*

Luke 1:1–4

1 FORASMUCH as many have taken in hand to draw up a narrative con-
2 cerning those matters which have been ¹fulfilled among us, even as they
delivered them unto us, which from the beginning were eyewitnesses
3 and ministers of the word, it seemed good to me also, having traced the
course of all things accurately from the first, to write unto thee in order,
4 most excellent Theophilus;† that thou mightest know the certainty concerning the ²things ³wherein thou wast instructed.

¹ Or, *fully established.*   ² Gr. *words.*   ³ Or, *which thou wast taught by word of mouth.*

---

* Luke is the first critic of the life of Christ whose criticism has been preserved to us. Others had drawn up narratives of certain portions of Christ's work. Others still had been eyewitnesses of the ministry of Jesus and gave Luke their oral testimony. Luke sifted it all with care and produced an orderly and reasonably full narrative of the earthly ministry of Jesus. We cannot reproduce all the sources that Luke had at his command, but it is clear that he followed in the main our Gospel of Mark, as any one can see for himself by comparing the two Gospels in this Harmony. Both Matthew and Luke made use of Mark. But they had other sources also. See note 2 on Synoptic Criticism at the close of the Harmony. See also Chapter IV, "Luke's Method of Research" in my *Luke the Historian in the Light of Research.*

† Luke alone follows the method of ancient historians in dedicating his Gospel, as also the Acts (1:1), to a patron who probably met the expense of publication. So Luke as a Gentile Christian writes an historical introduction in literary (*Koiné*) Greek after the fashion of Thucydides and Plutarch. Mark had no formal introduction. Matthew's introduction is genealogical because he is writing for Jewish readers to prove that Jesus is the Messiah of Jewish hope. John, writing last of all, has a theological introduction to meet the Gnostic and philosophical misconceptions concerning the Person of Christ. Thus he pictures Christ as the Eternal Logos, with God in his pre-incarnate state, who became flesh and thus revealed the Father to men.

PART II

THE PRE-EXISTENT STATE OF CHRIST AND HIS INCARNATION

§2. IN HIS INTRODUCTION JOHN PICTURES CHRIST AS THE WORD (LOGOS)

John 1:1-18

1 In the beginning was the Word,* and the Word was with God, and
2 the Word was God. The same was in the beginning with God. All
3 things were made ¹by him; and without him ²was not anything made
4 that hath been made. In him was life; and the life was the light of men.
5 And the light shineth in the darkness; and the darkness ³apprehended
6 it not. There came a man, sent from God, whose name was John. The
7 same came for witness, that he might bear witness of the light, that all
8 might believe through him. He was not the light, but *came* that he
9 might bear witness of the light. ⁴There was the true light, *even the light*
10 which lighteth ⁵every man, coming into the world. He was in the world,
and the world was made ¹by him, and the world knew him not. He
11 came unto ⁶his own, and they that were his own received him not. But
12 as many as received him, to them gave he the right to become children
13 of God, *even* to them that believe on his name: which were ⁷born, not
of ⁸blood, nor of the will of the flesh, nor of the will of man, but of God.
14 And the Word* became flesh, and ⁹dwelt among us (and we beheld his
glory, glory as of ¹⁰the only begotten from the Father), full of grace and
15 truth. John beareth witness of him, and crieth, saying, ¹¹This was he
of whom I said, He that cometh after me is become before me: for he
16 was ¹²before me. For of his fulness we all received, and grace for grace.
17 For the law was given ¹by Moses; grace and truth came ¹by Jesus Christ.
18 No man hath seen God at any time; ¹³the only begotten Son, which is in
the bosom of the Father, he hath declared *him*.

---

¹ Or, *through.* ² Or, *was not anything made. That which hath been made was life in him; and the life, &c.* ³ Or, *overcame.* ⁴ Or, *The true light, which lighteth every man, was coming.* ⁵ Or, *every man as he cometh.* ⁶ Gr. *his own things.* ⁷ Or, *begotten.* ⁸ Gr. *bloods.* ⁹ Gr. *tabernacled.* ¹⁰ Or, *an only begotten from a father.* ¹¹ Some ancient authorities read *this was he that said.* ¹² Gr. *first in regard of me.* ¹³ Many very ancient authorities read *God only begotten.*

---

* The Fourth Gospel makes no further use of the term Logos (Word) for Christ. No other Gospel employs the term, but in 1 John 1:1 we find "the Word of life" in this sense and in Rev. 19:14 we have: "and his name is called the Word of God." The Greek word has a double sense (reason and speech) and John seems to have both ideas in mind (1:18). Christ is the Idea of God and the Expression of God. The Stoics followed Plato in the philosophical use of Logos. Philo took it up and made it familiar to Jewish readers who were already used to the Hebrew *Mêmra* (Word) in a personal sense. But John carried the term further than any of his predecessors and placed it on a par with Messiah, Son of God, Son of Man, and other phrases that portray aspects of the Person of Christ. John writes his Gospel to prove the deity of Jesus (John 20:31) against Gnostics (Cerinthian) who denied it, as he wrote his First Epistle (1 John 1:1-4) to prove the humanity of Jesus against Docetic Gnostics who disclaimed it. See note 3 at end of Harmony.

PART III

THE TWO GENEALOGIES IN MATTHEW AND LUKE

§3. APPARENTLY JOSEPH'S GENEALOGY IN MATTHEW AND MARY'S IN LUKE*

Matt. 1:1–17. (*Cf.* 1 Chron. 1:34; 2:1–15; 3:1–19.)

1 ¹The book of the ²generation of Jesus Christ, the son of David, the son of Abraham.

2 Abraham begat Isaac; and Isaac begat Jacob; and Jacob begat Ju-
3 dah and his brethren; and Judah begat Perez and Zerah of Tamar; and Perez begat Hezron; and Hez-
4 ron begat ³Ram; and ³Ram begat Amminadab; and Amminadab begat Nahshon: and Nahshon
5 begat Salmon; and Salmon begat Boaz of Rahab; and Boaz begat
6 Obed of Ruth; and Obed begat Jesse; and Jesse begat David the king.

And David begat Solomon of her *that had been the wife* of Uriah;
7 and Solomon begat Rehoboam; and Rehoboam begat Abijah;
8 and Abijah begat ⁴Asa; and ⁴Asa begat Jehoshaphat; and Jehoshaphat begat Joram; and Joram
9 begat Uzziah; and Uzziah begat Jotham; and Jotham begat Ahaz;
10 and Ahaz begat Hezekiah; and Hezekiah begat Manasseh; and Manasseh begat ⁵Amon; and
11 ⁵Amon begat Josiah; and Josiah begat Jechoniah and his brethren, at the time of the ⁶carrying away to Babylon.

12 And after the ⁶carrying away

Luke 3:23–38. (*Cf.* 1 Chron. 1:1–4, 24–28; 2:1–15; 3:17; Ruth 4:18–22.)

Being the son (as was supposed)
24 of Joseph, the *son* of Heli, the *son* of Matthat, the *son* of Levi,
25 the *son* of Jannai, the *son* of Joseph, the *son* of Matthias, the *son* of Amos, the *son* of Nahum, the *son* of Esli, the *son* of Nag-
26 gai, the *son* of Maath, the son of Mattathias, the *son* of Semein, the *son* of Josech, the *son* of
27 Joda, the *son* of Joanan, the *son* of Rhesa, the *son* of Zerubbabel, the *son* of ⁷Shealtiel, the *son* of
28 Neri, the *son* of Melchi, the *son* of Addi, the *son* of Cosam, the
29 son of Elmadam, the *son* of Er, the *son* of Jesus, the *son* of Eliezer, the *son* of Jorim, the *son* of
30 Matthat, the *son* of Levi, the *son* of Symeon, the *son* of Judas, the *son* of Joseph, the *son* of Jonam,
31 the *son* of Eliakim, the *son* of Melea, the *son* of Menna, the *son* of Mattatha, the *son* of Nathan,
32 the *son* of David, the *son* of Jesse, the *son* of Obed, the *son* of Boaz, the *son* of ⁸Salmon, the *son* of
33 Nahshon, the *son* of Amminadab, ⁹the *son* of ¹⁰Arni, the *son* of Hez-
34 ron, the *son* of Perez, the *son* of Judah, the *son* of Jacob, the *son*
35 of Isaac, the *son* of Abraham, the son of Terah, the *son* of Nahor,

---

* This view is not accepted by all scholars, though it is found as early as Eusebius (*Hist. Eccl.* i, 7). See note 5 at end of Harmony.

Matt. 1:1–17

to Babylon, Jechoniah begat
⁷Shealtiel; and ⁷Shealtiel begat
13 Zerubbabel; and Zerubbabel begat Abiud; and Abiud begat Eli-
14 akim; and Eliakim begat Azor;
and Azor begat Sadoc; and Sa-
15 doc begat Achim; and Achim
begat Eliud; and Eliud begat
Eleazar; and Eleazar begat Matthan; and Matthan begat Jacob;
16 and Jacob begat Joseph the husband of Mary, of whom was born*
Jesus, who is called Christ.

Luke 3:23–38

the *son* of Serug, the *son* of Reu,
the *son* of Peleg, the *son* of Eber,
36 the *son* of Shelah, the *son* of Cainan, the *son* of Arphaxad, the
son of Shem, the *son* of Noah,
37 the *son* of Lamech, the *son* of
Methuselah, the *son* of Enoch,
the *son* of Jared, the *son* of Ma-
38 halaleel, the *son* of Cainan, the
son of Enos, the *son* of Seth, the
son of Adam, the *son* of God.

17   So all the generations from Abraham unto David are fourteen generations; and from David to the ⁶carrying away to Babylon fourteen
generations; and from the ⁶carrying away to Babylon unto the Christ
fourteen generations.†

¹ Or, *The Genealogy of Jesus Christ.*   ² Or, *the birth;* as in ver. 18.   ³ Gr. *Aram.*   ⁴ Gr. *Asaph.*
⁵ Gr. *Amos.*   ⁶ Or, *removal to Babylon.*   ⁷ Gr. *Salathiel.*   ⁸ Some ancient authorities write *Sala.*
⁹ Many ancient authorities insert *the son of Admin;* and one writes *Admin* for *Amminadab.*   ¹⁰ Some
ancient authorities write *Aram.*

* The Sinaitic Syriac, against all the early Greek manuscripts, reads in Matt. 1:16: "But
Joseph, to whom the Virgin Mary was betrothed, begat Jesus." This ancient Ebionitic text is
followed by Von Soden in his *Griechisches Neues Testament* and by Moffatt in his *New Translation
of the New Testament,* but it is difficult to believe it genuine, for in Matt. 1:18–22 the writer pictures
Joseph as on the point of putting Mary away privily. The two reports in the Sinaitic Syriac
flatly contradict each other. Those who accept it say that the writer of the Virgin Birth view in
1:18–20 overlooked 1:16 (certainly a serious oversight). It is easier to think that an Ebionitic
scribe in copying altered 1:16, but passed by 1:18–20. The Ebionites denied the deity of Jesus.
Both Matthew and Luke (1:26–38) give the Virgin Birth of Jesus, but they preserve separate
traditions on the subject.

† Observe that Matthew's three divisions of the genealogy represent three great periods in the
history of Israel. See note 5 at end of Harmony for discussion of the differences between the
genealogies in Matthew and in Luke.

PART IV

THE BIRTH AND CHILDHOOD OF THE BAPTIST AND OF JESUS

Probably B.C. 7 to A.D. 7

§§ 4–19. These sections include the annunciations, the birth, infancy, and childhood of both John and Jesus.

§ 4. THE ANNUNCIATION* OF THE BIRTH OF THE BAPTIST TO ZACHARIAS

Jerusalem, in the Temple. Probably B.C. 7

Luke 1:5–25†

5 There was in the days of Herod, king of Judea, a certain priest named Zacharias, of the course of Abijah: and he had a wife of the daughters
6 of Aaron, and her name was Elisabeth. And they were both righteous before God, walking in all the commandments and ordinances of the
7 Lord blameless. And they had no child, because that Elisabeth was barren, and they both were *now* ¹well stricken in years.
8 Now it came to pass, while he executed the priest's office before God
9 in the order of his course, according to the custom of the priest's office,
10 his lot was to enter into the ²temple of the Lord and burn incense. And the whole multitude of the people were praying without at the hour of
11 incense. And there appeared unto him an angel of the Lord standing
12 on the right side of the altar of incense. And Zacharias was troubled
13 when he saw *him*, and fear fell upon him. But the angel said unto him, Fear not, Zacharias: because thy supplication is heard, and thy wife
14 Elisabeth shall bear thee a son, and thou shalt call his name John. And
15 thou shalt have joy and gladness; and many shall rejoice at his birth. For he shall be great in the sight of the Lord, and he shall drink no wine nor ³strong drink [*see Num. 6:3; Judg. 13:4–6; 1 Sam. 1:11*]; and he shall
16 be filled with the ⁴Holy Ghost, even from his mother's womb. And many
17 of the children of Israel shall he turn unto the Lord their God. And he shall ⁵go before his face in the spirit and power of Elijah, to turn the hearts of the fathers to the children [*see Mal. 3:1; 4:5–6*], and the disobedient

* There are three annunciations: (1) to Zacharias § 4, (2) to Mary § 5, (3) to Joseph § 9. Luke gives the first two and Matthew the third. The Angel Gabriel is named by Luke (1:19, 26), but Matthew simply has "an angel of the Lord" (1:20).

† It is certain that Luke tells the infancy stories from the standpoint of Mary while Matthew writes from the standpoint of Joseph. Matthew gives the public account while Luke tells the private story from Mary herself (Ramsay, *Was Christ Born at Bethlehem?* p. 79). Luke could have seen Mary, if still alive, or could have obtained it from one of Mary's circle either orally or in manuscript form. Some scholars even suggest "Gospel of Mary" and even, "Gospel of the Baptist" as a written source for Luke in 1:5–2:52. Sanday (*The Life of Christ in Recent Research,* p. 166) says: "These two chapters—whatever the date at which they were first committed to writing—are essentially the most archaic thing in the whole New Testament" Certainly Luke reveals the use of Aramaic or Hebrew sources by the sudden changes in his style from 1:1–4. Luke, if familiar with the current account as seen in Matthew, apparently felt that he owed it to Mary to record her story of her great experience.

5

Luke 1:5-25

to walk in the wisdom of the just; to make ready for the Lord a people pre-
18 pared *for him*. And Zacharias said unto the angel, Whereby shall I
know this? for I am an old man, and my wife ⁶well stricken in years.
19 And the angel answering said unto him, I am Gabriel, that stand in the
presence of God [*see Dan. 8:16; 9:21*]; and I was sent to speak unto thee,
20 and to bring thee these good tidings. And behold, thou shalt be silent
and not able to speak, until the day that these things shall come to pass,
because thou believedst not my words, which shall be fulfilled in their
21 season. And the people were waiting for Zacharias, and they marvelled
22 ⁷while he tarried in the ²temple. And when he came out, he could not
speak unto them: and they perceived that he had seen a vision in the
²temple: and he continued making signs unto them, and remained dumb.
23 And it came to pass, when the days of his ministration were fulfilled, he
departed unto his house.
24 And after these days Elisabeth his wife conceived; and she hid her-
25 self five months, saying, Thus hath the Lord done unto me in the days
wherein he looked upon *me*, to take away my reproach among men.

¹ Gr. *advanced in their days.* ² Or,"*sanctuary* ³ Gr. *sikera.* ⁴ Or, *Holy Spirit;* and so throughout all the Gospels. ⁵ Some ancient authorities read *come nigh before his face.* ⁶ Gr. *advanced in her days.* ⁷ Or, *at his tarrying.*

§ 5. THE ANNUNCIATION TO THE VIRGIN MARY OF THE BIRTH OF JESUS

Nazareth. Probably B.C. 7 or 6

Luke 1:26-38

26 Now in the sixth month the angel Gabriel was sent from God unto
27 a city of Galilee, named Nazareth, to a virgin betrothed to a man whose
name was Joseph, of the house of David; and the virgin's name was Mary.
28 And he came in unto her, and said, Hail, thou that art ¹highly favoured,
29 the Lord *is* with thee.² But she was greatly troubled at the saying, and
30 cast in her mind what manner of salutation this might be. And the
angel said unto her, Fear not, Mary: for thou hast found ³favour with
31 God. And behold, thou shalt conceive in thy womb, and bring forth a
32 son, and shalt call his name Jesus [*see Isa. 7:14*]. He shall be great, and
shall be called the Son of the Most High: and the Lord God shall give unto
33 him the throne of his father David [*see 2 Sam. 7:12-17*]: and he shall reign
over the house of Jacob ⁴forever; and of his kingdom there shall be no end.
34 And Mary said unto the angel, How shall this be, seeing I know not a
35 man? And the angel answered and said unto her, The Holy Ghost shall
come upon thee, and the power of the Most High shall overshadow thee:
wherefore also ⁵that which ⁶is to be born ⁷shall be called holy [*see Ex. 13:12*],
36 the Son of God. And behold, Elisabeth thy kinswoman, she also hath
37 conceived a son in her old age: and this is the sixth month with her that
38 ⁸was called barren. For no word from God shall be void of power [*see Gen.
18:14*]. And Mary said, Behold, the ⁹handmaid of the Lord; be it unto
me according to thy word. And the angel departed from her.

¹ Or, *endued with grace.* ² Many ancient authorities add *blessed* art *thou among women.* (See ver. 42.) ³ Or, *grace.* ⁴ Gr. *unto the ages.* ⁵ Or, *the holy thing which is to be born shall be called the son of God.* ⁶ Or, *is begotten.* ⁷ Some ancient authorities insert *of thee.* ⁸ Or, *is.* ⁹ Gr. *bondmaid.*

§6. THE SONG* OF ELISABETH TO MARY UPON HER VISIT

Hill Country of Judea

Luke 1:39–45

39 And Mary arose in these days and went into the hill country with
40 haste, into a city of Judah; and entered into the house of Zacharias and
41 saluted Elisabeth. And it came to pass, when Elisabeth heard the salutation of Mary, the babe leaped in her womb; and Elisabeth was filled
42 with the Holy Ghost; and she lifted up her voice with a loud cry, and
said, Blessed *art* thou among women, and blessed *is* the fruit of thy womb
43 And whence is this to me, that the mother of my Lord should come unto
44 me? For behold, when the voice of thy salutation came into mine ears,
45 the babe leaped in my womb for joy. And blessed *is* she that ¹believed;
for there shall be a fulfilment of the things which have been spoken to
her from the Lord.

¹ Or, *believed that there shall be.*

§7. THE MAGNIFICAT OF MARY

Hill Country of Judea

Luke 1:46–56

And Mary said,

46 My soul doth magnify the Lord [*see 1 Sam. 2:1–10*],
47 And my spirit hath rejoiced in God my Saviour.
48 For he hath looked upon the low estate of his ¹handmaiden:
For behold, from henceforth all generations shall call me blessed
[*see 1 Sam 1:11*].
49 For he that is mighty hath done to me great things;
And holy is his name [*see 1 Sam. 2:2*].
50 And his mercy is unto generations and generations
On them that fear him [*see Ps. 103:17*].
51 He hath shewed strength with his arm;
He hath scattered the proud ²in the imagination of their heart [*see 1 Sam. 2:4; Ps. 89:10*].
52 He hath put down princes from *their* thrones,
And hath exalted them of low degree [*see Job 5:11; 12:19*].
53 The hungry he hath filled with good things;
And the rich he hath sent empty away [*see Ps. 107:9*].
54 He hath holpen Israel his servant,
That he might remember mercy [*see Isa. 41:8–9*].
55 (As he spake unto our fathers)
Toward Abraham and his seed for ever [*see Gen. 17:7; Mic. 7:20*].
56 And Mary abode with her about three months, and returned unto her house.

¹ Gr. *bondmaiden.* ² Or, *by.*

* This hymn or psalm springs from the omen to Elisabeth.

§ 8. THE BIRTH AND CHILDHOOD OF THE BAPTIST, AND HIS DESERT LIFE

Hill Country of Judea.   B.C. 7 or 6

Luke 1:57–80

57 Now Elisabeth's time was fulfilled that she should be delivered; and
58 she brought forth a son.   And her neighbors and her kinsfolk heard
that the Lord had magnified his mercy toward her; and they rejoiced
59 with her.   And it came to pass on the eighth day, that they came to
circumcise the child; and they would have called him Zacharias, after
60 the name of his father.   And his mother answered and said, Not so;
61 but he shall be called John.   And they said unto her, There is none of
62 thy kindred that is called by this name.   And they made signs to his
63 father, what he would have him called.   And he asked for a writing
64 tablet, and wrote, saying, His name is John.   And they marvelled all.
And his mouth was opened immediately, and his tongue *loosed*, and he
65 spake, blessing God.   And fear came on all that dwelt round about them:
and all these sayings were noised abroad throughout all the hill country
66 of Judea.   And all that heard them laid them up in their heart, saying,
What then shall this child be?   For the hand of the Lord was with him.
67 And his father Zacharias was filled with the Holy Ghost, and prophesied,
saying,
68 Blessed *be* the Lord, the God of Israel;
For he hath visited and wrought redemption for his people [*see Ps. 72:18;
111:9*],
69 And hath raised up a horn of salvation for us
In the house of his servant David [*see 1 Sam. 2:10; Ps. 18:3*],
70 (As he spake by the mouth of his holy prophets which have been since
the world began),
71 Salvation from our enemies, and from the hand of all that hate us
[*see Ps. 106:10*];
72 To show mercy towards our fathers,
And to remember his holy convenant;
73 The oath which he sware unto Abraham our father [*see Gen. 17:7; Lev.
26:42; Ps. 105:3; Mic. 7:20*],
74 To grant unto us that we being delivered out of the hand of our enemies
Should serve him without fear,
75 In holiness and righteousness before him all our days.
76 Yea and thou, child, shalt be called the prophet of the Most High:
For thou shalt go before the face of the Lord to make ready his ways
[*see Mal. 3:1*];
77 To give knowledge of salvation unto his people
In the remission of their sins,
78 Because of the ¹tender mercy of our God,
²Whereby the dayspring from on high ³shall visit us [*see Mal. 4:2*],
79 To shine upon them that sit in darkness and the shadow of death;
To guide our feet into the way of peace [*see Isa. 8:22; 9:2*].
80 And the child grew, and waxed strong in spirit, and was in the deserts
till the day of his shewing unto Israel.*

¹ Or, *heart of mercy.*   ² Or, *Wherein.*   ³ Many ancient authorities read *hath visited us.*

* Dwell on this summary statement as to John's retired life in the wild regions of Judea, whence
he will come forth thirty years later.

§ 9. THE ANNUNCIATION TO JOSEPH OF THE BIRTH OF JESUS

Nazareth

Matt. 1:18-25

18 Now the [1]birth [2]of Jesus Christ was on this wise: When his mother
    Mary had been betrothed to Joseph, before they came together she was
19 found with child of the [3]Holy Ghost. And Joseph her husband, being
    a righteous man, and not willing to make her a public example, was
20 minded to put her away privily. But when he thought on these things,
    behold, an angel of the Lord appeared unto him in a dream, saying,
    Joseph, thou son of David, fear not to take unto thee Mary thy wife:
21 for that which is [4]conceived in her is of the Holy Ghost. And she shall
    bring forth a son; and thou shalt call his name JESUS; for it is he that shall
22 save his people from their sins. Now all this is come to pass, that it
    might be fulfilled which was spoken by the Lord through the prophet,
    saying,
23   Behold, the virgin shall be with child, and shall bring forth a son [*see
    Isa. 7:14*], And they shall call his name [5]Immanuel;
24 which is, being interpreted, God with us. And Joseph arose from his
    sleep, and did as the angel of the Lord commanded him, and took unto
25 him his wife; and knew her not till she had brought forth a son: and he
    called his name Jesus.

[1] Or, *generation:* as in ver. 1 in § 3   [2] Some ancient authorities read *of the Christ.*   [3] Or, *Holy Spirit.*   [4] Gr. *begotten.*   [5] Gr. *Emmanuel.*

§ 10. THE BIRTH OF JESUS

Bethlehem.   Próbably B.C. 6 or 5

Luke 2:1-7

1 Now it came to pass in those days, there went out a decree from Cæsar
2 Augustus, that all the [1]world should be enrolled. This was the first
3 enrolment made when Quirinius was governor of Syria. And all went
   to enrol themselves, every one to his own city.* And Joseph also went
4 up from Galilee, out of the city of Nazareth, into Judea, to the city of
5 David, which is called Bethlehem, because he was of the house and family
   of David; to enrol himself with Mary, who was betrothed to him, being
6 great with child. And it came to pass, while they were there, the days
7 were fulfilled that she should be delivered. And she brought forth her
   firstborn son; and she wrapped him in swaddling clothes and laid him in a
   manger, because there was no room for them in the inn.

[1] Gr. *inhabited earth.*

*Observe how the ruler of the civilized world is unconsciously bringing it about that the Messiah, the son of David, shall be born at Bethlehem, though his mother's home was Nazareth. All the previous history of Rome and of Israel gathers about this manger. As to Quirinius, and as to the probable time of the Saviour's birth, see note 6 at the end of the book. The vindication of Luke's historical statements in these verses is one of the triumphs of modern research, as is shown in that note.

§ 11. THE PRAISE OF THE ANGELS AND THE HOMAGE OF THE SHEPHERDS

Near Bethlehem

Luke 2:8–20

8 And there were shepherds in the same country abiding in the field,
9 and keeping ¹watch by night over their flock. And an angel of the Lord
stood by them, and the glory of the Lord shone round about them, and
10 they were sore afraid. And the angel said unto them, Be not afraid;
11 for behold, I bring you good tidings of great joy which shall be to all the
people: for there is born to you this day in the city of David, a Saviour
12 which is ²Christ the Lord. And this *is* the sign unto you; Ye shall find a
13 babe wrapped in swaddling clothes, and lying in a manger. And suddenly
there was with the angel a multitude of the heavenly host praising* God,
and saying,
14   Glory to God in the highest,
   And on earth ³peace among ⁴men in whom he is well pleased.
15 And it came to pass, when the angels went away from them into heaven,
the shepherds said one to another, Let us now go even unto Bethlehem,
and see this ⁵thing that is come to pass, which the Lord hath made known
16 unto us. And they came with haste, and found both Mary and Joseph,
17 and the babe lying in the manger. And when they saw it, they made
known concerning the saying which was spoken to them about this child.
18 And all that heard it wondered at the things which were spoken unto
19 them by the shepherds. But Mary kept all these ⁶sayings, pondering
20 them in her heart. And the shepherds returned, glorifying and praising
God for all the things that they had heard and seen, even as it was spoken
unto them.

¹ Or, *night-watches.* ² Or, *Anointed Lord.* ³ Many ancient authorities read *peace, good pleasure
among men.* ⁴ Gr. *men of good pleasure.* ⁵ Or, *saying.* ⁶ Or, *things.*

§ 12. THE CIRCUMCISION OF JESUS

Bethlehem

Luke 2:21

21 And when eight days were fulfilled for circumcising him [*see Gen.
17:12; Lev. 12:3*], his name was called JESUS, which was so called by
the angel before he was conceived in the womb.

§ 13. THE PRESENTATION IN THE TEMPLE WITH THE HOMAGE OF SIMEON AND ANNA

Jerusalem

Luke 2:22–38

22 And when the days of their purification according to the law of Moses
23 were fulfilled, they brought him up to Jerusalem, to present him to the

* The Gloria in Excelsis.

Luke 2:22-38

Lord (as it is written in the law of the Lord, Every male that openeth the
womb, shall be called holy to the Lord) [*see Ex. 13:2, 12, 15; Lev. 12:1-8*],
24 and to offer a sacrifice according to that which is said in the law of the
25 Lord, A pair of turtledoves, or two young pigeons.   And behold, there was
a man in Jerusalem, whose name was Simeon; and this man was righteous
and devout, looking for the consolation of Israel: and the Holy Spirit
26 was upon him.   And it had been revealed unto him by the Holy Spirit,
27 that he should not see death, before he had seen the Lord's Christ.   And
he came in the Spirit into the temple: and when the parents brought in
the child Jesus, that they might do concerning him after the custom of the
28 law, then he received him into his arms, and blessed God and said,*

29   Now lettest thou thy ¹servant depart, O ²Lord,
       According to thy word, in peace;
30   For mine eyes have seen thy salvation [*see Isa. 52:10*].
31   Which thou hast prepared before the face of all the peoples;
32   A light for ³revelation to the Gentiles,
       And the glory of thy people Israel [*see Isa. 42:6; 49:6*].

33 And his father and his mother were marvelling at the things which
34 were spoken concerning him; and Simeon blessed them, and said unto
Mary his mother, Behold, this *child* is set for the falling and rising up
35 of many in Israel; and for a sign which is spoken against; yea and a sword
shall pierce through thine own soul; that thoughts out of many hearts
36 may be revealed.   And there was one Anna, a prophetess, the daughter
of Phanuel, of the tribe of Asher (she was ⁴of a great age, having lived
37 with a husband seven years from her virginity, and she had been a widow
even for four-score and four years), which departed not from the temple,
38 worshipping with fastings and supplications night and day.   And coming
up at that very hour she gave thanks unto God, and spake of him to all
them that were looking for the redemption of Jerusalem.

¹ Gr. *bond-servant*.   ² Gr. *Master*.   ³ Or, *the unveiling of the Gentiles*.   ⁴ Gr. *advanced in many days*.

§ 14. MAGI VISIT THE NEW-BORN KING OF THE JEWS

Jerusalem and Bethlehem

Matt. 2:1-12

1   Now when Jesus was born in Bethlehem of Judea in the days of Herod
2 the king, behold, ¹wise men from the east [*see Num. 24:17*] came to
Jerusalem, saying, ²Where is he that is born King of the Jews? for we saw
3 his star in the east, and are come to worship him.   And when Herod the
4 king heard it, he was troubled, and all Jerusalem with him.   And gathering together all the chief priests and scribes of the people, he inquired
5 of them where the Christ should be born.   And they said unto him, In
Bethlehem of Judea: for thus it is written ³by the prophet,

* The four New Testament psalms, given by Luke, breathe the atmosphere of Old Testament
piety, quite in contrast to the formalism of the Pharisees and yet thoroughly Jewish in background
and Christian in sentiment.   But it is primitive Christian feeling.   Section 7 gives the Magnificat of
Mary in response to the song of Elisabeth in § 6.   In § 8 we have the *Benedictus* of Zacharias and
in § 13 The *Nunc Dimittis* of Simeon.

11

Matt. 2:1–12

6   And thou Bethlehem, land of Judah,
      Art in no wise least among the princes of Judah;
      For out of thee shall come forth a governor [see *Mic. 5:1–2*],
      Which shall be shepherd of my people Israel.

7 Then Herod privily called the [1]wise men, and learned of them carefully
8 [4]what time the star appeared. And he sent them to Bethlehem, and said,
  Go and search out carefully concerning the young child; and when ye
  have found *him*, bring me word, that I also may come and worship him.
9 And they, having heard the king, went their way; and lo, the star, which
  they saw in the east, went before them, till it came and stood over where
10 the young child was. And when they saw the star, they rejoiced with
11 exceeding great joy. And they came into the house and saw the young
  child with Mary his mother; and they fell down and worshipped him; and
  opening their treasures they offered unto him gifts, gold and frankincense
12 and myrrh. And being warned *of God* in a dream that they should not
  return to Herod, they departed into their own country another way.

[1] Gr. *Magi.* Compare Esther 1:13; Dan. 2:12. [2] Or, *Where is the King of the Jews that is born?* [3] Or, *through.* [4] Or, *the time of the star that appeared.*

§ 15. THE CHILD JESUS CARRIED TO EGYPT, AND THE CHILDREN AT BETHLEHEM SLAIN

Probably B.C. 5

Matt. 2:13–18

13   Now when they were departed, behold, an angel of the Lord appeareth
  to Joseph in a dream, saying, Arise and take the young child and his
  mother, and flee into Egypt, and be thou there until I tell thee: for Herod
14 will seek the young child to destroy him. And he arose and took the
  young child by night, and departed into Egypt; and was there until the
15 death of Herod: that it might be fulfilled which was spoken by the Lord
  through the prophet, saying, Out of Egypt did I call my son [see *Hos. 11:1*].
16 Then Herod, when he saw that he was mocked of the [1]wise men, was
  exceeding wroth, and sent forth, and slew all the male children that were
  in Bethlehem, and in all the borders thereof, from two years old and under,
  according to the time which he had carefully learned of the [1]wise men.
17 Then was fulfilled that which was spoken [2]by Jeremiah the prophet,
  saying [see *Jer. 31:15*],
18   A voice was heard in Ramah,
      Weeping and great mourning
      Rachel weeping for her children;
      And she would not be comforted, because they are not.

[1] Gr. *Magi.* [2] Or, *through.*

§ 16. THE CHILD BROUGHT FROM EGYPT TO NAZARETH

Probably B.C. 4

Matt. 2:19–23	Luke 2:39
19 But when Herod was dead, behold, an angel of the Lord appeareth in a dream to Joseph in 20 Egypt, saying, Arise and take the young child and his mother, and go into the land of Israel: 21 for they are dead that sought the young child's life. And he arose and took the young child and his mother, and came into the land of Is- 22 rael. But when he heard that Archelaus was reigning over Judea in the room of his father Herod, he was afraid to go thither; and being 23 warned *of God* in a dream, he withdrew into the parts of Galilee, and came and dwelt in a city called Nazareth; that it might be fulfilled which was spoken ¹by the prophets,* that he should be called a Nazarene.	39 And when they had accomplished all things that were according to the law of the Lord, they returned into Galilee, to their own city Nazareth.

¹ Or, *through.*

§ 17. THE CHILDHOOD OF JESUS AT NAZARETH

Probably B.C. 4 to A.D. 7

Luke 2:40

40 And the child grew, and waxed strong, †filled with wisdom; and the grace of God was upon him.

§ 18. THE VISIT OF THE BOY JESUS TO JERUSALEM WHEN TWELVE YEARS OLD

Probably A.D. 7 or 8

Luke 2:41–50

41 And his parents went every year to Jerusalem at the feast of the pass-
42 over [see *Ex. 23:14–17; Deut. 16:1–8*]. And when he was twelve years old,
43 they went up after the custom of the feast; and when they had fulfilled the days, as they were returning, the boy Jesus tarried behind in Jerusalem;
44 and his parents knew it not; but supposing him to be in the company they went a day's journey; and they sought for him among their kinsfolk
45 and acquaintance: and when they found him not, they returned to Jeru-

---

* *Cf.* Isa. 11:1 where the Messiah is called *Netzer*, a Branch, though Nazareth is not mentioned in the Old Testament.

† This simple statement of Luke tells more in one sentence than all the apocryphal Gospels of the Infancy, with their silly legends about the miraculous prowess of the child Jesus.

Luke 2: 41–50

46 salem, seeking for him.   And it came to pass, after three days they found
   him in the temple, sitting in the midst of the [1]doctors, both hearing them,
47 and asking them questions: and all that heard him were amazed at his
48 understanding and his answers.   And when they saw him, they were
49 astonished: and his mother said unto him, [2]Son, why hast thou thus dealt
50 with us? behold, thy father and I sought thee sorrowing.   And he said
   unto them, How is it that ye sought me? wist ye not that I must be [3]in my
   Father's house?   And they understood not the saying which he spake
   unto them.

[1] Or, teachers.   [2] Gr. Child.   [3] Or, about my Father's business.

§ 19. THE EIGHTEEN YEARS* AT NAZARETH

Probably A.D. 7 to A.D. 26 (or 6 to 25)

Luke 2:51–52

51   And he went down with them, and came to Nazareth; and he was subject
     unto them: and his mother kept all *these* [1]sayings in her heart.
52   And Jesus advanced in wisdom and [2]stature, and in [3]favor with God
     and men [*see 1 Sam. 2:26*].

[1] Or, things.   [2] Or, age.   [3] Or, grace.

* After the return to Nazareth, we know nothing of Jesus' life at that place beyond the general
statements of Luke 2:52, with the knowledge and dispositions indicated in the narrative of § 18
and the fact that he was a carpenter, until he comes forth to be baptized by John, his forerunner.
The social and political conditions of this period in Galilee are described by Edersheim, D. Smith, and
other writers on the Life of Jesus, and briefly stated in Broadus's Commentary on Matthew, p. 30 f.
Dwell on the general statement of Luke 2:52.   Other passages throw light on the life in Nazareth
as to habits of worship (Luke 4:16), the family group of brothers and sisters (Mark 6:3 = Matt
13:55 f.), work as carpenter (*ibid.*).   A helpful book on this obscure period is Ramsay's *The Educa-
tion of Christ.*

PART V

THE BEGINNING OF THE BAPTIST'S MINISTRY

Probably six months and in A.D. 25. In the Wilderness of Judea and beside the Jordan, §§ 20–23

§ 20. THE TIME OF THE BEGINNING

Mark 1:1		Luke 3:1–2
1 The beginning of the gospel of Jesus Christ ¹the Son of God.		1 Now in the fifteenth *year of the reign of Tiberius Cæsar, Pontius Pilate being governor of Judea, and Herod being tetrarch of Galilee, and his brother Philip tetrarch of the region of Ituræa and Trachonitis, and Lysanias† tetrarch of Abilene, 2 in the highpriesthood of Annas and Caiaphas, the word of God came unto John the son of Zacharias in the wilderness.

¹ Some ancient authorities omit *the son of God.*

§ 21. THE MESSAGE AND THE MESSENGER

Mark 1:2–6	Matt. 3:1–6	Luke 3:3–6
2 Even as it is written ¹in Isaiah the prophet, Behold, I send my messenger before thy face [*see Mal. 3:1*],	1 And in those days cometh John the Baptist, preaching in the wilderness of 2 Judea, saying‡ Repent ye; for the kingdom of heaven is at	3 And he came into all the region round about Jordan, preaching the baptism of repentance unto re- 4 mission of sins; as it is written in the book

* See note 6 at end of Harmony.
† See note 6. Luke follows the custom of ancient historians in dating events by the names of the rulers. As the son of a priest John was probably thirty years old when he came forth.
‡ See Mark 1:15 (= Matt. 4:17); Matt. 10:7; Acts 2:38.

15

Mark 1:2–6	Matt. 3:1–6	Luke 3:3–6
Who shall prepare thy way;	3 hand. For this is he that was spoken of ²by Isaiah the proph-	of the words of Isaiah the prophet,
3 The voice of one crying in the wilderness [see Isa. 40: 3], Make ye ready the way of the Lord, Make his paths straight;	et, saying, The voice of one crying in the wilderness, Make ye ready the way of the Lord, Make his paths straight.	The voice of one crying in the wilderness, Make ye ready the way of the Lord, Make his paths straight.
4 John came, who baptized in the wilderness and preached the baptism of repentance unto re- 5 mission of sins. And there went out unto him all the country of Judea, and all they of Jerusalem; and they were baptized of him in the river Jordan, confessing their sins.	4 Now John himself had his raiment of camel's hair, and a leathern girdle about his loins; and his food was locusts and 5 wild honey. Then went out unto him Jerusalem, and all Judea, and all the region round about 6 Jordan; and they were baptized of him in the river Jordan, confessing their sins.	5 Every valley shall be filled, And every mountain and hill shall be brought low; And the crooked shall become straight, And the rough ways smooth; 6 And all flesh shall see the salvation of God [see Isa. 40:4–5].
6 And John was clothed with camel's hair, and *had* a leathern girdle about his loins, and did eat locusts and wild honey.		

¹ Some ancient authorities read *in the prophets.*   ² Or, *through*

§ 22. A SPECIMEN* OF JOHN'S PREACHING

Matt. 3:7–10	Luke 3:7–14
7 But when he saw many of the Pharisees and Sadducees coming to his baptism, he said unto them, Ye offspring of vipers, who warned you to flee from the wrath to 8 come? Bring forth therefore fruit 9 worthy of ¹repentance: and think not to say within yourselves, We have Abraham to our father: for I say unto you, that God is able of these stones to raise up children	7 He said therefore to the multitude that went out to be baptized of him, Ye offspring of vipers, who warned you to flee from the wrath 8 to come? Bring forth therefore fruits worthy of ¹repentance; and begin not to say within yourselves, We have Abraham to our father: for I say unto you, that God is able of these stones to raise up 9 children unto Abraham. And

* Here we see Matthew and Luke preserving a non-Markan section, as so frequently hereafter, an example of the so-called Logia (Discourses).

Matt. 3:10–10	Luke 3:9–14
10 unto Abraham. And even now is the axe laid unto the root of the trees: every tree therefore that bringeth not forth good fruit is hewn down, and cast into the fire.	even now is the axe also laid unto the root of the trees: every tree therefore that bringeth not forth good fruit is hewn down, and cast 10 into the fire. And the multitudes asked him, saying, What then must 11 we do? And he answered and said unto them, He that hath two coats, let him impart to him that hath none; and he that hath food, 12 let him do likewise. And there came also ²publicans to be baptized, and they said unto him, 13 ³Master, what must we do? And he said unto them, Extort no more than that which is appointed 14 you. And ⁴soldiers also asked him, saying, And we, what must we do? And he said unto them, Do violence to no man, neither ⁵exact *anything* wrongfully; and be content with your wages.

¹ Or, *your repentance*. ² That is, *collectors or renters of Roman taxes*. ³ Or, *Teacher*. ⁴ Gr. *Soldiers in service*. ⁵ Or, *accuse any one*.

§ 23. THE FORERUNNER'S PICTURE OF THE MESSIAH BEFORE SEEING HIM

Mark 1:7–8	Matt. 3:11–12	Luke 3:15–18
7 And he preached, saying, There cometh after me he that is mightier than I, the latchet of whose shoes I am not ²worthy to stoop down 8 and unloose. I baptized you ¹with water; but he shall baptize you ³with the Holy Ghost.	11 I indeed baptize you ¹with water unto repentance: but he that cometh after me is mightier than I, whose shoes I am not ²worthy to bear: he shall baptize you ³with the Holy Ghost 12 and *with* fire: whose fan is in his hand, and he will throughly cleanse his threshing-floor; and he will gather his wheat into the garner, but the chaff he will burn up with unquenchable fire.	15 And as the people were in expectation, and all men reasoned in their hearts concerning John, whether haply he were the Christ; 16 John answered, saying unto them all, I indeed baptize you with water; but there cometh he that is mightier than I, the latchet of whose shoes I am not ²worthy to unloose: he shall baptize you ¹with the ³Holy Ghost and *with* fire: whose 17 fan is in his hand,

17

Luke 3:15–18

throughly to cleanse his threshing-floor, and to gather the wheat into his garner: but the chaff he will burn up with unquenchable fire.

18   With many other exhortations therefore preached he [3]good tidings unto the people.*

[1]Or, *in.*   [2]Gr. *sufficient.*   [3]Or, *Holy Spirit.*   [4]Or, *the gospel.*

---

* One can easily put together all that we are told of John the Baptist in John 1:6-15 and in Sections 4, 6, 8, 20, 21, 22, 23, 24, 26, 27, 28, 33, 34, 49, 57, 71, 86, 132. See also Acts 1:5, 22; 10:37; 13:24; 18:25; 19:1-7. For a full discussion of the Baptist see my *John the Loyal.* These months of John's ministry prepared the way for the Messiah.

PART VI

THE BEGINNING OF CHRIST'S PUBLIC MINISTRY

The Year of Obscurity*

Probably Part of A.D. 26 and 27

In all parts of the Holy Land (the first Perean Ministry, the first Galilean Ministry, the first Judean Ministry, the first Samaritan Ministry). §§ 24–36. This early ministry includes the baptism, the temptation, John's witness to Jesus, the first disciples, the first miracle and work in Galilee, the first work in Judea, the arrest of John, the work in Samaria, and the return to Galilee.

§ 24. JESUS BAPTIZED BY JOHN IN THE JORDAN

Bethany beyond Jordan.   Probably A.D. 26

Mark 1:9–11	Matt. 3:13–17	Luke 3:21–23
9 And it came to pass in those days, that Jesus came from Nazareth of Galilee, and was baptized of John ⁴in the Jordan.	13 Then cometh Jesus from Galilee to the †Jordan unto John, to be baptized of him. 14 But John would have hindered him, saying, I have need to be baptized of thee, and comest thou to 15 me? But Jesus answering said unto him, Suffer ¹it now: for thus it becometh us to fulfil all right-eousness. Then he	Luke 3:21–23

---

* The precise duration of this early ministry cannot be determined. Our Lord's baptism must have been at least two months *before* the Passover, and may have been some weeks or months earlier. Then the highly successful ministry in Judea *after* the Passover must have lasted several months (John 3:22; 4:1–3). If the "yet four months" in John 4:35 be understood to be not a common saying as to the usual interval between seedtime and harvest, but a statement that it was *then* just four months before harvest, that would make the Judean ministry extend eight months after the Passover. But this interpretation is upon the whole improbable, and we can only say that the opening ministry lasted several months. The time occupied makes very little difference for our understanding the events and discourses. All of the incidents during this period after the temptation are given in John's Gospel. But for the Fourth Gospel we should not know that Jesus did not plunge at once into the great Galilee Ministry.

† The Gospel of the Hebrews (one of the apocryphal gospels) is quoted by Jerome (*adv. Pelag.* iii. 2) as having the following: "Behold, the Lord's mother and His brethren were saying to Him, John the Baptist baptizes unto the remission of sins; let us go and be baptized by him. But he said unto them, What sin have I done, that I should go and be baptized by him? unless perchance this very thing which I have said is an ignorance."

19

Mark 1:9–11	Matt. 3:13–17	Luke 3:21–23
10 And straightway coming up out of the water, he saw the heavens rent asunder,	16 suffereth him. And Jesus, when he was baptized, went up straightway from the water: and lo, the heavens were opened ²unto him, and he	21 Now it came to pass, when all the people were baptized, that Jesus also having been baptized, and praying, the
and the Spirit as a dove descending up-11 on him: and a voice came out of the heavens, Thou art my beloved Son, in thee I am well pleas-ed [see Ps. 2:7; Isa. 42:1].	saw the Spirit of God descending as a dove, and coming 17 upon him; and lo, a voice out of the heavens, saying, ³This is my beloved Son, in whom I am well pleased.	heaven was opened, 22 and the Holy Ghost *descended in a bodily form, as a dove, upon him [see John 1:32–34], and a voice came out of heaven, Thou art my beloved Son; in thee †I am well pleased. 23 And Jesus himself, when he began to teach, was about thirty years of age.

¹ Or, *me.* ² Some ancient authorities omit *unto him.* ³ Or, *This is my son; my beloved in whom I am well pleased.* ⁴ Gr. *into.*

§ 25. THE THREE TEMPTATIONS‡ OF JESUS

The Wilderness of Judea.   Probably A.D. 26

Mark 1:12–13	Matt. 4:1–11	Luke 4:1–13
12 And straightway the Spirit driveth him forth into the wilder-13 ness. And he was in the wilderness forty days tempted of Satan; and he was with the wild beasts;	1 Then was Jesus led up of the Spirit into the wilderness to be tempted of the devil. 2 And when he had fasted forty days and forty nights, he afterward hungered. 3 And the tempter came and said unto him, If thou art the Son of God, com-	1 And Jesus, full of the Holy Spirit, re-turned from the Jordan, and was led ³by the Spirit in the wilderness during forty 2 days, being tempted of the devil [see Heb. 4:15]. And he did eat nothing in those days: and when they were completed, he hun-

* The Gospel of John does not describe the baptism of Jesus, but refers to the event in a way that shows knowledge of the Synoptic Gospels.

† Codex Bezae (D) reads in Luke: "Thou art my beloved son, to-day have I begotten thee." The Gospel of the Ebionites has: "Thou art my beloved son, in thee I am well pleased, to-day I have begotten thee."

See §85 for similar language at the Transfiguration.

‡ Mark gives only a summary account while the Logia (the oldest known record) tells the temptations in detail. This early document reveals the Messianic consciousness of Jesus as distinctly as it appears in the Gospel of John. The record of the baptism in § 24 and of the temptation in § 25 goes back to the two oldest strata of the Gospel sources (Mark or the Memoirs of Peter and the Logia of Matthew) and shows that Jesus enters upon his Messianic work knowing that he had his Father's approval and the power of the Holy Spirit upon him.

Matt. 4:1–11	Luke 4:1–13

mand that these stones become ¹bread. 4 But he answered and said, It is written [*see Deut. 8:3*], Man shall not live by bread alone, but by every word that proceedeth out of the mouth 5 of God. Then the devil taketh him into the holy city; and he set him on the ²pinnacle of the tem- 6 ple, and saith unto him, If thou art the Son of God, cast thyself down: for it is written [*see Ps.91:11–12*],

He shall give his angels charge concerning thee: And on their hands they shall bear thee up, Lest haply thou dash thy foot against a stone.

7 Jesus said unto him, Again it is written [*see Deut.6:16*], Thou shalt not tempt the 8 Lord thy God. Again the devil taketh him unto an exceeding high mountain, and sheweth him all the kingdoms of the world, and the glory 9 of them; and he said unto him, All these things will I give thee, if thou wilt fall down and worship 10 me. Then saith Jesus unto him, Get thee hence, Satan: for it is written [*see Deut. 6: 13*], Thou shalt wor-

3 gered. And the devil said unto him, *If thou art the Son of God, command this stone that it become 4 ⁴bread.* And Jesus answered unto him, It is written [*see Deut. 8:3*], Man shall not live by bread alone. 5 And he led him up, and shewed him all the kingdoms of ⁵the world in a moment 6 of time. And the devil said unto him, To thee will I give all this authority, and the glory of them: for it hath been delivered unto me; and to whomsoever I will 7 I give it. If thou therefore wilt worship before me, it shall 8 all be thine. And Jesus answered and said unto him, It is written [*see Deut. 6: 13*], Thou shalt worship the Lord thy God, and him only shalt 9 thou serve. And he led him to Jerusalem, and set him on the pinnacle of the temple, and said unto him, If thou art the Son of God, cast thyself down from hence: 10 for it is written [*see Ps. 91:11–12*],

He shall give his angels charge concerning thee, to guard thee: 11 And on their hands they shall bear thee up, Lest haply thou

Mark 1:12–13	Matt. 4:1–11	Luke 4:1–13
	ship the Lord thy God, and him only shalt thou serve.	dash thy foot against a stone.
		12 And Jesus answering said unto him, It is said [*see Deut. 6:16*], Thou shalt not tempt the Lord thy God.
		13 And when the devil had completed every temptation, he departed from him [6]for a season.
and the angels ministered unto him.	11 Then the devil leaveth him; and behold angels came and ministered unto him.	

[1] Gr. *loaves.* [2] Gr. *wing.* [3] Gr. *in.* [4] Or, *a loaf.* [5] Gr. *the inhabited earth.* [6] Or, *until.*

§ 26. THE TESTIMONY OF THE BAPTIST TO THE COMMITTEE OF THE SANHEDRIN

At Bethany beyond Jordan

John 1:19–28

19 And this is the witness of John, when the Jews sent unto him from
20 Jerusalem priests and Levites to ask him, Who art thou? And he con-
21 fessed, and denied not: and he confessed, I am not the Christ. And
they asked him, What then? Art thou Elijah? And he saith, I am not.
22 Art thou the prophet? And he answered, No. They said therefore
unto him, Who art thou? that we may give an answer to them that sent
23 us. What sayest thou of thyself? He said, I am the voice of one crying
24 in the wilderness Make straight the way of the Lord, as said Isaiah the
25 prophet [*see Isa. 40:3*]. [1]And they had been sent from the Pharisees.* And
they asked him, and said unto him, Why then baptizest thou, if thou
art not the Christ, neither Elijah, neither the prophet? John answered
26 them, saying, I baptize [2]with water: in the midst of you standeth one
whom ye know not, *even* he that cometh after me, the latchet of whose
27 shoe I am not worthy to unloose. These things were done in [3]Bethany
28 beyond Jordan, where John was baptizing.

[1] Or, *And* certain *had been sent from among the Pharisees.* [2] Or, *in.* [3] Many ancient authorities read *Bethabarah,* some *Betharabah.*

§ 27. JOHN'S IDENTIFICATION OF JESUS AS THE MESSIAH

At Bethany beyond the Jordan

John 1:29–34

29 On the morrow he seeth Jesus coming unto him, and saith, Behold,
30 the Lamb of God, which [1]taketh away the sin of the world [*see Isa. 53:7*]!
This is he of whom I said, After me cometh a man which is become before

* In 1:19 the priests and Levites are Sadducees.   The idea seems to be that the Pharisees had the Sadducees sent on this embassy (*cf.* § 22).   Later Jesus will say that John was Elijah that was to come; some will even take Jesus to be Elijah.

John 1:29-34

31 me: for he was ²before me. And I knew him not; but that he should be
32 made manifest to Israel, for this cause came I baptizing ³with water.
And John bare witness, saying, I have beheld the Spirit descending as
33 a dove out of heaven; and it abode upon him. And I knew him not:
but he that sent me to baptize ³with water, he said unto me, Upon whomsoever thou shalt see the Spirit descending, and abiding upon him, the
34 same is he that baptizeth ³with the Holy Spirit. And I have seen, and
have borne witness that this is the son of God.*

¹ Or, *beareth the sin.* ² Gr. *first in regard of me.* ³ Or, *in.*

§ 28. JESUS MAKES HIS FIRST† DISCIPLES

At Bethany beyond the Jordan

John 1:35-51

35 Again on the morrow John was standing, and two of his disciples;
36 and he looked upon Jesus as he walked, and saith, Behold, the Lamb
37 of God [*see Isa. 53:7*]! And the two disciples heard him speak, and they
38 followed Jesus. And Jesus turned, and beheld them following, and saith
unto them, What seek ye? And they said unto him, Rabbi (which is to
39 say, being interpreted, ¹Master), where abidest thou? He saith unto
them, Come, and ye shall see. They came therefore and saw where he
abode; and they abode with him that day: it was about the tenth hour.
40 One of the two that heard John *speak*, and followed him, was Andrew,
41 Simon Peter's brother. He findeth first his own brother Simon, and
saith unto him, We have found the Messiah (which is, being interpreted,
42 ²Christ). He brought him unto Jesus. Jesus looked upon him, and
said, thou art Simon the son of ³John: thou shalt be called Cephas (which
is by interpretation, ¹Peter).
43 On the morrow he was minded to go forth into Galilee, and he findeth Philip: and Jesus saith unto him, Follow me. Now Philip was from
44 Bethsaida, of the city of Andrew and Peter. Philip findeth Nathanael,
45 and saith unto him, We have found him, of whom Moses in the law,
46 and the prophets, did write, Jesus of Nazareth, the son of Joseph. And
Nathanael said unto him, Can any good thing come out of Nazareth?
47 Philip saith unto him, Come and see. Jesus saw Nathanael coming to
him, and saith of him, Behold, an Israelite indeed, in whom is no guile!
48 Nathanael saith unto him, Whence knowest thou me? Jesus answered
and said unto him, Before Philip called thee, when thou wast under the
49 fig tree, I saw thee. Nathanael answered him, Rabbi, thou art the son

* Put together the Baptist's testimonies to Jesus in sections 21, 22, 23, 24, 26, 27, 28, 33, 57. Add
John 1:6-15. Note also the four testimonies of Jesus to John, sections 49, 57, 86, 132. Observe
the four successive days here in John 1:19, 29, 35, 43, and the third day from the last in John 2:1,
making a week that is covered in detail (*cf.* the Passion Week at the close). We have other glimpses
of special days in the ministry, as the Busy Day of the blasphemous accusation and the parables
(Matt. 12 and 13). In John 1:39 the very hour is preserved, probably Roman time (ten in the
morning), as John writes long after the destruction of Jerusalem and outside of Palestine and uses
the Roman reckoning (midnight to midnight) in John 20:19. But see note 11 at end of Harmony
for Ramsay's objections to this view.

† Notice here a series of First Things: first testimony of John, first disciples, first miracle, first
residence at Capernaum, first passover during his ministry, first extended discourse.

John 1:35–51

50 of God; thou art King of Israel* [see 2 Sam. 7:14; Ps. 2:7].   Jesus answered
and said unto him, Because I said unto thee, I saw thee underneath the
51 fig tree, believest thou? thou shalt see greater things than these.   And he
saith unto him, Verily, verily, I say unto you, Ye shall see the heaven
opened, and the angels of God ascending and descending upon the Son
of man† [see Gen. 28:12].

1 Or, *Teacher*.   2 That is, *Anointed*.   3 Gr. *Joanes:* called in Matt. 16:17 *Jonah*.   4 That is,
Rock or Stone.

§ 29. JESUS WORKS HIS FIRST MIRACLE

At Cana in Galilee

John 2:1–11

1   And the third day there was a marriage in Cana of Galilee: and the
2 mother of Jesus was there: and Jesus also was bidden, and his disciples,
3 to the marriage.   And when the wine failed, the mother of Jesus saith
4 unto him, They have no wine.   And Jesus saith unto her, Woman, what
5 have I to do with thee? mine hour is not yet come.   His mother saith
6 unto the servants, Whatsoever he saith unto you, do it.   Now there
were six waterpots of stone set there after the Jews' manner of purifying,
7 containing two or three firkins apiece.   Jesus saith unto them, Fill the
8 waterpots with water.   And they filled them up to the brim.   And he
saith unto them, Draw out now, and bear unto the 1ruler of the feast.
9 And they bare it.   And when the ruler of the feast tasted the water 2now
become wine, and knew not whence it was (but the servants which had
drawn the water knew), the ruler of the feast calleth the bridegroom,
10 and saith unto him, Every man setteth on first the good wine; and when
men have drunk freely, *then* that which is worse: thou hast kept the good
11 wine until now.   This beginning of his signs did Jesus in Cana of Galilee,
and manifested his glory; and his disciples believed on him.

1 Or, *steward*.   2 Or, *that it had become*.

§ 30. JESUS MAKES A FIRST SOJOURN AT CAPERNAUM, ACCOMPANIED BY HIS KINDRED AND HIS EARLY DISCIPLES

(Later Capernaum will become his home)

John 2:12

12   After this he went down to Capernaum, he, and his mother, and *his*
brethren, and his disciples: and there they abode not many days.

* Notice that these first disciples at once believed that Jesus was the Messiah (ver. 41, 45, 49).
Compare the confession of Jesus (§ 35) to the Woman at Jacob's well and the confessions of Peter in
Matt. 14:33; John 6:69; Matt. 16:16 (§§ 74, 76, 83).
† *Cf.* the close of the temptation in the wilderness and the experience in the Garden of Geth-
semane.

§ 31. THE FIRST* CLEANSING OF THE TEMPLE AT THE PASSOVER

Jerusalem.†   Probably A.D. 27

John 2:13–22

13 And the passover‡ of the Jews was at hand, and Jesus went up to
14 Jerusalem.   And he found in the temple those who sold oxen and sheep
15 and doves, and the changers of money sitting: and he made a scourge
   of cords, and cast all out of the temple, both the sheep and the oxen;
16 and he poured out the changers' money, and overthrew their tables;
   and to them that sold the doves he said, Take these things hence; make
17 not my Father's house a house of merchandise.   His disciples remembered
18 that it was written, The zeal of thine house shall eat me up [*see Ps. 69:9*].
   The Jews therefore answered and said unto him, What sign shewest
19 thou unto us, seeing thou doest these things?   Jesus answered and said
   unto them, Destroy this ¹temple, and in three days I will raise it up.
20 The Jews therefore said, Forty and six years was this ¹temple in building,
21 and wilt thou raise it up in three days?   But he spake of the ¹temple of
22 his body.   When therefore he was raised from the dead, his disciples
   remembered that he spake this; and they believed the scripture, and
   the word which Jesus had said.

¹ Or, *sanctuary*.

§ 32. THE INTERVIEW OF NICODEMUS WITH JESUS

At Jerusalem during the Passover

John 2:23 to 3:21

23 Now when he was in Jerusalem at the passover, during the feast, many
24 believed on his name, beholding his signs which he did.   But Jesus did
25 not trust himself unto them, for that he knew all men, and because he
   needed not that any one should bear witness concerning ¹man: for he
   himself knew what was in man.
1   Now there was a man of the Pharisees, named Nicodemus,§ a ruler
2 of the Jews: the same came unto him by night, and said to him, Rabbi,
   we know that thou art a teacher come from God: for no man can do
3 these signs that thou doest, except God be with him.   Jesus answered
   and said unto him, Verily, verily, I say unto thee, Except a man be born

---

* Many scholars consider this the same incident as that in the Synoptic Gospels and placed by
them in Passion Week (§ 129) probably on Monday.   It is urged that Jesus would not have repeated
such an act and hence one must follow either the order of John or of the Synoptics.   But there is no
inherent difficulty in the repetition of such an act when one reflects on the natural indignation of
Jesus at the desecration of the temple on his visit during his ministry and considers that Jesus may
have wished to make one last protest at the close of his ministry.   Certainty, of course, is not
possible in such an argument one way or the other.
    † Observe the successive *scenes* of this early ministry—beside the Jordan, on the eastern side,
at Cana of Galilee, at Capernaum, at Jerusalem, in Judea, in Samaria.
    ‡ This is the first of the passovers in John's Gospel (2:13; 6:4; 13:1).   There may have been
another.
    § Nicodemus appears as an exception to the statement of 2:24, as one whom Jesus did trust,
and who amid all difficulties of temperament and station proved not unworthy of the trust.

John 2:23 to 3:21

4 ²anew, he cannot see the kingdom of God. Nicodemus saith unto him,
How can a man be born when he is old? can he enter a second time into
5 his mother's womb, and be born? Jesus answered, Verily, verily, I say
unto thee, Except a man be born of water and the Spirit, he cannot enter
6 into the kingdom of God. That which is born of the flesh is flesh; and
that which is born of the Spirit is spirit. Marvel not that I said unto
7 thee, Ye must be born ²anew. ³The wind bloweth where it listeth, and
8 thou hearest the voice thereof, but knowest not whence it cometh, and
9 whither it goeth: so is every one that is born of the Spirit. Nicodemus
10 answered and said unto him, How can these things be? Jesus answered
and said unto him, Art thou the teacher of Israel, and understandest not
11 these things? Verily, verily, I say unto thee, We speak that we do know,
12 and bear witness of that we have seen; and ye receive not our witness. If
I told you earthly things, and ye believe not, how shall ye believe, if I
13 tell you heavenly things? And no man hath ascended into heaven, but
he that descended out of heaven, *even* the Son of man, ⁴which is in heaven.
14 And as Moses lifted up the serpent in the wilderness [*see Num. 21:8-9*],
even so must the Son of man be lifted up: that whosoever ⁵believeth may
15 in him have eternal life.
16   For God so loved the world, that he gave his only begotten Son, that
whosoever believeth on him should not perish, but have eternal life.
17 For God sent not the Son into the world to judge the world; but that
18 the world should be saved through him. He that believeth on him is
not judged; he that believeth not has been judged already, because he
19 hath not believed on the name of the only begotten Son of God. And this
is the judgment, that the light is come into the world, and men loved the
20 darkness rather than the light; for their works were evil. For every one
that ⁶doeth ill hateth the light, and cometh not to the light, lest his works
21 should be ⁷reproved. But he that doeth the truth cometh to the light,
that his works may be made manifest, ⁸that they have been wrought in
God.

¹ Or, *a man, for . . . the man.*   ² Or, *from above.*   ³ Or, *The Spirit breatheth.*   ⁴ Many ancient
authorities omit *which is in heaven.*   ⁵ Or, *believeth in him may have.*   ⁶ Or, *practiseth.*   ⁷ Or, *con-
victed.*   ⁸ Or, *because.*

§ 33. THE PARALLEL *MINISTRY OF JESUS AND JOHN WITH JOHN'S LOYALTY TO JESUS

John 3:22-36

22   After these things came Jesus and his disciples into the land of Judea;
23 and there he tarried with them, and baptized. And John also was baptizing in Ænon near to Salim, because there ¹was much water there; and
24 they came, and were baptized. For John was not yet cast into prison.
25 There arose therefore a questioning on the part of John's disciples with a
26 Jew about purifying. And they came unto John, and said to him, Rabbi,
he that was with thee beyond Jordan, to whom thou hast borne witness,
27 behold, the same baptizeth, and all men come to him. John answered and

* Jesus gained his first disciples from John at Bethany beyond Jordan and many in Jerusalem.
Now he is surpassing John. On John's loyalty to Jesus see my *John the Loyal.*

John 3:22–36

said, A man can receive nothing, except it have been given him from
28 heaven. Ye yourselves bear me witness, that I said, I am not the Christ,
29 but, that I am sent before him. He that hath the bride is the bridegroom:
but the friend of the bridegroom, which standeth and heareth him, rejoiceth greatly because of the bridegroom's voice: this my joy therefore is
30 fulfilled. He must increase, but I must decrease.
31 He that cometh from above is above all: he that is of the earth is of
the earth, and of the earth he speaketh: ²he that cometh from heaven
32 is above all. What he hath seen and heard, of that he beareth witness;
33 and no man receiveth his witness. He that hath received his witness
34 hath set his seal to *this*, that God is true. For he whom God hath sent
speaketh the words of God: for he giveth not the Spirit by measure.
35 The Father loveth the Son, and hath given all things into his hand. He
36 that believeth on the Son hath eternal life; but he that ³obeyeth not the
Son shall not see life, but the wrath of God abideth on him.

¹ Gr. *were many waters.* ² Some ancient authorities read *he that cometh from heaven beareth
witness of what he hath seen and heard.* ³ Or, *believeth not.*

§ 34. CHRIST'S REASONS FOR LEAVING JUDEA

John 4:1–4

1 When therefore the Lord knew how that the Pharisees had heard that
2 Jesus was making and baptizing more disciples than John (although
3 Jesus himself baptized not, but his disciples), he left Judea, and departed
4 again into Galilee. And he must needs pass through Samaria.

Luke 3:19, 20

19 But Herod the tetrarch, being reproved by him for Herodias his
brother's wife, and for all the evil things which Herod had done, added
20 yet this above all, that he shut up John in prison.*

Mark 1:14	Matt. 4:12	Luke 4:14
14 Now after that John was delivered up Jesus came into Galilee.	12 Now when he heard that John was delivered up he withdrew into Galilee.	14 And Jesus return-ed in the power of the Spirit into Gali-lee.

§ 35. JESUS IN SAMARIA.†

At Jacob's Well and in Sychar

John 4:5–42

5 So he cometh to a city of Samaria, called Sychar, near to the parcel of
ground that Jacob gave to his son Joseph: and Jacob's ¹well was there
6 [*see Josh. 24:32*]. Jesus therefore, being wearied with his journey, sat ²thus

* The place of John's imprisonment was Machærus, east of the Dead Sea. See Josephus,
War, Ch. VII, vi. In *Antiquities,* Ch. XVIII, v, 2 Josephus gives the public and political reason
for John's imprisonment because of Herod's fear of a revolution. He "feared lest the great influ-
ences John had over the people might put it into his power and inclination to raise a rebellion."
† Notice that John also had recently been preaching to Samaritans (§ 33) and compare hereafter Philip's work in the city of Samaria (Acts 8:5 ff.)

John 4:5–42

7 by the well.[1] It was about the sixth hour. There cometh a woman of
8 Samaria to draw water: Jesus saith unto her, Give me to drink. For
9 his disciples were gone away into the city to buy food. The Samaritan
woman therefore saith unto him, How is it that thou, being a Jew, askest
drink of me, which am a Samaritan woman? ([3]For Jews have no dealings
10 with Samaritans.) Jesus answered and said unto her, If thou knewest
the gift of God, and who it is that saith to thee, Give me to drink; thou
wouldest have asked of him, and he would have given thee living water.
11 The woman saith unto him, [4]Sir, thou hast nothing to draw with, and the
12 well is deep: from whence then hast thou that living water? Art thou
greater than our father Jacob, which gave us the well, and drank thereof
13 himself, and his sons, and his cattle? Jesus answered and said unto her,
14 Every one that drinketh of this water shall thirst again: but whosoever
drinketh of the water that I shall give him shall never thirst; but the water
that I shall give him shall become in him a well of water springing up unto
15 eternal life. The woman saith unto him, [5]Sir, give me this water, that
16 I thirst not, neither come all the way hither to draw. Jesus saith unto
17 her, Go, call thy husband, and come hither. The woman answered and
18 said unto him, I have no husband. Jesus saith unto her, Thou saidst well,
I have no husband: for thou hast had five husbands; and he whom thou
19 now hast is not thy husband: this hast thou said truly. The woman
20 saith unto him, [6]Sir, I perceive that thou art a prophet. Our fathers
worshipped in this mountain; and ye say, that in Jerusalem is the place
21 where men ought to worship. Jesus saith unto her, Woman, believe me,
the hour cometh, when neither in this mountain, nor in Jerusalem, shall
22 ye worship the Father. Ye worship that which ye know not; we worship
23 that which we know: for salvation is from the Jews. But the hour cometh,
and now is, when the true worshippers shall worship the Father in spirit
24 and truth: [5]for such doth the Father seek to be his worshippers. [6]God is a
25 Spirit: and they that worship him must worship in spirit and truth. The
woman saith unto him, I know that Messiah cometh (which is called
26 Christ): when he is come, he will declare unto us all things. Jesus saith
unto her, I that speak unto thee am *he*.
27   And upon this came his disciples; and they marvelled that he was
speaking with a woman; yet no man said, What seekest thou? or, Why
28 speakest thou with her? So the woman left her waterpot, and went
29 away into the city, and saith to the men, Come, see a man, which told
30 me all things that *ever* I did: can this be the Christ? They went out of
31 the city, and were coming to him. In the mean while the disciples
32 prayed him, saying, Rabbi, eat. But he said to them, I have meat to
33 eat that ye know not. The disciples therefore said one to another, Hath
34 any man brought him *aught* to eat? Jesus saith unto them, My meat is
35 to do the will of him that sent me, and to accomplish his work. Say not
ye, There are yet four months, and *then* cometh the harvest? behold, I
say unto you, Lift up your eyes, and look on the fields, that they are
36 [7]white already unto harvest. He that reapeth receiveth wages, and
gathereth fruit unto life eternal; that he that soweth and he that reapeth
37 may rejoice together. For herein is the saying true, One soweth and
38 another reapeth. I sent you to reap that whereon ye have not laboured:
others have laboured, and ye are entered into their labour.

John 4:5–42

39 And from that city many of the Samaritans believed on him *because
40 of the word of the woman, who testified, He told me all things that *ever* I
 did. So when the Samaritans came unto him, they besought him to abide
41 with them: and he abode there two days. And many more believed
42 because of his word; and they said to the woman, Now we believe, not
 because of thy speaking: for we have heard for ourselves, and know that
 this is indeed the Saviour of the world.†

¹ Gr. *spring:* and so in ver. 14; but not in ver. 11, 12.　² Or, *as he was.*　³ Some ancient authorities
omit *For Jews have no dealings with Samaritans.*　⁴ Or, *Lord.*　⁵ Or, *for such the Father also seeketh.*
⁶ Or, *God's spirit.*　⁷ Or, *white unto harvest. Already he that reapeth, &c.*

§ 36. THE ARRIVAL OF JESUS IN GALILEE

John 4:43–45

43 And after the two days he went forth from thence into Galilee. For
44 Jesus himself testified, that a prophet hath no honour in his own country
45 [*see Luke 4:24; Mark 6:4; Matt. 13:57*]. So when he came into Galilee, the
 Galileans received him, having seen all the things that he did in Jerusalem
 at the feast: for they also went unto the feast.

* See note on p. 27.
† In this early ministry Jesus allowed himself to be regarded as the Messiah by his first disciples
(§ 28), and personally declared that he was the Messiah to the woman at the well (§ 35) (John 4:26),
which many other Samaritans also personally believed (John 4:39, 42). He never declared this
to the Jewish rulers at Jerusalem till the very end (§ 156), doubtless because such an avowal would
lead them to kill him, and so must not be made till his work in teaching the people and training his
disciples should be completed. Compare what he says later to Peter in Matt. 16:17–20 (§ 82). At
the baptism and the temptation of Jesus it was clear that Jesus knew that he was the Son of God,
the Messiah, and was so regarded by the Baptist. Events in Judea and Galilee change the early
policy of Jesus and lead to silence on his part in the use of the word Messiah, though many of the
people know that he makes Messianic claims and the rulers in Jerusalem come to suspect him and to
fear him. See my volume on *The Pharisees and Jesus.*

PART VII

THE GREAT GALILEAN MINISTRY

Probably* Autumn of A.D. 27 to Spring of 29

(Apparently about a year and a half)

§§ 37-71. Great fulness of detail in Mark for this period and condensed report in Luke while Matthew is chiefly topical in this portion. Mark's Gospel plunges at once into the Great Galilean Ministry (cf. Peter's summary of Christ's life in Acts 10:36-43 to the household of Cornelius). The mass of material makes clear grouping difficult, but there is progress† in the development of events.

1. The Rejection at Nazareth and the New Home in Capernaum, §§ 37-43.
2. The First Tour of Galilee with the Four Fishermen and the Call of Matthew (Levi) on the Return with the Growing Fame of Jesus, §§ 44-48.
3. The Sabbath Controversy in Jerusalem and in Galilee, §§ 49-51.
4. The Choice of the Twelve and the Sermon on the Mount, §§ 52-54.
5. The Spread of Christ's Influence and the Inquiry from John in Prison, §§ 55-59.
6. The Second Tour of Galilee (now with the Twelve) and the Intense Hostility of the Pharisees, §§ 60-63.
7. The First Great Group of Parables with the Visit to Gerasa (Khersa) and to Nazareth (final one), §§ 64-69.
8. The Third Tour of Galilee (Following the Twelve) and the Effect on Herod Antipas, §§ 70-71.

---

* We cannot confidently determine the length of the ministry in Galilee. We are not sure whether it *began* in summer or late autumn (see footnote 7 in Explanatory Notes at end of Harmony). If the feast of John 5:1 was a passover or there is an unknown passover, the Galilean ministry lasted at least sixteen months, for it *ended* when another passover was near (John 6:4). Otherwise we should not certainly know that it lasted more than some six or eight months. About the two subsequent periods of our Lord's ministry we shall find no room to question that each lasted six months; but *here* we have to admit much uncertainty as to the time. After all, a determination of the time employed would be a matter of very little importance to our study of this period. But the immense amount of material in this period argues for a length of over a year.

† Throughout this great ministry in Galilee, and the periods that will follow after, the reader ought to trace carefully the *progress* of the history along several lines: (1) the Saviour's progressive self-manifestation; (2) the gradual training of the Twelve who are to carry on his teaching and work after his death; (3) the deepening and spreading hostility of the Jewish influential classes and official rulers. By constantly observing these parallel lines of progress, it will be seen that the history and teachings of our Lord exhibit a vital growth, moving on to an end by him foreseen (Luke 12:50), when the hostility of the rulers will culminate as he before the Sanhedrin avows himself to be the Messiah, and the Twelve will be almost prepared to succeed him.

§ 37. GENERAL ACCOUNT OF HIS TEACHING IN GALILEE

Mark 1:14–15	Matt. 4:17	Luke 4:14–15
14 [Now after that John was delivered up, Jesus came into Galilee], preaching the gospel of God, 15 and saying, The time is fulfilled, and the kingdom of God is at hand: repent ye, and believe in the gospel.	17 From that time began Jesus to preach, and to say, Repent ye; for the kingdom of heaven is at hand.	14 [And Jesus returned in the power of [see John 4:3, 43] the Spirit into Galilee]: and a fame went out concerning him through all the region round about. And 15 he taught in their synagogues, being glorified of all.

In sections 38–43 (the Rejection at Nazareth and the New Home in Capernaum) Jesus revisits Cana and Nazareth, recalls the four fishermen by the Sea of Galilee, and begins his ministry of teaching and healing in Capernaum.

§ 38. THE HEALING AT CANA OF THE SON OF A COURTIER OF CAPERNAUM

John 4:46–54

46 He came therefore again unto Cana of Galilee, where he made the
47 water wine. And there was a certain 1nobleman, whose son was sick at
Capernaum. When he heard that Jesus was come out of Judea into
Galilee, he went unto him, and besought *him* that he would come down,
48 and heal his son; for he was at the point of death. Jesus therefore said
49 unto him, Except ye see signs and wonders, ye will in no wise believe.
50 The 1nobleman saith unto him. 2Sir, come down ere my child die. Jesus
saith unto him, Go thy way; thy son liveth. The man believed the word
51 that Jesus spake unto him, and he went his way. And as he was now
52 going down, his 3servants met him, saying, that his son lived. So he
inquired of them the hour when he began to amend. They said therefore
53 unto him, Yesterday at the seventh hour the fever left him. So the
father knew that *it was* at that hour in which Jesus said unto him, Thy
54 son liveth: and himself believed, and his whole house. This is again the
second sign that Jesus did, having come out of Judea into Galilee.

1 Or, *king's officer.* 2 Or, *Lord.* 3 Gr. *bond-servants.*

§ 39. THE FIRST REJECTION AT NAZARETH

Luke 4:16–31

16 And he came to Nazareth, where he had been brought up: and he
entered, as his custom was, into the synagogue on the sabbath day, and
17 stood up to read. And there was delivered unto him 1the book of the

Luke 4:16–31

prophet Isaiah. And he opened the ²book, and found the place where it was written,

18 The Spirit of the Lord is upon me,
    ³Because he anointed me to preach ⁴good tidings to the poor:
    He hath sent me to proclaim release to the captives,
    And recovering of sight to the blind,
    To set at liberty them that are bruised

19 To proclaim the acceptable year of the Lord [*see Isa. 58:6; 61:1–2*].

20 And he closed the ²book, and gave it back to the attendant, and sat down:

21 and the eyes of all in the synagogue were fastened on him. And he began to say unto them, To-day hath this scripture been fulfilled in your

22 ears. And all bare him witness, and wondered at the words of grace which proceeded out of his mouth: and they said, Is not this Joseph's son?

23 And he said unto them, Doubtless ye will say unto me this parable, Physician, heal thyself [*see John 6:42; 7:15*]: whatsoever we have heard done

24 at Capernaum, do also here in thine own country. And he said, Verily I say unto you, No prophet is acceptable in his own country [*see John 4:44*].

25 But of a truth I say unto you, There were many widows in Israel in the days of Elijah, when the heaven was shut up three years and six months, when there came a great famine over all the land [*see 1 Kings 17:1; 18:1–2*];

26 and unto none of them was Elijah sent, but only to ⁵Zarephath, in the land of Sidon, unto a woman that was a widow [*see 1 Kings 17:8–9*]. And

27 there were many lepers in Israel in the time of Elisha the prophet; and none of them was cleansed, but only Naaman the Syrian [*see 2 Kings 5:1, 14*].

28 And they were all filled with wrath in the synagogue, as they heard these

29 things; and they rose up, and cast him forth out of the city, and led him unto the brow of the hill whereon their city was built, that they might

30 throw him down headlong. But he passing through the midst of them

31 went his way. And he came down to Capernaum, a city of Galilee.

¹ Or, *a roll.*   ² Or, *roll.*   ³ Or, *wherefore.*   ⁴ Or, *the gospel.*   ⁵ Gr. *Sarepta.*

§ 40. THE NEW HOME IN CAPERNAUM

Matt. 4:13–16

13 And leaving Nazareth* he came and dwelt in Capernaum, which is by

14 the sea, in the borders of Zebulun and Naphtali; that it might be fulfilled which was spoken ¹by Isaiah the prophet [*see Isa. 8:23; 9:1–2*], saying,

15 The land of Zebulun and the land of Naphtali,
    ²Toward the sea, beyond Jordan,
    Galilee of the ³Gentiles,

16 The people which sat in darkness
    Saw a great light
    And to them which sat in the region and shadow of death,
    To them did light spring up.

¹ Or, *through.*   ² Gr. *the way of the sea.*   ³ *Nations,* and so elsewhere.

* Nazareth was never the Saviour's residence during his public ministry. After the wedding at Cana he lived a short time at *Capernaum,* and henceforth that city will be his abode, till he leaves Galilee six months before the crucifixion—most of the time, however, being actually spent in several journeys throughout Galilee, together with a trip to Jerusalem, and retirement to districts around Galilee.

§ 41. JESUS FINDS FOUR FISHERS OF MEN IN FOUR FISHERMEN*

By the Sea of Galilee, near Capernaum

Mark 1:16–20	Matt. 4:18–22	Luke 5:1–11
16 And passing along by the sea of Galilee, he saw Simon and Andrew the brother of Simon casting a net in the sea: for they were fishers. 17 And Jesus said unto them, Come ye after me, and I will make you to become fishers 18 of men. And straightway they left the nets, and followed 19 him. And going on a little further, he saw James the *son* of Zebedee, and John his brother, who were also in the boat mend-20 ing the nets. And straightway he called them: and they left their father Zebedee in the boat with the hired servants, and went after him.	18 And walking by the sea of Galilee, he saw two brethren, Simon who is called Peter, and Andrew his brother, casting a net into the sea; for they were fishers. 19 And he saith unto them, Come ye after me, and I will make you fishers of men. 20 And they straightway left the nets, and 21 followed him. And going on from thence he saw other two brethren, ¹James the *son* of Zebedee, and John his brother, in the boat with Zebedee their father, mending their nets; and he 22 called them. And they straightway left the boat and their father, and followed him.*	1 Now it came to pass, while the multitude pressed upon him, and heard the word of God, that he was standing by the lake of Gennesaret; 2 and he saw two boats standing by the lake: but the fishermen had gone out of them, and were washing their 3 nets. And he entered into one of the boats, which was Simon's, and asked him to put out a little from the land. And he sat down and taught the multitudes out of 4 the boat. And when he had left speaking, he said unto Simon, Put out into the deep, and let down your nets for a 5 draught. And Simon answered and said, Master, we toiled all

6 night, and took nothing: but at thy word I will let down the nets. And when they had this done, they inclosed a great multitude of fishes; and 7 their nets were breaking; and they beckoned unto their partners in the other boat, that they should come and help them. And they came, and 8 filled both the boats, so that they began to sink. But Simon Peter, when he saw it, fell down at Jesus' knees, saying, Depart from me; for I am a 9 sinful man, O Lord. For he was amazed, and all that were with him, 10 at the draught of the fishes which they had taken; and so were also James and John, sons of Zebedee, which were partners with Simon. And Jesus 11 said unto Simon, Fear not; from henceforth thou shalt ²catch men. And when they had brought their boats to land, they left all, and followed him.

¹ Or, *Jacob:* and so elsewhere. ² Gr. *take alive.*

* Three of these two pairs of brothers (Andrew and Peter, John and James) had already become disciples of Jesus at Bethany beyond Jordan (James probably soon afterwards), but now they leave their prosperous fish business and follow Jesus continuously as many business men since have given up a lucrative business for the ministry. They, along with Philip and Nathaniel, had been with Jesus in the early ministry (the year of obscurity).

§ 42. THE EXCITEMENT IN THE SYNAGOGUE BECAUSE OF THE TEACHING OF JESUS AND THE HEALING OF A DEMONIAC ON THE SABBATH

Mark 1:21-28	Luke 4:31-37
21 And they go into Capernaum; and straightway on the sabbath day he entered into the synagogue and taught. And they were astonished at his teaching: for he taught them as having authority, and not as the scribes. 23 And straightway there was in their synagogue a man with an unclean spirit, and he cried out, 24 saying, What have we to do with thee, thou Jesus of Nazareth? art thou come to destroy us? I know thee who thou art, the 25 Holy One of God. And Jesus rebuked ¹him, saying, hold thy peace, and come out of him. 26 And the unclean spirit, ²tearing him and crying with a loud voice, 27 came out of him. And they were all amazed, insomuch that they questioned among themselves, saying, What is this? a new teaching! with authority he commandeth even the unclean spirits, and 28 they obey him. And the report of him went out straightway everywhere into all the region of Galilee round about.	31 [And he came down to Capernaum, a city of Galilee.] And he was teaching them on the sabbath day: and they were astonished at his teaching; for his 33 word was with authority. And in the synagogue there was a man, which had a spirit of an unclean ³devil; and he cried out 34 with a loud voice, ⁴Ah! what have we to do with thee, thou Jesus of Nazareth? art thou come to destroy us? I know thee who thou art [see Ps. 16:10], the Holy One 35 of God. And Jesus rebuked him, saying, Hold thy peace, and come out of him. And when the ³devil had thrown him down in the midst, he came out of him, having done him 36 no hurt. And amazement came upon all, and they spake together, one with another, saying, What is ⁵this word? for with authority and power he commandeth the unclean spirits, and they come 37 out. And there went forth a rumour concerning him into every place of the region round about.

¹ Or, it. ² Or, convulsing. ³ Gr. demon. ⁴ Or, let alone. ⁵ Or, this word, that with authority—come out?

§ 43. HE HEALS PETER'S MOTHER-IN-LAW AND MANY OTHERS

At Capernaum, in Peter's Home

Mark 1:29-34	Matt. 8:14-17	Luke 4:38-41
29 And straightway ³when they were come out of the synagogue, they came into the house of Simon and Andrew, with James 30 and John. Now Si-		38 And he rose up from the synagogue and entered into the house of Simon. And Simon's wife's mother was holden with a

Mark 1:29-34	Matt. 8:14-17	Luke 4:38-41
mon's wife's mother lay sick of a fever; and straightway they 31 tell him of her: and he came and took her by the hand, and raised her up; and the fever left her, and she ministered unto them.	14 And when Jesus was come into Peter's house, he saw his wife's mother lying sick of a fever 15 And he touched her hand, and the fever left her; and she arose, and ministered unto him.	great fever; and they besought him for 39 her. And he stood over her, and rebuked the fever; and it left her: and immediately she rose up and ministered unto them.
32 And at even, when the sun did set, they brought unto him all that were sick, and them that were ¹possessed with 33 devils. And all the city was gathered together at the door. 34 And he healed many that were sick with divers diseases, and cast out many ⁴devils; and he suffered not the ⁴devils to speak, because they knew him.⁵	16 And when even was come, they brought unto him many ¹possessed with devils: and he cast out the spirits with a word, and healed all that 17 were sick: that it might be fulfilled which was spoken ²by Isaiah the prophet [*see Isa. 53:4*], saying, Himself took our infirmities, and bare our diseases.	40 And when the sun was setting, all they that had any sick with divers diseases brought them unto him; and he laid his hands on every one of them, and healed 41 them. And ⁴devils also came out from many, crying out, and saying, Thou art the Son of God. And rebuking them, he suffered them not to speak, because they knew that he was the Christ.

¹ Or, *demoniacs.* ² Or, *through.* ³ Some ancient authorities read *when he was come out of the synagogue, he came, &c.* ⁴ Gr. *demons.* ⁵ Many ancient authorities add *to be Christ.* See Luke 4:41.

In sections 44–52 Jesus makes his first tour of Galilee with the Four Fishermen whom he has now called to follow him continuously. On the return to Capernaum Matthew is called and various miracles arouse the enthusiasm of the multitudes and the hostility of the Pharisees to Christ's teachings.

§44. THE FIRST TOUR OF GALILEE WITH THE FOUR FISHERMEN

Mark 1:35-39	Luke 4:42-44
35 And in the morning, a great while before day, he rose up and went out, and departed into a desert place, and	42 And when it was day, he came out and went into a desert place: and the multitudes sought after him, and came unto

Mark 1:35–39	Matt. 4:23–25	Luke 4:42–44
36 there prayed. And Simon and they that were with him fol- 37 lowed after him; and they found him, and say unto him, All are seeking thee. 38 And he saith unto them, Let us go elsewhere into the next towns, that I may preach there also; for to this end came I		him, and would have stayed him, that he should not go from 43 them. But he said unto them, I must preach the ⁵good tidings of the kingdom of God to the other cities also; for therefore was I sent.
39 forth. And he went into their synagogues throughout all Galilee, preaching and casting out ⁴devils.	23 And ¹Jesus went about in all Galilee,* teaching in their synagogues, and preaching the ²gospel of the kingdom, and healing all manner of disease and all manner of sickness	44 And he was preaching in the synagogues of ⁶Galilee.
24 among the people. And the report of him went forth into all Syria: and they brought unto him all that were sick, holden with divers diseases and torments, ³possessed with devils, and epileptic, and	25 palsied; and he healed them. And there followed him great multitudes from Galilee and Decapolis and Jerusalem and Judea and *from* beyond Jordan.	

¹ Some ancient authorities read *he.* ² Or, *good tidings:* and so elsewhere. ³ Or, *demoniac·*
⁴ Gr. *demons.* ⁵ Or, *Gospel.* ⁶ Very many ancient authorities read *Judea.*

§ 45. A LEPER HEALED, AND MUCH POPULAR EXCITEMENT

Mark 1:40–45	Matt. 8:2–4	Luke 5:12–16
40　And there cometh to him a leper, beseeching him, ¹and kneeling down to him, and saying unto him, If thou wilt, thou canst make me clean.	2　And behold, there came to him a leper and worshipped him, saying, Lord, if thou wilt thou canst make me clean,	12　And it came to pass, while he was in one of the cities, behold, a man full of leprosy: and when he saw Jesus, he fell on his face, and besought him, saying,
41 And being moved with compassion, he	3 And he stretched forth his hand, and	Lord, if thou wilt,

* This journey about all Galilee included a *great mass* of teaching and healing (dwell on Matt. 4:23–25), of which only a few specimens are recorded, and these apparently occurred at Capernaum, his headquarters.　The journey given by Luke only (8:1–3) is probably distinct from this, and if so it would be a *second*, while that of Luke 9:1–6(=Mark 6:6–13=Matt. 9:35, 11:1), which is quite certainly distinct, would then be a *third* journey about Galilee.　The reader ought to expand his imagination and take in these extended labors.

Mark 1:40–45	Matt. 8:2–4	Luke 5:12–16
stretched forth his hand, and touched him, and saith unto him, I will; be thou 42 made clean. And straightway the leprosy departed from him, and he was 43 made clean. And he ²strictly charged him, and straightway sent 44 him out, and saith unto him, See thou say nothing to any man: but go thy way, shew thyself to the priest, and offer for thy cleansing the things which Moses commanded, for a testimony unto them.	touched him, saying, I will; be thou made clean. And straightway his leprosy was cleansed.	thou canst make me 13 clean. And he stretched forth his hand, and touched him, saying, I will; be thou made clean. And straightway the leprosy departed from him.
	4 And Jesus saith unto him, See thou tell no man; but go thy way, shew thyself to the priest, and offer the gift that Moses commanded, for a testimony unto them.	14 And he charged him to tell no man: but go thy way, and shew thyself to the priest, and offer for thy cleansing, according as Moses commanded, for a testimony unto them [*see Lev. 13: 49; 14:2–32*].
45 But he went out, and began to publish it much, and to spread abroad the ³matter, insomuch that ⁴Jesus could no more openly enter into ⁵a city, but was without in desert places: and they came to him from every quarter.		15 But so much the more went abroad the report concerning him: and great multitudes came together to hear, and to be healed of their in- 16 firmities. But he withdrew himself in the deserts, and prayed.

¹ Some ancient authorities omit *and kneeling down to him.*   ² Or, *sternly.*   ³ Gr. *word.*   ⁴ Gr. *he.*
⁵ Or, *the city.*

§ 46. THRONGED IN CAPERNAUM, HE HEALS A PARALYTIC LOWERED THROUGH THE ROOF OF PETER'S HOUSE

Mark 2:1–12	Matt. 9:1–8	Luke 5:17–26
1 And when he entered again into Capernaum after some days, it was noised that he was ⁴in the 2 house. And many were gathered together, so that there	1 And he entered into a boat, and crossed over, and came into his own city.	17 And it came to pass on one of those days, that he was teaching; and there were Pharisees and doctors of the law sitting by, which were come out of every

37

Mark 2:1–12	Matt. 9:1–8	Luke 5:17–26
was no longer room *for them*, no, not even about the door: and he spake the word un- 3 to them. And they come bringing unto him a man sick of the palsy, borne of four. 4 And when they could not ⁵come nigh unto him for the crowd, they uncovered the roof where he was: and when they had broken it up, they let down the bed where- on the sick of the	2 And behold they brought to him a man sick of the palsy, lying on a bed;	village of Galilee and Judea and Jerusalem: and the power of the Lord was with him 18 ⁶to heal. And be- hold, men bring on a bed a man that was palsied: and they sought to bring him in, and to lay him 19 before him. And not finding by what *way* they might bring him in because of the multitude, they went up to the housetop, and let him down through the tiles with his couch into the midst before Jesus.
5 palsy lay. And Jesus seeing their faith saith unto the sick of 6 the palsy, ¹Son, thy sins are forgiven. But there were certain of the scribes sit- ting there, and rea- soning in their hearts, 7 Why doth this man thus speak? he blas- phemeth: who can forgive sins but one, 8 *even* God? And straightway Jesus, perceiving in his spirit that they so reasoned within themselves, saith unto them, Why reason ye these things in your hearts? 9 Whether is easier, to say to the sick of the palsy, Thy sins are forgiven; or to say, Arise, and take up thy bed, and walk? 10 But that ye may know that the Son of man hath ³power	and Jesus seeing their faith said unto the sick of the palsy, ¹Son, be of good cheer; thy sins are 3 forgiven. And be- hold, certain of the scribes said within themselves, This man blasphemeth. 4 And Jesus ²knowing their thoughts said, Wherefore think ye evil in your hearts? 5 For whether is easier, to say, Thy sins are forgiven; or to say, 6 Arise and walk? But that ye may know that the Son of man hath ³power on earth	20 And seeing their faith, he said, Man, thy sins are forgiven 21 thee. And the scribes and the Pharisees be- gan to reason, saying, Who is this that speaketh blasphem- ies? Who can for- give sins but God alone? 22 But Jesus per- ceiving their reason- ings, answered and said unto them, ⁷What reason ye in your hearts? 23 Whether is easier to say, Thy sins are forgiven thee; or to say, Arise and walk? 24 But that ye may know that the Son of man hath ³power

Mark 2:1-12	Matt. 9:1-8	Luke 5:17-26
on earth to forgive sins (he saith to the sick of the palsy),* I 11 say unto thee, Arise, take up thy bed, and go unto thy house.	to forgive sins (then saith he to the sick of the palsy), Arise, and take up thy bed, and go unto thy	on earth to forgive sins (he said unto him that was palsied), I say unto thee, Arise, and take up thy couch, and go 25 unto thy house. And
12 And he arose, and straightway took up the bed, and went forth before them all; insomuch that they were all amazed, and glorified God, saying, We never saw it on this fashion.	7 house. And he arose, and departed to his house. 8 But when the multitudes saw it, they were afraid, and glorified God, which had given such ³power unto men.	immediately he rose up before them, and took up that whereon he lay, and departed to his house, 26 glorifying God. And amazement took hold on all, and they glorified God; and they were filled with fear, saying, We have seen strange things to-day.

¹ Gr. *Child*. ² Many ancient authorities read *seeing*. ³ Or, *authority*. ⁴ Or, *at home*. ⁵ Many ancient authorities read *bring him unto him*. ⁶ Gr. *that he should heal*. Many ancient authorities read *that* he *should heal them*. ⁷ Or, *Why*.

§47. THE CALL OF MATTHEW (LEVI) AND HIS RECEPTION IN HONOR OF JESUS

Capernaum

Mark 2:13-17	Matt. 9:9-13	Luke 5:27-32
13 And he went forth again by the sea side; and all the multitude resorted unto him, and he taught them.		27 And after these things he went forth, and beheld a publican, named Levi, sitting at the place of toll, and said unto him, Follow me.
14 And as he passed by, he saw Levi the *son* of Alphæus sitting at the place of toll, and he saith unto him, Follow me. And he arose and followed	9 And as Jesus passed by from thence, he saw a man, called Matthew, sitting at the place of toll: and he saith unto him, Follow me. And he arose, and followed him.	28 And he forsook all, and rose up and followed him.
15 him. And it came to pass, that he was sitting at meat in his house, and many	10 And it came to pass, as he ¹sat at meat in the house, behold, many publi-	29 And Levi made him a great feast in his house: and there was

* Note the parenthetic explanation of the writers in the middle of the saying of Jesus. It is proof that each of the Gospels had the same written source here or rather, as we know otherwise, that Matthew and Luke had Mark before them.

Mark 2:13–17	Matt. 9:9–13	Luke 5:27–32
⁴publicans and sinners sat down with Jesus and his disciples: for there were many, and they followed him.	cans and sinners came and sat down with Jesus and his disciples.	a great multitude of publicans and of others that were sitting at meat with them.
16 And the scribes⁵ of the Pharisees, when they saw that he was eating with the sinners and publicans, said unto his disciples, ⁶He eateth ⁷and drinketh with publicans and sinners.	11 And when the Pharisees saw it, they said unto his disciples, Why eateth your ²Master with the publicans and sinners?	30 And ⁸the Pharisees and their scribes murmured against his disciples, saying, Why do ye eat and drink with the publicans and sinners?
17 And when Jesus heard it, he saith unto them, They that are ³whole have no need of a physician, but they that are sick: I came not to call the righteous but sinners.	12 But when he heard it, he said, They that are ³whole have no need of a physician, but they that are 13 sick. But go ye and learn what *this* meaneth,* I desire mercy, and not sacrifice: for I came not to call the righteous, but sinners.	31 And Jesus answering said unto them, They that are ³whole have no need of a physician; but they that are sick. 32 I am not come to call the righteous but sinners to repentance.

¹ Gr. *reclined:* and so always.   ² Or, *Teacher.*   ³ Gr. *strong.*   ⁴ That is, *collectors or renters of Roman taxes:* and so elsewhere.   ⁵ Some ancient authorities read *and the Pharisees.*   ⁶ Or, *how is it that he eateth . . . sinners?*   ⁷ Some ancient authorities omit *and drinketh.*   ⁸ Or, *the Pharisees and the scribes among them.*

§ 48. JESUS IN THREE PARABLES DEFENDS HIS DISCIPLES FOR FEASTING† INSTEAD OF FASTING

Mark 2:18–22	Matt. 9:14–17	Luke 5:33–39
18 And John's disciples and the Pharisees were fasting: and they come and say unto him, Why do John's disciples and the disciples of the Pharisees fast, but thy disciples fast not?	14 Then come to him the disciples of John, saying, Why do we and the Pharisees fast ¹oft, but thy disciples	33 And they said unto him, The disciples of John fast often, and make supplications; likewise also the *disciples* of the Pharisees; but thine
19 And Jesus said unto them, Can the sons of the bride-chamber	15 fast not? And Jesus said unto them, Can the sons of the bride-chamber mourn, as	34 eat and drink. And Jesus said unto them, Can ye make the sons of the bride-chamber fast while

* Hos. 6:6.

† It was probably the presence of the disciples of Christ at Matthew's feast on one of the Jewish fast days that occasioned the complaint of John's disciples and the Pharisees. It is sad to see disciples of John aligned with the Pharisees against Jesus.

Mark 2:18–22	Matt. 9:14–17	Luke 5:33–39
fast, while the bride-groom is with them? as long as they have the bride-groom with them they cannot 20 fast. But the days will come, when the bride-groom shall be taken away from them, and then they will fast in that day.	long as the bride-groom is with them? But the days will come, when the bride-groom shall be taken away from them, and then will they fast.	the bride-groom is with them? 35 But the days will come; and when the bride-groom shall be taken away from them, then will they fast in those days. 36 And he spake also a parable* unto
21 No man seweth a piece of undressed cloth on an old garment; else that which should fill it up taketh from it, the new from the old, and a worse rent 22 is made. And no man putteth new wine into old ²wine-skins: else the wine will burst the skins, and the wine perish-eth, and the skins: but *they put* new wine into fresh wine-skins.	16 And no man putteth a piece of undressed cloth upon an old garment; for that which should fill it up taketh from the garment, and a worse rent is made. 17 Neither do *men* put new wine into old ²wine-skins: else the skins burst and the wine is spilled, and the skins perish; but they put new wine into fresh wine-skins, and both are pre-served.	them; No man rend-eth a piece from a new garment and put-teth it upon an old garment; else he will rend the new, and also the piece from the new will not agree with the old. And 37 no man putteth new wine into old ²wine-skins; else the new wine will burst the skins, and itself will be spilled, and the skins will perish. 38 But new wine must be put into fresh 39 wine-skins. And no man having drunk old *wine* desireth new: for he saith, The old is ³good.

¹ Some ancient authorities omit *oft.*   ² That is, *skins used as bottles.*   ³ Many ancient authorities read *better.*

In sections 49 to 51 we see the Pharisees attacking Jesus both in Jerusalem and in Galilee with great hostility and with the purpose of killing him because of violation of the Pharisaic regulations about the Sabbath. Jesus defends himself and his disciples by various arguments and personal claims.

---

* Note the use of the term parable in Luke. There are three parables (the sons of the bride-chamber, the new patch on an old garment, the new wine in old wine-skins) here together. A few isolated ones have already occurred as in John 2:19.

§ 49. AT A FEAST IN JERUSALEM (POSSIBLY THE PASSOVER) JESUS HEALS A LAME MAN ON THE SABBATH AND DEFENDS THIS ACTION TO THE PHARISEES IN A GREAT DISCOURSE

John 5:1–47

1 After these things there was ¹a feast* of the Jews; and Jesus went up to Jerusalem.†

2 Now there is in Jerusalem by the sheep *gate* a pool, which is called in
3 Hebrew ²Bethesda, having five porches. In these lay a multitude of them
5 that were sick, blind, halt, withered.³ And a certain man was there,
6 which had been thirty and eight years in his infirmity. When Jesus saw him lying, and knew that he had been now a long time *in that case*, he
7 saith unto him, Wouldst thou be made whole? The sick man answered him, ⁴Sir, I have no man, when the water is troubled, to put me into the
8 pool: but while I am coming, another steppeth down before me. Jesus
9 saith unto him, Arise, take up thy bed, and walk. And straightway the man was made whole, and took up his bed and walked.

10 Now it was the sabbath on that day. So the Jews said unto him that was cured, It is the sabbath, and it is not lawful for thee to take up thy
11 bed [*see Ex. 20:10; Deut. 5:14*]. But he answered them, He that made me
12 whole, the same said unto me, Take up thy bed, and walk. They asked
13 him, Who is the man that said unto thee, Take up *thy bed*, and walk? But he that was healed wist not who it was: for Jesus had conveyed himself
14 away, a multitude being in the place. Afterward Jesus findeth him in the temple, and said unto him, Behold, thou art made whole: sin no more,
15 lest a worse thing befall thee. The man went away, and told the Jews
16 that it was Jesus which had made him whole. And for this cause did the Jews persecute Jesus, because he did these things on the sabbath. But
17 Jesus answered them, My Father worketh even until now, and I work.
18 For this cause therefore the Jews sought the more to kill him, because he not only brake the sabbath, but also called God his own Father, making himself equal with God.

19 Jesus therefore answered and said unto them,

Verily, verily, I say unto you, The Son can do nothing of himself, but what he seeth the Father doing: for what things soever he doeth, these
20 the Son also doeth in like manner. For the Father loveth the Son, and sheweth him all things that himself doeth; and greater works than these
21 will he shew him, that ye may marvel. For as the Father raiseth the dead and quickeneth them, even so the Son also quickeneth whom he will.

---

* This feast of John 5:1 was *most probably* a Passover (see note at end of volume, note 7). If so, we should know that our Lord's public ministry lasted three years and a fraction, and that the great ministry in Galilee lasted some 18 to 20 months. Otherwise, we should know of only two years and a fraction for the former, and 6 to 8 months for the latter: as John gives three passovers beyond question (John 2:13; 6:4; 12:1), and our Lord's ministry began some time before the first of these. If the feast of 5:1 was not a passover, it is quite impossible to determine what other feast it was. While one would be glad to settle these questions, if it were possible, yet it really does not matter as regards understanding our Lord's *recorded* history and teachings during the great ministry in Galilee, the only point of difference being that if this feast was a Passover (or if there is an unmentioned Passover) we should conceive of the three journeys about Galilee as occupying a longer time, and including more extensive *unrecorded* labors in preaching and healing.

† It is to be noted that John's Gospel gives the Jerusalem Ministry of Jesus almost entirely except Galilee in ch. 2, Samaria and Galilee in ch. 4, Galilee in ch. 6 and again in ch. 21. It seems clear that John wrote with full knowledge of the Synoptic Gospels and supplements them at certain points. Both Luke and John were thus critics of the Gospel records.

John 5:1–47

22 For neither doth the Father judge any man, but he hath given all judgement unto the Son; that all may honour the Son, even as they honour the
23 Father. He that honoureth not the Son honoureth not the Father which
24 sent him. Verily, verily, I say unto you, He that heareth my word, and
believeth him that sent me, hath eternal life, and cometh not into judge-
25 ment, but hath passed out of death into life. Verily, verily, I say unto
you, The hour cometh, and now is, when the dead shall hear the voice
26 of the Son of God; and they that hear shall live. For as the Father hath
life in himself, even so gave he to the Son also to have life in himself: and
27 he gave him authority to execute judgement, because he is ⁵the Son of
28 man. Marvel not at this: for the hour cometh, in which all that are in
29 the tombs shall hear his voice, and shall come forth; they that have done
good, unto the resurrection of life; and they that have ⁶done ill, unto the
resurrection of judgement.
30 I can of myself do nothing: as I hear, I judge: and my judgement is
righteous; because I seek not mine own will, but the will of him that sent
31 me. If I bear witness of myself, my witness is not true. It is another
32 that beareth witness of me; and I know that the witness which he wit-
33 nesseth of me is true. Ye have sent unto John, and he hath borne witness
34 unto the truth. But the witness which I receive is not from man: howbeit
35 I say these things, that ye may be saved. He was the lamp that burneth
36 and shineth: and ye were willing to rejoice for a season in his light. But the
witness which I have is greater than *that* of John: for the works which the
Father hath given me to accomplish, the very works that I do, bear
37 witness of me, that the Father hath sent me. And the Father which sent
me, he hath borne witness of me. Ye have neither heard his voice at any
38 time, nor seen his form. And ye have not his word abiding in you: for
39 whom he sent, him ye believe not. ⁷Ye search the scriptures, because
ye think that in them ye have eternal life; and these are they which bear
40 witness of me; and ye will not come to me, that ye may have life. I
41 receive not glory from men. But I know you, that ye have not the love
42 of God in yourselves. I am come in my Father's name, and ye receive
43 me not; if another shall come in his own name, him ye will receive. How
44 can ye believe, which receive glory one of another, and the glory that
45 *cometh* from ⁸the only God ye seek not? Think not that I will accuse you
to the Father: there is one that accuseth you, *even* Moses, on whom ye have
46 set your hope. For if ye believed Moses, ye would believe me; for he wrote
47 of me. But if ye believe not his writings, how shall ye believe my words?*

¹ Many ancient authorities read *the feast.* ² Some ancient authorities read *Bethsaida,* others
Bethzatha. ³ Many ancient authorities insert, wholly or in part, *waiting for the moving of the water:*
4 *for an angel of the Lord went down at certain seasons into the pool, and troubled the water: whosoever
then first after the troubling of the water stepped in was made whole, with whatsoever disease he was
holden.* ⁴ Or, *Lord.* ⁵ Or, *a son of man.* ⁶ Or, *practised.* ⁷ Or, *Search the scriptures.* ⁸ Some
ancient authorities read *the only one.*

---

* Observe that here more than a year before the crucifixion, and probably two years (*i.e.* if
the feast of 5:1 was a passover or if an unnamed passover is granted), the hostility of the Jews *at*
Jerusalem (comp. John 4:1) has reached the point of a desire to kill him, as a sabbath-breaker and a
blasphemer (5:16–18). So we shall find him staying away from Jerusalem at the passover of John
6:4, and until the Tabernacles six months before the crucifixion (John 7:1–10). Meantime, the
hostility will go on increasing in other parts of the country (Mark 3:6, etc.).—Notice also that in
this discourse at Jerusalem our Lord repeatedly declares himself in a high sense the Son of God,
and the appointed judge of mankind (ver. 27), and says that Moses wrote concerning him (ver. 46).
All this indicated that he was the Messiah, but he did not here expressly assert it as he did in Samaria
(John 4:26). That would have precipitated the collision, for to claim to be the Messiah would *in*
the view of the Jewish rulers involve *political* consequences. Comp. John 11:48.

§ 50. ANOTHER SABBATH CONTROVERSY WITH THE PHARISEES WHEN THE DISCIPLES PLUCK EARS OF GRAIN IN THE FIELDS

Probably in Galilee on the Way Back from Jerusalem*

Mark 2:23–28	Matt. 12:1–8	Luke 6:1–5
23 And it came to pass, that he was going on the sabbath day through the corn-fields; and his disciples ³began, as they went, to pluck the 24 ears of corn. And the Pharisees said unto him, Behold, why do they on the sabbath day that which is not lawful? 25 And he said unto them, Did ye never read what David did, when he had need, and was an hungred, he, and they that were with 26 him? How he entered into the house of God ⁴when Abiathar was high priest, and did eat the shewbread, which is not lawful to eat, save for the priests, and gave also to them that were with him?	1 At that season Jesus went on the sabbath-day through the corn-fields: and his disciples were an hungred, and began to pluck ears of corn, 2 and to eat. But the Pharisees, when they saw it, said unto him, Behold, thy disciples do that which it is not lawful to do upon the sabbath. 3 But he said unto them, Have ye not read what David did, when he was an hungred, and they that were with him; how 4 he entered into the house of God, and ¹did eat the shewbread, which it was not lawful for him to eat, neither for them that were with them, but only for 5 the priests? Or have ye not read in the law, how that on the sabbath day the priests in the temple profane the sabbath [see *Num. 28:9–10*], 6 and are guiltless? But I say unto you, that ²one greater than 7 the temple is here. But if ye had known what this meaneth [see *Hos. 6:6*], I	1 Now it came to pass, on a ⁵sabbath, that he was going through the corn-fields [see *Deut. 23: 25*]; and his disciples plucked the ears of corn, and did eat, rubbing them in their 2 hands. But certain of the Pharisees said, Why do ye that which it is not lawful to do on the sabbath day [see *John 5:10; Ex.20:* 3 *10; Deut. 5:14*]? And Jesus answering them said, Have ye not read even this, what David did, when he was an hungred, he, and they that were with him [see *Lev. 24: 9; 1 Sam.21:1–6*]; how 4 he entered into the house of God, and did take and eat the shewbread, and gave also to them that were with him; which it is not lawful to eat save for the priests alone?
27 And he said unto them, The sab-		

---

* Because in Mark 3:7 Jesus withdraws to the Sea of Galilee.

Mark 2:23-28	Matt. 12:1-8	Luke 6:1-5
bath was made for man, and not man for 28 the sabbath: so that the Son of man is lord even of the sabbath.*	desire mercy, and not sacrifice, ye would not have condemned the 8 guiltless. For the Son of man is lord of the sabbath.	5 And he said unto them, The Son of man is lord of the sabbath.

¹ Some ancient authorities read *they did eat.* ² Gr. *a greater thing.* ³ Gr. *began to make* their *way plucking.* ⁴ Some ancient authorities read *in the days of Abiathar the high priest.* ⁵ Many ancient authorities insert *second-first.*

§51. A THIRD† SABBATH CONTROVERSY WITH THE PHARISEES OVER THE HEALING OF A MAN WITH A WITHERED HAND IN A SYNAGOGUE

In Galilee

Mark 3:1-6	Matt. 12:9-14	Luke 6:6-11
1 And he entered again into the synagogue; and there was a man there which had his hand withered	9 And he departed thence, and went into 10 their synagogue; and behold, a man having a withered hand.	6 And it came to pass on another sabbath, that he entered into the synagogue and taught: and there was a man there, and his right hand 7 was withered. And the scribes and the Pharisees watched him, whether he would heal on the sabbath; that they might find how to 8 accuse him. But he knew their thoughts; and he said to the man that had his hand withered, Rise up, and stand forth in the midst. And he arose and stood 9 forth. And Jesus said unto them, I ask you, Is it lawful on
2 And they watched him, whether he would heal him on the sabbath day; that they might accuse him.	And they asked him, saying, Is it lawful to heal on the sabbath day? that they might accuse him.	
3 And he saith unto the man that had his hand withered, ¹Stand 4 forth. And he saith unto them, Is it lawful on the sabbath day to do good, or to do harm? to save a life, or to kill? But they held their peace. 5 And when he had looked round about	11 And he said unto them, What man shall there be of you, that shall have one sheep, and if this fall into a pit on the sabbath day, will he not lay hold on it, and lift it out? 12 How much then is a man of more value than a sheep! Wherefore it is lawful to do	

* Note the five arguments made by Jesus in defence of the conduct of the disciples on the Sabbath (the historical appeal in the conduct of David, the appeal to the law about the temple service, the voice of prophecy, the purpose of God in the Sabbath, and the lordship of the Messiah over the Sabbath). Jesus had already (John 5:17) argued that he was equal to the Father and hence had the right to do certain things (acts of mercy) on the Sabbath.

† On three other later occasions controversies arise with the Pharisees concerning Sabbath observance (John 9:1-34; Luke 13:10-21; 14:1-24). In John 7:20-24 Jesus refers to the miracle in John 5 and adds another argument (circumcision on the Sabbath) for his conduct on the Sabbath.

Mark 3:1–6	Matt. 12:9–14	Luke 6:6–11
on them with anger, being grieved at the hardening of their hearts, he saith unto the man, Stretch forth thy hand. And he stretched it forth: and his hand was restored.	good on the sabbath day. 13 Then saith he to the man, Stretch forth thy hand. And he stretched it forth; and it was restored whole,	the sabbath to do good, or to do harm? to save a life, or to 10 destroy it? And he looked round about on them all, and said unto him, Stretch forth thy hand. And he did *so:* and his hand was restored.
6 And the Pharisees went out and straightway with the Herodians took counsel against him, how they might destroy him.*	14 as the other. But the Pharisees went out, and took counsel against him, how they might destroy him.	11 But they were filled with ²madness; and communed one with another what they might do to Jesus.

¹ Gr. *Arise into the midst.*   ² Or, *foolishness.*

In sections 52 to 54 we see Christ choosing the Twelve Apostles and delivering the Sermon on the Mount to them and to the multitudes.

§ 52. JESUS TEACHES AND HEALS GREAT MULTITUDES BY THE SEA OF GALILEE

Mark 3:7–12	Matt. 12:15–21
7 And Jesus with his disciples withdrew to the sea: and a great multitude from Galilee followed: 8 and from Judea, and from Jerusalem, and from Idumæa, and beyond Jordan, and about Tyre and Sidon,† a great multitude, hearing ²what great things he 9 did, came unto him. And he spake to his disciples, that a little boat should wait on him because of the crowd, lest they 10 should throng him, for he had healed many; insomuch that as many as had ³plagues ⁴pressed upon him that they might touch 11 him. And the unclean spirits, whensoever they beheld him, fell down before him, and cried,	15 And Jesus perceiving *it*, withdrew from thence: and many followed him; 16 and he healed them all,

* Here at some point near the sea of Galilee, there is already a plot to kill him, as some had wished to do in Jerusalem (comp. on § 49).
 † Note the wide territory from which the crowds now come, from Idumea in the south to Phœnicia in the north and from Perea in the east.

Mark 3:7–12	Matt. 12:15–21

saying, Thou art the Son of God.
12 And he charged them much that they should not make him known.
	and
	charged them that they should
	17 not make him known: that it might be fulfilled which was spoken ¹by Isaiah* the prophet, saying,
	18 Behold, my servant whom I have chosen;
	    My beloved in whom my soul is well pleased:
	    I will put my Spirit upon him,
	    And he shall declare judgement to the Gentiles.
	19 He shall not strive, nor cry aloud;
	    Neither shall any one hear his voice in the streets.
	20 A bruised reed shall he not break,
	    And smoking flax shall he not quench,
	    Till he send forth judgement unto victory.
	21 And in his name shall the Gentiles hope.

¹ Or, *through.* ² Or, *all the things that he did.* ³ Gr. *scourges.* ⁴ Gr. *fell.*

§ 53. AFTER A NIGHT OF PRAYER, JESUS SELECTS TWELVE APOSTLES

Mark 3:13–19	Luke 6:12–16
13 And he goeth up into the mountain, and calleth unto him whom he himself would: and they went 14 unto him. And he appointed twelve¹, that they might be with him, and that he might send 15 them forth to preach, and to have 16 authority to cast out ²devils; ³and 17 Simon he surnamed Peter; and James the *son* of Zebedee, and John the brother of James; and them he surnamed Boanerges, 18 which is, Sons of thunder: and	12 And it came to pass in these days, that he went out into the mountain to pray; and he continued all night in prayer to 13 God. And when it was day, he called his disciples: and he chose from them twelve, whom also he named Apostles;† 14 Simon, whom he also named Peter, and Andrew his brother, and James and John, and Philip and Bartholomew,

* Isaiah 42:1–4.
† Matthew postpones giving the names of the Twelve till they are sent out to preach in Galilee (Matt. 10 :1:4. § 70). There is a fourth list in Acts 1:13. See the four compared in note at the end of this volume, note 8.

Mark 3:13–19	Luke 6:12–16
Andrew, and Philip, and Bartholomew, and Matthew, and Thomas, and James the *son* of Alphæus, and Thaddæus, and Simon the ⁴Cananæan, 19 and Judas Iscariot, which also betrayed him.	15 and Matthew and Thomas, and James *the son* of Alphæus, and Simon which was 16 called the Zealot, and Judas, *the son* of ⁵James, and Judas Iscariot, which was the traitor.

¹ Some ancient authorities add *whom also he named apostles.* See Luke 6:13.   ³ Gr. *demons.*
⁸ Some ancient authorities insert *and he appointed twelve.*   ⁴ Or, *Zealot.*   See Luke 6:15; Acts 1:13.
¹ Or, *brother.* See Jude 1.

§ 54. THE SERMON ON THE MOUNT. PRIVILEGES AND REQUIREMENTS OF THE MESSIANIC REIGN. CHRIST'S STANDARD OF RIGHTEOUSNESS

Matthew, chapters 5–7.   Luke 6:17–49.*

A level place on a mountain, not far from Capernaum
The Place and the Audience

Matt. 5:1–2	Luke 6:17–19
1 And seeing the multitudes, he went up into the mountain: and when he had sat down, his disci- 2 ples came unto him: and he opened his mouth and taught them, saying,	17 And he came down with them, and stood on a level place, and a great multitude of his disciples, and a great number of the people from all Judea and Jerusalem, and the sea coast of Tyre and Sidon, which came to hear him, and to be healed of their diseases; 18 and they that were troubled with unclean spirits were healed. 19 And all the multitude sought to touch him: for power came forth from him, and healed *them* all.

1. *The Introduction: The Beatitudes and the Woes. Privileges of the Messiah's Subjects*

Matt. 5:3–12	Luke 6:20–26
3 Blessed are the poor in spirit: for theirs is the kingdom of 4 heaven. ¹Blessed are they that	20 And he lifted up his eyes on his disciples, and said, Blessed *are* ye poor: for yours is the

* There is little doubt that the discourses given by Matthew and Luke are the same, Matthew locating it on "the mountain," and Luke "on a level place," which might easily be a level spot on a mountain. (See note at end of this book, note 9.) Observe that they begin and end alike, and pursue the same general order. Luke omits various matters of special interest to Matthew's Jewish readers (*e.g.* Matt. 5:17–42), and other matters that he himself will give elsewhere (*e.g.* Luke 11:1–4; 12:22–31); while Luke has a few sentences (as ver. 24–26, 38–40), which are not given by Matthew.

Matt. 5:3–12	Luke 6:20–26
mourn [*see Isa. 61:3*]: for they shall 5 be comforted. Blessed are the meek: for they shall inherit the 6 earth [*see Ps. 37:11*]. Blessed are they that hunger and thirst after righteousness: for they shall be 7 filled [*see Ps. 55*]. Blessed are the merciful: for they shall obtain mercy [*see Ps. 18:25; Prov. 11:17*]. 8 Blessed are the pure in heart: for they shall see God [*see Ps. 24:3–5*]. 9 Blessed are the peacemakers: for they shall be called sons of God. 10 Blessed are they that have been persecuted for righteousness' sake: for theirs is the kingdom of 11 heaven. Blessed are ye when *men* shall reproach you, and persecute you, and say all manner of evil against you falsely, for my 12 sake. Rejoice, and be exceeding glad: for great is your reward in heaven: for so persecuted they the prophets which were before you.	21 kingdom of God. Blessed *are* ye that hunger now: for ye shall be filled. Blessed *are* ye that weep now: for ye shall laugh. 22 Blessed are ye, when men shall hate you, and when they shall separate you *from their company*, and reproach you, and cast out your name as evil, for the Son of 23 man's sake. Rejoice in that day, and leap *for joy:* for behold, your reward is great in heaven: for in the same manner did their fath- 24 ers unto the prophets. But woe unto you that are rich! for ye have received your consolation. 25 Woe unto you, ye that are full now! for ye shall hunger. Woe *unto you*, ye that laugh now! for ye 26 shall mourn and weep. Woe *unto you*, when all men shall speak well of you! for in the same manner did their fathers to the false prophets.

[1] Some ancient authorities transpose verses 4 and 5.

2. *The Theme of the Sermon: Christ's Standard of Righteousness in Contrast with that of the Scribes and Pharisees*

Matt. 5:13–20

13 Ye are the salt of the earth: but if the salt have lost its savour, where-
14 with shall it be salted? it is thenceforth good for nothing, but to be cast
15 out and trodden under foot of men [*see Mark 9:50; Jesus often repeated his sayings*]. Ye are the light of the world. A city set on a hill cannot be
16 hid. Neither do *men* light a lamp, and put it under the bushel, but on the stand; and it shineth unto all that are in the house [*see Mark 4:21; Luke 8:16*]. Even so let your light shine before men, that they may see your good works, and glorify your Father which is in heaven.
17 Think not that I came to destroy the law or the prophets: I came not
18 to destroy but to fulfil. For verily I say unto you, Till heaven and earth pass away, one jot or one tittle shall in no wise pass away from the
19 law, till all things be accomplished. Whosoever therefore shall break one of these least commandments, and shall teach men so, shall be called least in the kingdom of heaven: but whosoever shall do and teach them,
20 he shall be called great in the kingdom of heaven. For I say unto you, that except your righteousness shall exceed *the righteousness* of the scribes and Pharisees, ye shall in no wise enter into the kingdom of heaven.

3. *Christ's Ethical Teaching Superior to that of the Scribes (both the Old Testament and the Oral Law) in Six Items or Illustrations (Murder, Adultery, Divorce, Oaths, Retaliation, Love of Enemies)*

Matt. 5:21–48

21   Ye have heard that it was said to them of old time, Thou shalt not
22 kill; and whosoever shall kill shall be in danger of the judgement [*see Ex. 20:13; Deut. 5:17*]: but I say unto you, that every one who is angry with his brother [1]shall be in danger of the judgement: and whosoever shall say to his brother [2]Raca, shall be in danger of the council; and whosoever shall
23 say, [3]Thou fool, shall be in danger [4]of the [5]hell of fire. If therefore thou art offering thy gift at the altar, and there rememberest that thy brother
24 hath aught against thee, leave there thy gift before the altar, and go thy way, first be reconciled to thy brother, and then come and offer thy gift.
25 Agree with thine adversary quickly, whiles thou art with him in the way; lest haply the adversary deliver thee to the judge, and the judge [6]deliver
26 thee to the officer, and thou be cast into prison. Verily I say unto thee, Thou shalt by no means come out thence, till thou have paid the last farthing.
27   Ye have heard that it was said, Thou shalt not commit adultery [*see Ex.*
28 *20: 14; Deut. 5:18*]: but I say unto you, that every one that looketh on a woman to lust after her hath committed adultery with her already in his
29 heart. And if thy right eye causeth thee to stumble, pluck it out, and cast it from thee; for it is profitable for thee that one of thy members should
30 perish, and not thy whole body be cast into [7]hell. And if thy right hand causeth thee to stumble, cut it off, and cast it from thee: for it is profitable for thee that one of thy members should perish, and not thy whole body
31 go into [7]hell. It was said also, Whosoever shall put away his wife, let
32 him give her a writing of divorcement [*see Deut. 24:1*]: but I say unto you, that every one that putteth away his wife, saving for the cause of fornication, maketh her an adulteress: and whosoever shall marry her when she is put away committeth adultery.*
33   Again, ye have heard that it was said to them of old time, Thou shalt
34 not forswear thyself, but shalt perform unto the Lord thine oaths [*see Lev. 19:12; Num. 30:2; Ex. 20:7; Deut. 5:11; 23:21*]: but I say unto you, Swear not at all [*see Matt. 26: 63–64*]; neither by the heaven, for it is the throne
35 of God; nor by the earth, for it is the footstool of his feet; nor [8]by Jerusalem,
36 for it is the city of the great King [*see Isa. 66:1*]. Neither shalt thou swear by thy head, for thou canst not make one hair white or black
37 [*see Ps. 48:2*]. [9]But let your speech be, Yea, yea; Nay, nay: and whatsoever is more than these is of [10]the evil *one*.
38   Ye have heard that it was said, An eye for an eye, and a tooth for a
39 tooth [*see Ex. 21:24; Lev. 24:20; Deut. 19:21*]: but I say unto you, Resist not
40 [11]him that is evil; but whosoever smiteth thee on thy right cheek, turn to him the other also [*see John 18:23*]. And if any man would go to law with
41 thee, and take away thy coat, let him have thy cloke also. And whosoever
42 shall [12]compel thee to go one mile, go with him twain. Give to him that asketh thee, and from him that would borrow of thee turn not thou away.
43   Ye have heard that it was said, Thou shalt love thy neighbour [*see Lev. 19: 18; Deut. 23:6; 25:19*].

* See further Mark 9:43–47; 10:11–12; Matt. 18:8–9; 19:9.

Matt. 5:21–48	Luke 6:27–30, 32–36
44 and hate thine enemy: But I say unto you [*see Luke 23:34*], Love your enemies, and pray for them that **45** persecute you; that ye may be sons of your Father which is in heaven: for he maketh his sun to rise on the evil and the good, and sendeth rain on the just and the unjust.	**27** But I say unto you which hear, Love your enemies, do good to them that **28** hate you, bless them that curse you, pray for them that despite-**29** fully use you. To him that smiteth thee on the *one* cheek offer also the other; and from him that taketh away thy cloke withhold not thy coat also. **30** Give to every one that asketh thee; and of him that taketh away thy goods ask them not
46 For if ye love them that love you, what reward have ye? do not even the [13]publicans the **47** same? And if you salute your brethren only, what do ye more *than others?* do not even the **48** Gentiles the same? Ye therefore shall be perfect, as your heavenly Father is perfect.	**32** again. And if ye love them that love you, what thank have ye? for even sinners love those **33** that love them. And if ye do good to them that do good to you, what thank have ye? for **34** even sinners do the same. And if ye lend to them of whom ye hope to receive, what thank have ye? even sinners lend to sinners, **35** to receive again as much. But love your enemies, and do *them* good, and lend, [14]never despairing; and your reward shall be great, and ye shall be sons of the Most High: for he is kind toward **36** the unthankful and evil. Be ye merciful, even as your Father is merciful.

[1] Many ancient authorities insert *without cause.* [2] An expression of contempt. [3] Or, *Moreh,* a Hebrew expression of condemnation. [4] Gr. *unto* or *into.* [5] Gr. *Gehenna of fire.* [6] Some ancient authorities omit *deliver thee.* [7] Gr. *Gehenna.* [8] Or, *toward.* [9] Some ancient authorities read *But your speech* shall be. [10] Or, *evil:* as in ver. 39; 6:13. [11] Or, *evil.* [12] Gr. *impress.* [13] That is, *collectors or renters of Roman taxes:* and so elsewhere. [14] Some ancient authorities read, *despairing of no man.*

4. *The Practice of Real Righteousness unlike the Ostentatious Hypocrisy of the Pharisees, as in Almsgiving, Prayer, Fasting*

Matt. 6:1–18

1   Take heed that ye do not your righteousness before men, to be seen of them: else ye have no reward with your Father which is in heaven.
2   When therefore thou doest alms, sound not a trumpet before thee, as the hypocrites do in the synagogues and in the streets, that they may have glory of men. Verily I say unto you, They have received their **3** reward. But when thou doest alms, let not thy left hand know what **4** thy right hand doeth: that thine alms may be in secret: and thy Father which seeth in secret shall recompense thee.

Matt. 6:1-18

5 And when ye pray, ye shall not be as the hypocrites: for they love to
stand and pray in the synagogues and in the corners of the streets, that
they may be seen of men. Verily I say unto you, They have received
6 their reward. But thou, when thou prayest, enter into thine inner
chamber, and having shut thy door, pray to thy Father which is in secret,
7 and thy Father which seeth in secret shall recompense thee. And in
praying use not vain repetitions, as the Gentiles do: for they think that
8 they shall be heard for their much speaking. Be not therefore like unto
them: for [1]your Father knoweth what things ye have need of, before ye
9 ask him. After this manner therefore pray ye: Our Father which art in
10 heaven, Hallowed by thy name. Thy kingdom come. Thy will be done,
11 as in heaven, so on earth. Give us this day [2]our daily bread. And
12 forgive us our debts, as we also have forgiven our debtors. And bring us
13 not into temptation, but deliver us from [3]the evil *one*. [4]For if ye forgive
14 men their trespasses, your heavenly Father will also forgive you. But
15 if ye forgive not men their trespasses, neither will your Father forgive
your trespasses.

16 Moreover when ye fast, be not, as the hypocrites, of a sad countenance:
for they disfigure their faces, that they may be seen of men to fast.
17 Verily I say unto you, They have received their reward. But thou,
18 when thou fastest, anoint thy head, and wash thy face; that thou be not
seen of men to fast, but of thy Father which is in secret: and thy
Father, which seeth in secret, shall recompense thee.

[1] Some ancient authorities read *God your Father*. [2] Gr. *our bread for the coming day*. [3] Or, *evil*.
[4] Many authorities, some ancient, but with variations, add *For thine is the kingdom, and the power,
and the glory, for ever, Amen.*

5. *Single-hearted Devotion to God, as Opposed to Worldly Aims and Anxieties*

Matt. 6:19-34

19 Lay not up for yourselves treasures upon the earth, where moth and
20 rust doth consume, and where thieves [1]break through and steal: but lay
up for yourselves treasures in heaven, where neither moth nor rust doth
21 consume, and where thieves do not [1]break through nor steal: for where
22 thy treasure is, there will thy heart be also. The lamp of the body is the
eye: if therefore thine eye be single, thy whole body shall be full of light.
23 But if thine eye be evil, thy whole body shall be full of darkness. If
therefore the light that is in thee be darkness, how great is the darkness!
24 No man can serve two masters: for either he will hate the one, and love
the other; or else he will hold to one, and despise the other. Ye cannot
25 serve God and mammon. Therefore I say unto you, Be not anxious for
your life, what ye shall eat, or what ye shall drink; nor yet for your body,
what ye shall put on. Is not the life more than the food, and the body
26 than the raiment? Behold, the birds of the heaven, that they sow not,
neither do they reap, nor gather into barns; and your heavenly Father
27 feedeth them. Are not ye of much more value than they? And which
28 of you by being anxious can add one cubit unto his [2]stature? And why
29 are ye anxious concerning raiment? Consider the lilies of the field, how
they grow; they toil not, neither do they spin: yet I say unto you, that

Matt. 6:19–34

30 even Solomon in all his glory was not arrayed like one of these. But if God doth so clothe the grass of the field, which to-day is, and to-morrow is cast into the oven, *shall he* not much more *clothe* you, O ye of little faith?
31 Be not therefore anxious, saying, What shall we eat? or, What shall we
32 drink? or, Wherewithal shall we be clothed? For after all these things do the Gentiles seek; for your heavenly Father knoweth that ye have need of
33 all these things. But seek ye first his kingdom, and his righteousness;
34 and all these things shall be added unto you. Be not therefore anxious for the morrow: for the morrow will be anxious for itself. Sufficient unto the day is the evil thereof.

¹ Gr. *dig through.* ² Or, *age.*

6. *Captious Criticism, or Judging Others*

Matt. 7:1–6	Luke 6:37–42
1 Judge not, that ye be not judged. 2 For with what judgement ye judge, ye shall be judged: and with what measure ye mete, it shall be measured unto you.	37 And judge not, and ye shall not be judged: and condemn not, and ye shall not be condemned: release, and ye shall be released: 38 give, and it shall be given unto you; good measure, pressed down, shaken together, running over, shall they give into your bosom. For with what measure ye mete it shall be measured to you again. 39 And he spake also a parable unto them, Can the blind guide the blind? shall they not both 40 fall into a pit? The disciple is not above his ¹master: but every one when he is perfected shall 41 be as his ¹master. And why beholdest thou the mote that is in thy brother's eye, but considerest not the beam that is in thine 42 own eye? Or how canst thou say to thy brother, Brother, let me cast out the mote that is in thine eye, when thou thyself beholdest not the beam that is in thine own eye? Thou hypocrite, cast out first the beam out of thine own eye, and then shalt thou see clearly to cast out the mote that is in thy brother's eye.
3 And why beholdest thou the mote that is in thy brother's eye, but considerest not the beam that 4 is in thine own eye? Or how wilt thou say to thy brother, Let me cast out the mote out of thine eye; and lo, the beam is in thine 5 own eye? Thou hypocrite, cast out first the beam out of thine own eye; and then shalt thou see clearly to cast out the mote out of thy brother's eye.	
6 Give not that which is holy unto the dogs, neither cast your pearls before the swine, lest hap-	

ly they trample them under their feet, and turn and rend you.

¹ Or, *teacher.*

7. *Prayer, and the Golden Rule*

Matt. 7:7-12

7 Ask, and it shall be given you: seek, and ye shall find: knock, and it
8 shall be opened unto you, for every one that asketh receiveth; and he
9 that seeketh findeth; and to him that knocketh it shall be opened. Or
what man is there of you, who, if his son shall ask him for a loaf, will give
10 him a stone; or if he shall ask him for a fish, will give him a serpent?
11 If ye then, being evil, know how to give good gifts unto your children,
how much more shall your Father which is in heaven give good things
12 to them that ask him? All things

therefore whatsoever ye would that men should do unto you, even so do ye also unto them: for this is the law and the prophets.	**Luke 6:31** 31 And as ye would that men should do to you, do ye also to them likewise.

8. *The Conclusion of the Sermon. The Lesson of Personal Righteousness Driven Home by Powerful Parables*

Matt. 7:13 to 8:1.

13 Enter ye in by the narrow gate: for wide ¹is the gate, and broad is
the way, that leadeth to destruction, and many be they that enter in
14 thereby. ²For narrow is the gate, and straitened the way, that leadeth
unto life, and few be they that find it.
15 Beware of false prophets, which come to you in sheep's clothing,
16 but inwardly are ravening wolves. By their fruits ye shall know
17 them. Do *men* gather grapes of thorns, or figs of thistles? Even so

every good tree bringeth forth good fruit: but the corrupt tree 18 bringeth forth evil fruit. A good tree cannot bring forth evil fruit, neither can a corrupt tree bring 19 forth good fruit. Every tree that bringeth not forth good fruit is hewn down, and cast into the fire. 20 Therefore by their fruits ye shall 21 know them. Not every one that saith unto me, Lord, Lord, shall enter the kingdom of heaven; but he that doeth the will of my Father 22 which is in heaven. Many will say to me in that day, Lord, Lord, did we not prophesy by thy name, and by thy name cast out ³devils, and by thy name do many ⁴mighty 23 works? And then will I profess unto them, I never knew you: depart from me, ye that work iniquity.	**Luke 6:43-49** 43 For there is no good tree that bringeth forth corrupt fruit; nor again a corrupt tree that bring-44 eth forth good fruit. For each tree is known by its own fruit. For of thorns men do not gather figs, nor of a bramble bush gather 45 they grapes. The good man out of the good treasure of his heart bringeth forth that which is good. and the evil *man* out of the evil *treasure* bringeth forth that which is evil; for out of the abundance of the heart his mouth speaketh. 46 And why call ye me, Lord, Lord, and do not the things which I say?

Matt. 7:13 to 8:1 | Luke 6:43–49

24 Every one therefore which heareth these words of mine, and doeth them, shall be likened unto a wise man, which built his
25 house upon the rock: and the rain descended, and the floods came, and the winds blew, and beat upon that house; and it fell not: for it was founded upon
26 the rock. And every one that heareth these words of mine, and doeth them not, shall be likened unto a foolish man, which built his house upon the
27 sand: and the rain descended, and the floods came, and the winds blew, and smote upon that house; and it fell: and great was the fall thereof.
28 And it came to pass, when Jesus ended these words, the multitudes were astonished at his
29 teaching: for he taught them as *one* having authority, and not as their scribes.
1 And when he was come down from the mountain, great multitudes followed him.

47 Every one that cometh unto me, and heareth my words, and doeth them, I will shew you to
48 whom he is like: he is like a man building a house, who digged and went deep, and laid a foundation upon the rock: and when a flood arose, the stream brake against that house, and could not shake it: ⁵because it had been well
49 builded. But he that heareth, and doeth not, is like a man that built a house upon the earth without a foundation; against which the stream brake, and straightway it fell in; and the ruin of that house was great.

¹ Some ancient authorities omit *is the gate.* ² Many ancient authorities read *How narrow is the gate, &c.* ³ Gr. *demons.* ⁴ Gr. *powers.* ⁵ Many ancient authorities read *for it had been founded upon the rock:* as in Matt. 7:25.

*In sections 55 to 58 we see the rapid spread of Christ's influence and the inquiry from the Baptist in prison.***

§ 55. JESUS HEALS A CENTURION'S SERVANT AT CAPERNAUM

Matt. 8:5–13 | Luke 7:1–10

5 And when he was entered into Capernaum, there came unto him a centurion,

1 After he had ended all his sayings in the ears of the people, he entered into Capernaum.
2 And a certain centurion's ⁵servant, who was ³dear unto him, was sick and at the point of
3 death. And when he heard concerning Jesus, he sent unto him elders of the Jews, asking

* Here we have only Matthew and Luke, a block from the Logia of Matthew.

Matt. 8:5–13	Luke 7:1–10
6　　　　　beseeching him, and saying, Lord, my [1]servant lieth in the house sick of the palsy, grievously tormented.	him that he would come and 4 save his [5]servant. And they, when they came to Jesus, besought him earnestly, saying, He is worthy that thou shouldst 5 do this for him: for he loveth our nation, and himself built us 6 our synagogue. And Jesus went with them. And when he was now not far from the house, the centurion sent friends to him, saying unto him, Lord, trouble not thyself: for I am not [2]worthy that thou shouldst come under 7 my roof: wherefore neither thought I myself worthy to come unto thee: but [3]say the word, and my [1]servant shall be healed. 8 For I also am a man set under authority, having under myself soldiers: and I say to this one, Go, and he goeth; and to another, Come, and he cometh; and to my [5]servant, Do this, and he doeth 9 it. And when Jesus heard these things, he marvelled at him, and turned and said unto the multitude that followed him, I say unto you, I have not found so great faith, no, not in Israel.
7　　　　　　And he saith unto him, I will come and heal him.	
8　And the centurion answered and said, Lord, I am not [2]worthy that thou shouldest come under my roof: but only [3]say the word, and my [1]servant shall be healed.	
9　For I also am a man [4]under authority, having under myself soldiers: and I say to this one, Go, and he goeth; and to another, Come, and he cometh; and to my [5]servant, Do this, and he doeth it. 10　And when Jesus heard it, he marvelled, and said to them that followed, Verily I say unto you, [6]I have not found so great 11 faith, no, not in Israel. And I say unto you, that many shall come from the east and the west, and shall [7]sit down with Abraham, and Isaac, and Jacob, in the kingdom 12 of heaven [see Ps. 107:3; Isa. 49: 12]: but the sons of the kingdom shall be cast forth into the outer darkness: there shall be weeping 13 and gnashing of teeth. And Jesus said unto the centurion, Go thy way; as thou hast believed so be it done unto thee. And the [1]servant was healed in that hour.	
	10 And they that were sent, returning to the house, found the [5]servant whole.

[1] Or, boy.　[2] Gr. sufficient.　[3] Gr. say with a word.　[4] Some ancient authorities insert set: as in Luke 7:8.　[5] Gr. bond-servant.　[6] Many ancient authorities read With no man in Israel have I found so great faith.　[7] Gr. recline.　[8] Or, precious to him; or, honourable with him.

§ 56. HE RAISES A WIDOW'S SON AT NAIN
Luke 7:11–17

11　And it came to pass [1]soon afterwards, that he went to a city called 12 Nain; and his disciples went with him, and a great multitude. Now

Luke 7:11–17

when he drew near to the gate of the city, behold, there was carried out
one that was dead, the only son of his mother, and she was a widow:
13 and much people of the city was with her. And when the Lord
saw her, he had compassion on her, and said unto her, Weep not.
14 And he came nigh and touched the bier: and the bearers stood still.
15 And he said, Young man, I say unto thee, Arise. And he that was
dead sat up, and began to speak. And he gave him to his mother.
16 And fear took hold on all; and they glorified God, saying, A great prophet
17 is arisen among us: and, God hath visited his people. And this report
went forth concerning him in the whole of Judea, and the region round
about.

¹ Many ancient authorities read *on the next day.*

§ 57. THE MESSAGE* FROM THE BAPTIST AND THE EULOGY OF JESUS

Galilee

Matt. 11:2–19	Luke 7:18–35
2 Now when John heard in the prison† the works of the Christ, he sent by his disciples, and said 3 unto him, Art thou he that cometh, or look we for another?	18 And the disciples of John told 19 him all of these things. And John calling unto him ¹⁰two of his disciples sent them to the Lord, saying, Art thou he that cometh, or look we for another? 20 And when the men were come unto him, they said, John the Baptist hath sent us unto thee, saying, Art thou he that cometh, 21 or look we for another? In that hour he cured many of diseases and ¹¹plagues and evil spirits; and on many that were blind he 22 bestowed sight. And he answered and said unto them, Go your
4 And Jesus answered and said unto them, Go your way and tell John the things which ye do 5 hear and see: the blind receive their sight, and the lame walk, the lepers are cleansed, and the deaf hear, and the dead are raised up, and the poor have ¹good tidings preached to them. 6 And blessed is he, whosoever shall find none occasion of stumbling in me.	way, and tell John what things ye have seen and heard [*see Isa. 29:18–19; 35:5–6; 61:1*]: the blind receive their sight, the lame walk, the lepers are cleansed, and the deaf hear, the dead are raised up, the poor have ¹good 23 tidings preached to them. And blessed is he, whosoever shall find none occasion of stumbling in me.

* Observe that his fame as having raised the dead, and as being "a great prophet," spread widely, and reaching John, led to his message of inquiry (connect Luke 7:17 and 18).
† John's prison was at Machærus, east of the Dead Sea. Jesus was somewhere in Galilee, probably near Nain, which was in the southern part of Galilee.

Matt. 11:2–19

7 And as these went their way, Jesus began to say unto the multitudes concerning John, What went ye out into the wilderness to behold? a reed shaken with
8 the wind? But what went ye out for to see? a man clothed in soft *raiment?* Behold, they that wear soft *raiment* are in
9 kings' houses. ²But wherefore went ye out? to see a prophet? Yea, I say unto you, and much
10 more than a prophet. This is he, of whom it is written,

Behold, I send my messenger before thy face,
Who shall prepare thy way before thee.

11 Verily I say unto you, Among them that are born of women there hath not arisen a greater than John the Baptist: yet he that is ³but little in the kingdom of heaven is greater than he.
12 And from the days of John the Baptist until now the kingdom of heaven suffereth violence, and men of violence take it by force
13 [*see Luke 16:17*]. For all the prophets and the law prophesied until
14 John. And if ye are willing to re-
15 ceive ⁴*it*, this is Elijah, which is to come [*see Mal. 4:5*]. He that hath ears ⁵to hear, let him hear.

16 But whereunto shall I liken this generation? It is like* unto children sitting in the marketplaces, which call un-
17 to their fellows, and say, We piped unto you, and ye did not dance; we wailed, and ye did not ⁶mourn.

Luke 7:18–35

24 And when the messengers of John were departed, he began to say unto the multitudes concerning John, What went ye out into the wilderness to behold? a
25 reed shaken with the wind? But what went ye out to see? a man clothed in soft raiment? Behold, they which are gorgeously apparelled, and live delicately, are
26 in kings' courts. But what went ye out to see? a prophet? Yea, I say unto you, and much more
27 than a prophet. This is he of whom it is written,

Behold, I send my messenger before thy face.
Who shall prepare thy way before thee [*see Mal. 3:1*].

28 I say unto you, Among them that are born of women there is none greater than John: yet he that is ³but little in the kingdom of God is greater than he.

29 And all the people when they heard, and the publicans, justified God, ¹²being baptized with the baptism of
30 John. But the Pharisees and the lawyers rejected for themselves the counsel of God ¹³being
31 not baptized of him. Whereunto then shall I liken the men of this generation, and to what are
32 they like? They are like unto children that sit in the marketplace, and call one to another; which say, We piped unto you, and ye did not dance; we wailed,

---

* Parable of the Children Playing in the Market Place.

Matt. 11:2–19	Luke 7:18–35
18 For John came neither eating nor drinking, and 19 they say, He hath a ⁷devil. The Son of man came eating and drinking, and they say, Behold, a gluttonous man, and a winebibber, a friend of publicans and sinners!	33 and ye did not weep. For John the Baptist is come eating no bread nor drinking wine; and ye 34 say, He hath a ⁷devil. The Son of man is come eating and drinking; and ye say, Behold, a gluttonous man, and a winebibber, a friend of publicans and sinners!
And wisdom ⁸is justified by her ⁹works.	35 And wisdom ⁸is justified of all her children.

¹ Or, *the gospel.* ² Many ancient authorities read *But what went ye out to see? a prophet?* ³ Gr. *lesser.* ⁴ Or, *him.* ⁵ Some ancient authorities omit *to hear.* ⁶ Gr. *beat the breast.* ⁷ Gr. *demon.* ⁸ Or, *was.* ⁹ Many ancient authorities read *children:* as in Luke vii, 35. ¹⁰ Gr. *certain two.* ¹¹ Gr. *scourges.* ¹² Or, *having been.* ¹³ Or, *not having been.*

---

§ 58. WOES UPON THE CITIES OF OPPORTUNITY. THE CLAIMS OF CHRIST AS THE TEACHER ABOUT THE FATHER.

Galilee

Matt. 11:20–30

20   Then began he to upbraid the cities wherein most of his mighty works
21 were done, because they repented not. Woe unto thee, Chorazin! woe unto thee, Bethsaida! for if the ¹mighty works had been done in Tyre and Sidon which were done in you, they would have repented long ago in sack-
22 cloth and ashes. Howbeit I say unto you, it shall be more tolerable
23 for Tyre and Sidon in the day of judgement, than for you [*see Isa. 14:13–15*]. And thou, Capernaum, shalt thou be exalted unto heaven? thou shalt ²go down unto Hades: for if the ¹mighty works had been done in Sodom which
24 were done in thee, it would have remained until this day. Howbeit I say unto you, that it shall be more tolerable for the land of Sodom in the day of judgement, than for thee [*see Gen. 19:24*].
25   At that season Jesus answered and said, I ³thank thee, O Father [*see John 3:35; 17:2*], Lord of heaven and earth, that thou didst hide these things
26 from the wise and understanding, and didst reveal them unto babes: yea,
27 Father, ⁴for so it was well-pleasing in thy sight. All things have been delivered unto me of my Father: and no one knoweth the Son, save the Father: neither doth any know the Father, save the Son, and he to whom-
28 soever the Son willeth to reveal *him.* Come unto me, all ye that labour
29 and are heavy laden, and I will give you rest. Take my yoke* upon you, and learn of me; for I am meek and lowly in heart: and ye shall find rest
30 unto your souls. For my yoke is easy, and my burden is light [*see Jer. 6:16; Sirach 51:23*].

¹ Gr. *powers.* ² Many ancient authorities read *be brought down.* ³ Or, *praise.* ⁴ Or, *that.*

---

* Rabbinical figure for going to school. Jesus thus definitely pictures himself as the expert on God in a Johannean passage (*cf.* Luke 10:21–24). He conceives himself as the Teacher who alone is able to interpret the Father.

§ 59. THE ANOINTING* OF CHRIST'S FEET BY A SINFUL WOMAN IN THE HOUSE OF SIMON A PHARISEE. THE PARABLE OF THE TWO DEBTORS

Galilee

Luke 7:36–50

36 And one of the Pharisees desired him that he would eat with him.
37 And he entered into the Pharisee's house, and sat down to meat. And behold, a woman which was in the city, a sinner; and when she knew that he was sitting at meat in the Pharisee's house, she brought [1]an
38 alabaster cruse of ointment, and standing behind at his feet, weeping, she began to wet his feet with her tears, and wiped them with the hair of her head, and [2]kissed his feet, and anointed them with the ointment.
39 Now when the Pharisee which had bidden him saw it, he spake within himself, saying, This man, if he were [3]a prophet, would have perceived who and what manner of woman this is which toucheth him, that she is
40 a sinner. And Jesus answering said unto him, Simon, I have somewhat
41 to say unto thee. And he saith, [4]Master, say on. A certain lender had two debtors: the one owed five hundred [5]pence, and the other fifty.
42 When they had not *wherewith* to pay, he forgave them both. Which
43 of them therefore will love him most? Simon answered and said, He, I
44 suppose, to whom he forgave the most. And he said unto him, Thou hast rightly judged. And turning to the woman, he said unto Simon, Seest thou this woman? I entered into thine house, thou gavest me no water for my feet: but she hath wetted my feet with her tears, and wiped
45 them with her hair. Thou gavest me no kiss: but she, since the time I
46 came in, hath not ceased to [6]kiss my feet. My head with oil thou didst
47 not anoint: but she hath anointed my feet with ointment. Wherefore I say unto thee, Her sins, which are many, are forgiven: for she loved much:
48 but to whom little is forgiven, *the same* loveth little. And he said unto
49 her, Thy sins are forgiven. And they that sat at meat with him began
50 to say [7]within themselves, Who is this that even forgiveth sins? And he said unto the woman, Thy faith hath saved thee; go in peace.

[1] Or, *a flask.* [2] Gr. *kissed much.* [3] Some ancient authorities read *the prophet.* See John 1:21, 25. [4] Or, *Teacher.* [5] The word in the Greek denotes a coin worth about seventeen cents. [6] Gr. *kiss much.* [7] Or, *among.*

In sections 60 to 63 Jesus makes a second (three in all) tour of Galilee, this time with all the Twelve. Intense hostility of the Pharisees is aroused by the work. They make the blasphemous accusation that Jesus is in league with Satan. Even the kindred of Jesus fear that he is beside himself because of the excitement and the charges.

---

* This anointing in Galilee must be distinct from the anointing at Bethany, near Jerusalem, more than a year later. This sinful and penitent woman is represented by a very late tradition as being Mary Magdalene, and hence all the popular uses of the term Magdalen. But that notion has no historical support whatever, and it becomes violently improbable when we find that in the very next paragraph Luke introduces Mary Magdalene as a new figure in the history. Some men even identify Mary of Bethany with this woman that was a sinner and also with Mary Magdalen, a medley of medieval mysticism.

§ 60. THE SECOND TOUR OF GALILEE

Luke 8:1-3

1 And it came to pass soon afterwards, that he went about through cities and villages, preaching and bringing the ¹good tidings of the king-
2 dom of God, and with him the twelve, and certain women which had been healed of evil spirits and infirmities, Mary that was called Magdalene,
3 from whom seven ²devils had gone out, and Joanna the wife of Chuza Herod's steward, and Susanna, and many others, which ministered unto ³them of their substance.

¹ Or, gospel.   ² Gr. demons.   ³ Many ancient authorities read him.

Notice that the events of §§ 61–66 all occurred on the same day, called the Busy Day*

§ 61. BLASPHEMOUS ACCUSATION OF LEAGUE WITH BEELZEBUB

Galilee

Mark 3:19-30	Matt. 12:22-37

19 And he cometh into a house.
20 And the multitude cometh together again, so that they could
21 not so much as eat bread. And when his friends heard it, they went out to lay hold on him: for they said, He is beside himself.

22 Then was brought unto him ¹one possessed with a devil, blind and dumb: and he healed him, insomuch that the dumb man

22 And the scribes which came down from Jerusalem said, He hath Beelzebub, and, ³By the prince of the ²devils casteth he
23 out the ²devils. And he called them unto him, and said unto them in parables, How can Satan
24 cast out Satan? And if a kingdom be divided against itself,
25 that kingdom cannot stand. And if a house be divided against itself, that house will not be able

23 spake and saw. And all the multitudes were amazed, and said,
24 Is this the son of David? But when the Pharisees heard it, they said, †This man doth not cast out ²devils, but ³by Beelzebub the prince of the ²devils
25 [*see John 7:20; 8:48, 52; 10:20*]. And knowing their thoughts he said unto them, Every kingdom di-

---

* This "Busy Day" is just one of many such days in the Master's Ministry. See, for instance, the last day of his public ministry in the temple in Jerusalem. Observe Jesus in the *forenoon* teaching a crowded audience (Mark 3:19), some of whom insult and blaspheme him, and others demand a sign, and at length his mother and brethren try to carry him off as insane (comp. Mark 3:21); in the *afternoon* giving a group of most remarkable parables, several of which he interprets; towards night crossing the Lake in a boat, so tired and worn that he sleeps soundly amid the alarming storm; then healing the Gadarene demoniacs, and returning by boat, apparently the same evening. What a day of toil and trial.

† Luke (11:14–36) gives another blasphemous accusation later in Judea. Matthew (9:27–34) also has another blasphemous accusation. Note Christ's use of parables in replying to the accusations.

Mark 3:19–30

26 to stand. And if Satan hath risen up against himself, and is divided, he cannot stand, but hath an end.

27 But no one can enter into the house of the strong *man,* and spoil his goods, except he first bind the strong *man;* and then he will spoil his house.

28 Verily I say unto you, All their sins shall be forgiven unto the sons of men, and their blasphemies wherewith so-
29 ever they shall blaspheme: but whosoever shall blaspheme against the Holy Spirit hath never forgiveness, but is guilty
30 of an eternal sin: because they said, He hath an unclean spirit.

Matt. 12:22–37

vided against itself is brought to desolation; and every city or house divided against itself shall
26 not stand: and if Satan casteth out Satan, he is divided against himself; how then shall his king-
27 dom stand? And if I [3]by Beelzebub cast out [2]devils, [3]by whom do your sons cast them out? therefore shall they be your judges.
28 But if I [3]by the Spirit of God cast out [2]devils, then is the kingdom of
29 God come upon you. Or how can one enter into the house of the strong *man,* and spoil his goods, except he first bind the strong *man?* and then he will spoil his
30 house. He that is not with me is against me; and he that gather-
31 eth not with me scattereth. Therefore I say unto you, every sin and blasphemy shall be forgiven [4]unto men; but the blasphemy against the Spirit shall not be forgiven.
32 And whosoever shall speak a word against the Son of man, it shall be forgiven him; but whosoever shall speak against the Holy Spirit it shall not be forgiven him, neither in this [5]world, nor

33 in that which is to come. Either make the tree good, and its fruit good;
or make the tree corrupt, and its fruit corrupt: for the tree is known by
34 its fruit. Ye offspring of vipers, how can ye, being evil, speak good
35 things? for out of the abundance of the heart the mouth speaketh. The
good man out of his own good treasure bringeth forth good things: and the
36 evil man out of his evil treasure bringeth forth evil things. And I say
unto you, that every idle word that men shall speak, they shall give
37 account thereof in the day of judgement. For by thy words thou shalt
be justified, and by thy words thou shalt be condemned.

[1] Or, *a demoniac.* [2] Gr. *demons.* [3] Or, *in.* [4] Some ancient authorities read *unto you men.*
[5] Or, *age.*

§ 62. SCRIBES AND PHARISEES DEMAND A SIGN

Same day. Galilee

Matt. 12:38–45

38 Then certain of the scribes and Pharisees answered him, saying, [1]Master,
39 we would see a sign from thee. But he answered and said unto them,
An evil and adulterous generation seeketh after a sign; and there shall no

Matt. 12:38–45

40 sign be given to it but the sign of Jonah the prophet: for as Jonah was three days and three nights in the belly of the [2]whale; so shall the Son of man be three days and three nights in the heart of the earth [*see Jonah 1:17;*

41 *2:1–2; 3:5; 4:3; 1 Kings 10:1–10*]. The men of Nineveh shall stand up in the judgement with this generation, and shall condemn it: for they repented at the preaching of Jonah; and behold, [3]a greater than Jonah is

42 here. The queen of the south shall rise up in the judgement with this generation, and shall condemn it: for she came from the ends of the earth to hear the wisdom of Solomon; and behold, [3]a greater than Solomon is

43 here. But the unclean spirit, when [4]he is gone out of the man, passeth

44 through waterless places, seeking rest, and findeth it not. Then [4]he saith, I will return into my house whence I came out; and when [4]he is

45 come, [4]he findeth it empty, swept, and garnished. Then goeth [4]he, and taketh with [5]himself seven other spirits more evil than [5]himself, and they enter in and dwell there: and the last state of that man becometh worse than the first. Even so shall it be also unto this evil generation.

[1] Or, *Teacher.*   [2] Gr. *sea-monster.*   [3] Gr. *more than.*   [4] Or, *it.*   [5] Or, *itself.*

§63. CHRIST'S MOTHER AND BRETHREN SEEK TO TAKE HIM HOME

Same day. Galilee

Mark 3:31–35	Matt. 12:46–50	Luke 8:19–21
31 And there come his mother and his brethren; and, standing without, they sent unto him, calling him. 32 And a multitude was sitting about him; and they say unto him, Behold, thy mother and thy brethren without seek 33 for thee. And he answereth them, and saith, Who is my mother and my brethren? 34 And looking round on them which sat round about him, he saith, Behold, my mother and my brethren!	46 While he was yet speaking to the multitudes, behold, his mother and his brethren stood without, seeking to speak to 47 him. [1]And one said unto him, Behold, thy mother and thy brethren stand without, seeking to speak to thee. 48 But he answered and said unto him that told him, Who is my mother? and who are my 49 brethren? And he stretched forth his hand towards his disciples, and said, Behold, my mother and 50 my brethren! For	19 And there came to him his mother and brethren, and they could not come at him for the crowd. 20 And it was told him, Thy mother and thy brethren stand without, desiring to see thee. 21 But he answered and said unto them,

Mark 3:31–35	Matt. 12:46–50	Luke 8:19–21
35 For whosoever shall do the will of God, the same is my brother, and sister, and mother.	whosoever shall do the will of my Father which is in heaven, he is my brother, and sister, and mother.	My mother and my brethren are these which hear the word of God, and do it [see John 15:14].

[1] Some ancient authorities omit ver. 47.

In §§ 64 to 69 we have the first great group of Parables with the visit to Gerasa and the return to Nazareth

§ 64. THE FIRST GREAT GROUP OF PARABLES*

Same day.   Beside the Sea of Galilee.   Introduction to the Group

Mark 4:1, 2	Matt. 13:1–3	Luke 8:4
1 And again he began to teach by the sea side. And there is gathered unto him a very great multitude, so that he entered into a boat, and sat in the sea; and all the multitude were by the sea on the land. 2 And he taught them many things in parables, and said unto them in his teaching, Hearken:	1 On that day went Jesus out of the house, and sat by the 2 sea side. And there were gathered unto him great multitudes, so that he entered into a boat, and sat; and all the multitude stood on the beach. 3 And he spake to them many things in parables, saying,	4 And when a great multitude came together, and they of every city resorted unto him, he spake by a parable:

1. *To the Crowds by the Sea*

(a) Parable of the Sower

Mark 4:3–25	Matt. 13:3–23	Luke 8:5–18
3 Behold, the sower went forth to sow; 4 and it came to pass, as he sowed, some *seed* fell by the way side, and the birds came and devoured 5 it. And other fell on the rocky *ground*, where it had not	3 Behold, the sower went forth to sow; 4 and as he sowed, some *seeds* fell by the way side, and the birds came and de- 5 voured them; and others fell upon the rocky places, where they had not much	5 The sower went forth to sow his seed: and as he sowed some fell by the way side; and it was trodden under foot, and the birds of the heaven 6 devoured it. And other fell on the rock; and as soon as it

* We have met various *separate* parables heretofore, but here is a *group* of at least ten. Two other great groups will occur hereafter, one group given in Luke only, and the last group during the last week of our Lord's public ministry.

Mark 4:3–25	Matt. 13:3–23	Luke 8:5–18

much earth: and straightway it sprang up, because it had no
6 deepness of earth: and when the sun was risen, it was scorched; and because it had no root, it with-
7 ered away. And other fell among the thorns, and the thorns grew up, and choked it, and it yielded no
8 fruit. And others fell into the good ground, and yielded fruit, growing up and increasing; and brought forth, thirtyfold, and sixtyfold, and a hun-
9 dredfold. And he said, Who hath ears to hear, let him hear.
10 And when he was alone, they that were about him with the twelve asked of him the parables.
11 And he said unto them, Unto you is given the mystery of the kingdom of God: but unto them that are without, all things are done in parables: that

12 seeing they may see, and not perceive; and hearing they may hear, and not understand; lest haply they

earth: and straightway they sprang up, because they had no deepness of earth:
6 and when the sun was risen, they were scorched; and because they had no root, they withered away.
7 And others fell upon the thorns; and the thorns grew up, and choked them: and
8 others fell upon the good ground, and yielded fruit, some a hundredfold, some sixty, some thirty.

9 He that hath ears[1], let him hear.
10 And the disciples came, and said unto him, Why speakest thou unto them in parables?
11 And he answered and said unto them, Unto you it is given to know the mysteries of the kingdom of heaven, but to them it is not
12 given. For whosoever hath, to him shall be given, and he shall have abundance: but whosoever hath not, from him shall be taken away even that which he hath.
13 Therefore speak I to them in parables; because seeing they see not, and hearing they hear not, neither do
14 they understand. And unto them is fulfilled

grew, it withered away, because it had no moisture.

7 And other fell amidst the thorns; and the thorns grew with it, and
8 choked it. And other fell into the good ground, and grew, and brought forth fruit a hundredfold. As he said these things, he cried,

He that hath ears to hear, let him hear.

9 And his disciples asked him what this parable might be.
10 And he said, Unto you it is given to know the mysteries of the kingdom of God: but to the rest

in parables; that seeing they may not see, and hearing they may
11 not understand. Now the parable is this:

Mark 4:3–25	Matt. 13:3–23	Luke 8:5–18
should turn again, and it should be for- 13 given* them. And he saith unto them, Know ye not this parable? and how shall ye know all the 14 parables? The sower soweth the word. 15 And these are they by the way side, where the word is sown; and when they have heard, straightway cometh Satan, and taketh away the word which hath been 16 sown in them. And these in like manner are they that are	the prophecy of Isaiah, which saith, By hearing ye shall hear, and shall in no wise understand; And seeing ye shall see, and shall in no wise perceive: 15 For this people's heart is waxed gross, And their ears are dull of hearing, And their eyes they have closed Lest haply they should perceive with their eyes, And hear with their ears, And understand with their heart, And should turn again, And I should heal them [see *Isa. 6:9–10*];	12 The seed is the word of God. And those by the way side are they that have heard; then cometh the devil, and taketh away the word from their heart, that they may not believe and be saved.

16   But blessed are your eyes, for they see; and your ears, for they hear.
17 For verily I say unto you, that many prophets and righteous men desired
to see the things which ye see, and saw them not; and to hear the things
18 which ye hear, and heard them not. Hear then ye the parable of the
19 sower. When any one heareth the word of the kingdom, and under-
standeth it not, *then* cometh the evil *one*, and snatcheth away that
which hath been sown in his heart. This is he that was sown by the

	20 way side. And he	13
	that was sown upon	And
sown upon the rocky *places*, who, when they have heard the word, straightway re- 17 ceive it with joy; and they have no root in themselves, but endure for a while; then, when tribulation or persecution ariseth because of the word, straightway 18 they stumble. And others are they that are sown among the thorns; these are they	the rocky places, this is he that heareth the word, and straight- way with joy receiv- 21 eth it; yet hath he not root in himself, but endureth for a while; and when trib- ulation or persecution ariseth because of the word, straighway he 22 stumbleth. And he that was sown among the thorns, this is he that heareth the	those on the rock *are* they which, when they have heard, re- ceive the word with joy; and these have no root, which for a while believe, and in time of temptation fall away. 14 And that which fell among the thorns, these are they that have heard, and as

Mark 4:3-25	Matt. 13:3-23	Luke 8:5-18
that have heard the 19 word, and the cares of the ²world, and the deceitfulness of riches, and the lusts of other things entering in, choke the word, and it becometh unfruit- 20 ful. And those are they that were sown upon the good ground; such as hear the word, and accept it, and bear fruit, thirtyfold, and sixty- fold, and a hundred- fold.	word; and the care of the ²world, and the deceitfulness of riches, choke the word, and he becom- 23 eth unfruitful. And he that was sown up- on the good ground, this is he that heareth the word, and un- derstandeth it: who verily beareth fruit, and bringeth forth, some a hundredfold, some sixty, some thirty.	they go on their way they are choked with cares and riches and pleasures of *this* life, and bring no fruit to perfection. 15 And that in the good ground, these are such as in an honest and good heart, hav- ing heard the word, hold it fast, and bring forth fruit with pa- tience.
21 And he said unto them, Is the *lamp brought to be put under the bushel, or under the bed, *and* not to be put on the stand? 22 For there is nothing hid, save that it should be mani- fested; neither was *anything* made 23 secret, but that it should come to light. If any man hath ears to 24 hear, let him hear. And he said unto them, Take heed what ye hear: with what measure ye mete it shall be measured unto you: and 25 more shall be given unto you. For he that hath, to him shall be given: and he that hath not, from him shall be taken away even that which he hath.	16 And no man, when he hath lighted a lamp, covereth it with a vessel, or putteth it under a bed; but putteth it on a stand, that they which enter in may see the light. 17 For nothing is hid, that shall not be made manifest; nor *anything* secret, that shall not be known and 18 come to light. Take heed there- fore how ye hear: for whosoever hath, to him shall be given, and whosoever hath not, from him shall be taken away even that which he ³thinketh he hath.	

¹ Some ancient authorities add here, and in ver. 43, *to hear:* as in Mark 4:9; Luke 8:8.   ² Or, *age.*
³ Or, *seemeth to have.*

(b) Parable of the Seed Growing of Itself

Mark 4:26-29

26 And he said, So is the kingdom of God, as if a man should cast seed
27 upon the earth; and should sleep and rise night and day, and the seed
28 should spring up and grow, he knoweth not how. The earth ¹beareth
fruit of herself; first the blade, then the ear, then the full corn in the ear.

* Note here another brief parable of the lamp to enforce the lesson of the parable of the Sower. Preachers to-day sometimes tell one story to illustrate another.

Mark 4:26–29

29 But when the fruit ²is ripe, straightway he ³putteth forth the sickle, because the harvest is come [*see Joel 3:13*].

¹ Or, *yieldeth.*   ² Or, *alloweth.*   ³ Or, *sendeth forth.*

(c) Parable of the Tares

Matt. 13:24–30

24 Another parable set he before them, saying, The kingdom of heaven
25 is likened unto a man that sowed good seed in his field: but while men
slept, his enemy came and sowed ¹tares also among the wheat, and went
26 away. But when the blade sprang up, and brought forth fruit, then
27 appeared the tares also. And the ²servants of the householder came and
said unto him, Sir, didst thou not sow good seed in thy field? whence then
28 hath it tares? And he said unto them, ³An enemy hath done this. And
the ²servants say unto him, Wilt thou then that we go and gather them
29 up? But he saith, Nay; lest haply while ye gather up the tares, ye root
30 up the wheat with them. Let both grow together until the harvest:
and in the time of the harvest I will say to the reapers, Gather up first
the tares, and bind them in bundles to burn them: but gather the wheat
into my barn.

¹ Or, *darnel.*   ² Gr. *bond-servants.*   ³ Gr. *A man* that is an *enemy.*

(d) Parable of the Mustard Seed

Mark 4:30–32	Matt. 13:31–32
30 And he said, How shall we liken the kingdom of God? or in what 31 parable shall we set it forth? ¹It is like a grain of mustard seed, which, when it is sown upon the earth, though it be less than all the seeds that are upon the earth, 32 yet when it is sown, groweth up, and becometh greater than all the herbs, and putteth out great branches; so that the birds of the heaven can lodge under the shadow thereof.	31 Another parable set he before them, saying, The kingdom of heaven is like unto a grain of mustard seed, which a man took, 32 and sowed in his field: which indeed is less than all seeds: but when it is grown, it is greater than the herbs, and becometh a tree [*see Dan. 4:12, 21*], so that the birds of the heaven come and lodge in the branches thereof.

¹ Gr. *As, unto.*

(e) Parable of the Leaven and many such Parables

Mark 4:33–34	Matt. 13:33–35
	33 Another parable spake he unto them; The kingdom of heaven is like unto leaven, which a woman took, and hid in three ¹measures of meal, till it was all leavened.
33 And with many* such parables	34 All these things spake Jesus

* See note, p. 69.

Mark 4:33–34	Matt. 13:33–35
spake he the word unto them, as 34 they were able to hear it: and without a parable spake he not unto them: but privately to his disciples he expounded all things.	in parables unto the multitudes; and without* a parable spake he 35 nothing unto them: that it might be fulfilled which was spoken ²by the prophet, saying, I will open my mouth in parables; I will utter things hidden from the foundation ³of the world [see Ps. 78:2].

¹ The word in the Greek denotes the Hebrew seah, a measure containing nearly a peck and a half. ² Or, *through.* ³ Many ancient authorities omit *of the world.*

2. *To the Disciples in the House*

(a) Explanation of the Parable of the Tares

Matt. 13:36–43

36 Then he left the multitudes, and went into the house: and his disciples came unto him, saying, Explain unto us the parable of the tares of the
37 field.   And he answered and said, He that soweth the good seed is the
38 Son of man; and the field is the world; and the good seed, these are the
39 sons of the kingdom; and the tares are the sons of the evil *one;* and the enemy that sowed them is the devil: and the harvest is ¹the end of the
40 world; and the reapers are angels.   As therefore the tares are gathered
41 up and burned with fire; so shall it be in the end of the world.   The Son of man shall send forth his angels, and they shall gather out of his kingdom all things that cause stumbling, and them that do iniquity, and shall
42 cast them into the furnace of fire: there shall be the weeping and gnashing
43 of teeth.   Then shall the righteous shine forth as the sun in the kingdom of their Father [see Dan. 12:3].   He that hath ears, let him hear.

¹ Or, *the consummation of the age.*

(b) The Parable of the Hid Treasure

Matt. 13:44

44 The kingdom of heaven is like unto a treasure hidden in the field; which a man found, and hid; and ¹in his joy he goeth and selleth all that he hath, and buyeth that field.

¹ Or, *for joy thereof.*

(c) The Parable of the Pearl of Great Price

Matt. 13:45–46

45 Again, the kingdom of heaven is like unto a man that is a merchant
46 seeking goodly pearls: and having found one pearl of great price, he went and sold all that he had, and bought it.

* Note the expression.   Matthew gives nine in Chapter 13 and Mark another.   There may have been still others on this day.

(d) The Parable of the Net

Matt. 13:47–50

47 Again, the kingdom of heaven is like unto a ¹net, that was cast into
48 the sea, and gathered of every kind: which, when it was filled, they drew
up on the beach; and they sat down, and gathered the good into vessels,
49 but the bad they cast away. So shall it be in ²the end of the world:
the angels shall come forth, and sever the wicked from among the right-
50 eous, and shall cast them into the furnace of fire: there shall be the weeping and gnashing of teeth.

¹ Gr. *dragnet.*   ² Or, *consummation of the age.*

(e) The Parable of the Householder

Matt. 13:51–53

51 Have ye understood all these things? They say unto him, Yea.
52 And he said unto them, Therefore every scribe who hath been made a
disciple to the kingdom of heaven is like unto a man that is a
householder, which bringeth forth out of his treasure things new and old.
53 And it came to pass, when Jesus had finished these *parables, he departed thence.

§ 65. IN CROSSING THE LAKE, JESUS STILLS THE TEMPEST

Same day. Sea of Galilee

Mark 4:35–41	Matt. 8:18, 23–27	Luke 8:22–25
35 And on that day, when even was come, he saith unto them, Let us go over unto the other side.	18 Now when Jesus saw great multitudes about him, he gave commandment to depart unto the other side.	
36 And leaving the multitude, they take him with them, even as he was, in the boat. And other boats were with him.	23 And when he was entered into a boat, his disciples followed him.	22 Now it came to pass on one of those days, that he entered into a boat, himself and his disciples; and he said unto them, Let us go over to the other side of the lake: and they launched 23 forth. But as they sailed he fell asleep:

* Eight of these ten parables go in pairs (the sower and the seed growing of itself, the tares and the net, the mustard seed and the leaven, the hid treasure and the pearl of great price). But nothing can be made out of the number of the parables spoken on this day. We do not even know what the number was. Jesus had spoken various shorter and more or less isolated parables before this occasion. An immediate occasion for the use of so many and such extended parables at this point was the hostility of the Pharisees and the need of special instruction for the disciples who were taught by Jesus how to interpret parables, though they had much difficulty later in applying the instruction about the parabolic teaching.

Mark 4:35-41	Matt. 8:18, 23-27	Luke 8:22-25
37 And there ariseth a great storm of wind, and the waves beat into the boat, insomuch that the boat 38 was now filling. And he himself was in the stern, asleep on the cushion: and they awake him, and say unto him, Master, carest thou not that 39 we perish? And he awoke, and rebuked the wind, and said unto the sea, Peace, be still. And the wind ceased, and there was a great 40 calm. And he said unto them, Why are ye fearful? have ye not yet faith?	24 And behold, there arose a great tempest in the sea, insomuch that the boat was covered with the waves: but 25 he was asleep. And they came to him, and awoke him, saying, Save, Lord; we perish. 26 And he saith unto them, Why are ye fearful, O ye of little faith? Then he arose, and rebuked the winds and the sea; and there was a great calm.	and there came down a storm of wind on the lake: and they were filling *with water*, and were in jeopardy. 24 And they came to him, and awoke him, saying, Master, master, we perish, And he awoke, and rebuked the wind and the raging of the water: and they ceased, and there was a calm. 25 And he said unto them, Where is your faith?
41 And they feared exceedingly, and said one to another, Who then is this, that even the wind and the sea obey him?	27 And the men marvelled, saying, What manner of man is this, that even the winds and the sea obey him?	And being afraid they marvelled, saying one to another, Who then is this, that he commandeth even the winds and the water, and they obey him?

§ 66. BEYOND THE LAKE JESUS HEALS THE GERASENE* DEMONIAC†

Gerasa (Khersa). Same day

Mark 5:1-20	Matt. 8:28-34	Luke 8:26-39
1 And they came to the other side of the sea, into the country 2 of the Gerasenes. And when he was come out of the boat, straightway there	28 And when he was come to the other side into the country of the Gadarenes, there met him two ¹possessed with devils, coming forth out	26 And they arrived at the country of the ⁴Gerasenes, which is over against Galilee. 27 And when he was come forth upon the land, there met him

* The long famous instance of "discrepancy" as to the *place* in this narrative has been cleared up in recent years by the decision of textual critics that the correct text in Luke is Gerasenes, as well as in Mark, and by Dr. Thomson's discovery of a ruin on the lake shore, named Khersa (Gerasa). If this village was included (a very natural supposition) in the district belonging to the city of Gadara, some miles south-eastward, then the locality could be described as either in the country of the Gadarenes, or in the country of the Gerasenes.

† Matthew mentions two demoniacs, Mark and Luke describe one, who was probably the prominent and leading one.

Mark 5:1–20	Matt. 8:28–34	Luke 8:26–39
met him out of the tombs a man with 3 an unclean spirit, who had his dwelling in the tombs: and no man could any more bind him, no, not 4 with a chain; because that he had been often bound with fetters and chains, and the chains had been rent asunder by him, and the fetters broken in pieces: and no man had strength to tame 5 him. And always, night and day, in the tombs and in the mountains, he was crying out, and cutting himself with 6 stones. And when he saw Jesus from afar, he ran and worshipped him; and cry- 7 ing out with a loud voice, he saith, What have I to do with thee, Jesus, thou Son of the Most High God? I adjure thee by God, torment me 8 not. For he said unto him, Come forth, thou unclean spirit, out of the man.	of the tombs, exceeding fierce, so that no man could pass by that way.	a certain man out of the city, who had ²devils; and for a long time he had worn no clothes, and abode not in *any* house, but in the tombs.
	29 And behold, they cried out, saying, What have we to do with thee, thou Son of God? art thou come hither to torment us before the time?	28 And when he saw Jesus, he cried out, and fell down before him, and with a loud voice said, What have I to do with thee, Jesus, thou Son of the Most High God? I beseech thee, torment 29 me not. For he commanded the unclean spirit to come out of the man. For ⁵oftentimes it had seized him: and he was kept under guard, and bound with chains and fetters; and breaking the bands asunder, he was driven of the ⁶devil into the deserts. And 30 Jesus asked him, What is thy name? And he said, Legion; ⁷or many ²devils were entered into him.
9 And he asked him, What is thy name? And he saith unto him, My name is Legion; for we are		

72

Mark 5:1-20	Matt. 8:28-34	Luke 8:26-39
10 many. And he besought him much that he would not send them away out of 11 the country. Now there was there on the mountain side a great herd of swine 12 feeding. And they besought him, saying, Send us into the swine, that we may enter into them. 13 And he gave them leave. And the unclean spirits came out, and entered into the swine: and the herd rushed down the steep into the sea, *in number* about two thousand; and they were choked in the 14 sea. And they that fed them fled, and told it in the city, and in the country. And they came to see what it was that had 15 come to pass. And they come to Jesus, and behold ³him that was possessed with devils sitting, clothed and in his right mind, *even* he that had the legion: and they were 16 afraid. And they that saw it declared unto them how it befell ³him that was possessed with devils, and concerning the 17 swine. And they began to beseech him to depart from their 18 borders. And as he was entering into the boat, he that had been possessed with	30 Now there was afar off from them a herd of many 31 swine feeding. And the ²devils besought him, saying, If thou cast us out, send us 32 of swine. And he said unto them, Go. And they came out, and went into the swine: and behold, the whole herd rushed down the steep into the sea, and perished in the waters. 33 And they that fed them fled, and went away into the city, and told everything, and what was befallen to them that were ¹possessed with 34 devils. And behold, all the city came out to meet Jesus· and when they saw him, they besought *him* that he would depart from their borders.	31 And they intreated him that he would not command them to depart into the 32 abyss. Now there was there a herd of many swine feeding on the mountain: and they intreated him that he would give them leave to enter into them. And he gave 33 them leave. And the ²devils came out from the man, and entered into the swine: and the herd rushed down the steep into the lake and were choked. 34 And when they that fed them saw what had come to pass, they fled, and told it in the city and in the 35 country. And they went out to see what had come to pass: and they came to Jesus, and found the man, from whom the ²devils were gone out, sitting, clothed and in his right mind, at the feet of Jesus: and they were afraid. 36 And they that saw it told them how he that was possessed with ²devils was 37 ⁷made whole. And all the people of the country of the ⁴Gerasenes round about asked him to depart from them; for they were holden with great fear: and he entered into a boat,

Mark 5:1–20		Luke 8:26–39
²devils besought him that he might be with 19 him. And he suffered him not, but saith unto him, Go to thy house unto thy friends, and tell them how great things the Lord hath done for thee, and *how* he had 20 mercy on thee. And he went his way, and began to publish in Decapolis how great things Jesus had done for him: and all men did marvel.*		38 and returned. But the man from whom the ²devils were gone out prayed him that he might be with him: but he sent him 39 away, saying, Return to thy house, and declare how great things God hath done for thee. And he went his way, publishing throughout the whole city how great things Jesus had done for him.

¹ Or, *demoniacs.*　² Gr. *demons.*　³ Or, *the demoniac.*　⁴ Many ancient authorities read *Gergesenes;* others *Gadarenes.*　⁵ Or, *of a long time.*　⁶ Gr. *demon.*　⁷ Or, *saved.*

§ 67. THE RETURN AND THE HEALING OF JAIRUS' DAUGHTER AND OF THE WOMAN WHO ONLY TOUCHED CHRIST'S GARMENT

Probably Capernaum

Mark 5:21–43	Matt. 9:18–26	Luke 8:40–56
21 And when Jesus had crossed over again in the boat unto the other side, a great multitude was gathered unto him: and he was by the sea. 22 And there cometh one of the rulers of the synagogue, Jairus by name; and seeing him, he falleth at his 23 feet, and beseecheth him much, saying, My little daughter is at the point of death: *I pray thee*, that thou	18 While he s p a k e these things unto them,† behold, there came ¹a ruler, and worshipped him, saying, My daughter is even now dead: but come and lay thy	40 And as Jesus returned, the multitude welcomed him; for they were all waiting for him. 41 And behold there came a man named Jairus, and he was a ruler of the synagogue: and he fell down at Jesus' feet, and besought him to come into his house;

* Note in Mark the numerous vivid details and fulness of narrative.
† Broadus felt that the language in Matt. 9:18 compelled him to place 9:18 after 9:17. I do not think so, for "while he spake" may be merely an introductory phrase for a new paragraph. It is best to follow Mark's order, as Luke does, for Matthew is not chronological in this part of his Gospel.

Mark 5:21-43	Matt. 9:18-26	Luke 8:40-56
come and lay thy hands on her, that she may be ²made 24 whole, and live. And he went with him; and a great multitude followed him, and they thronged him.	hand upon her, and 19 she shall live. And Jesus arose, and followed him, and *so did* his disciples.	42 for he had an only daughter, a b o u t twelve years of age, and she lay a dying. But as he went the multitudes thronged him.
25 And a woman, which had an issue 26 of blood twelve years, and had suffered many things of many physicians, and had spent all that she had, and was nothing bettered, but rather 27 grew worse, having heard the things concerning Jesus, came in the crowd behind, and touched his gar- 28 ment. For she said, If I touch but his garments, I shall be 29 ²made whole. And straightway the fountain of her blood was dried up; and she felt in her body that she was healed of her 30 ⁵plague. And straightway Jesus, perceiving in himself that the power *proceeding* from him had gone forth, turned him about in the crowd, and said, Who touched my gar- 31 ments? And his disciples said unto him, Thou seest the multitude thronging thee, and sayest thou, Who 32 touched me? And he looked round about to see her that had 33 done this thing. But the woman fearing and trembling, know-	20 And behold, a woman, who had an issue of blood twelve years, came behind him, and touched the border of his gar- 21 ment: for she said within herself, If I do but touch his garment, I shall be ²made whole.	43 And a woman having an issue of blood twelve years, which ⁸had spent all her living upon physicians, and could not be healed of any, 44 came behind him, and touched the border of his garment: and immediately the issue of her blood stanched. 45 And Jesus said, Who is it that touched me? And when all denied, Peter said, ⁹and they that were with him, Master, the multitudes press thee and crush *thee*. 46 But Jesus said, Some one did touch me; for I perceived that power had gone forth

Mark 5:21–43	Matt. 9:18–26	Luke 8:40–56
ing what had been done to her, came and fell down before him, and told him 34 all the truth. And he said unto her, Daughter, thy faith hath ³made thee whole; go in peace, and be whole of thy ⁵plague. 35 While he yet spake, they come from the ruler of the synagogue's *house,* saying, Thy daughter is dead: why troublest thou the ⁶Master any further? 36 But Jesus, ⁷not heeding the word spoken, saith unto the ruler of the synagogue, Fear not, 37 only believe. And he suffered no man to follow with him, save Peter, and James, and John the brother of 38 James. And they come to the house of the ruler of the synagogue; and he beholdeth a tumult, and *many* weeping and wailing greatly. 39 And when he was entered in, he saith unto t h e m, W h y make ye a tumult and weep? the child is not dead, but sleep- 40 eth. And they laughed him to scorn. But he, having put them all forth, taketh the father of the child and her mother and them that were with him, and goeth in where the child was.	22 But Jesus turning and seeing her said, Daughter, be of good cheer; thy faith hath ³made thee whole. And the woman was ²made whole from that hour.\n\n23 And when Jesus came into the ruler's house, and saw the flute-players, and the crowd making a tu- 24 mult, he said, Give place: for the damsel is not dead, but sleepeth. And they laugh- 25 ed him to scorn. But when the crowd was put forth, he entered	47 from me. And when the woman saw that she was not hid, she came trembling, and falling down before him declared in the presence of all the people for what cause she touched him, and how she was healed 48 immediately. And he said unto her, Daughter, thy faith hath ³made thee whole; go in peace.\n\n49 While he yet spake, there cometh one from the ruler of the synagogue's *house,* saying, Thy daughter is dead; trouble not 50 the ⁶Master. But Jesus hearing it, answered him, Fear not: only believe, and she shall be ²made whole. 51 And when he came to the house, he suffered not any man to enter in with him, save Peter, and John, and James, and the father of the maiden and her mother. 52 And all were weeping, and bewailing her: but he said, Weep not; for she is not dead, but sleepeth. 53 And they laughed him to scorn, knowing that she was dead.

Mark 5:21-43	Matt. 9:18-26	Luke 8:40-56
41 And taking the child by the hand, he saith unto her, Talitha cumi; which is being interpreted, Damsel, I say unto thee, Arise. 42 And straightway the damsel rose up, and walked; for she was twelve years old. And they were amazed straightway with a great amazement. 43 And he charged them much that no man should know this: and he commanded that *something* should be given her to eat.	in, and took her by the hand; and the 26 damsel arose. And ⁴the fame hereof went forth into all that land.	54 But he, taking her by the hand, called, saying, Maiden, arise. 55 And her spirit returned, and she rose up immediately: and he commanded that *something* be given 56 her to eat. And her parents were amazed but he charged them to tell no man what had been done.

¹ Gr. *one ruler.* ² Or, *saved.* ³ Or, *saved thee.* ⁴ Gr. *this fame.* ⁵ Gr. *scourge.* ⁶ Or, *Teacher.*
⁷ Or, *overhearing.* ⁸ Some ancient authorities omit *had spent all her living upon physicians, and.*
⁹ Some ancient authorities omit *and they that were with him.*

§ 68. HE HEALS TWO BLIND MEN, AND A DUMB DEMONIAC. A BLASPHEMOUS ACCUSATION

Matt. 9:27-34

27 And as Jesus passed by from thence, two blind men followed him, cry-
28 ing out, and saying, Have mercy on us, thou son of David. And when he was come into the house, the blind men came to him: and Jesus saith unto them, Believe ye that I am able to do this? They say unto him,
29 Yea, Lord. Then touched he their eyes, saying, According to your faith
30 be it done unto you. And their eyes were opened. And Jesus ¹strictly
31 charged them, saying, See that no man know it. But they went forth, and spread abroad his fame in all that land.
32 And as they went forth, behold, there was brought to him a dumb
33 man possessed with a ²devil. And when the ²devil was cast out, the dumb man spake: and the multitudes marvelled, saying, It was never so
34 seen in Israel. But the Pharisees said, ³By the prince of the ⁴devils casteth he out ⁴devils.

¹ Or, *sternly.* ² Gr. *demon.* ³ Or, *In.* ⁴ Gr. *demons.*

§ 69. THE LAST* VISIT TO NAZARETH

Mark 6:1-6	Matt. 13:54-58
1 And he went out from thence; and he cometh into his own	54 And coming into his own coun-

* There is no sufficient occasion to identify this visit to Nazareth with that described by Luke. That was at the very beginning of the great ministry in Galilee, and this is near its close. The details are quite different. It is perfectly natural that after a long interval he should give the Nazarenes another opportunity to hear his teaching, and to witness miracles, which he would not work for them when demanded, but now voluntarily works in a few cases, so far as their now *wonderful* unbelief left it appropriate.

Mark 6:1–6	Matt. 13:54–58
country; and his disciples follow 2 him. And when the sabbath was come, he began to teach in the synagogue: and ³many hearing him were astonished, saying, Whence hath this man these things? and, What is the wisdom that is given unto this man, and *what mean* such ¹mighty works 3 wrought by his hands? Is not this the carpenter, the son of Mary, and brother of James, and Joses, and Judas, and Simon? and are not his sisters here with us? And they were ²offended in 4 him. And Jesus said unto them, A prophet is not without honour, save in his own country, and among his own kin, and in his 5 own house. And he could there do no ⁴mighty work, save that he laid his hands upon a few 6 sick folk, and healed them. And he marvelled because of their unbelief.	try he taught them in their synagogue, insomuch that they were astonished, and said, Whence hath this man this wisdom, and these ¹mighty works? 55 Is not this the carpenter's son? is not his mother called Mary? and his brethren, James, and Joseph, and 56 Simon, and Judas? And his sisters, are they not all with us? 57 Whence then hath this man all these things? And they were ²offended in him. But Jesus said unto them, a prophet is not without honour, save in his own country, and in his own house. 58 And he did not many ¹mighty works there because of their unbelief.

¹ Gr. *powers*. ² Gr. *caused to stumble*. ³ Some ancient authorities insert *the*. ⁴ Gr. *power*.

In Sections 70 to 71 we have the Third Tour of Galilee (Jesus following the Twelve) and the effect on Herod Antipas.

§ 70. THE THIRD TOUR OF GALILEE AFTER INSTRUCTING THE TWELVE AND SENDING THEM FORTH BY TWOS

Mark 6:6–13	Matt. 9:35 to 11:1
6 And he went round about the villages teaching.	35 And Jesus went about all the cities and the villages* teaching in their synagogues, and preaching the gospel of the kingdom, and healing all manner of disease and all manner of 36 sickness. But when

* This is certainly a *second*, and probably a *third* journey about Galilee. Dwell on Matt. 9:35 and 11:1 (end of this section), and try to realize the extent of the Saviour's work in teaching and healing. He "crowded into three short years actions and labours of love that might have adorned a century." (Ro. Hall.)

Mark 6:6–13	Matt. 9:35 to 11:1	Luke 9:1–6
	he saw the multitudes, he was moved with compassion for them, because they were distressed and scattered, as sheep not having a shepherd [*see Num.*	
	37 *27:17; Ezek. 34:5*]. Then saith he unto his disciples, the harvest truly is plenteous, but the labourers are few.	
	38 Pray ye therefore the Lord of the harvest, that he send forth labourers into his harvest.	
7 And he called unto him the twelve, and began to send them forth by two and two; and he gave them authority over the unclean spirits;	1 And he called unto him his twelve disciples, and gave them authority over unclean spirits, to cast them out, and to heal all manner of disease and all manner of sickness.	1 And he called the twelve together, and gave them power and authority over all ²devils, and to cure
8 and he charged them		2 diseases. And he sent them forth to preach the kingdom of God, and to heal
	2 Now the names of the twelve apostles are these: The first, Simon, who is called Peter, and Andrew his brother; James the *son* of Zebedee, and John his brother;	3 ¹ªthe sick. And he said unto them,
	3 Philip, and Bartholomew; Thomas, and Matthew the publican; James the *son* of Alphæus, and	
	4 Thaddæus; Simon the ¹Cananæan, and Judas Iscariot, who also	
	5 ²betrayed him. These twelve Jesus sent forth, and charged them, saying, Go not into *any* way of the Gentiles, and enter not into any city of	
	6 the Samaritans: but	

Mark 6:6-13	Matt. 9:35 to 11:1	Luke 9:1-6

Matt. 9:35 to 11:1

go rather to the lost sheep of the house of
7 Israel. And as ye go, preach, saying, The kingdom of heaven is
8 at hand. Heal the sick, raise the dead, cleanse the lepers, cast out ³devils: freely ye received, freely
9 give. Get you no gold, nor silver, nor brass in your ⁴purses;
10 no wallet for *your* journey, neither two coats, nor shoes, nor staff: for the labourer is worthy of his food.
11 And into whatsoever city or village ye shall enter, search out who in it is worthy; and there abide till ye go forth.
12 And as ye enter into the house, salute it.
13 And if the house be worthy, let your peace come upon it: but if it be not worthy, let your peace return to you.
14 And whosoever shall not receive you, nor hear your words, as ye go forth out of that house or that city, shake off the dust of your feet.
15 Verily, I say unto you, It shall be more tolerable for the land of Sodom and Gomorrah in the day of judgement, than for that city.

Mark 6:6-13

that they should take nothing for *their* journey, save a staff only; no bread, no wallet, no ¹⁷money in their ¹⁸purse; but
9 *to go* shod with sandals: and, *said he*, put not on two coats.

10   And he said unto them, Wheresoever ye enter into a house, there abide till ye depart thence.
11 And whatsoever place shall not receive you, and they hear you not, as ye go forth thence, shake off the dust that is under your feet for a testimony unto them.

Luke 9:1-6

Take nothing for your journey, neither staff, nor wallet, nor bread, nor money; neither have two coats.

4   And into whatsoever house ye enter, there abide, and thence de-
5 part. And as many

as receive you not, when ye depart from that city,

shake off the dust from your feet for a testimony against them.

16   Behold, I send you forth as sheep in the midst of wolves: be ye there-
17 fore wise as serpents, and ⁵harmless as doves. But beware of men: for they will deliver you up to councils, and in their synagogues they
18 will scourge you; yea and before governors and kings shall ye be brought

Matt. 9:35 to 11:1

19 for my sake, for a testimony to them and to the Gentiles. But when they
deliver you up, be not anxious how or what ye shall speak: for it shall be
20 given you in that hour what ye shall speak. For it is not ye that speak,
21 but the Spirit of your Father that speaketh in you. And brother shall
deliver up brother to death, and the father his child: and children shall
22 rise up against parents, and ᶜcause them to be put to death. And ye shall
be hated of all men for my name's sake: but he that endureth to the end,
23 the same shall be saved. But when they persecute you in this city, flee
into the next: for verily I say unto you, Ye shall not have gone through
the cities of Israel, till the Son of man be come.
24   A disciple is not above his ⁷master, nor a ⁸servant above his lord.
25 It is enough for the disciple that he be as his ⁷master, and the ⁸servant
as his lord. If they have called the master of the house ⁹Beelzebub, how
26 much more *shall they call* them of his household! Fear them not therefore: for there is nothing covered, that shall not be revealed; and hid,
27 that shall not be known. What I tell you in the darkness, speak ye in
the light: and what ye hear in the ear, proclaim upon the housetops.
28 And be not afraid of them which kill the body, but are not able to kill
the soul: but rather fear him which is able to destroy both soul and body
29 in ¹⁰hell. Are not two sparrows sold for a farthing? and not one of them
30 shall fall on the ground without your Father: but the very hairs of your
31 head are all numbered. Fear not, therefore; ye are of more value than
32 many sparrows. Every one therefore who shall confess ¹¹me before men,
33 ¹²him will I also confess before my Father which is in heaven. But whosoever shall deny me before men, him will I also deny before my Father
which is in heaven.
34   Think not that I came to ¹³send peace on the earth: I came not to
35 ¹³send peace, but a sword. For I came to set a man at variance against
his father, and the daughter against her mother, and the daughter in
36 law against her mother in law: and a man's foes *shall be* they of his own
37 household [*see Micah. 7:6*]. He that loveth father or mother more than me
is not worthy of me: and he that loveth son or daughter more than me is
38 not worthy of me. And he that doth not take his cross and follow after
39 me, is not worthy of me. He that ¹⁴findeth his ¹⁵life shall lose it; and he
that ¹⁶loseth his ¹⁵life for my sake shall find it [*see John 12: 25*].
40   He that receiveth you receiveth me, and he that receiveth me re-
41 ceiveth him that sent me [*see John 13: 20*]. He that receiveth a prophet in
the name of a prophet shall receive a prophet's reward; and he that receiveth a righteous man in the name of a righteous man shall receive a
42 righteous man's reward. And whosoever shall give to drink unto one of
these little ones a cup of cold water only, in the name of a disciple, verily
I say unto you, he shall in no wise lose his reward.

Mark 6:6–13	Matt. 9:35 to 11:1	Luke 9:1–6
12 And they went out, and preached that *men* should repent.	1 And it came to pass, when Jesus had made an end of command-	
13 And they cast out many ³devils, and anointed with oil	ing his twelve disci- ples, he departed thence to teach and	6 And they departed, and went throughout the villages, preach-

81

Mark 6:6-13	Matt. 9:35 to 11:1	Luke 9:1-6
many that were sick, and healed them.	preach in their cities.	ing the gospel, and healing everywhere.

[1] Or, *Zealot.* See Luke 6:15; Acts 1:13. [2] Or, *delivered him up,* and so always. [3] Gr. *demons.* [4] Gr. *girdles.* [5] Or, *simple.* [6] Or, *put them to death.* [7] Or, *teacher.* [8] Gr. *bond-servant.* [9] Gr. *Beelzebul:* and so elsewhere. [10] Gr. *Gehenna.* [11] Gr. *in me.* [12] Gr. *in him.* [13] Gr. *cast.* [14] Or, *found.* [15] Or, *soul.* [16] Or, *lost.* [17] Gr. *brass.* [18] Gr. *girdle.* [19] Some ancient authorities omit *the sick.*

§71. THE GUILTY FEARS OF HEROD ANTIPAS IN TIBERIAS ABOUT JESUS BECAUSE HE HAD BEHEADED THE BAPTIST IN MACHÆRUS

Mark 6:14-29

14 And king Herod heard* *thereof;* for his name had become known: and [1]he said, John [2]the Baptist is risen from the dead, and therefore do these powers work in him. 15 But others said, It is Elijah. And others said, *It is* a prophet, *even* as one of the 16 prophets. But Herod, when he heard *thereof,* said, John, whom I beheaded, he 17 is risen. For Herod himself had sent forth and laid hold upon John, and bound him in prison for the sake of Herodias, his brother Philip's wife: for he had married 18 her. For John said unto Herod.† It is not lawful for thee to have thy brother's wife [*see Lev. 18:16;* 19 *20:21*]. And Herodias set herself against

Matt. 14:1-12

1 At that season Herod the tetrarch heard the report con- 2 cerning Jesus, and said unto his servants, This is John the Baptist; he is risen from the dead; and therefore do these powers work in him. 3 For Herod had laid hold on John, and bound him, and put him in prison for the sake of Herodias, his brother Philip's wife.

4 For John said unto him, It is not lawful for thee to have her. 5 And when he would have put him to death, he feared the multitude, because

Luke 9:7-9

7 Now Herod the tetrarch heard of all that was done: and he was much perplexed, because that it was said by some, that John was risen 8 from the dead; and by some, that Elijah had appeared; and by others, that one of the old prophets was risen again. And 9 Herod said, John I beheaded: but who is this, about whom I hear such things? And he sought to see him.

* Mark's connection shows that Herod Antipas was impressed by the account of miracles which the disciples had wrought, as well as by those of Jesus himself.

† Josephus (*Antiquities,* Book XVIII, v., 2) says of John that Herod "thought it best, by putting him to death, to prevent any mischief he might cause, and not bring himself into difficulties, by sparing a man who might make him repent of it when it should be too late." Josephus in no wise controverts the picture in Mark where Herodias appears as the one who prods Antipas to put John out of the way to satisfy her resentment against him for his rebuke of her adulterous marriage. Josephus merely presents the public and political aspects of the imprisonment and death of John.

Mark 6:14–29	Matt. 14:1–12
him; and desired to 20 kill him; and she could not; for Herod feared John, knowing that he was a righteous man and a holy, and kept him safe. And when he heard him, he *was much perplexed; and he heard him gladly.	they counted him as a prophet.
21 And when a convenient d a y w a s come, that Herod on his birthday made a supper to his lords, and the *high captains, and the chief	
22 men of Galilee: and when *the daughter of Herodias herself came in and danced, *she pleased Herod and them that sat at meat with him; and the king said unto the damsel, Ask of me whatsoever thou wilt, and I will give it thee.	6 But when Herod's birthday came, the daughter of Herodias danced in the midst, and pleased Herod.
23 And he sware unto her, Whatsoever thou shalt ask of me, I will give it thee, unto the half of my king-	7 Whereupon he promised with an oath to give her whatsoever
24 dom. And she went out, and said unto her mother, What shall I ask? And she said, The head of John the Baptist.	8 she should ask. And she, being put forward by her mother,
25 And she came in straightway w i t h haste unto the king, and asked, saying, I will that thou forthwith give me in a charger the head of	saith, Give me here in a charger the head
26 John the Baptist. And the king was exceeding sorry; but for the	of John the Baptist. 9 And the king was grieved: but for the

Mark 6:14–29	Matt. 14:1–12
sake of his oaths, and of them that sat at meat, he would not 27 reject her. And straightway the king sent forth a soldier of his guard, and commanded to bring his head: and he went and beheaded him in 28 the prison, and brought his head in a charger, and gave it to the damsel; and the damsel gave it to 29 her mother. And when his disciples heard *thereof*, they came and took up his corpse, and laid it in a tomb.	sake of his oaths, and of them which sat at meat with him, he commanded it to be 10 given: and he sent, and beheaded John 11 in the prison. And his head was brought in a charger, and given to the damsel: and she brought it to 12 her mother. And his disciples came, and took up the corpse, and buried him; and they went and told Jesus.

¹ Some ancient authorities read *they*. ² Gr. *the Baptizer*. ³ Many ancient authorities read *did many things*. ⁴ Or, *military tribunes*. Gr. *chiliarch*. ⁵ Some ancient authorities read *his daughter Herodias*. ⁶ Or, *it*.

PART VIII

THE SPECIAL TRAINING OF THE TWELVE IN DISTRICTS AROUND GALILEE

Probably Passover in A.D. 29* to near Tabernacles in A.D. 29 or a year earlier (six months from spring to autumn). Just a year from the beginning of this Period till the Crucifixion. Emphasis now on the King of the Kingdom (the Person of the Messiah).

§§ 72–95. Four separate withdrawals† from Galilee are given, in §§ 72, 78, 79, 81. Notice that in every case he keeps out of Herod's territory, and in every case he goes to the mountains.

§ 72. THE FIRST RETIREMENT. THE TWELVE RETURN, AND JESUS RETIRES WITH THEM BEYOND THE LAKE TO REST. FEEDING OF THE FIVE THOUSAND

Mark 6:30–44		Luke 9:10–17	
30 And the apostles gather themselves together unto Jesus; and they told him all things, whatsoever they had done, and whatsoever they had 31 taught. And he saith unto them, Come ye yourselves apart into a desert place, and rest a		10 And the apostles, when they were returned, declared unto him what things they had done.	

---

* If the ministry of Jesus was three and a half years in length. If there were only three passovers in the ministry, then the year would be A.D. 28. This period begins just before a passover (John 6:4).

† There are five reasons for the withdrawals from Galilee. He withdraws from the jealousy of Herod Antipas (§ 71), from the fanaticism of would-be followers in Galilee (John 6:15), and the hostility of the Jewish rulers; and leaving the hot shores of the Lake of Galilee, he spent the summer in mountain districts around, resting, and *instructing the Twelve.*

Mark 6:30–44	Matt. 14:13–21	Luke 9:10–17	John 6:1–13
while. For there were many coming and going, and they had no leisure so much as to eat. 32 And they went away in the boat to a desert place apart. 33 And *the people* saw them going, and many knew *them*, and they ran there together ¹on foot from all the cities, and outwent 34 them. And he came forth and saw a great multitude, and he had compassion on them, because they were as sheep not having a shepherd, and he began to teach them many things. 35 And when the day was now far spent, his disciples came unto him, and said, The place is desert, and the day is now 36 far spent; send them away that they may go into the country and villages round	13 Now when Jesus heard *it,* he withdrew from thence in a boat, to a desert place apart. And when the multitudes heard *thereof,* they followed him ¹on foot from 14 the cities. And he came forth, and saw a great multitude, and he had compassion on them, and healed their sick. 15 And when even was come, the disciples came to him, saying, The place is desert, and the time is already past; send the multitudes away, that they may go into the villages, and buy them-	And he took them, and withdrew apart to a city called Bethsaida.* 11 But the multitudes perceiving it followed him: and he welcomed them, and spake to them of the kingdom of God, and them that had need of healing he healed. 12 And the day began to wear away; and the twelve came and said unto him, Send the multitude away, that they may go into the villages and country round about, and lodge, and get victuals: for we are here	1 After these things Jesus went away to the other side of the sea of Galilee, which is *the sea* of Tiberias. 2 And a great multitude followed him, because they beheld the signs which he did on them that 3 were sick. And Jesus went up into the mountain, and there he sat with his disciples. 4 Now the passover, the feast of the Jews, was at hand. 5 Jesus therefore lifting up his eyes, and seeing that a great multitude cometh unto him, saith unto Philip, Whence are we to buy

* The Bethsaida of Luke 9:10 was evidently the eastern Bethsaida, which the Tetrarch Philip had named Bethsaida Julias, while that of Mark 6:45 was the western Bethsaida, near Capernaum. The territory belonging to Bethsaida Julias would naturally extend some distance down the lake.

Mark 6:30-44	Matt. 14:13-21	Luke 9:10-17	John 6:1-13
about, and buy themselves somewhat to	selves food.	in a desert	4bread, that these may eat?
37 eat. But he answered and said unto them, Give ye them to eat. And they say unto him, Shall we go and buy two hundred ²pennyworth of bread, and give them to 38 eat? And he saith unto them,	16 But Jesus said unto them, They have no need to go a-way; give ye them to eat.	13 place. But he said unto them, Give ye them to eat.	6 And this he said to prove him: for he himself knew what he would 7 do. Philip answered him, Two hundred ²pennyworth of ⁴bread is not sufficient for them, that every one may take a little.
How many loaves have ye? go *and* see. And when they knew, they say, Five, and two fishes.	17 And they say unto him, We have here but five loaves, and 18 two fishes. And he said, Bring them hither	And they said, We have no more than five loaves and two fishes; except we should go and buy food for all this peo-	8 One of his disciples, Andrew, Simon Peter's brother, saith unto him, 9 There is a lad here, which hath five barley loaves, and two fishes: but what are these
39 And he commanded them that all should ³sit down by companies upon the green 40 grass. And they sat down in ranks, by hundreds, and 41 by fifties. And he took the	19 to me. And he commanded the multitudes to ³sit down on the grass;	14 ple. For they were about five thousand. And he said unto his disciples, Make them ²sit down in companies, about fifty 15 each. And they did so, and made them all	among so 10 many? Jesus said, Make the people sit down. Now there was much grass in the place. So the men sat down, in number about five
he took the five loaves and the two fishes, and looking up to heaven, he blessed, and brake the loaves; and he gave to the disciples to set before them; and the two fishes divided	and he took the five loaves, and the two fishes, and looking up to heaven, he blessed, and brake and gave the loaves to the disciples, and the disciples to 20 the multi- tudes. And	16 ²sit down. And he took the five loaves and the two fishes, and looking up to heaven, he blessed them, and brake; and gave to the disciples to set before the multitude. 17 And they did eat, and were	11 thousand. Je- sus therefore took the loaves: and having given thanks, dis- tributed to them that were set down; likewise also of the fishes as

Mark 6:30–44	Matt. 14:13–21	Luke 9:10–17	John 6:1–13
he among 42 them all. And they did all eat, and were 43 filled. And they took up broken pieces, twelve basketfuls, and also of the fishes. 44 And they that ate the loaves were five thousand men.	they did all eat, and were filled: and they took up that which remained over of the broken pieces, twelve baskets 21 full. And they that did eat were about five thousand men, besides women and children.	all filled: and there was taken up that which remained over to them of broken pieces, twelve baskets.	much as they 12 would. And when they were filled, he saith unto his disciples, Gather up the broken pieces which remain over, that nothing be 13 lost. So they gathered them up, and filled twelve baskets with broken pieces from the five barley loaves, which remained over unto them that had eaten.*

¹ Or, *by land.*   ² Gr. *recline.*   ³ The word in the Greek denotes a coin worth about seventeen cents.
⁴ Gr. *loaves.*

§ 73. THE PREVENTION⸗ OF THE REVOLUTIONARY PURPOSE TO PROCLAIM JESUS KING (A POLITICAL MESSIAH)

Mark 6:45–46	Matt. 14:22–23	John 6:14–15
45 And straightway he constrained his disciples to enter into the boat, and to go before *him* unto the other side to Bethsaida, while he himself sendeth the multitude away. 46 And after he had taken leave of them, he departed into the mountain to pray.	22 And straightway he constrained the disciples to enter into the boat, and to go before him unto the other side, till he should send the multitudes away. 23 And after he had sent the multitudes away, he went up into the mountain apart to pray: and when even was come, he was there alone.	14 When therefore the people saw the sign that he did they said, This is of a truth the prophet that cometh unto the world [*see Deut. 18:15*]. 15 Jesus therefore perceiving that they were about to come and take him by force, to make him king, withdrew again into the mountain himself alone.

* Note that here for the first time John runs parallel with all the synoptic gospels. All four report this incident. See Passion Week.

§74. THE PERIL TO THE TWELVE IN THE STORM AT SEA AND CHRIST'S COMING TO THEM ON THE WATER IN THE DARKNESS

Mark 6:47–52

47 And when even was come, the boat was in the midst of the sea, and he alone on
48 the land. And seeing them distressed in rowing, for the wind was contrary unto them, about the fourth watch of the night he cometh unto them, walking on the sea; and he would have passed by them:
49 but they, when they saw him walking on the sea, supposed that it was an apparition,
50 and cried out: for they all saw him, and were troubled. But he straightway spake with them, and saith unto them, Be of good cheer: it is I; be not afraid.

Matt. 14:24–33

24 But the boat ¹was now in the midst of the sea, distressed by the waves; for the wind was contrary.

25 And in the fourth watch of the night he came unto them, walking upon the sea.

26 And when the disciples saw him walking on the sea, they were troubled, saying, It is an apparition; and they cried
27 out for fear. But straightway Jesus spake unto them, saying, Be of good cheer; it is I; be not
28 afraid. And Peter answered him, and said, Lord, if it be thou, bid me come unto thee upon the
29 waters. And he said, Come. And Peter went down from the boat, and walked upon the waters, ²to
30 come to Jesus. But when he saw the ³wind, he was afraid, and beginning to sink, he cried out, saying,
31 Lord, save me. And immediately Jesus stretched forth his hand, and took hold of him, and saith un-

John 6:16–21

16 And when evening came, his disciples went down unto the
17 sea; and they entered into a boat, and were going over the sea unto Capernaum. And it was now dark, and Jesus had not yet come to them.
18 And the sea was rising by reason of a great wind that blew.
19 When therefore they had rowed about five and twenty or thirty furlongs, they behold Jesus walking on the sea, and drawing nigh unto the boat: and they were afraid.
20 But he saith unto them, It is I; be not afraid.

Mark 6:47-52	Matt. 14:24-33	John 6:16-21
	to him, O thou of little faith, wherefore didst thou doubt?	
51 And he went up unto them into the boat; and the wind ceased: and they were sore amazed in themselves 52 for they understood not concerning the loaves, but their heart was hardened.	32 And when they were gone up into the boat, the wind ceased. 33 And they that were in the boat worshipped him, saying, Of a truth thou art the Son of God.	21 They were willing therefore to receive him into the boat: and straightway the boat was at the land whither they were going.

¹ Some ancient authorities read *was many furlongs distant from the land.* ² Some ancient authorities read *and came.* ³ Many ancient authorities add *strong.*

§ 75. THE RECEPTION AT GENNESARET

Mark 6:53-56	Matt. 14:34-36
53 And when they had ¹crossed over, they came to the land unto Gennesaret, and moored to the 54 shore. And when they were come out of the boat, straightway *the* 55 *people* knew him, and ran about that whole region, and began to carry about on their beds those that were sick, where they heard 56 he was. And wheresoever* he entered, into villages, or into cities, or into the country, they laid the sick in the marketplaces, and besought him that they might touch if it were but the border of his garment: and as many as touched ²him were made whole.	34 And when they crossed over, they came to the land, unto Gennesaret. 35 And when the men of that place knew him, they sent unto all that region round about, and brought unto 36 him all that were sick; and they besought him that they might only touch the border of his garment: and as many as touched were made whole.

¹ Or, *crossed over to the land, they came unto Gennesaret.* ² Or, *it.*

§ 76. THE COLLAPSE OF THE GALILEAN CAMPAIGN BECAUSE JESUS WILL NOT CONFORM TO POPULAR MESSIANIC EXPECTATIONS

The next day in the Synagogue in Capernaum. The same crowd that had eaten the Loaves and the Fishes leave Christ in disgust on learning that He is the Bread of Life and not a Political Messiah.

John 6:22-71

22 On the morrow the multitude which stood on the other side of the sea saw that there was none other ¹boat there, save one, and that Jesus

* This general characterization applies to the Galilean work as a whole in Part VII rather than to the precise time at this juncture. But one must allow his imagination to enlarge upon the scope of Christ's work.

John 6:22–71

entered not with his disciples into the boat, but *that* his disciples went
23 away alone (howbeit there came ²boats from Tiberias nigh unto the place
where they ate the bread after the Lord had given thanks): when the
24 multitude therefore saw that Jesus was not there, neither his disciples,
they themselves got into the ²boats, and came to Capernaum, seeking
25 Jesus. And when they found him on the other side of the sea, they said
26 unto him, Rabbi, when camest thou hither? Jesus answered them and
said, Verily, verily, I say unto you, Ye seek me, not because ye saw signs,
27 but because ye ate of the loaves and were filled. Work not for the meat
which perisheth, but for the meat which abideth unto eternal life, which
the Son of man shall give unto you: for him the Father, *even* God, hath
28 sealed. They said therefore unto him, What must we do, that we may
29 work the works of God? Jesus answered and said unto them, This is the
30 work of God, that ye believe on him whom ³he hath sent. They said
therefore unto him, What then doest thou for a sign, that we may see,
31 and believe thee? what workest thou? Our fathers ate the manna in
32 the wilderness; as it is written, He gave them bread out of heaven to eat
[*see Ex. see 16:4, 15; Ps. 78:24; Neh. 9:15*]. Jesus therefore said unto them,
Verily, verily, I say unto you, It was not Moses that gave you the bread
out of heaven: but my Father giveth you the true bread out of heaven.
33 For the bread of God is that which cometh down out of heaven, and
34 giveth life unto the world. They said therefore unto him, Lord, ever-
35 more give us this bread. Jesus said unto them, I am the bread of life:
he that cometh to me shall not hunger, and he that believeth on me shall
36 never thirst. But I said unto you, that ye have seen me, and yet believe
37 not. All that which the Father giveth me shall come unto me; and him
38 that cometh to me I will in no wise cast out. For I am come down from
39 heaven, not to do mine own will, but the will of him that sent me. And
this is the will of him that sent me, that of all that which he hath given me
40 I should lose nothing, but should raise it up at the last day. For this is
the will of my Father, that every one that beholdeth the Son, and believeth on him, should have eternal life; ⁴I will raise him up at the last day.
41 The Jews therefore murmured concerning him, because he said, I am
42 the bread which came down out of heaven. And they said, Is not this
Jesus, the son of Joseph, whose father and mother we know? how doth
43 he now say, I am come down out of heaven? Jesus answered and said
44 unto them, Murmur not among yourselves. No man can come to me,
except the Father which sent me draw him: and I will raise him up in the
45 last day. It is written in the prophets [*see Isa. 54:13*], And they shall all be
taught of God. Every one that hath heard from the Father, and hath
46 learned, cometh unto me. Not that any man hath seen the Father,
47 save he which is from God, he hath seen the Father. Verily, verily, I
48 say unto you, He that believeth hath eternal life. I am the bread of life.
49 Your fathers did eat the manna in the wilderness, and they died. This
50 is the bread which cometh down out of heaven, that a man may eat
51 thereof, and not die. I am the living bread which came down out of
heaven: if any man eat of this bread, he shall live for ever: yea and the
bread which I will give is my flesh, for the life of the world.
52 The Jews therefore strove one with another, saying, How can this man
53 give us his flesh to eat? Jesus therefore said unto them, Verily, verily,

John 6:22–71

I say unto you, Except ye eat the flesh of the Son of man and drink his
54 blood, ye have not life in yourselves. He that eateth my flesh and
55 drinketh my blood hath eternal life; and I will raise him up at the last
day. For my flesh is ⁵meat indeed, and my blood is ⁶drink indeed.
56 He that eateth my flesh and drinketh my blood abideth in me, and I in
57 him. As the living Father sent me, and I live because of the Father;
58 so he that eateth me, he also shall live because of me. This is the bread
which came down out of heaven: not as the fathers did eat, and died:
59 he that eateth this bread shall live for ever. These things said he in ⁷the
synagogue, as he taught in Capernaum.
60   Many therefore of his disciples, when they heard *this*, said, This is a
61 hard saying; who can hear ⁸it? But Jesus knowing in himself that his
disciples murmured at this, said unto them, Doth this cause you to
62 stumble? *What* then if ye should behold the Son of man ascending where
63 he was before? It is the spirit that quickeneth; the flesh profiteth noth-
64 ing: the words that I have spoken unto you are spirit, and are life. But
there are some of you that believe not. For Jesus knew from the beginning who they were that believed not, and who it was that should
65 betray him. And he said, For this cause have I said unto you, that no
man can come unto me, except it be given unto him of the Father.
66   Upon this many of his disciples went back, and walked no more with
67 him. Jesus said therefore unto the twelve, Would ye also go away?
68 Simon Peter answered him, Lord, to whom shall we go? thou ⁹hast the
69 words of eternal life. And we have believed and know that thou art the
70 Holy One of God. Jesus answered them, Did not I choose you the
71 twelve, and one of you is a devil? Now he spake of Judas *the son* of
Simon Iscariot, for he it was that should betray him, *being* one of the
twelve.

¹ Gr. *little boat.* ² Gr. *little boats.* ³ Or, *he sent.* ⁴ Or, *that I should raise him up.* ⁵ Gr. *true meat.*
⁶ Gr. *true drink.* ⁷ Or, *a synagogue.* ⁸ Or, *him.* ⁹ Or, *hast words.*

§ 77. PHARISEES FROM JERUSALEM REPROACH JESUS FOR ALLOWING HIS DISCIPLES TO DISREGARD THEIR TRADITIONS ABOUT CEREMONIAL DEFILEMENT OF THE HANDS. A PUZZLING PARABLE IN REPLY

Probably in Capernaum

Mark 7:1–23	Matt. 15:1–20	John 7:1
1 And there are gathered together unto him the Pharisees, and cer- tain of the scribes, which had come 2 from Jerusalem, and had seen that some of his disciples ate their bread with ⁶defiled, that is un- 3 washen, hands. For the Phari- sees, and all the Jews, except they wash their hands ⁷diligently, eat not, holding the tradition of 4 the elders: and *when they come*	1 Then there came to Je- sus from Jerusalem Pharisees and scribes, 2 saying, Why do thy disciples	1 And after these things Jesus walked in Galilee: for he would not walk in Judea, because the Jews sought to kill him.

Mark 7:1-23

from the marketplace, except they ³wash themselves, they eat not: and many other things there be, which they have received to hold, ⁹washings of cups, and pots, and 5 brasen vessels.¹⁰ And the Pharisees and the scribes ask him, Why walk not thy disciples according to the tradition of the elders, but eat their bread with ⁶defiled 6 hands? And he said unto them, Well did Isaiah prophesy of you hypocrites, as it is written,

This people honoureth me with their lips,
But their heart is far from me.
7 But in vain do they worship me, Teaching *as their* doctrines the precepts of men.
8 Ye leave the commandment of God, and hold fast the tradition
9 of men. And he said unto them, Full well do ye reject the commandment of God, that ye may
10 keep your tradition. For Moses [*see Ex. 20:12; Deut. 5:16*] said, Honour thy father and thy mother; and, He that speaketh evil of father or mother, let him ¹die the
11 death; but ye say, If a man shall say to his father or his mother, That wherewith thou mightest have been profited by me is Corban, that is to say, Given *to God;*
12 [*see Ex. 21:17; Lev. 20:9*]; ye no longer suffer him to do aught for his father or his mother; making void the word of God by your tradition, which ye have de-
13 livered: and many such like things
14 ye do. And he called to him the multitude again, and said unto them, Hear me all of you, and
15 understand: there is nothing from without the man, that going into him can defile him: but the things which proceed out of the man are those that defile the man.¹¹
17 And when he was entered into the house from the multitude, his

Matt. 15:1-20

transgress the tradition of the elders? for they wash not their 3 hands when they eat bread. And he answered and said unto them, 7 Ye hypocrites, well did Isaiah prophesy of you, saying [*see Isa. 29:13*],
8   This people honoureth me with their lips;
But their heart is far from me.
9   But in vain do they worship me, Teaching *as their* doctrines the precepts of men.
3 Why do ye also transgress the commandment of God, because of your tradition?

4   For God said, Honour thy father and thy mother: and, He that speaketh evil of father or mother, let him 5 ¹die the death. But ye say, Whosoever shall say to his father or his mother, That wherewith thou mightest have been profited by 6 me is given *to God;* he shall not honour his father.² And ye have

made void the ³word of God because of your tradition.

10   And he called to him the multitude, and said unto them, Hear, and under-11 stand: Not that which entereth

into the mouth defileth the man, but that which proceedeth out of the mouth, this defileth the man.

Mark 7:1–23	Matt. 15:1–20
disciples asked of him the parable.	12 Then came the disciples, and said unto him, Knowest thou that the Pharisees were ⁴offended, when 13 they heard this saying? But he answered and said, Every ⁵plant which my heavenly Father plant-14 ed not, shall be rooted up. Let them alone: they are blind guides. And if the blind guide the blind, 15 both shall fall into a pit. And Peter answered and said unto
18 And he saith unto them, Are ye so without understanding also? Perceive ye not, that whatsoever from without goeth into the man, 19 *it* cannot defile him; because it goeth not into his heart, but into his belly, and goeth out into the draught? *This he said*, making 20 all meats clean. And he said, That which proceedeth out of the man, that defileth the man. 21 For from within, out of the heart of men, ¹²evil thoughts proceed, 22 fornications, thefts, murders, adulteries, covetings, wickednesses, deceit, lasciviousness, an evil eye, 23 railing, pride, foolishness: all these evil things proceed from within, and defile the man.	him, Declare unto us the parable. 16 And he said, Are ye also even yet 17 without understanding? Perceive ye not, that whatsoever goeth into the mouth passeth into the belly, and is cast out into 18 the draught? But the things which proceed out of the mouth come forth out of the heart; and 19 they defile the man. For out of the heart come forth evil thoughts, murders, adulteries, fornications, thefts, false witness, railings: 20 these are the things which defile the man: but to eat with unwashen hands defileth not the man.

¹ Or, *surely die.* ² Some ancient authorities add *or his mother.* ³ Some ancient authorities read *law.* ⁴ Gr. *caused to stumble.* ⁵ Gr. *planting.* ⁶ Or, *common.* ⁷ Or, *up to the elbow.* Gr. *with the fist.* ⁸ Gr. *baptize.* Some ancient authorities read *sprinkle themselves.* ⁹ Gr. *baptizings.* ¹⁰ Many ancient authorities add *and couches.* ¹¹ Many ancient authorities insert ver. 16, *If any man hath ears to hear, let him hear.* ¹² Gr. *thoughts that are evil.*

§78. THE SECOND WITHDRAWAL TO THE REGION OF TYRE AND SIDON AND THE HEALING OF THE DAUGHTER OF A SYRO–PHŒNICIAN WOMAN

Mark 7:24–30	Matt. 15:21–28
24 And from thence he arose, and went away into the borders of Tyre ³and Sidon. And he entered	21 And Jesus went out thence, and withdrew into the parts of Tyre and Sidon.*

* It used to be questioned whether he actually left the land of Israel. Matthew's expression ought to have settled the question, and the corrected text of Mark 7:31 leaves no doubt.

Mark 7:24–30	Matt. 15:21–28
into a house, and would have 25 no man know it: and he could not be hid. But straightway a woman, whose little daughter had an unclean spirit, having heard of him, came and fell down 26 at his feet. Now the woman was a ⁴Greek, a Syrophœnician by race. And she besought him that he would cast forth the ¹devil out of her daughter. 27 And he said unto her, Let the children first be filled: for it is not meet to take the children's ²bread and 28 cast it to the dogs. But she answered and saith unto him, Yea, Lord: even the dogs under the table eat of the children's crumbs. 29 And he said unto her, For this saying go thy way; the ¹devil is 30 gone out of thy daughter. And she went away unto her house, and found the child laid upon the bed, and the ¹devil gone out.	22 And behold, a Canaanitish woman came out from those borders, and cried, saying, Have mercy on me, O Lord, thou son of David, my daughter is grievously vexed with 23 a ¹devil. But he answered her not a word. And his disciples came and besought him, saying, Send her away; for she crieth 24 after us. But he answered and said, I was not sent but unto the lost sheep of the house of Is-25 rael. But she came and worshipped him, saying, Lord, help 26 me. And he answered and said, It is not meet to take the children's ²bread and cast it to the 27 dogs. But she said, Yea, Lord: for even the dogs eat of the crumbs which fall from their 28 masters' table. Then Jesus answered and said unto her, O woman, great is thy faith; be it done unto thee even as thou wilt. And her daughter was healed from that hour.

¹ Gr. *demon*.   ² Or, *loaf*.   ³ Some ancient authorities omit *and Sidon*.   ⁴ Or, *Gentile*.

§ 79. THE THIRD WITHDRAWAL NORTH THROUGH PHŒNICIA AND EAST TOWARDS HERMON AND SOUTH INTO DECAPOLIS (KEEPING OUT OF THE TERRITORY OF HEROD ANTIPAS) WITH THE HEALING OF THE DEAF AND DUMB MAN AND THE FEEDING OF THE FOUR THOUSAND

Mark 7:31–8:9	Matt. 15:29–38
31 And again he went out from the borders of Tyre, and came through Sidon unto the sea of Galilee, through the midst of the 32 borders of Decapolis.* And they	29 And Jesus departed thence, and came nigh unto the sea of Galilee; and he went up into the mountain, and sat there.

* Observe how carefully he keeps away from the territory ruled by Herod Antipas. The tetrarch Philip, who governed the districts east of the Lake of Galilee and of the upper Jordan, was a better man than Antipas, and moreover had no cause to feel uneasy about Jesus

Mark 7:31–8:9

bring unto him one that was deaf, and had an impediment in his speech; and they beseech him to 33 lay his hand upon him. And he took him aside from the multitude privately, and put his fingers into his ears, and he spat, and touched 34 his tongue; and looking up to heaven, he sighed, and saith unto him, Ephphatha, that is, Be 35 opened. And his ears were opened, and the bond of his tongue was 36 loosed, and he spake plain. And he charged them that they should tell no man: but the more he charged them, so much the more a 37 great deal they published it. And they were beyond measure astonished, saying, He hath done all things well: he maketh even the deaf to hear, and the dumb to speak.

1 In those days, when there was again* a great multitude, and they had nothing to eat, he called unto him his disciples, and saith 2 unto them, I have compassion on the multitude, because they continue with me now three days, and have nothing to eat; and 3 if I send them away fasting to their home, they will faint in the way; and some of them are 4 come from far. And his disciples answered him, Whence shall one be able to fill these men with ¹bread here in a desert place? 5 And he asked them, How many loaves have ye? And they said, 6 Seven. And he commanded the multitude to sit down on the ground: and he took the seven loaves, and having given thanks, he brake, and gave to his disciples, to set before them; and they set 7 them before the multitude. And

Matt. 15:29–38

30 And there came unto him great multitudes, having with them the lame, blind, dumb, maimed, and many others, and they cast 31 them down at his feet; and he healed them: insomuch that the multitude wondered, when they saw the dumb speaking, the maimed whole, and the lame walking, and the blind seeing: and they glorified the God of Israel. 32 And Jesus called unto him his disciples, and said, I have compassion on the multitude, because they continue with me now three days and have nothing to eat: and I would not send them away fasting, lest haply they faint in the way.

33 And the disciples say unto him, Whence should we have so many loaves in a desert place, as to fill so great a multi-34 tude? And Jesus saith unto them, How many loaves have ye? And they said, Seven, and a few small 35 fishes. And he commanded the multitude to sit down on the 36 ground: and he took the seven loaves and the fishes; and he gave thanks and brake, and gave to the disciples, and the disciples to the multitudes.

---

¹ It is to be noted that Mark and Matthew give the feeding of the five thousand and of the four thousand. Mark and Matthew likewise report Jesus as referring to both incidents (Mark 8:19–20 = Matt. 16:9–10). Hence, it is hard to think of a mere confusion in the use of the data. There is no real reason why both incidents could not be true.

Mark 7:31–8:9	Matt. 15:29–38
they had a few small fishes: and having blessed them, he commanded to set these also before 8 them. And they did eat, and were filled: and they took up, of broken pieces that remained over, 9 seven baskets. And they were about four thousand: and he sent them away.	37 And they did all eat, and were filled: and they took up that which remained over the broken pieces, seven baskets full. And they 38 that did eat were four thousand men, beside women and children.

¹ Gr. loaves.

§ 80. THE BRIEF VISIT TO MAGADAN (DALMANUTHA) IN GALILEE AND THE SHARP ATTACK BY THE PHARISEES AND THE SADDUCEES (NOTE THEIR APPEARANCE NOW AGAINST JESUS)

Mark 8:10–12	Matt. 15:39–16:4
10 And straightway he entered into the boat with his disciples, and came into the parts of Dalmanutha.	39 And he sent away the multitudes, and entered into the boat, and came into the borders of Magadan.*
11 And the Pharisees came forth, began to question with him, seeking of him a sign from heaven, tempting him.	1 And the Pharisees and Sadducees came, and tempting him† asked him to shew them a sign 2 from heaven. But he answered and said unto them, ¹When it is evening, ye say, *It will be* fair 3 weather: for the heaven is red. And in the morning, *It will be* foul weather to-day: for the heaven is red and lowring. Ye know how to discern the face of the heaven; but ye cannot *discern* the signs of 4 the times. An evil and adulterous generation seeketh after a sign; and there shall no sign be given unto it, but the sign of Jonah [see *Jonah 3:4*]. And he left them, and departed.
12 And he sighed deeply in his spirit, and saith, Why doth this generation seek a sign? verily I say unto you, There shall no sign be given unto this generation.	

¹ The following words, to the end of ver. 3, are omitted by some of the most ancient and other important authorities.

* The situation of Magadan was unknown to some early students or copyists, as it is to us, and so they changed it to the familiar Magdala, found in our common texts.
† The moment he returns to Galilee the Jewish leaders begin to attack him.

§ 81. THE FOURTH RETIREMENT TO BETHSAIDA JULIAS IN THE TETRARCHY OF HEROD PHILIP WITH SHARP REBUKE OF THE DULNESS OF THE DISCIPLES ON THE WAY ACROSS AND THE HEALING OF A BLIND MAN IN BETHSAIDA

Mark 8:13-26

13 And he left them, and again entering into *the boat* departed to the other ʳside.

14 And they forgot to take bread; and they had not in the boat with them more than one loaf.

15 And he charged them, saying, Take heed, beware of the leaven of the Pharisees and the leaven

16 of Herod. And they reasoned one with another, ⁴saying. ⁵We

17 have no bread. And Jesus perceiving it saith unto them, Why reason ye, because ye have no bread? do ye not yet perceive, neither understand? have ye your

18 heart hardened? having eyes, see ye not? and having ears, hear ye not? and do ye not remember

19 [*see Jer. 5:21; Ezek. 12:2*]? When I brake the five loaves among the five thousand, how many ⁶baskets full of broken pieces took ye up?

20 They say unto him, Twelve. And when the seven among the four thousand, how many ⁶basketfuls of broken pieces took ye up?

21 And they say unto him, Seven. And he said unto them, Do ye not yet understand?

22 And they come unto Bethsaida.* And they bring to him a blind man, and beseech him to touch

23 him. And he took hold of the blind man by the hand, and brought him out of the village;

Matt. 16:5-12

5 And the disciples came to the other side and forgot to take

6 ¹bread. And Jesus said unto them, Take heed and beware of the leaven of the Pharisees and

7 Sadducees. And they reasoned among themselves, saying, ²We

8 took no ¹bread. And Jesus perceiving it said, O ye of little faith, why reason ye among yourselves

9 because ye have no ¹bread? Do ye not yet perceive, neither remember the five loaves of the five thousand, and how many ³baskets

10 ye took up? Neither the seven loaves of the four thousand, and how many ³baskets ye took up?

11 How is it that ye do not perceive that I spake not to you concerning ¹bread? But beware of the leaven of the Pharisees and Sadducees.

12 Then they understood how that he bade them not beware of the leaven of ¹bread, but of the teaching of the Pharisees and Sadducees.

---

* Jesus goes on to the region of Cæsarea Philippi on Mount Hermon, where no hostility had been aroused, and he could quietly instruct the Twelve. He probably remained in that vicinity several months, as this whole period of retirement lasted six months. He was near Bethsaida Julias in the First Retirement and now he stops here again on his way to Cæsarea Philippi. Each of the four retirements is into heathen territory (Ituræa twice, Phœnicia, Decapolis), where Greek influence prevails, and where the Greek language is dominant.

Mark 8:13–26

and when he had spit on his eyes, and laid his hands upon him, he asked him, Seest thou aught?

24 And he looked up, and said, I see men; for I behold *them* as trees,

25 walking. Then again he laid his hands upon his eyes; and he looked stedfastly, and was restored, and saw all things clearly.

26 And he sent him away to his home, saying, Do not even enter into the village.

¹ Gr. *loaves*. ² Or, It is *because we took no bread*. ³ *Basket* in ver. 9 and 10 represents different Greek words. ⁴ Some ancient authorities read *because they had no bread*. ⁵ Or, It is *because we have no bread*. ⁶ *Basket* in ver. 19 and 20 represents different Greek words.

§ 82. NEAR CÆSAREA PHILIPPI JESUS TESTS THE FAITH OF THE TWELVE IN HIS MESSIAHSHIP

Mark 8:27–30

27 And Jesus went forth, and his disciples, into the villages of Cæsarea Philippi: and in the way he asked his disciples, saying unto them, Who do men say that

28 I am? And they told him, saying, John the Baptist: and others, Elijah: but others, One of the

29 prophets. And he asked them, But who say ye that I am? Peter answereth and saith unto him, Thou art the Christ.

Matt. 16:13–20

13 Now when Jesus came into the parts of Cæsarea Philippi, he asked his disciples, saying, Who do men say ¹that the

14 Son of man is? And they said, Some *say* John the Baptist; some, Elijah; and others, Jeremiah, or one of the prophets.

15 He saith unto them, But who say ye that

16 I am? And Simon Peter answered and said, Thou art the Christ,* the Son of

17 the living God. And Jesus answered and said unto him, Blessed art thou, Simon Bar-Jonah: for flesh

Luke 9:18–21

18 And it came to pass, as he was praying alone, the disciples were with him: and he asked them, saying, Who do the multitudes say that I am?

19 And they answering said, John the Baptist; but others *say*, Elijah; and others, that one of the old prophets is risen

20 again. And he said unto them, But who say ye that I am? And Peter answering said, The Christ of God.

* Some understand ver. 16f. as showing that they had never before believed him to be the Messiah, and so hold that the other Gospels here utterly conflict with John, who represents the first disciples (§§ 28, 35) as believing Jesus to be the Messiah. But it is easy to suppose that their early faith in his Messiahship was shaken by his continued failure to gather armies and set up the expected temporal kingdom, and while still believing him to have a divine mission they had questioned whether he was the Messiah, as John the Baptist did in prison (§ 57). Observe that in Matthew and Luke he long before this time distinctively *implied* that he was the Messiah, in response to the Forerunner's inquiries (§ 57). Besides, at the Baptism and the Temptation, the Synoptic Gospels represent Jesus as the Son of God.

Mark 8:27–30	Matt. 16:13–20	Luke 9:18–21
	and blood hath not revealed it unto thee, but my Father which 18 is in heaven. And I also say unto thee, that thou art ²Peter, and upon this ³rock I will build* my church [see Ps. 89:4, 26, 38, 48]; and the gates of Hades shall not prevail against it. 19 I will give unto thee the keys of the king-dom of heaven: and whatsoever thou shalt bind on earth shall be bound in heaven: and whatsoever thou shalt loose on earth shall be loosed in heaven. 20 Then charged he the	
30 And he charged them that they should tell no man of him.	disciples that they should tell no man that he was the Christ.	21 But he charged them, and command-ed them to tell this to no man;

¹ Many ancient authorities read that I the Son of man am. See Mark 8:27; Luke 9:18. ² Gr. Petros. ³ Gr. petra.

§83. JESUS DISTINCTLY FORETELLS THAT HE, THE MESSIAH, WILL BE REJECTED AND KILLED AND WILL RISE THE THIRD DAY

Mark 8:31–37	Matt. 16:21–26	Luke 9:22–25
31 And he began to teach them, that the Son of man must suf-fer many things, and be rejected by the elders, and the chief priests, and the scribes, and be killed, and after three days 32 rise again. And he	21 From that time be-gan ¹Jesus to shew unto his disciples, how that he must go unto Jerusalem, and suffer many things of the elders and chief priests and scribes, and be killed, and the third day be raised up.	22 saying, The Son of man must suffer many things, and be rejected of the elders and chief priests and scribes, and be killed, and the third day be raised up.

* It is interesting to note that the imagery employed by Jesus here all appears in Ps. 89, a Mes-sianic Psalm built on 2 Sam. 7. Thus note "build" in Ps. 89:4, "rock" in 89:26, "anointed" in 89:38, "the power of Sheol" in 89:48, and the Psalm discusses the perpetuity of the Davidic throne (Kingdom). Jesus applies this imagery to the spiritual Kingdom that He is building.

Mark 8:31-37	Matt. 16:21-26	Luke 9:22-25
spake the saying openly. And Peter took him, and began 33 to rebuke him. But he turning about, and seeing his disciples, rebuked Peter, and saith, Get thee behind me, Satan: for thou mindest not the things of God, but the things of men. 34 And he called unto him the multitude with his disciples, and said unto them, If any man would come after me, let him deny himself, and take up his cross, 35 and follow me. For whosoever would save his [3]life shall lose it; and whosoever shall lose his [3]life for my sake and the gospel's 36 shall save it. For what doth it profit a man, to gain the whole world, and forfeit his [3]life? For 37 what should a man give in exchange for his [3]life?	22 And Peter took him, and began to rebuke him, saying, [2]Be it far from thee, Lord: this shall never be unto 23 thee. But he turned, and said unto Peter, Get thee behind me, Satan: thou art a stumbling-block unto me: for thou mindest not the things of God, but the things 24 of men. Then said Jesus unto his disciples, If any man would come after me, let him deny himself, and take up his cross, 25 and follow me. For whosoever would save his [3]life shall lose it: and whosoever shall lose his [3]life for my sake shall find it. 26 For what shall a man be profited, if he shall gain the whole world, and forfeit his [3]life? or what shall a man give in exchange for his [3]life?	23 And he said unto all, If any man would come after me, let him deny himself, and take up his cross daily, and 24 follow me. For whosoever would save his [3]life shall lose it; but whosoever shall lose his [3]life for my sake, the same shall 25 save it. For what is a man profited, if he gain the whole world, and lose or forfeit his own self?

[1] Some ancient authorities read *Jesus Christ.*   [2] Or, God *have mercy on thee.*   [3] Or, *soul.*

§84. THE COMING OF THE SON OF MAN IN THAT GENERATION

Mark 8:38-9:1	Matt. 16:27-28	Luke 9:26-27
38 For whosoever shall be ashamed of me and of my words in this adulterous and sinful generation, the Son of man also shall be ashamed of him, when he cometh in the glory of his Father	27 For the Son of man shall come in the glory of his Father with his angels and then shall	26 For whosoever shall be ashamed of me and of my words, of him shall the Son of man be ashamed, when he cometh in his own glory, and *the glory* of the Father, and of 27 the holy angels. But

Mark 8:38–9:1	Matt. 16:27–28	Luke 9:26–27
with the holy angels. 1 And he said unto them, Verily I say unto you, There be some here of them that stand *by*, which shall in no wise taste of death, till they see the kingdom of God come with power.	he render unto every man according to his 28 [1]deeds [*see Ps. 62:12; Prov. 24:12*]. Verily I say unto you, There be some of them that stand here, which shall in no wise taste of death, till they see the Son of man coming in his kingdom.	I tell you of a truth, There be some of them that stand here, which shall in no wise taste of death, till they see the kingdom of God.

[1] Or, *doings*.

§ 85. THE TRANSFIGURATION OF JESUS ON A MOUNTAIN (PROBABLY HERMON*) NEAR CÆSAREA PHILIPPI

Mark 9:2–8	Matt. 17:1–8	Luke 9:28–36
2 And after six days Jesus taketh with him Peter, and James, and John, and bringeth them up into a high mountain apart by themselves: and he was transfigured be- 3 fore them: and his garments became glistering, exceeding white; so as no fuller on earth can whiten 4 them. And there appeared unto them Elijah with Moses: and they were talking with Jesus.	1 And after six days Jesus taketh with him Peter, and James, and John his brother, and bringeth them up into a high mountain 2 apart: and he was transfigured before them; and his face did shine as the sun, and his garments became white as the light. 3 And behold, there appeared unto them Moses and Elijah talking with him.	28 And it came to pass, about eight days after these sayings, he took with him Peter and John and James, and went up into the mountain to pray. 29 And as he was praying, the fashion of his countenance was altered, and his raiment *became* white 30 *and* dazzling. And behold, there talked with him two men, which were Moses 31 and Elijah; who appeared in glory, and spake of his [2]decease which he was about to accomplish at 32 Jerusalem. Now Peter and they that were with him, were heavy with sleep: but [3]when they were fully awake, they saw his

* The tradition which places the Transfiguration on Mount Tabor is beyond question false.

Mark 9:2-8	Matt. 17:1-8	Luke 9:28-36
5 And Peter answereth and saith unto Jesus, Rabbi, it is good for us to be here: and let us make three ¹tabernacles,* one for thee, and one for Moses, and one for 6 Elijah. For he wist not what to answer; for they became sore 7 afraid. And there came a cloud overshadowing them: and there came a voice out of the cloud, This is my beloved Son: hear ye him [*see Deut. 18:15; Isa. 42:1; Ps. 2:7*].†	4 And Peter answered, and said unto Jesus, Lord, it is good for us to be here: if thou wilt, I will make here three ¹tabernacles; one for thee, and one for Moses, and one for Elijah. 5 While he was yet speaking, behold, a bright cloud overshadowed them: and behold, a voice out of the cloud, saying, This is my beloved Son, in whom I am well pleased; hear ye 6 him. And when the disciples heard it, they fell on their face, and were sore 7 afraid. And Jesus came and touched them and said, Arise, and be not afraid.	glory, and the two men that stood with 33 him. And it came to pass, as they were parting from him, Peter said unto Jesus, Master, it is good for us to be here: and let us make three ¹tabernacles; one for thee, and one for Moses, and one for Elijah: not knowing what he 34 said. And while he said these things, there came a cloud, and overshadowed them: and they feared as they entered 35 into the cloud. And a voice came out of the cloud, saying, This is ⁴my Son, my chosen: hear ye him.
8 And suddenly looking round about, they saw no one any more, save Jesus only with themselves.	8 And lifting up their eyes, they saw no one, save Jesus only.	36 And when the voice ⁵came, Jesus was found alone.

¹ Or, *booths*. ² Or, *departure*. ³ Or, *having remained awake*. ⁴ Many ancient authorities read *my beloved Son*. See Matt. 17:5; Mark 9:7. ⁵ Or, *was past*.

§ 86. THE PUZZLE OF THE THREE DISCIPLES ABOUT THE RESURRECTION AND ABOUT ELIJAH ON THEIR WAY DOWN THE MOUNTAIN

Mark 9:9-13	Matt. 17:9-13	Luke 9:36
9 And as they were coming down from the mountain, he charged them that they should tell no man what things they had seen, save when the Son of man	9 And as they were coming down from the mountain, Jesus commanded them, saying, Tell the vision to no man, until the Son of man be risen from the dead.	36 And they held their peace, and told no man in those days any of the things which they had seen.

* Probably not long before the feast of tabernacles (near end of September) and Peter may have meant that they celebrate the feast on the mountains instead of going to Jerusalem.
† See § 24 for similar language at the Baptism of Jesus.

103

Mark 9:9–13	Matt. 17:9–13	
should have risen again from the dead. 10 And they kept the saying, questioning among themselves what the rising again from the dead should 11 mean. And they asked him, saying, ¹The scribes say that Elijah must first 12 come. And he said unto them, Elijah indeed cometh first, and restoreth all things: and how is it written of the Son of man, that he should suffer many things and be 13 set at naught? But I say unto you, that Elijah is come, and they have also done unto him whatsoever they listed, even as it is written of him.	10 And his disciples asked him, saying, Why then say the scribes that Elijah must first come [*see* [*Mal. 4:5–6*]? And he answered and said, Elijah indeed cometh, and shall restore all 12 things: but I say unto you, that Elijah is come already,* and they knew him not, but did unto him whatsoever they listed [*see 1 Kings 19:2, 10*]. Even so shall the Son of man also suffer 13 of them. Then understood the disciples that he spake unto them of John the Baptist.	

¹ Or, *How is it that the scribes say . . . come!*

§ 87. THE DEMONIAC BOY, WHOM THE DISCIPLES COULD NOT HEAL

In the region of Cæsarea Philippi

Mark 9:14–29	Matt. 17:14–20	Luke 9:37–43
14 And when they came to the disciples, they saw a great multitude about them, and scribes questioning 15 with them. And straightway all the multitude, when they saw him, were greatly amazed, and running to him sa- 16 luted him. And he asked them, What question ye with	14 And when they were come to the multitude, there came to	37 And it came to pass, on the next day, when they were come down from the mountain, a great multitude met him.

* The Baptist's disclaimer about being Elijah (John 1:21) means only that he was not Elijah in person come back to earth according to popular expectation.

104

Mark 9:14–29	Matt. 17:14–20	Luke 9:37–43
17 them? And one of the multitude answered him, ³Master, I brought unto thee my son, which hath a dumb spirit; and 18 wheresoever it taketh him, it ⁴dasheth him down: and he foameth, and grindeth his teeth, and pineth away: and I spake to thy disciples that they should cast it out; and they were 19 not able. And he answereth them and saith, O faithless generation, how long shall I be with you? how long shall I bear with you? bring him 20 unto me. And they brought him unto him: and when he saw him, straightway the spirit ⁵tare him grievously; and he fell on the ground, and wallowed foam- 21 ing. And he asked his father, How long time is it since this hath come unto him? And he said, From 22 a child. And ofttimes it hath cast him both into the fire and into the waters, to destroy him: but if thou canst do anything, have compassion on us, and help 23 us. And Jesus said unto him, If thou canst! All things are possible to him that 24 believeth. Straightway the father of the child cried out, and	him a man, kneeling to him, and saying, 15 Lord, have mercy on my son: for he is epileptic, and suffereth grievously: for ofttimes he falleth into the fire, and ofttimes into the water. 16 And I brought him to thy disciples, and they could not cure him. 17 And Jesus answered and said, O faithless and perverse generation, how long shall I bear with you? bring him hither to me.	38 And behold, a man from the multitude cried, saying, ³Master, I beseech thee to look upon my son; for he is mine only 39 child: and behold, a spirit taketh him and he suddenly crieth out; and it ⁹teareth him that he foameth, and it hardly departeth from him, bruis- 40 ing him sorely. And I besought thy disciples to cast it out; and they could not. 41 And Jesus answered and said, O faithless and perverse generation, how long shall I be with you, and bear with you? bring 42 hither thy son. And as he was yet a coming, the ¹devil ¹⁰dashed him down, and ⁵tare *him* grievously.

105

Mark 9:14–29	Matt. 17:14–20	Luke 9:37–43
said⁶, I believe; help thou mine unbelief. 25 And when Jesus saw that a multitude came running together, he rebuked the unclean spirit, saying unto him, Thou dumb and deaf spirit, I command thee, come out of him, and enter no 26 more into him. And having cried out, and ⁹torn him much, he came out: and *the child* became as one dead; insomuch that the more part said, 27 He is dead. But Jesus took him by the hand, and raised him up; and he arose. 28 And when he was come into the house, his disciples asked him privately, ⁷*saying,* We could not cast 29 it out. And he said unto them, This kind can come out by nothing, save by prayer.⁸	18 And Jesus rebuked him; and the ¹devil went out from him: and the boy was cured from that hour. 19 Then came the disciples to Jesus apart, and said, Why could not we cast it out? 20 And he said unto them, Because of your little faith: for verily I say unto you, If ye have faith as a grain of mustard seed, ye shall say unto this mountain, Remove hence to yonder place; and it shall remove; and nothing shall be impossible unto you.²	But Jesus rebuked the unclean spirit, and healed the boy, and gave him back 43 to his father. And they were all astonished at the majesty of God.

¹ Gr. *demon.* ² Many authorities, some ancient, insert ver. 21 *But this kind goeth not out save by prayer and fasting.* See Mark 9:29. ³ Or, *Teacher.* ⁴ Or, *rendeth him.* ⁵ Or, *convulsed.* ⁶ Many ancient authorities add *with tears.* ⁷ Or, How is it *that we could not cast it out?* ⁸ Many ancient authorities add *and fasting.* ⁹ Or, *convulseth.* ¹⁰ Or, *rent him.*

§ 88. RETURNING PRIVATELY THROUGH GALILEE, HE AGAIN FORETELLS HIS DEATH AND RESURRECTION

Mark 9:30–32	Matt. 17:22–23	Luke 9:43–45
30 And they went forth from thence, and passed through Galilee; and he would not that any man 31 should know it. For he taught his disciples, and said unto them, The Son of man is delivered up into the hands of men, and they shall kill him; and when he is killed, after three days he shall 32 rise again. But they understood not the saying, and were afraid to ask him	22 And while they ¹abode in Galilee, Jesus said unto them, The Son of man shall be delivered up into the hands of men; 23 and they shall kill him, and the third day he shall be raised up. And they were exceeding sorry.	43 But while all were marvelling at all the things which he did, he said unto his disciples, 44 Let these words sink into your ears: for the Son of man shall be delivered up into the hands of men. 45 But they understood not this saying, and it was concealed from them, that they should not perceive it: and they were afraid to ask him about this saying.

¹ Some ancient authorities read *were gathering themselves together.*

The season of retirement from Galilee is now ended (§§72–88). The remaining events at this time (§§89–95) probably occupied only a few days.

§ 89. JESUS, THE MESSIAH, PAYS THE HALF–SHEKEL FOR THE TEMPLE

Capernaum

Matt. 17:24–27

24 And when they were come to Capernaum, they that received the ¹half-shekel came to Peter, and said, Doth not your ²master pay the 25 ¹half-shekel [*see Ex. 30:11–15*]? He saith, Yea. And when he came into the house, Jesus spake first to him, saying, What thinkest thou, Simon? the kings of the earth, from whom do they receive toll or tribute? from their 26 sons, or from strangers? And when he said, From strangers, Jesus said 27 unto him, Therefore the sons are free. But, lest we cause them to stumble,

107

Matt. 17:24–27

go thou to the sea and cast a hook, and take up the fish that first cometh up; and when thou hast opened his mouth, thou shalt find a ³shekel: that take, and give unto them for me and thee.

¹ Gr. *didrachma.*   ² Or, *teacher.*   ³ Gr. *stater.*

§ 90. THE TWELVE CONTEND AS TO WHO SHALL BE THE GREATEST UNDER THE MESSIAH'S REIGN. HIS SUBJECTS MUST BE CHILDLIKE

Capernaum

Mark 9:33–37	Matt. 18:1–5	Luke 9:46–48
33 And they came to Capernaum: a n d when he was in the house he asked them, What were ye reasoning in the way? 34 But they held their peace: for they had disputed one with another in the way, who *was* the ¹greatest. 35 And he sat down, and called the twelve; he saith unto them, If any man would be first, he shall be last of all, and minister 36 of all. And he took a little child, and set him in the midst of them: and taking him in his arms, he said unto them,	1 In that hour came the disciples unto Jesus, saying, who then is ¹greatest in the kingdom of heaven? 2 And he called to him a little child, and set him in the midst of 3 them, and said, Verily I say unto you, Except ye turn, and become as little children, ye shall in no wise enter into the kingdom of heaven. 4 Whosoever therefore shall humble himself as this little child, the same is the ¹greatest in the king- 5 dom of heaven. And	46 And there arose a reasoning a m o n g them, which of them should be ¹greatest. 47 But when Jesus saw the reasoning of their heart, he took a little child, and set him by his side, and said unto them,
37 Whosoever shall receive one of such little children in my name, receiveth me: and whosoever receiveth me, receiveth not me, but him that sent me.	whoso shall receive one such little child in my name receiveth me:	48 Whosoever shall receive this little child in my name receiveth me: and whosoever shall receive me receiveth him that sent me: for he that is ²least among you all, the same is great.

¹ Gr. *greater.*   ² Gr. *lesser*

§91. THE MISTAKEN ZEAL OF THE APOSTLE JOHN REBUKED BY JESUS IN PERTINENT PARABLES

Capernaum

Mark 9:38–50	Matt. 18:6–14	Luke 9:49–50
38 John said unto him, [7]Master, we saw one casting out [8]devils in thy name: and we forbade him, because he followed not us. 39 But Jesus said, Forbid him not: for there is no man which shall do a [9]mighty work in my name, and be able quickly to speak evil 40 of me. For he that is not against us is 41 for us. For whosoever shall give you a cup of water to drink [10]because ye are Christ's, verily I say unto you, he shall in no wise lose his re- 42 ward. And whosoever shall cause one of these little ones that believe [11]on me to stumble, it were better for him if [2]a great millstone were hanged about his neck, and he were cast into the sea.		49 And John answered and said, Master, we saw one casting out [8]devils in thy name; and we forbade him, because he followeth not with 50 us. But Jesus said unto him, Forbid *him* not: for he that is not against you is for you.
	6 but whoso shall cause one of these little ones which believe on me to stumble, it is profitable for him that [2]a great millstone should be hanged about his neck, and *that* he should be sunk in the depth of 7 the sea. Woe unto the world because of occasions of stumbling! for it must needs be that the occasions come; but woe to that man through whom the occasion 8 cometh! And if thy	
43 And if thy hand cause thee to stumble, cut it off: it is good for thee to enter into life	hand or thy foot causeth thee to stumble, cut it off, and cast it from thee: it	

Mark 9:38–50

maimed, rather than having thy two hands to go into [12]hell, into the unquenchable 45 fire.[13] And if thy foot cause thee to stumble, cut it off: it is good for thee to enter into life halt, rather than having thy two feet to be 47 cast into [12]hell. And if thine eye cause thee to stumble, cast it out: it is good for thee to enter into the kingdom of God with one eye, rather than having two eyes to be cast into [12]hell; 48 where their worm dieth not, and the fire is not quenched [*see Isa. 66:24*]. For 49 every one shall be salted with fire[14] [*see* 50 *Lev. 2:13*]. Salt is good: but if the salt have lost its saltness, wherewith will ye season it? Have salt in yourselves, and be at peace one with another.

Matt. 18:6–14

is good for thee to enter into life maimed or halt, rather than having two hands or two feet to be cast into the eternal fire.

9 And if thine eye causeth thee to stumble, pluck it out, and cast it from thee: it is good for thee to enter into life with one eye, rather than having two eyes to be cast into the [3]hell of fire.

10 See that ye despise not one of these little ones; for I say unto you, that in heaven their angels do always behold the face of my Father which 12 is in heaven.[4] How think ye? if any man have a hundred sheep,* and one of them be gone astray, doth he not leave the ninety and nine, and go unto the mountains, and seek that

13 which goeth astray? And if so be that he find it, verily I say unto you, he rejoiceth over it more than over the ninety and nine which have not 14 gone astray. Even so it is not [5]the will of [6]your Father which is in heaven, that one of these little ones should perish.

[1] Gr. *greater*. [2] Gr. *a millstone turned by an ass.* [3] Gr. *Gehenna of fire.* [4] Many authorities, some ancient, insert ver. 11 *For the Son of man came to save that which was lost.* See Luke 19:10. [5] Gr. *a thing willed before your father.* [6] Some ancient authorities read *my.* [7] Or, *teacher.* [8] Gr. *demons.* [9] Gr. *power.* [10] Gr. *in name that ye are.* [11] Many ancient authorities omit *on me.* [12] Gr. *Gehenna.* [13] Ver. 44 and 46 (which are identical with ver. 48) are omitted by the best ancient authorities. [14] Many ancient authorities add *and every sacrifice shall be salted with salt.* See Lev. 2:13. [15] Gr. *lesser.*

* Parable of the Lost Sheep.

§ 92. RIGHT TREATMENT OF A BROTHER WHO HAS SINNED AGAINST ONE, AND DUTY OF PATIENTLY FORGIVING A BROTHER (PARABLE OF THE UNMERCIFUL SERVANT)

Matt. 18:15–35

15 And if thy brother sin [1]against thee, go, shew him his fault between
16 thee and him alone: if he hear thee, thou hast gained thy brother. But
if he hear *thee* not, take with thee one or two more, that at the mouth
17 of two witnesses or three every word may be established [*see Deut. 19:15*].
And if he refuse to hear them, tell it unto the [2]church: and if he refuse to
hear the [2]church also, let him be unto thee as the Gentile and the publican.
18 Verily I say unto you, What things soever ye shall bind on earth shall be
bound in heaven: and what things soever ye shall loose on earth shall be
19 loosed in heaven. Again I say unto you, that if two of you shall agree
on earth as touching anything that they shall ask, it shall be done for
20 them of my Father which is in heaven. For where two or three are
gathered together in my name, there am I in the midst of them.
21 Then came Peter, and said to him, Lord, how oft shall my brother sin
22 against me, and I forgive him? until seven times? Jesus saith unto him,
I say not unto thee, Until seven times; but, Until [3]seventy times seven.
23 Therefore is the kingdom of heaven likened* unto a certain king, which
24 would make a reckoning with his [4]servants. And when he had begun
to reckon, one was brought unto him, which owed him ten thousand
25 [5]talents. But forasmuch as he had not *wherewith* to pay, his lord commanded him to be sold, and his wife, and children, and all that he had,
26 and payment to be made. The [6]servant therefore fell down and worshipped him, saying, Lord, have patience with me, and I will pay thee all.
27 And the lord of that [6]servant, being moved with compassion, released him,
28 and forgave him the debt. But that [6]servant went out, and found one
of his fellow-servants, which owed him a hundred [8]pence: and he laid hold
29 on him, and took *him* by the throat, saying, Pay what thou owest. So his
fellow-servant fell down and besought, him, saying, Have patience with
30 me, and I will pay thee. And he would not: but went and cast him into
31 prison, till he should pay that which was due. So when his fellow-servants
32 saw what was done, they were exceedingly sorry, and came and told unto
their lord all that was done. Then his lord called him unto him, and
33 saith unto him, Thou wicked [6]servant, I forgave thee all that debt,[7]
34 because thou besoughtest me: shouldest not thou also have had mercy
on thy fellow-servant, even as I had mercy on thee?† And his lord was
35 wroth, and delivered him to the tormentors, till he should pay all that
was due. So shall also my heavenly Father do unto you, if ye forgive
not every one his brother from your hearts.

[1] Some ancient authorities omit *against thee*. [2] Or, *congregation*. [3] Or, *seventy times and seven*.
[4] Gr. *bond-servants*. [5] This talent was probably worth about $1200. [6] Gr. *bond-servant*. [7] Or,
loan. [8] The word in the Greek denotes a coin worth about seventeen cents.

---

* Parable of the Unforgiving Servant.
† The king forgave the servant $1,200,000; the servant refused to forgive $17. We might say in round numbers, a million, and ten dollars.

§ 93. THE MESSIAH'S FOLLOWERS MUST GIVE UP EVERYTHING FOR HIS SERVICE

Matt. 8:19-22	Luke 9:57-62
19 And there came [1]a scribe, and said unto him, [2]Master, I will follow thee whithersoever thou 20 goest. And Jesus saith unto him, the foxes have holes, and the birds of the heaven *have* [3]nests; but the Son of man hath not 21 where to lay his head. And another of the disciples saith unto him, Lord, suffer me first to go 22 and bury my father. But Jesus saith unto him, Follow me; and leave the dead to bury their own dead.	57 And as they went in the way, a certain man said unto him, I will follow thee whithersoever thou 58 goest. And Jesus said unto him, the foxes have holes, and the birds of the heaven *have* [3]nests; but the Son of man hath not 59 where to lay his head. And he said unto another, Follow me. But he said, Lord, suffer me first 60 to go and bury my father. But he said unto him, Leave the dead to bury their own dead; but go thou and publish abroad the 61 kingdom of God. And another also said, I will follow thee, Lord; but first suffer me to bid farewell to them that are at my house. 62 But Jesus said unto him, No man, having put his hand to the plough, and looking back, is fit for the kingdom of God

[1] Gr. *one scribe.*   [2] Or, *Teacher.*   [3] Gr. *lodging-places.*

§ 94. THE UNBELIEVING BROTHERS OF JESUS COUNSEL HIM TO EXHIBIT HIMSELF IN JUDEA, AND HE REJECTS THE ADVICE

John 7:2-9

2 Now the feast of the Jews, the feast of tabernacles, was at hand.
3 His brethren therefore said unto him, Depart hence, and go into Judea,
4 that thy disciples also may behold thy works which thou doest. For no man doeth anything in secret, [1]and himself seeketh to be known openly.
5 If thou doest these things, manifest thyself to the world. For even his
6 brethren did not believe on him. Jesus therefore saith unto them, My
7 time is not yet come; but your time is always ready. The world cannot hate you; but me it hateth, because I testify of it, that its works are evil.
8 Go ye up unto the feast: I go not up [2]yet unto this feast; because my
9 time is not yet fulfilled. And having said these things unto them, he abode *still* in Galilee.

[1] Some ancient authorities read *and seeketh it to be known openly.*   [2] Many ancient authorities omit *yet.*

§ 95. HE GOES PRIVATELY TO JERUSALEM THROUGH SAMARIA

Luke 9:51–56

51 And it came to pass, when the days ¹were well-nigh come that he should be received up, he stedfastly set his face to go to Je-
52 rusalem,* and sent messengers before his face: and they went, and entered into a village of the Samaritans, to make ready for him.
53 And they did not receive him, because his face was as *though he*
54 *were* going to Jerusalem. And when his disciples James and John saw *this*, they said, Lord, wilt thou that we bid fire to come down from heaven, and consume
55 them [*see 2 Kings 1:10–12*]?² But he turned, and rebuked them.³
56 And they went to another village.

John 7:10

10 But when his brethren were gone up unto the feast, then went he also up, not publicly, but as it were in secret.

¹ Gr. *were being fulfilled.* ² Many ancient authorities add, *even as Elijah did.* ³ Some ancient authorities add, *and said, Ye know not what manner of spirit ye are of.* Some, but fewer, add also *For the Son of man came not to destroy men's lives, but to save them.*

* See note 10 at end of Harmony for the combination of Luke and John and the three journeyings in Luke toward Jerusalem.

PART IX

THE LATER JUDEAN MINISTRY

(Probably Tabernacles to Dedication, about three months, in A.D. 29 or 28 if Ministry only two and a half years in length)

This ministry is given only by John and Luke. John gives the Jerusalem ministry and Luke that in the country of Judea. §§ *96–111.*

§ 96. THE COMING OF JESUS TO THE FEAST OF TABER-NACLES CREATES INTENSE EXCITEMENT CONCERNING THE MESSIAHSHIP

The attempt of the rulers (the Jews, the chief priests, and Pharisees) to arrest him. Division of sentiment in the Galilean multitude at the feast. Impressions of the Jerusalem populace and the Roman officers and of Nicodemus.

John 7:11–52

11 The Jews therefore sought him at the feast, and said, Where is he?
12 And there was much murmuring among the multitudes concerning him. Some said, He is a good man; others said, Nay, but he leads the multitude
13 astray. Yet no one spoke openly concerning him, for fear of the Jews.
14 But when it was now the midst of the feast Jesus went up into the
15 temple, and taught. The Jews therefore marvelled, saying, How knoweth
16 this man letters, having never learned? Jesus therefore answered them,
17 and said, My teaching is not mine, but his that sent me. If any man willeth to do his will, he shall know of the teaching, whether it be of God,
18 or *whether* I speak from myself. He that speaketh from himself seeketh his own glory: but he that seeketh the glory of him that sent him, the
19 same is true, and no unrighteousness is in him. Did not Moses give you the law, and *yet* none of you doeth the law? Why seek ye to kill me?
20 The multitude answered, Thou hast a ¹devil: who seeketh to kill thee?
21 Jesus answered and said unto them, I did one work, and ye all ²marvel.
22 For this cause hath Moses given you circumcision (not that it is of Moses, but of the fathers); and on the sabbath ye circumcise a man [*see Gen. 17:*
23 *9–14; Lev. 12:1–3*]. If a man receiveth circumcision on the sabbath, that the law of Moses may not be broken; are ye wroth with me, because I made a
24 man every whit whole on the sabbath? Judge not according to appearance, but judge righteous judgement.
25 Some therefore of them of Jerusalem said, Is not this he whom they
26 seek to kill? And lo, he speaketh openly, and they say nothing unto him.
27 Can it be that the rulers indeed know that this is the Christ? Howbeit we know this man whence he is: but when the Christ cometh, no one
28 knoweth whence he is. Jesus therefore cried in the temple, teaching and saying, Ye both know me, and know whence I am; and I am not

John 7:11-52

29 come of myself, but he that sent me is true, whom ye know not. I know
30 him; because I am from him, and he sent me. They sought therefore to
　　take him: and no man laid his hands on him, because his hour was not yet
31 come. But of the multitude many believed on him; and they said, When
　　the Christ shall come, will he do more signs than those, which this man
32 hath done? The Pharisees heard the multitude murmuring these things
　　concerning him; and the chief priests and the Pharisees sent officers to
33 take him. Jesus therefore said, Yet a little while am I with you, and I
34 go unto him that sent me. Ye shall seek me, and shall not find me: and
35 where I am, ye cannot come. The Jews therefore said among themselves,
　　Whither will this man go that we shall not find him? will he go unto
36 the Dispersion ²among the Greeks, and teach the Greeks? What is this
　　word that he said, Ye shall seek me, and shall not find me: and where I
　　am, ye cannot come?

37 　　Now on the last day, the great *day* of the feast, Jesus stood and cried,
38 saying, If any man thirst, let him come unto me, and drink. He that be-
　　lieveth on me, as the scripture hath said, out of his belly shall flow rivers
39 of living water. But this spake he of the Spirit, which they that believed
　　on him were to receive: ⁴for the Spirit was not yet *given;* because Jesus
40 was not yet glorified. *Some* of the multitude therefore, when they heard
41 these words, said, This is of a truth the prophet. Others said, This is the
　　Christ. But some said, What, doth the Christ come out of Galilee?
42 Hath not the scripture said that the Christ cometh out of the seed of David,
　　and from Bethlehem [*see 2 Sam. 7:12,17; Mic. 5:2*], the village where David
43 was? So there arose a division in the multitude because of him. And
44 some of them would have taken him; but no man laid his hands on him.
45 　　The officers therefore came to the chief priests* and Pharisees; and
46 they said unto them, Why did ye not bring him? The officers answered,
47 Never man so spake. The Pharisees therefore answered them, Are ye
48 also led astray? Hath any of the rulers believed on him, or of the Phari-
49 sees? But this multitude which knoweth not the law are accursed.
50 Nicodemus saith unto them (he that came to him before, being one of
51 them), Doth our law judge a man, except it first hear from himself and
52 know what he doeth? They answered and said unto him, Art thou also
　　of Galilee? Search, and ⁵see that out of Galilee ariseth no prophet.

¹ Gr. *demon.* ² Or, *marvel because of this. Moses hath given you circumcision.* ³ Gr. *of.* ⁴ Some
ancient authorities read *for the Holy Spirit was not yet given.* ⁵ Or, *see; for out of Galilee, etc.*

§ 97. STORY OF AN ADULTERESS BROUGHT TO JESUS FOR JUDGMENT

John 7:53 to 8:11†

53, 1[¹And they went every man unto his own house: but Jesus went unto
2 the mount of Olives. And early in the morning he came again into

* The Sanhedrin included both Sadducees (chief priests) and Pharisees. Nicodemus was a mem-
ber of the Sanhedrin and a Pharisee. Now both parties in the Sanhedrin were united against Jesus
and the purpose was to bring Jesus before the Sanhedrin for trial.
　† This paragraph can no longer be considered a part of the Gospel of John, but it is in all probability a true story of Jesus, very likely drawn by early students from the collection of Papias,
published about A.D. 140. See Hovey on John (American Comm. on N. T.). Observe that without
it § 98 goes right on after § 96.

John 7:53 to 8:11

the temple, and all the people came unto him; and he sat down, and
3 taught them. And the scribes and the Pharisees bring a woman taken
4 in adultery; and having set her in the midst, they say unto him, ²Master,
5 this woman hath been taken in adultery, in the very act. Now in the law
  Moses commanded us to stone such [*see Lev. 20:10; Deut. 22:22–24*]: what
6 then sayest thou of her? And this they said, ³tempting him, that they
  might have *whereof* to accuse him. But Jesus stooped down, and with his
7 finger wrote on the ground. But when they continued asking him, he
  lifted up himself, and said unto them, He that is without sin among you,
8 let him first cast a stone at her. And again he stooped down, and with
9 his finger wrote on the ground. And they, when they heard it, went
  out one by one, beginning from the eldest, *even* unto the last: and Jesus
10 was left alone, and the woman, where she was, in the midst. And Jesus
11 lifted up himself, and said unto her, Woman, where are they? did no man
  condemn thee? And she said, No man, Lord. And Jesus said, Neither
  do I condemn thee: go thy way; from henceforth sin no more.]

¹ Most of the ancient authorities omit John 7:53–8:11. Those which contain it vary much
from each other. ² Or, *Teacher*. ³ Or, *trying*.

§ 98. AFTER THE FEAST OF TABERNACLES IN THE TEMPLE JESUS ANGERS THE PHARISEES BY CLAIMING TO BE THE LIGHT OF THE WORLD

John 8:12–20

12   Again therefore Jesus spake unto them, saying, I am the light of the
  world: he that followeth me shall not walk in the darkness, but shall
13 have the light of life. The Pharisees therefore said unto him, Thou
14 bearest witness of thyself; thy witness is not true. Jesus answered and
  said unto them, Even if I bear witness of myself, my witness is true; for
  I know whence I came, and whither I go; but ye know not whence I come,
15 or whither I go. Ye judge after the flesh; I judge no man. Yea and
16 if I judge, my judgement is true; for I am not alone, but I and the Father
17 that sent me. Yea and in your law it is written, that the witness of two
18 men is true [*see Deut. 17:6; 19:15*]. I am he that beareth witness of myself,
19 and the Father that sent me beareth witness of me. They said therefore
  unto him, Where is thy Father? Jesus answered, Ye know neither me,
20 nor my Father: if ye knew me, ye would know my Father also. These
  words spake he in the treasury, as he taught in the temple: and no man
  took him; because his hour was not yet come.

§ 99. THE PHARISEES ATTEMPT TO STONE JESUS WHEN HE EXPOSES THEIR SINFULNESS

Jerusalem, probably in the Temple

John 8:21–59

21   He said therefore again unto them, I go away, and ye shall seek me,
22 and shall die in your sin: whither I go, ye cannot come. The Jews therefore said, Will he kill himself, that he saith, Whither I go. ye cannot come?

John 8:21-59

23 And he said unto them, Ye are from beneath; I am from above: ye are of
24 this world; I am not of this world. I said therefore unto you, that ye
    shall die in your sins: for except ye believe that ¹I am *he*, ye shall die in
25 your sins. They said therefore unto him, Who art thou? Jesus said
    unto them, ²Even that which I have also spoken unto you from the be-
26 ginning. I have many things to speak and to judge concerning you:
    howbeit he that sent me is true; and the things which I heard from him,
27 these speak I ³unto the world. They perceived not that he spake to them
28 of the Father. Jesus therefore said, When ye have lifted up the Son of
    man, then shall ye know that ⁴I am *he*, and *that* I do nothing of myself,
29 but as the Father taught me, I speak these things. And he that sent me
    is with me: he hath not left me alone; for I do always the things that are
30 pleasing to him. As he spake these things, many believed on him.
31   Jesus therefore said to those Jews which had believed him, If ye abide
32 in my word, *then* are ye truly my disciples; and ye shall know the truth,
33 and the truth shall make you free. They answered unto him, We be
    Abraham's seed, and have never yet been in bondage to any man: how
34 sayest thou, Ye shall be made free? Jesus answered them, Verily, verily,
    I say unto you, Every one that committeth sin is the bondservant of sin.
35 And the bondservant abideth not in the house for ever: the son abideth
36 for ever. If therefore the Son shall make you free, ye shall be free indeed.
37 I know that ye are Abraham's seed; yet ye seek to kill me, because my
38 word ⁵hath not free course in you. I speak the things which I have seen
    with ⁶*my* Father; and ye also do the things which ye heard from *your*
    father. They answered and said unto him, Our Father is Abraham.
39 Jesus saith unto them, If ye ⁷were Abraham's children, ⁸ye would do the
40 works of Abraham. But now ye seek to kill me, a man that hath told
41 you the truth, which I heard from God; this did not Abraham. Ye do the
    works of your father. They said unto him, We were not born of fornica-
42 tion; we have one Father, *even* God. Jesus said unto them, If God were
    your Father, ye would love me: for I came forth and am come from God;
43 for neither have I come of myself, but he sent me. Why do ye not ⁹under-
44 stand my speech? *Even* because ye cannot hear my word. Ye are of
    your father, the devil, and the lusts of your father it is your will to do.
    He was a murderer from the beginning, ¹⁰and stood not in the truth, be-
    cause there is no truth in him. ¹¹When he speaketh a lie, he speaketh of
45 his own: for he is a liar, and the father thereof. But because I say the
46 truth, ye believe me not. Which of you convicteth me of sin? If I say
47 truth, why do ye not believe me? He that is of God heareth the words
48 of God: for this cause ye hear *them* not, because ye are not of God. The
    Jews answered and said unto him, Say we not well that thou art a Samari-
49 tan, and hast a ¹²devil? Jesus answered, I have not a ¹²devil; but I honour
50 my Father, and ye dishonour me. But I seek not mine own glory: there
51 is one that seeketh and judgeth. Verily, verily, I say unto you, If a man
52 keep my word, he shall never see death. The Jews said unto him, Now
    we know that thou hast a ¹²devil. Abraham is dead, and the prophets;
    and thou sayest, If a man keep my word, he shall never taste of death.
53 Art thou greater than our father Abraham, which is dead? and the prophets
54 are dead: whom makest thou thyself? Jesus answered, If I glorify my-
    self, my glory is nothing: it is my Father that glorifieth me: of whom ye

John 8:21:59

55 say, that he is your God; and ye have not known him: but I know him;
and if I should say, I know him not, I shall be like unto you, a liar: but
56 I know him, and keep his word.   Your father Abraham rejoiced [13]to see
57 my day; and he saw it, and was glad.   The Jews therefore said unto him,
58 Thou art not yet fifty years old, and hast thou seen Abraham?   Jesus
said unto them, Verily, verily, I say unto you, Before Abraham [14]was, I
59 am.   They took up stones therefore to cast at him: but Jesus [15]hid himself,
and went out of the temple.[16]

[1] Or, *I am.* [2] Or, How is it *that I even speak to you at all?* [3] Gr. *into.* [4] Or, *I am,* or [*I am he:
and I do.* [5] Or, *hath no place in you.* [6] Or, *the Father: do ye also therefore the things which ye heard
from the Father.* [7] Gr. *are.* [8] Some ancient authorities read *ye do the works of Abraham.* [9] Or,
know. [10] Some ancient authorities read *standeth.* [11] Or, *When one speaketh a lie, he speaketh of
his own; for his father also is a liar.* [12] Gr. *demon.* [13] Or, *that he should see.* [14] Gr. *was born.* [15]Or,
was hidden, and went, etc. [16] Many ancient authorities add *and going through the midst of them went
his way, and so passed by.*

§ 100. JESUS HEALS A MAN BORN BLIND WHO OUT- WITS THE PHARISEES.   THE RULERS FORBID THE RECOGNITION OF JESUS AS THE MESSIAH. THE CONVERSION OF THE HEALED MAN

Jerusalem

John 9:1–41

1, 2 And as he passed by, he saw a man blind from his birth.   And his
disciples asked him, saying, Rabbi, who did sin, this man, or his parents,
3 that he should be born blind?   Jesus answered, Neither did this man sin,
nor his parents: but that the works of God should be made manifest in
4 him.   We must work the works of him that sent me, while it is day:
5 the night cometh, when no man can work.   When I am in the world,
6 I am the light of the world.   When he had thus spoken, he spat on the
ground, and made clay of the spittle, and [1]anointed his eyes with the clay,
7 and said unto him, Go, wash in the pool of Siloam (which is by inter-
8 pretation, Sent).   He went away therefore, and washed, and came seeing.
The neighbours therefore, and they which saw him aforetime, that he was
9 a beggar, said, Is not this he that sat and begged?   Others said, It is he:
10 others said, No, but he is like him.   He said, I am *he*.   They said there-
11 fore unto him, How then were thine eyes opened?   He answered, the man
that is called Jesus made clay, and anointed mine eyes, and said unto
me, Go to Siloam, and wash: so I went away and washed, and I received
12 sight.   And they said unto him, Where is he?   He saith, I know not.
13, 14 They bring to the Pharisees him that aforetime was blind.   Now
it was the sabbath on the day when Jesus made the clay, and opened his
15 eyes.   Again therefore the Pharisees also asked him how he received his
sight.   And he said unto them, He put clay upon mine eyes, and I washed,
16 and do see.   Some therefore of the Pharisees said, This man is not from God,
because he keepeth not the sabbath.   But others said, How can a man
17 that is a sinner do such signs?   And there was a division among them.
They say therefore unto the blind man again, What sayest thou of him,
18 in that he opened thine eyes?   And he said, He is a prophet.   The Jews
therefore did not believe concerning him, that he had been blind, and had

118

John 9:1–41

received his sight, until they called the parents of him that had received
19 his sight, and asked them, saying, Is this your son, who ye say was born
20 blind? how then doth he now see? His parents answered and said, We
21 know that this is our son, and that he was born blind: but how he now
seeth, we know not; or who opened his eyes, we know not; ask him; he is of
22 age; he shall speak for himself. These things said his parents, because
they feared the Jews: for the Jews had agreed already, that if any man
should confess him *to be* Christ, he should be put out of the synagogue.
23 Therefore said his parents, He is of age; ask him. So they called the
24 second time the man that was blind, and said unto him, Give glory to
25 God: we know that this man is a sinner. He therefore answered, Whether
he be a sinner, I know not: one thing I know, that, whereas I was blind,
26 now I see. They said therefore unto him, What did he to thee? how
27 opened he thine eyes? He answered them, I told you even now, and ye
did not hear: wherefore would ye hear it again? would ye also become his
28 disciples? And they reviled him, and said, Thou art his disciple, but we
29 are disciples of Moses. We know that God hath spoken unto Moses:
30 but as for this man, we know not whence he is. The man answered and
said unto them, Why, herein is the marvel, that ye know not whence he is,
31 and *yet* he opened mine eyes. We know that God heareth not sinners:
but if any man be a worshipper of God, and do his will, him he heareth.
32 Since the world began it was never heard that any one opened the eyes of
33 a man born blind. If this man were not from God, he could do nothing.
34 They answered and said unto him, Thou wast altogether born in sins,
and dost thou teach us? And they cast him out.
35   Jesus heard that they had cast him out; and finding him, he said,
36 Dost thou believe on [2]the Son of God? He answered and said, And who
37 is he, Lord, that I may believe on him? Jesus said unto him, Thou hast
38 both seen him, and he it is that speaketh with thee. And he said, Lord,
39 I believe. And he worshipped him. And Jesus said, For judgement came
I into this world, that they which see not may see; and that they which
40 see may become blind. Those of the Pharisees which were with him
41 heard these things, and said unto him, Are we also blind? Jesus said unto
them, If ye were blind, ye would have no sin: but now ye say, We see:
your sin remaineth.

[1] Or, *and with the clay thereof anointed his eyes.*   [2] Many ancient authorities read *the Son of man.*

§ 101. IN THE PARABLE (ALLEGORY) OF THE GOOD SHEPHERD JESUS DRAWS THE PICTURE OF THE HOSTILE PHARISEES AND INTIMATES THAT HE IS GOING TO DIE FOR HIS FLOCK AND COME TO LIFE AGAIN

Jerusalem

John 10:1–21

1   Verily, verily, I say unto you, He that entereth not by the door into the
fold of the sheep, but climbeth up some other way, the same is a thief
2 and a robber. But he that entereth in by the door is [1]the shepherd of the

John 10:1-21

3 sheep. To him the porter openeth; and the sheep hear his voice: and
4 he calleth his own sheep by name, and leadeth them out. When he hath
   put forth all his own, he goeth before them, and the sheep follow him:
5 for they know his voice. And a stranger will they not follow, but will
6 flee from him: for they know not the voice of strangers. This [2]parable
   spake Jesus unto them: but they understood not what things they were
   which he spake unto them.

7   Jesus therefore said unto them again, Verily, verily, I say unto you,
8 I am the door of the sheep. All that came before me are thieves and
9 robbers: but the sheep did not hear them. I am the door: by me if any
   man enter in, he shall be saved, and shall go in and go out, and shall
10 find pasture. The thief cometh not, but that he may steal, and kill, and
   destroy: I came that they may have life, and may [3]have it abundantly.
11 I am the good shepherd: the good shepherd layeth down his life for the
12 sheep. He that is a hireling, and not a shepherd, whose own the sheep
   are not, beholdeth the wolf coming, and leaveth the sheep, and fleeth, and
13 the wolf snatcheth them, and scattereth *them: he fleeth* because he is a
14 hireling, and careth not for the sheep. I am the good shepherd; and I
15 know mine own, and mine own know me, even as the Father knoweth
   me, and I know the Father; and I lay down my life for the sheep.
16 And other sheep I have, which are not of this fold [*see Ezek. 34:23; 37:24*]:
   them also I must [4]bring, and they shall hear my voice; and [5]they shall
17 become one flock, one shepherd. Therefore doth the Father love me, be-
18 cause I lay down my life, that I may take it again. No one [6]taketh it
   away from me, but I lay it down of myself. I have [7]power to lay it down,
   and I have [7]power to take it again. This commandment received I from
   my Father.

19   There arose a division again among the Jews because of these words.
20 And many of them said, He hath a [8]devil, and is mad; why hear ye him?
21 Others said, These are not the sayings of one possessed with ⸱ [8]devil.
   Can a [8]devil open the eyes of the blind?

[1] Or, *a shepherd.* [2] Or, *proverb.* [3] Or, *have abundance.* [4] Or, *lead.* [5] Or, *there shall be one flock.*
[6]Some ancient authorities read *took it away.* [7] Or, *right.* [8] Gr. *demon.*

*In §§102-110 we have matters given by Luke only, which probably
occurred in Judea. Several of them are similar to events and discourses of the ministry in Galilee, given by Matthew and Mark.**

§ 102. MISSION OF THE SEVENTY. CHRIST'S JOY IN THEIR WORK ON THEIR RETURN

(Compare Mission of the Twelve in § 70.)

Probably in Judea

Luke 10:1-24

1   Now after these things the Lord appointed seventy[1] others, and sent
   them two and two before his face into every city and place, whither he

---

* Observe that here, as in previous portions of the history, we possess only a few specimens from
what must have been the great mass of our Lord's doings and sayings.

Luke 10:1-24

2 himself was about to come. And he said unto them, The harvest is
plenteous, but the labourers are few: pray ye therefore the Lord of the
3 harvest, that he send forth labourers into his harvest. Go your ways:
4 behold, I send you forth as lambs in the midst of wolves. Carry no purse,
5 no wallet, no shoes; and salute no man on the way. And into whatsoever
6 house ye shall ²enter, first say, Peace *be* to this house. And if a son of
7 peace be there, your peace shall rest upon ³him: but if not, it shall turn to
you again. And in that same house remain, eating and drinking such
8 things as they give: for the labourer is worthy of his hire. Go not from
house to house. And into whatsoever city ye enter, and they receive
you, eat such things as are set before you: and heal the sick that are
9 therein, and say unto them, The kingdom of God is come nigh unto you.
10 But into whatsoever city ye shall enter, and they receive you not, go out
11 into the streets thereof and say, Even the dust from your city, that
cleaveth to our feet, we do wipe off against you: howbeit know this, that
12 the kingdom of God is come nigh. I say unto you, It shall be more toler-
13 able in that day for Sodom, than for that city [*see Gen. 19:24*]. Woe unto
thee, Chorazin! woe unto thee, Bethsaida! for if the ⁴mighty works had
been done in Tyre and Sidon, which were done in you, they would have
14 repented long ago, sitting in sackcloth and ashes. Howbeit it shall be
more tolerable for Tyre and Sidon in the judgement, than for you.
15 And thou, Capernaum, shalt thou be exalted unto heaven? thou shalt
16 be brought down unto Hades [*see Isa. 14:13-15*]. He that heareth you
heareth me; and he that rejecteth you rejecteth me; and he that rejecteth
me rejecteth him that sent me.
17 And the seventy returned with joy, saying, Lord, even the ⁵devils are
18 subject unto us in thy name. And he said unto them, I beheld Satan
19 fallen as lightning from heaven. Behold, I have given you authority
to tread upon serpents and scorpions, and over all the power of the
20 enemy: and nothing shall in any wise hurt you. Howbeit in this rejoice
not, that the spirits are subject unto you; but rejoice that your names are
written in heaven.
21 In that same hour he rejoiced ⁶in the Holy Spirit, and said, I ⁷thank
thee, O Father, Lord of heaven and earth, that thou didst hide these
things from the wise and understanding, and didst reveal them unto
22 babes: yea, Father; ⁸for so it was well-pleasing in thy sight. All things
have been delivered unto me of my Father: and no one knoweth who
the Son is, save the Father; and who the Father is, save the Son, and
23 he to whomsoever the Son willeth to reveal *him*. And turning to the
disciples, he said privately, Blessed are the eyes which see the things that
24 ye see: for I say unto you, that many prophets and kings desired to see
the things which ye see, and saw them not: and to hear the things which
ye hear, and heard them not.

¹ Many ancient authorities add *and two;* and so in verse 17. ² Or, *enter first, say.* ³ Or, *it.* ⁴ Gr.
powers. ⁵ Gr. *demons.* ⁶ Or, *by.* ⁷ Or, *praise.* ⁸ Or, *that.*

§ 103. JESUS ANSWERS A LAWYER'S QUESTION AS TO ETERNAL LIFE, GIVING THE PARABLE OF THE GOOD SAMARITAN

Probably in Judea

Luke 10:25–37

25 And behold, a certain lawyer stood up and tempted him, saying,
26 ¹Master, what shall I do to inherit eternal life? And he said unto him,
27 What is written in the law? how readest thou? And he answering said,
Thou shalt love the Lord thy God ²with all thy heart, and with all thy
soul, and with all thy strength, and with all thy mind; and thy neighbour
28 as thyself [*see Deut. 6:5; Lev. 19:18*]. And he said unto him, Thou hast
29 answered right: do this, and thou shalt live [*see Lev. 18:5*]. But he, desiring
30 to justify himself, said unto Jesus, And who is my neighbour? Jesus
made answer and said, A certain man was going down from Jerusalem to
Jericho; and he fell among robbers, which both stripped him and beat
31 him, and departed, leaving him half dead. And by chance a certain
priest was going down that way: and when he saw him, he passed by
32 on the other side. And in like manner a Levite also, when he came to
33 the place, and saw him, passed by on the other side. But a certain
Samaritan, as he journeyed, came where he was: and when he saw him,
34 he was moved with compassion, and came to him, and bound up his
wounds, pouring on *them* oil and wine; and he set him on his own beast, and
35 brought him to an inn, and took care of him. And on the morrow he took
out two ³pence, and gave them to the host, and said, Take care of him;
and whatsoever thou spendest more, I, when I come back again, will
36 repay thee. Which of these three, thinkest thou, proved neighbour to
37 him that fell among the robbers? And he said, He that shewed mercy on
him. And Jesus said unto him, Go, and do thou likewise.

¹ Or, *Teacher.*   ² Gr *from.*   ³ The word in the Greek denotes a coin worth about seventeen cents.

§ 104. JESUS THE GUEST OF MARTHA AND MARY

Bethany, near Jerusalem*

Luke 10:38–42

38 Now as they went on their way, he entered into a certain village:
and a certain woman named Martha received him into her house.
39 And she had a sister called Mary, which also sat at the Lord's feet, and
40 heard his word. But Martha was ¹cumbered about much serving; and
she came up to him, and said, Lord, dost thou not care that my sister
did leave me to serve alone? bid her therefore that she help me.
41 But the Lord answered and said unto her, ²Martha, Martha, thou art
42 anxious and troubled about many things: ³but one thing is needful: for
Mary hath chosen the good part, which shall not be taken away from her.

¹ Gr. *distracted.*   ² A few ancient authorities read, *Martha, Martha, thou art troubled; Mary hath chosen, etc.*   ³ Many ancient authorities read *but few things are needful, or one.*

* There was another Bethany beyond Jordan (John 1:28, § 26). We shall see Jesus in Bethany near Jerusalem again (John 12:1–8). It was his Jerusalem home in the early days of Passion Week.

§ 105. JESUS AGAIN GIVES A MODEL OF PRAYER (COMP. § 54), AND ENCOURAGES HIS DISCIPLES TO PRAY. PARABLE OF THE IMPORTUNATE FRIEND

Probably in Judea

Luke 11:1–13

1 And it came to pass, as he was praying in a certain place, that when he ceased, one of his disciples said unto him, Lord, teach us to pray, even 2 as John also taught his disciples. And he said unto them, When ye pray, 3 say, ¹Father, Hallowed be thy Name. Thy kingdom come.² Give us 4 day by day ³our daily bread. And forgive us our sins; for we ourselves also forgive every one that is indebted to us. And bring us not into temptation⁴.*

5 And he said unto them, Which of you shall have a friend, and shall go unto him at midnight, and say to him, Friend, lend me three loaves; for 6 a friend of mine is come to me from a journey, and I have nothing to set 7 before him; and he from within shall answer and say, Trouble me not: the door is now shut, and my children are with me in bed; I cannot rise 8 and give thee? I say unto you, Though he will not rise and give him, because he is his friend, yet because of his importunity he will arise and 9 give him ⁵as many as he needeth. And I say unto you, Ask, and it shall be given you; seek, and ye shall find; knock, and it shall be opened unto 10 you. For every one that asketh receiveth; and he that seeketh findeth; 11 and to him that knocketh it shall be opened. And of which of you that is a father shall his son ask a ⁶loaf, and he give him a stone? or a fish, and 12 he for a fish give him a serpent? Or if he shall ask an egg, will he give 13 him a scorpion? If ye then, being evil, know how to give good gifts unto your children, how much more shall *your* heavenly Father give the Holy Spirit to them that ask him?

¹ Many ancient authorities read *Our Father, which art in heaven.* See Matt. 6:9. ² Many ancient authorities add *Thy will be done, as in heaven, so on earth.* See Matt. 6:10. ³ Gr. *our bread for the coming day.* ⁴ Many ancient authorities add *but deliver us from the evil* one (or, *from evil*). See Matt. 6:13. ⁵ Or, *whatsoever things.* ⁶ Some ancient authorities omit *a loaf, and he gave him a stone? or.*

§ 106. BLASPHEMOUS ACCUSATION OF LEAGUE WITH BEELZEBUB

(Compare § 61) †

Probably in Judea

Luke 11:14–36

14 And he was casting out a ¹devil which was dumb. And it came to pass, when the ¹devil was gone out, the dumb man spake; and the multitudes

---

* The language here is different from that in Matt. 6 (§ 54), but the ideas are the same. Evidently the disciples were slow to learn Christ's teaching about prayer.

† It is perfectly natural that the blasphemous accusation made in Galilee (§ 61), and probably more than once (§ 68, Matt. 9:34), should be repeated a year or so afterward in Judea or Perea.

Luke 11:14–36

15 marvelled. But some of them said, ³By Beelzebub the prince of the
16 ³devils casteth he out devils. And others, tempting him, sought of him
17 a sign from heaven. But he, knowing their thoughts, said unto them,
Every kingdom divided against itself is brought to desolation; ⁴and a
18 house divided against a house falleth. And if Satan also is divided against
himself, how shall his kingdom stand? because ye say that I cast out
19 ³devils ²by Beelzebub. And if I ²by Beelzebub cast out ³devils, by whom
20 do your sons cast them out? therefore shall they be your judges. But if
I by the finger of God cast out ³devils, then is the kingdom of God come
21 upon you. When the strong *man* fully armed guardeth his own court,
22 his goods are in peace: but when a stronger than he shall come upon him,
and overcome him, he taketh from him his whole armour wherein he
23 trusted, and divideth his spoils. He that is not with me is against me; and
24 he that gathereth not with me scattereth. The unclean spirit when
⁵he is gone out of the man, passeth through waterless places, seeking
rest; and finding none, ⁵he saith, I will turn back unto my house whence
25 I came out. And when he is come, ⁵he findeth it swept and garnished.
26 Then goeth ⁵he, and taketh *to him* seven other spirits more evil than
⁶himself; and they enter in and dwell there: and the last state of that man
becometh worse than the first.
27   And it came to pass, as he said these things, a certain woman out of
the multitude lifted up her voice, and said unto him, Blessed is the
28 womb that bare thee, and the breasts which thou didst suck. But
he said, Yea rather, blessed are they that hear the word of God, and
keep it.
29   And when the multitudes were gathering together unto him, he began
to say, This generation is an evil generation: it seeketh after a sign; and
there shall no sign be given to it but the sign of Jonah [*see Jonah 3:1–4*].
30 For even as Jonah became a sign unto the Ninevites, so shall also the
31 Son of man be to this generation. The queen of the south shall rise up
in the judgement with the men of this generation, and shall condemn
them: for she came from the ends of the earth to hear the wisdom of
32 Solomon [*see 1 Kings 10:1–3*]; and behold, ⁷a greater than Solomon is here.
The men of Nineveh shall stand up in the judgement with this generation
and shall condemn it: for they repented at the preaching of Jonah [*see Jonah
3:5–10*]; and behold, ⁷a greater than Jonah is here.
33   No man, when he·hath lighted a lamp, putteth it in a cellar, neither
under the bushel, but on the stand, that they which enter in may see
34 the light. The lamp of thy body is thine eye: when thine eye is single,
thy whole body also is full of light; but when it is evil, thy body also is full of
35 darkness. Look therefore whether the light that is in thee be not darkness.
36 If therefore thy whole body be full of light, having no part dark, it shall

---

and that Jesus should make substantially the same argument in reply. This sort of thing occurs
to every travelling religious teacher. Our Lord does not here give the solemn warning that such
an accusation is really blaspheming against the Holy Spirit, and is unpardonable. (See Luke
12:10.) And the subsequent occurrences are quite different in the two cases. In § 64 he afterwards
goes out by the lake-side and gives the great group of parables, presently explaining some of them
to the disciples in a house, and then crosses the lake to Gerasa, etc. Here in § 107 he breakfasts
with a Pharisee, and utters such solemn woes against the Pharisees as are found only in the closing
months of his ministry, and then gives to vast multitudes a series of instructions wholly unlike
the great group of parables. So it is quite unsuitable to identify this occurrence with that of § 61.

Luke 11:14-36

be wholly full of light, as when the lamp with its bright shining doth give
the light.

¹ Gr. *demon.* ² Or, *in.* ³ Gr. *demons.* ⁴ Or, *and house falleth upon house.* ⁵ Or, *it.* ⁶ Or, *itself.*
⁷ Gr. *more than.*

§ 107. WHILE BREAKFASTING WITH A PHARISEE, JESUS SEVERELY DENOUNCES THE PHARISEES AND LAWYERS, AND EXCITES THEIR ENMITY

Probably in Judea

Luke 11:37-54

37 Now as he spake, a Pharisee asketh him to ¹dine with him: and he went
38 in, and sat down to meat. And when the Pharisee saw it, he marvelled
39 that he had not washed before ¹dinner. And the Lord said unto him,
Now do ye Pharisees cleanse the outside of the cup and of the platter;
40 but your inward part is full of extortion and wickedness. Ye foolish ones,
41 did not he that made the outside make the inside also? Howbeit give for
alms those things which ²are within; and behold, all things are clean
unto you.
42 But woe unto you Pharisees! for ye tithe mint and rue and every herb,
and pass over judgement and the love of God [*see Lev. 27:30; Mic. 6:8*]: but
43 these ought ye to have done, and not to leave the other undone. Woe
unto you Pharisees! for ye love the chief seats in the synagogues, and the
44 salutations in the marketplaces. Woe unto you! for ye are as the tombs
which appear not, and the men that walk over *them* know it not.
45 And one of the lawyers answering saith unto him, ³Master, in saying
46 this thou reproachest us also. And he said, Woe unto you lawyers also!
for ye lade men with burdens grievous to be borne, and ye yourselves
47 touch not the burdens with one of your fingers. Woe unto you! for ye
48 build the tombs of the prophets, and your fathers killed them. So ye are
witnesses and consent unto the works of your fathers: for they killed them,
49 and ye build *their tombs.* Therefore also said the wisdom of God, I will
50 send unto them prophets and apostles; and *some* of them they shall kill
and persecute; that the blood of all the prophets, which was shed from
51 the foundation of the world, may be required of this generation; from the
blood of Abel unto the blood of Zachariah [*see Gen. 4:8; 2 Chron. 24:20-21*],
who perished between the altar and the ⁴sanctuary: yea, I say unto you,
52 it shall be required of this generation. Woe unto you lawyers! for ye
took away the key of knowledge: ye entered not in yourselves, and them
that were entering in ye hindered.
53 And when he was come out from thence, the scribes and the Pharisees
began to ⁵press upon *him* vehemently, and to provoke him to speak of
54 ⁶many things; laying wait for him, to catch something out of his mouth.

¹ Gr. *breakfast.* ² Or, *ye can.* ³ Or, *Teacher.* ⁴ Gr. *house.* ⁵ Or, *set themselves vehemently against*
him. ⁶ Or, *more.*

§ 108. HE SPEAKS TO HIS DISCIPLES AND A VAST THRONG, ABOUT HYPOCRISY, COVETOUSNESS (PARABLE OF THE RICH FOOL), WORLDLY ANXIETIES, WATCHFULNESS (PARABLE OF THE WAITING SERVANTS, AND OF THE WISE STEWARD), AND HIS OWN APPROACHING PASSION*

Probably in Judea

Luke 12

1   In the mean time, when ¹the many thousands of the multitude were gathered together, insomuch that they trode one upon another, he began to ²say unto his disciples first of all, Beware ye of the leaven of the Phari-
2 sees, which is hypocrisy.   But there is nothing covered up; that shall
3 not be revealed: and hid, that shall not be known.   Wherefore whatsoever ye have said in the darkness shall be heard in the light; and what ye have spoken in the ear in the inner chambers shall be proclaimed upon the
4 housetops.   And I say unto you my friends, Be not afraid of them which
5 kill the body, and after that have no more that they can do.   But I will warn you whom ye shall fear: Fear him, which after he hath killed hath
6 ³power to cast into ⁴hell; yea, I say unto you, Fear him.   Are not five sparrows sold for two farthings? and not one of them is forgotten in the
7 sight of God.   But the very hairs of your head are all numbered.   Fear
8 not: ye are of more value than many sparrows.   And I say unto you, Every one who shall confess ⁵me before men, ⁶him shall the Son of man also
9 confess before the angels of God: but he that denieth me in the presence
10 of men shall be denied in the presence of the angels of God.   And every one who shall speak a word against the Son of man, it shall be forgiven him: but unto him that blasphemeth against the Holy Spirit it shall not
11 be forgiven.   And when they bring you before the synagogues, and the rulers, and the authorities, be not anxious how or what ye shall answer,
12 or what ye shall say: for the Holy Spirit shall teach you in that very hour what ye ought to say.
13   And one out of the multitude said unto him, ⁷Master, bid my brother
14 divide the inheritance with me.   But he said unto him, Man, who made
15 me a judge or a divider over you?   And he said unto them, Take heed, and keep yourselves from all covetousness: ⁸for a man's life consisteth
16 not in the abundance of the things which he possesseth.   And he spake
17 a parable unto them, saying, The ground of a certain rich man brought forth plentifully: and he reasoned within himself, saying, What shall I do,
18 because I have not where to bestow my fruits?   And he said, This will
   I do: I will pull down my barns, and build greater; and there will I bestow
19 all my corn and my goods.   And I will say to my ⁹soul, ⁹Soul, thou hast much goods laid up for many years; take thine ease, eat, drink, be merry.
20 But God said unto him, Thou foolish one, this night ¹⁰is thy ⁹soul required

---

* Here we have a series of discourses to the disciples (1–12), to one of the crowd (13–21), to the disciples (22–40), to Peter (41–53), to the multitudes (54–59). The constant interruption is typical of the teaching of Jesus.   This address, as often, repeats some of Christ's favorite sayings.
   Besides the Parable of the Rich Fool (12:16–21) note those of the Waiting Servants (37–40) and of the Wise Steward (42–48).

Luke 12

21 of thee; and the things which thou hast prepared, whose shall they be?
So is he that layeth up treasure for himself, and is not rich toward God.

22   And he said unto his disciples, Therefore I say unto you, Be not anxious
for *your* [11]life, what ye shall eat; nor yet for your body, what ye shall put
23 on.   For the [11]life is more than the food, and the body than the raiment.
24. Consider the ravens, that they sow not, neither reap; which have no
store-chamber nor barn; and God feedeth them: of how much more
25 value are ye than the birds!   And which of you by being anxious can
26 add a cubit unto his [12]stature?   If then ye are not able to do even that
27 which is least, why are ye anxious concerning the rest?   Consider the
lilies, how they grow: they toil not, neither do they spin; yet I say unto
you, Even Solomon in all his glory was not arrayed like one of these.
28 But if God doth so clothe the grass in the field, which to-day is, and to-
morrow is cast into the oven; how much more *shall he clothe* you, O ye
29 of little faith?   And seek not ye what ye shall eat, and what ye shall
30 drink, neither be ye of doubtful mind.   For all these things do the nations
of the world seek after: but your Father knoweth that ye have need of
31 these things.   Howbeit seek ye [13]his kingdom, and these things shall be
added unto you.   Fear not, little flock; for it is your Father's good pleas-
33 ure to give you the kingdom.   Sell that ye have, and give alms; make
for yourselves purses which wax not old, a treasure in the heavens that
34 faileth not, where no thief draweth near, neither moth destroyeth.   For
where your treasure is, there will your heart be also.

35, 36   Let your loins be girded about, and your lamps burning; and be
ye yourselves like unto men looking for their lord, when he shall return
from the marriage feast; that, when he cometh and knocketh, they may
37 straightway open unto him.   Blessed are those [14]servants, whom the lord
when he cometh shall find watching: verily I say unto you, that he shall
gird himself, and make them sit down to meat, and shall come and serve
38 them.   And if he shall come in the second watch, and if in the third, and
39 find *them* so, blessed are those *servants*.   [15]But know this, that if the master
of the house had known in what hour the thief was coming, he would have
40 watched, and not have left his house to be [16]broken through.   Be ye also
ready: for in an hour that ye think not the Son of man cometh.

41   And Peter said, Lord, speakest thou this parable unto us, or even unto
42 all?   And the Lord said, Who then is [17]the faithful and wise steward,
whom his lord shall set over his household, to give them their portion
43 of food in due season?   Blessed is that [18]servant, whom his lord when he
44 cometh shall find so doing.   Of a truth I say unto you, that he will set
45 him over all that he hath.   But if that [18]servant shall say in his heart,
My lord delayeth his coming; and shall begin to beat the menservants
and the maidservants, and to eat and drink, and to be drunken; the
46 lord of that [18]servant shall come in a day when he expecteth not, and in
an hour when he knoweth not, and shall [19]cut him asunder, and appoint
47 his portion with the unfaithful.   And that [18]servant, which knew his
lord's will, and made not ready, nor did according to his will, shall be
48 beaten with many *stripes;* but he that knew not, and did things worthy
of stripes, shall be beaten with few *stripes*.   And to whomsoever much
is given, of him shall much be required: and to whom they commit much,
of him will they ask the more.

Luke 12

49 I came to cast fire upon the earth; and what will I, if it is already
50 kindled?   But I have a baptism to be baptized with; and how am I
51 straitened till it be accomplished!   Think ye that I am come to give
52 peace in the earth?   I tell you, Nay; but rather division: for there shall
   be from henceforth five in one house divided, three against two, and two
53 against three [*see Mic. 7:6*].   They shall be divided, father against son,
   and son against father; mother against daughter, and daughter against
   her mother; mother in law against her daughter in law, and daughter in
   law against her mother in law.
54   And he said to the multitudes also, When ye see a cloud rising in the
   west, straightway ye say, There cometh a shower; and so it cometh to
55 pass.   And when *ye see* a south wind blowing, ye say, There will be a
56 ²⁰scorching heat; and it cometh to pass.   Ye hypocrites, ye know how to
   ²¹interpret the face of the earth and the heaven; but how is it that ye know
57 not how to ²¹interpret this time?   And why even of yourselves judge ye
58 not what is right?   For as thou art going with thine adversary before the
   magistrate, on the way give diligence to be quit of him; lest haply he
   hale thee unto the judge, and the judge shall deliver thee to the ²²officer,
59 and the ²²officer shall cast thee into prison.   I say unto thee, Thou shalt
   by no means come out thence, till thou have paid the very last mite.

¹ Gr. *the myriads of.* ² Or, *say unto his disciples, First of all beware ye.* ³ Or, *authority.* ⁴ Gr. *Gehenna.* ⁵ Gr. *in me.* ⁶ Gr. *in him.* ⁷ Or, *Teacher.* ⁸ Gr. *for not in a man's abundance consisteth his life, from the things which he possesseth.* ⁹ Or, *life.* ¹⁰ Gr. *they require thy soul.* ¹¹ Or, *soul.* ¹² Or, *age.* ¹³ Many ancient authorities read *the kingdom of God.* ¹⁴ Gr. *bond-servants.* ¹⁵ Or, *But this ye know.* ¹⁶ Or, *digged through.* ¹⁷ Or, *the faithful steward, the wise man whom, etc.* ¹⁸ Gr. *bond-servant.* ¹⁹ Or, *severely scourge him.* ²⁰ Or, *hot wind.* ²¹ Gr. *prove.* ²² Gr. *exactor.*

§ 109. ALL MUST REPENT OR PERISH (TWO CURRENT TRAGEDIES); PARABLE OF THE BARREN FIG TREE

Probably in Judea

Luke 13:1-9

1   Now there were some present at that very season which told him of
   the Galileans, whose blood Pilate had mingled with their sacrifices.
2 And he answered and said unto them, Think ye that these Galileans were
   sinners above all the Galileans, because they have suffered these things?
3 I tell you, Nay: but, except ye repent, ye shall all in like manner perish.
4 Or those eighteen, upon whom the tower in Siloam fell, and killed them,
   think ye that they were ¹offenders above all the men that dwell in Jeru-
5 salem?   I tell you, Nay: but, except ye repent, ye shall all likewise perish.
6   And he spake this parable; A certain man had a fig tree planted in his
7 vineyard; and he came seeking fruit thereon, and found none.   And he
   said unto the vinedresser, Behold, these three years I come seeking fruit
   on this fig tree, and find none: cut it down; why doth it also cumber the
8 ground?   And he answering saith unto him, Lord, let it alone this year
9 also, till I shall dig about it, and dung it: and if it bear fruit thenceforth,
   well; but if not, thou shalt cut it down.

¹ Gr. *debtors.*

§ 110. JESUS HEALS A CRIPPLED WOMAN ON THE SABBATH AND DEFENDS HIMSELF AGAINST THE RULER OF THE SYNAGOGUE (COMP. §§ 49 TO 51 AND 114). REPETITION OF THE PARABLES OF THE MUSTARD SEED AND OF THE LEAVEN

Luke 13:10–21

10 And he was teaching in one of the synagogues on the sabbath day.
11 And behold, a woman which had a spirit of infirmity eighteen years;
12 and she was bowed together, and could in no wise lift herself up. And when Jesus saw her, he called her, and said to her, Woman, thou art
13 loosed from thine infirmity. And he laid his hands upon her: and im-
14 mediately she was made straight, and glorified God. And the ruler of the synagogue, being moved with indignation because Jesus had healed on the sabbath [*see Ex. 20:8–11; Deut. 5:12–15*], answered and said to the multitude, There are six days in which men ought to work: in them
15 therefore come and be healed, and not on the day of the sabbath.   But the Lord answered him, and said, Ye hypocrites, doth not each one of you on the sabbath loose his ox or his ass from the ¹stall, and lead him away to
16 watering? And ought not this woman, being a daughter of Abraham, whom Satan had bound, lo, *these* eighteen years, to have been loosed from
17 this bond on the day of the sabbath? And as he said these things, all his adversaries were put to shame: and all the multitude rejoiced for all the glorious things that were done by him.
18 He said therefore, Unto what is the kingdom of God like? and where-
19 unto shall I liken it? It is like unto a grain of mustard seed, which a man took, and cast into his own garden; and it grew, and became a tree; and the birds of the heaven lodged in the branches thereof [*see Dan. 4:
20 10–12; 20–22*]. And again he said, Whereunto shall I liken the king-
21 dom of God? It is like unto leaven, which a woman took and hid in three ²measures of meal, till it was all leavened.

¹ Gr. *manger*. ² The word in the Gr. denotes the Hebrew **seah**, a measure containing nearly a peck and a half (cf. in Matt. 13:33).

Here again the Gospel of John takes us up, and carries us to Jerusalem, and then to Perea.

§ 111. AT THE FEAST OF DEDICATION, JESUS WILL NOT YET OPENLY SAY THAT HE IS THE MESSIAH. THE JEWS TRY TO STONE HIM

Jerusalem

John 10:22–39

22 ¹And it was the feast of the dedication at Jerusalem:* it was winter;
23 and Jesus was walking in the temple in Solomon's porch. The Jews

* Some scholars think that the events in John 9 and 10:1–21 belong to the time of the feast of dedication rather than soon after tabernacles. But the language of John 10:24 seems to call for an interval

John 10:22–39

24 therefore came round about him, and said unto him, How long dost thou
25 hold us in suspense? If thou art the Christ, tell us plainly. Jesus
    answered them, I told you, and ye believe not: the works that I do in my
26 Father's name, these bear witness of me. But ye believe not, because
27 ye are not of my sheep. My sheep hear my voice, and I know them,
28 and they follow me: and I give unto them eternal life; and they shall
29 never perish, and no one shall snatch them out of my hand. ²My Father,
    which hath given *them* unto me, is greater than all; and no one is able to
30, 31 snatch ³*them* out of the Father's hand. I and the Father are one. The
32 Jews took up stones again to stone him. Jesus answered them, Many
    good works have I shewed you from the Father; for which of those works
33 do ye stone me? The Jews answered him, For a good work we stone thee
    not, but for blasphemy; and because that thou, being a man, makest
34 thyself God. Jesus answered them, Is it not written in your law, I said,
35 ye are gods [*see Ps. 82:6*]? If he called them gods, unto whom the word
36 of God came (and the scripture cannot be broken), say ye of him, whom
    the Father ⁴sanctified and sent into the world, Thou blasphemest; because
37 I said, I am *the* Son of God? If I do not the works of my Father, believe
38 me not. But if I do them, though you believe not me, believe the works:
    that ye may know and understand that the Father is in me, and I in the
39 Father. They sought again to take him: and he went forth out of their
    hand.

¹ Some ancient authorities read *At that time was the feast.* ² Some ancient authorities read *That
which my Father hath given unto me.* ³ Or, *aught.* ⁴ Or, *consecrated.*

PART X

THE LATER PEREAN MINISTRY

Probably Dedication in A.D. *29 to Last Journey in* A.D. *30 (about three and a half months),* §§ *112–127.*

§ 112. THE WITHDRAWAL FROM JERUSALEM TO BETHANY BEYOND JORDAN

Perea

John 10:40–42

40 And he went away again beyond Jordan into the place where John was
41 at the first baptizing; and there he abode. And many came unto him;
and they said, John indeed did no sign: but all things whatsoever John
42 spake of this man were true. And many believed on him there.

§ 113. TEACHING IN PEREA, ON A JOURNEY* TOWARD JERUSALEM. WARNED AGAINST HEROD ANTIPAS

Luke 13:22–35

22 And he went on his way through cities and villages, teaching, and
23 journeying on unto Jerusalem.† And one said unto him, Lord, are they
24 few that be saved? And he said unto them, Strive to enter in by the
narrow door: for many, I say unto you, shall seek to enter in, and shall
25 not be ¹able. When once the master of the house is risen up, and hath
shut to the door, and ye begin to stand without, and to knock at the door,
saying, Lord, open to us; and he shall answer and say to you, I know
26 you not whence ye are; then shall ye begin to say, We did eat and drink
in thy presence, and thou didst teach in our streets; and he shall say,
27 I tell you, I know not whence ye are; depart from me, all ye workers of
28 iniquity [*see Ps. 6:8*]. There shall be weeping and gnashing of teeth,
when ye shall see Abraham, and Isaac, and Jacob, and all the prophets,
29 in the kingdom of God, and yourselves cast forth without. And they
shall come from the east and west, and from the north and south, and
30 shall ²sit down in the kingdom of God [*see Ps. 107:3; Isa. 49: 12*]. And

---

* See note 10 at end of Harmony for the combination of Luke and John. After the Feast of the
Dedication Jesus retired beyond Jordan (John 10:40), whence he goes to the raising of Lazarus
(John 11:17). Luke seems to give incidents that belong to this journey.
† The period of three to four months from the Dedication to the final Passover is divided by
another visit to Jerusalem. We cannot tell how many weeks preceded this event. All along here
we have only a few specimens of the Saviour's teaching and works.

131

Luke 13:22-35

behold, there are last which shall be first, and there are first which shall be
last.

31   In that very hour there came certain Pharisees, saying to him, Get
32 thee out, and go hence: for Herod would fain kill thee.   And he said unto
     them, Go and say to that fox, Behold, I cast out ³devils and perform cures
33 to-day and to-morrow, and the third *day* I am perfected.   Howbeit I must
34 go on my way to-day and to-morrow and the *day* following: for it cannot
     be that a prophet perish out of Jerusalem.   O Jerusalem, Jerusalem,
     which killeth the prophets, and stoneth them that are sent unto her! how
     often would I have gathered thy children together, even as a hen *gathereth*
35 her own brood under her wings, and ye would not!   Behold, your house
     is left unto you *desolate:* and I say unto you, Ye shall not see me, until ye
     shall say, Blessed *is* he that cometh in the name of the Lord [*see Ps. 118:26;
     Jer. 12:7; 22:5*].

¹ Or, *able, when once.*   ² Gr. *recline.*   ³ Gr. *demons.*

§ 114. WHILE DINING (BREAKFASTING) WITH A CHIEF PHARISEE, HE AGAIN HEALS ON THE SABBATH, AND DEFENDS HIMSELF (COMP. §§ 49 TO 51 AND 110).   THREE PARABLES SUGGESTED BY THE OCCASION

Probably in Perea

Luke 14:1-24

1   And it came to pass, when he went into the house of one of the rulers
     of the Pharisees on a sabbath to eat bread, that they were watching him.
2 And behold, there was before him a certain man which had the dropsy.
3 And Jesus answering spake unto the lawyers and Pharisees, saying, Is
4 it lawful to heal on the sabbath, or not?   But they held their peace.   And
5 he took him, and healed him, and let him go.   And he said unto them,
     Which of you shall have ¹an ass or an ox fallen into a well, and will not
6 straightway draw him up on a sabbath day?   And they could not answer
     again unto these things.
7   And he spake a parable unto those which were bidden, when he marked
8 how they chose out the chief seats; saying unto them, When thou art
     bidden of any man to a marriage feast, ²sit not down in the chief seat;
     lest haply a more honourable man than thou be bidden of him, and he
9 that bade thee and him shall come and say to thee, Give this man place;
10 and then thou shalt begin with shame to take the lowest place.   But when
     thou art bidden, go and sit down in the lowest place; that when he that
     hath bidden thee cometh, he may say to thee, Friend, go up higher: then
     shalt thou have glory in the presence of all that sit at meat with thee.
11 For every one that exalteth himself shall be humbled; and he that hum-
     bleth himself shall be exalted.
12   And he said to him also that had bidden him, When thou makest a

Luke 14:1-24

dinner or a supper,* call not thy friends, nor thy brethren, nor thy kins-
men, nor rich neighbours; lest haply they also bid thee again, and a recom-
13 pense be made thee. But when thou makest a feast, bid the poor, the
maimed, the lame, the blind: and thou shalt be blessed; because they
14 have not *wherewith* to recompense thee: for thou shalt be recompensed in
the resurrection of the just.

15 And when one of them that sat at meat with him heard these things,
he said unto him, Blessed is he that shall eat bread in the kingdom of
16 God. But he said unto him, A certain man made a great supper; and he
17 bade many: and he sent forth his ¹servant at supper time to say to them
18 that were bidden, Come, for *all* things are now ready. And they all
with one *consent* began to make excuse. The first said unto him, I have
bought a field, and I must needs go out and see it: I pray thee have me
19 excused. And another said, I have bought five yoke of oxen, and I go to
20 prove them: I pray thee have me excused. And another said, I have
21 married a wife, and therefore I cannot come. And the ²servant came,
and told his lord these things. Then the master of the house being angry
said to his ³servant, Go out quickly into the streets and lanes of the
22 city, and bring in hither the poor and maimed and blind and lame. And
the ³servant said, Lord, what thou didst command is done, and yet there
23 is room. And the Lord said unto the ³servant, Go out into the highways
and hedges, and constrain *them* to come in, that my house may be filled.
24 For I say unto you, that none of those men which were bidden shall taste
of my supper.

¹ Many ancient authorities read *a son.* See ch. 13:15.   ² Gr. *recline not.*   ³ Gr. *bond-servant.*

§ 115. GREAT CROWDS FOLLOW HIM, AND HE WARNS THEM TO COUNT THE COST OF DISCIPLE-SHIP TO HIM (COMP. §§ 70 and 83)

Probably in Perea

Luke 14:25-35

25 Now there went with him great multitudes: and he turned, and said
26 unto them, If any man cometh unto me, and hateth not his own father,
and mother, and wife, and children, and brethren, and sisters, yea, and
27 his own life also, he cannot be my disciple. Whosoever doth not bear
28 his own cross, and come after me, cannot be my disciple. For which of
you, desiring to build a tower, doth not first sit down and count the cost,
29 whether he have *wherewith* to complete it? Lest haply, when he hath
laid a foundation, and is not able to finish, all that behold begin to mock
30 him, saying, This man began to build, and was not able to finish. Or
31 what king, as he goeth to encounter another king in war, will not sit
down first and take counsel whether he is able with ten thousand to meet

* More exactly, "a breakfast or a dinner." The two principal meals of the Jews answered to
the present English breakfast (in the forenoon and often near noon), and dinner (at or after dark);
and so in our cities. In the time of King James, as in many of our country homes now, the meal
towards noon answered to dinner, and the night meal to supper. Hence a certain confusion in the
older and more recent English versions. In verses 16, 17 the right word would be dinner, according to city usage, and so elsewhere.

Luke 14:25–35

32 him that cometh against him with twenty thousand?   Or else, while the other is yet a great way off, he sendeth an ambassage, and asketh con-
33 ditions of peace.   So therefore whosoever he be of you that renounceth
34 not all that he hath, he cannot be my disciple.   Salt therefore is good;
35 but if even the salt have lost its savour, wherewith shall it be seasoned?   It is fit neither for the land nor for the dunghill: *men* cast it out.   He that hath ears to hear, let him hear.

§ 116.   THE PHARISEES AND THE SCRIBES MURMUR AGAINST JESUS FOR RECEIVING SINNERS.   HE DEFENDS HIMSELF BY THREE GREAT PARABLES (THE LOST SHEEP, THE LOST COIN, THE LOST SON)

Probably in Perea

Luke 15:1–32

1   Now all the publicans and sinners were drawing near unto him for to
2 hear him.   And both the Pharisees and the scribes murmured, saying, This man receiveth sinners, and eateth with them.
3, 4   And he spake unto them this parable, saying, What man of you, having a hundred sheep, and having lost one of them, doth not leave the ninety and nine in the wilderness, and go after that which is lost, until
5 he find it?   And when he hath found it, he layeth it on his shoulders,
6 rejoicing.   And when he cometh home, he calleth together his friends and his neighbours, saying unto them, Rejoice with me, for I have found my
7 sheep which was lost.   I say unto you, that even so there shall be joy in heaven over one sinner that repenteth, *more* than over ninety and nine righteous persons, which need no repentance.
8   Or what woman having ten ¹pieces of silver, if she lose one piece, doth not light a lamp, and sweep the house, and seek diligently until she find
9 it?   And when she hath found it, she calleth together her friends and neighbours, saying, Rejoice with me, for I have found the piece which I
10 had lost.   Even so, I say unto you, there is joy in the presence of the angels of God over one sinner that repenteth.
11, 12   And he said, A certain man had two sons: and the younger of them said to his father, Father, give me the portion of ²*thy* substance that falleth
13 to me.   And he divided unto them his living.   And not many days after the younger son gathered all together, and took his journey into a far
14 country; and there he wasted his substance with riotous living.   And when he had spent all, there arose a mighty famine in that country; and
15 he began to be in want.   And he went and joined himself to one of the citizens of that country; and he sent him into his fields to feed swine.
16 And he would fain have been filled with ³the husks that the swine did eat:
17 and no man gave unto him.   But when he came to himself he said, How many hired servants of my father's have bread enough and to spare, and
18 I perish here with hunger!   I will arise and go to my father, and will say
19 unto him, Father, I have sinned against heaven, and in thy sight: I am no

Luke 15:1-32

more worthy to be called thy son: make me as one of thy hired servants.
20 And he arose, and came to his father. But while he was yet afar off,
his father saw him, and was moved with compassion, and ran, and fell
21 on his neck, and ⁴kissed him. And the son said unto him, Father, I have
sinned against heaven, and in thy sight; I am no more worthy to be called
22 thy son.⁵ But the father said to his ⁶servants, Bring forth quickly the
best robe, and put it on him; and put a ring on his hand, and shoes on his
23 feet: and bring the fatted calf, *and* kill it, and let us eat, and make merry:
24 for this my son was dead, and is alive again; he was lost, and is found.
25 And they began to be merry. Now his elder son was in the field: and as
26 he came and drew nigh to the house, he heard music and dancing. And
he called to him one of the ⁶servants, and inquired what these things might
27 be. And he said unto him, Thy brother is come; and thy father hath
killed the fatted calf, because he hath received him safe and sound.
28 But he was angry, and would not go in: and his father came out, and
29 entreated him. But he answered and said to his father, Lo, these many
years do I serve thee, and I never transgressed a commandment of thine:
and *yet* thou never gavest me a kid, that I might make merry with my
30 friends: but when this thy son came, which hath devoured thy living with
31 harlots, thou killedst for him the fatted calf. And he said unto him,
32 ⁷Son, thou art ever with me, and all that is mine is thine. But it was meet
to make merry and be glad: for this thy brother was dead, and is alive
again; and *was* lost, and is found.

¹ Gr. *drachma*, a coin worth about sixteen cents. ² Gr. *the.* ³ Gr. *the pods of the carob-tree.*
⁴ Gr. *kissed him much.* ⁵ Some ancient authorities add *make me as one of thy hired servants.* See
ver. 19. ⁶ Gr. *bond-servants.* ⁷ Gr. *Child.*

§ 117. THREE PARABLES ON STEWARDSHIP (TO THE DISCIPLES, THE PARABLE OF THE UNJUST STEWARD; TO THE PHARISEES, THE PARABLE OF THE RICH MAN AND LAZARUS; TO THE DISCIPLES, THE PARABLE OF THE UNPROFITABLE SERVANTS)

Probably in Perea

Luke 16:1-17:10

16 And he said unto the disciples, There was a certain rich man, which
had a steward; and the same was accused unto him that he was wasting
2 his goods. And he called him, and said unto him, What is this that I
hear of thee? render the account of thy stewardship; for thou canst be no
3 longer steward. And the steward said within himself, What shall I do,
4 seeing that my lord taketh away the stewardship from me? I have
not strength to dig; to beg I am ashamed. I am resolved what to do,
that, when I am put out of the stewardship, they may receive me into their
5 houses. And calling to him each one of his lord's debtors, he said to the
6 first, How much owest thou unto my lord? And he said, A hundred
¹measures of oil. And he said unto him, Take thy ²bond, and sit down

135

Luke 16:1–17:10

7 quickly and write fifty. Then said he to another, And how much owest
   thou? And he said, A hundred ³measures of wheat. He saith unto him,
8 Take thy ⁹bond, and write fourscore. And his lord commended ⁴the
   unrighteous steward because he had done wisely: for the sons of this
   ⁵world are for their own generation wiser than the sons of the light.
9 And I say unto you, make to yourselves friends ⁶by means of the mammon
   of unrighteousness; that, when it shall fail, they may receive you into
10 the eternal tabernacles. He that is faithful in a very little is faithful
11 also in much. If therefore ye have not been faithful in the unrighteous
12 mammon, who will commit to your trust the true *riches?* And if ye
   have not been faithful in that which is another's, who will give you that
13 which is ⁷your own? No ⁸servant can serve two masters: for either he
   will hate the one, and love the other; or else he will hold to one, and
   despise the other. Ye cannot serve God and mammon.
14   And the Pharisees, who were lovers of money, heard all these things;
15 and they scoffed at him. And he said unto them, Ye are they that
   justify yourselves in the sight of men; but God knoweth your hearts: for
   that which is exalted among men is an abomination in the sight of God.
16 The law and the prophets *were* until John: from that time the gospel of
   the kingdom of God is preached, and every man entereth violently into it
17 [*see Matt. 11:12*]. But it is easier for heaven and earth to pass away,
18 than for one tittle of the law to fall. Every one that putteth away his
   wife, and marrieth another, committeth adultery: and he that marrieth
   one that is put away from a husband committeth adultery.
19   Now there was a certain rich man, and he was clothed in purple and
20 fine linen, ⁹faring sumptuously every day: and a certain beggar named
21 Lazarus was laid at his gate, full of sores, and desiring to be fed with the
   crumbs that fell from the rich man's table; yea, even the dogs came and
22 licked his sores. And it came to pass, that the beggar died, and that he
   was carried away by the angels into Abraham's bosom: and the rich man
23 also died, and was buried. And in Hades he lifted up his eyes, being in
24 torments, and seeth Abraham afar off, and Lazarus in his bosom. And he
   cried and said, Father Abraham, have mercy on me, and send Lazarus,
   that he may dip the tip of his finger in water, and cool my tongue; for I
25 am in anguish in this flame. But Abraham said, ¹⁰Son, remember that
   thou in thy lifetime receivedst thy good things, and Lazarus in like manner
26 evil things: but now here he is comforted, and thou art in anguish. And
   ¹¹beside all this, between us and you there is a great gulf fixed, that they
   which would pass from hence to you may not be able, and that none may
27 cross over from thence to us. And he said, I pray thee therefore, father,
28 that thou wouldest send him to my father's house: for I have five brethren;
   that he may testify unto them; lest they also come into this place of tor-
29 ment. But Abraham saith, They have Moses and the prophets; let them
30 hear them. And he said, Nay, father Abraham: but if one go to them
31 from the dead, they will repent. And he said unto him, If they hear not
   Moses and the prophets, neither will they be persuaded, if one rise from
   the dead.
1   And he said unto his disciples, It is impossible but that occasions of
   stumbling should come: but woe unto him, through whom they come!
2 It were well for him if a millstone were hanged about his neck, and he

Luke 16:1–17:10

were thrown into the sea, rather than that he should cause one of these
3 little ones to stumble. Take heed to yourselves: if thy brother sin,
4 rebuke him; and if he repent, forgive him. And if he sin against thee
seven times in the day, and seven times turn again to thee, saying, I
repent; thou shalt forgive him.
5, 6 And the apostles said unto the Lord, Increase our faith. And the
Lord said, If ye have faith as a grain of mustard seed, ye would say unto
this sycamine tree, Be thou rooted up, and be thou planted in the sea;
7 and it would have obeyed you. But who is there of you, having a [12]ser-
vant plowing or keeping sheep, that will say unto him, when he is come in
from the field, Come straightway and sit down to meat; and will not
8 rather say unto him, Make ready wherewith I may sup, and gird thyself,
and serve me, till I have eaten and drunken; and afterward thou shalt
9 eat and drink? Doth he thank the [12]servant because he did the things
10 that were commanded? Even so ye also, when ye shall have done all
the things that are commanded you, say, We are unprofitable [13]servants;
we have done that which it was our duty to do.

[1] Or, baths, the bath being a Hebrew measure. See Ezek. 45:10, 11, 14. [2] Gr. *writings*. [3] Gr.
cors, the cor being a Hebrew measure. See Ezek. 45:14. [4] Gr. *the steward of unrighteousness*.
[5] Or, *age*. [6] Gr. *out of*. [7] Some ancient authorities read, *our own*. [8] Gr. *household servant*. [9] Or,
living in mirth and splendor every day. [10] Gr. *Child*. [11] Or, *in all these things*. [12] Gr. *bond-servant*.
[13] Gr. *bond-servants*.

§ 118. JESUS RAISES LAZARUS FROM THE DEAD

From Perea* to Bethany near Jerusalem

John 11:1–44

1 Now a certain man was sick, Lazarus of Bethany, of the village of
2 Mary and her sister Martha. And it was that Mary, which anointed
the Lord with ointment, and wiped his feet with her hair, whose brother
3 Lazarus was sick. The sisters therefore sent unto him, saying, Lord,
4 behold, he whom thou lovest is sick. But when Jesus heard it, he said,
this sickness is not unto death, but for the glory of God, that the Son of
5 God may be glorified thereby. Now Jesus loved Martha, and her sister,
6 and Lazarus. When therefore he heard that he was sick, he abode at
7 that time two days in the place where he was. Then after this he saith
8 to the disciples, Let us go into Judea again. The disciples say unto him,
Rabbi, the Jews were but now seeking to stone thee; and goest thou thither
9 again? Jesus answered, Are there not twelve hours in the day? If a
man walk in the day, he stumbleth not, because he seeth the light of this
10 world. But if a man walk in the night, he stumbleth, because the light
11 is not in him. These things spake he: and after this he saith unto them,
Our friend Lazarus is fallen asleep; but I go, that I may awake him out of
12 sleep. The disciples therefore said unto him, Lord, if he is fallen asleep,
13 he will [1]recover. Now Jesus had spoken of his death: but they thought

* Our Lord was apparently at a distance of two or three days' journey (verses 6, 17) from
Bethany; and he was probably in Perea. This visit to Bethany, a suburb of Jerusalem, may be that
to which Luke pointed in 13:22.

John 11:1–44

14 that he spake of taking rest in sleep. Then Jesus therefore said unto
15 them plainly, Lazarus is dead. And I am glad for your sakes that I was
   not there, to the intent ye may believe; nevertheless let us go unto him.
16 Thomas therefore, who is called ²Didymus, said unto his fellow-disciples,
   Let us also go, that we may die with him.
17   So when Jesus came, he found that he had been in the tomb four days
18 already. Now Bethany was nigh unto Jerusalem, about fifteen furlongs
19 off; and many of the Jews had come to Martha and Mary, to console
20 them concerning their brother. Martha therefore, when she heard
   that Jesus was coming, went and met him: but Mary still sat in the house.
21 Martha therefore said unto Jesus, Lord, if thou hadst been here, my
22 brother had not died. And even now I know that whatsoever thou shalt
23 ask of God, God will give thee. Jesus saith unto her, Thy brother shall
24 rise again. Martha saith unto him, I know that he shall rise again in
25 the resurrection at the last day. Jesus said unto her, I am the resur-
26 rection, and the life: he that believeth on me, though he die, yet shall he
27 live: and whosoever liveth and believeth on me shall never die. Believest
   thou this? She saith unto him, Yea, Lord: I have believed that thou art
28 the Christ, the Son of God, *even* he that cometh into the world. And when
   she had said this, she went away, and called Mary ³her sister secretly,
29 saying, The ⁴Master is here, and calleth thee. And she, when she heard
30 it, arose quickly, and went unto him. (Now Jesus was not yet come into the
31 village, but was still in the place where Martha met him.) The Jews then
   which were with her in the house, and were comforting her, when they
   saw Mary, that she rose up quickly and went out, followed her, supposing
32 that she was going unto the tomb to ⁵weep there. Mary therefore, when
   she came where Jesus was, and saw him, fell down at his feet, saying unto
33 him, Lord, if thou hadst been here, my brother had not died. When
   Jesus therefore saw her ⁶weeping, and the Jews *also* ⁶weeping, which
34 came with her, he ⁷groaned in the spirit, and ⁸was troubled, and said, Where
35 have ye laid him? They say unto him, Lord, come and see. Jesus wept.
36, 37 The Jews therefore said, Behold how he loved him! But some of
   them said, Could not this man, which opened the eyes of him that was
38 blind, have caused that this man also should not die? Jesus therefore
   again ⁹groaning in himself cometh to the tomb. Now it was a cave, and
39 a stone lay ¹⁰against it. Jesus saith, Take ye away the stone. Martha,
   the sister of him that was dead, saith unto him, Lord, by this time he
40 stinketh: for he hath been *dead* four days. Jesus saith unto her,
   Said I not unto thee, that, if thou believedst, thou shouldest
41 see the glory of God? So they took away the stone. And Jesus lifted
   up his eyes, and said, Father, I thank thee that thou heardest me.
42 And I knew that thou hearest me always: but because of the multitude
   which standeth around I said it, that they may believe that thou didst
43 send me. And when he had thus spoken, he cried with a loud voice,
44 Lazarus, come forth. He that was dead came forth, bound hand and
   foot with ¹¹grave-clothes; and his face was bound about with a napkin.
   Jesus saith unto them, Loose him, and let him go.

¹ Gr. *be saved.*   ² That is, *Twin.*   ³ Or, *her sister, saying secretly.*   ⁴ Or, *Teacher.*   ⁵ Gr. *wail.*
⁶ Gr. *wailing.*   ⁷ Or, *was moved with indignation in the spirit.*   ⁸ Gr. *troubled himself.*   ⁹ Or, *being
moved with indignation in himself.*   ¹⁰ Or, *upon.*   ¹¹ Or, *grave-bands.*

§ 119. THE EFFECT OF THE RAISING OF LAZARUS (ON THE PEOPLE, ON THE SANHEDRIN, ON THE MOVEMENTS OF JESUS)

Jerusalem and Ephraim in Judea

John 11:45–54

45 Many therefore of the Jews, which came to Máry and beheld [1]that
46 which he did, believed on him. But some of them went away to the
Pharisees, and told them the thing which Jesus had done.
47 The chief priests therefore and the Pharisees gathered a council, and
48 said, What do we? for this man doeth many signs. If we let him thus
alone, all men will believe on him: and the Romans will come and take
49 away both our place and our nation. But a certain one of them, Caiaphas,
being high priest that year, said unto them, Ye know nothing at all,
50 nor do ye take account that it is expedient for you that one man should
51 die for the people, and that the whole nation perish not. Now this he
52 said not of himself: but being high priest that year, he prophesied that
Jesus should die for the nation; and not for the nation only, but that he
might also gather together into one the children of God that are scattered
53 abroad. So from that day forth they took counsel that they might put
him to death.
54 Jesus therefore walked no more openly among the Jews, but departed
thence into the country near to the wilderness, into a city called Ephraim;
and there he tarried with the disciples.

[1] Many ancient authorities read *the things which he did*.

§ 120. JESUS STARTS ON THE LAST JOURNEY TO JERU-SALEM BY WAY OF SAMARIA AND GALILEE

He heals the Ten Lepers and explains the Nature of the Kingdom of God to the Pharisees and the Disciples.

In Samaria or Galilee

Luke 17:11–37

11 And it came to pass, [1]as they were on the way to Jerusalem, that he
12 was passing [2]through the midst of Samaria and Galilee.* And as he
entered into a certain village, there met him ten men that were lepers,
13 which stood afar off [*see Lev. 13:45–46*]: and they lifted up their voices,
14 saying, Jesus, Master, have mercy on us. And when he saw them, he

* As Ephraim (§ 119) was pretty certainly in the northern part of Judea, it has been reasonably supposed (Wieseler, Clark, and others) that, when the Passover was approaching, Jesus went from that region northward through Samaria into the southern or southeastern part of Galilee, so as to fall in with the pilgrims going from Galilee through Perea to Jerusalem. We thus again combine Luke's account with that of John in easy agreement. And this explains Luke's mention of Samaria first, which would be strange in describing a journey from Galilee through Samaria to Jerusalem, while the marginal translation, "between Samaria and Galilee," would be obscure and hard to account for. From this point he is making his final journey to Jerusalem, for the Passover of the crucifixion.

Luke 17:11-37

said unto them, Go and shew yourselves unto the priests [see Lev. 13:49;
15 14:1-3]. And it came to pass, as they went, they were cleansed. And
one of them, when he saw that he was healed, turned back, with a loud
16 voice glorifying God; and he fell upon his face at his feet, giving him
17 thanks: and he was a Samaritan. And Jesus answering said, Were not
18 the ten cleansed? but where are the nine? ³Were there none found that
19 returned to give glory to God, save this ⁴stranger? And he said unto
him, Arise, and go thy way: thy faith hath ⁵made thee whole.
20   And being asked by the Pharisees, when the kingdom of God cometh,
he answered them and said, the kingdom of God cometh not with obser-
21 vation: neither shall they say, Lo, here! or, There! for lo, the kingdom of
God is ⁶within you.
22   And he said unto the disciples, The days will come, when ye shall
desire to see one of the days of the Son of man, and ye shall not see it.
23 And they shall say to you, Lo, there! Lo, here! go not away, nor follow
24 after *them:* for as the lightning, when it lighteneth out of the one part
under the heaven, shineth unto the other part under heaven; so shall
25 the Son of man be ⁷in his day. But first must he suffer many things and
26 be rejected of this generation. And as it came to pass in the days of Noah,
even so shall it be also in the days of the Son of man [see Gen. 6:11-13;
27 7, 21-23]. They ate, they drank, they married, they were given in marriage, until the day that Noah entered the ark, and the flood came, and
28 destroyed them all. Likewise even as it came to pass in the days of Lot;
they ate, they drank, they bought, they sold, they planted, they builded
29 [see Gen 18:20-22]: but in the day that Lot went out from Sodom [see Gen.
30 19:24-25] it rained fire and brimstone from heaven, and destroyed them
all: after the same manner shall it be in the day that the Son of
31 man is revealed. In that day, he which shall be on the housetop, and his
goods in the house, let him not go down to take them away: and let him
32, 33 that is in the field likewise not return back. Remember Lot's wife [see
Gen. 19:26]. Whosoever shall seek to gain his ⁸life shall lose it: but who-
34 soever shall lose *his life* shall ⁹preserve it. I say unto you, In that night
there shall be two men on one bed; the one shall be taken and the other
35 shall be left. There shall be two women grinding together; the one shall
37 be taken, and the other shall be left ¹⁰. And they answering say unto
him, Where, Lord? And he said unto them, Where the body *is*, thither
will the ¹¹eagles also be gathered together.

¹ Or, *as he was.*   ² Or, *between.*   ³ Or, *There were none found . . . save this stranger.*   ⁴ Or, *alien.*
⁵ Or, *saved thee.*   ⁶ Or, *in the midst of you.*   ⁷ Some ancient authorities omit *in his day.*   ⁸ Or, *soul.*
⁹ Or, *save it alive.*   ¹⁰ Some ancient authorities add ver. 36 *There shall be two men in the field: the one
shall be taken, and the other shall be left.*   ¹¹ Or, *vultures.*

§ 121. TWO PARABLES ON PRAYER (THE IMPORTUNATE WIDOW, THE PHARISEE AND THE PUBLICAN)

Luke 18:1-14

1   And he spake a parable unto them to the end that they ought always
2 to pray, and not to faint; saying, There was in a city a judge, which
3 feared not God, and regarded not man: and there was a widow in that

Luke 18:1–14

city; and she came oft unto him, saying, ¹Avenge me of mine adversary.
4 And he would not for a while: but afterward he said within himself,
5 Though I fear not God, nor regard man; yet because this widow troubleth
me, I will avenge her, lest she ²wear me out by her continual coming.
6 And the Lord said, Hear what ³the unrighteous judge saith. And shall
7 not God avenge his elect, which cry to him day and night, and he is long-
8 suffering over them? I say unto you, that he will avenge them speedily.
Howbeit when the Son of man cometh, shall he find ⁴faith on the earth?
9   And he spake also this parable unto certain which trusted in them-
10 selves that they were righteous, and set ⁵all others at nought: Two men
went up into the temple to pray; the one a Pharisee, and the other a
11 publican. The Pharisee stood and prayed thus with himself, God, I
thank thee, that I am not as the rest of men, extortioners, unjust, adulter-
12 ers, or even as this publican. I fast twice in the week; I give tithes of all
13 that I get. But the publican, standing afar off, would not lift up so much
as his eyes unto heaven, but smote his breast, saying, God, ⁶be merciful
14 to me ⁷a sinner. I say unto you, This man went down to his house
justified rather than the other: for every one that exalteth himself shall be
humbled; but he that humbleth himself shall be exalted.

---

¹ Or, *Do me justice of;* and so in verses 5, 7, 8.   ² Gr. *bruise.*   ³ Gr. *the judge of unrighteousness.*
⁴ Or, *the faith.*   ⁵ Gr. *the rest.*   ⁶ Or, *be propitiated.*   ⁷ Or, *the sinner.*

---

§ 122. GOING FROM GALILEE THROUGH PEREA,* HE TEACHES CONCERNING DIVORCE

Perea

Mark 10:1–12	Matt. 19:1–12
1 And he arose from thence, and cometh into the borders of Judea and beyond Jordan: and multitudes come together unto him again; and, as he was wont, he taught them again.	1 And it came to pass, when Jesus had finished these words, he departed from Galilee, and came into the borders of Judea beyond 2 Jordan; and great multitudes followed him; and he healed them there.
2 And there came unto him Pharisees, and asked him, Is it lawful for a man to put away *his* 3 wife? tempting him. And he answered and said unto them, What did Moses command you 4 [*see Deut. 24:1*]? And they said,	3 And there came unto him ¹Pharisees, tempting him, and saying, Is it lawful *for a man* to put away his wife for every cause? 4 And he answered and said, Have

---

* Matthew expressly states that he went from Galilee through Perea, and soon afterwards carries him forward to Jericho and Jerusalem. (Comp. Mark also.) Yet he says that Jesus did this when he had finished the parable of the unforgiving servant, which we have placed nearly six months earlier (§ 92). Luke here presently agrees with Matthew and Mark, and they go on together to the end, while heretofore Matthew and Mark have given us nothing since Jesus went to the Feast of Tabernacles. In one way or another we must suppose quite a break in their narrative. See Broadus' commentary on Matthew 19:1, and compare note 10 at end of Harmony.

Mark 10:1–12

Moses suffered to write a bill of divorcement, and to put her
5 away. But Jesus said unto them, For your hardness of heart he wrote you this commandment.
6 But from the beginning of the creation, Male and female made
7 he them [*see Gen. 1:27*]. For this cause shall a man leave his father and mother, ⁵and shall
8 cleave to his wife; and the twain shall become one flesh [*see Gen. 2:24*]: so that they are no more
9 twain, but one flesh. What therefore God hath joined together, let
10 not man put asunder. And in the house the disciples asked him again of this matter.

11 And he saith unto them, Whosoever shall put away his wife, and marry another, committeth
12 adultery against her: and if she herself shall put away her husband, and marry another, she committeth adultery.

Matt. 19:1–12

ye not read, that he which ²made *them* from the beginning made
5 them male and female, and said, For this cause shall a man leave his father and mother, and shall cleave to his wife; and the twain
6 shall become one flesh? So that they are no more twain, but one flesh. What therefore God hath joined together, let not man put asunder.
7 They say unto him, Why then did Moses command to give a bill of divorce-
8 ment, and to put *her* away? He saith unto them, Moses for your hardness of heart suffered you to put away your wives: but from the beginning it hath not been
9 so. And I say unto you, Whosoever shall put away his wife, ³except for fornication, and shall marry another, committeth adultery: ⁴and he that marrieth her when she is put away committeth
10 adultery. The disciples say unto him, If the case of the man is so with his wife, it is not expedient
11 to marry. But he said unto them, All men cannot receive this saying, but they to whom it is given.
12 For there are eunuchs which were so born from their mother's womb: and there are eunuchs, which were made eunuchs by men: and there are eunuchs, which made themselves eunuchs for the kingdom of heaven's sake. He that is able to receive it, let him receive it.

---

¹ Many authorities, some ancient, insert *the*. ² Some ancient authorities read *created*. ³ Some ancient authorities read *saving for the cause of fornication, maketh her an adulteress;* as in ch. 5:32, § 43. ⁴ The following words, to the end of the verse, are omitted by some ancient authorities. ⁵ Some ancient authorities omit *and shall cleave to his wife*.

§ 123. CHRIST AND CHILDREN AND THE FAILURE OF THE DISCIPLES TO UNDERSTAND THE ATTITUDE OF JESUS

Perea

Mark 10:13-16	Matt. 19:13-15	Luke 18:15-17*
13 And they brought unto him little children, that he should touch them: and the disciples r e b u k e d 14 them. But when Jesus saw it, he was moved with indignation. and said unto them, Suffer the little children to come unto me; forbid them not: for of such is the kingdom of God. 15 Verily I say unto you, Whosoever shall not receive the kingdom of God as a little child, he shall in no wise enter therein. 16 And he took them in his arms, and blessed them, laying his hands upon them.	13 Then were there brought unto him little children, that he should lay his hands on them, and pray: and the disciples rebuked them. 14 But Jesus said, Suffer the little children, and forbid them not, to come unto me: for of such is the kingdom of heaven. 15 And he laid his hands on them, and departed thence.	15 And they brought unto him also their babes, that he should touch them: but when the disciples saw it, they rebuked them. 16 But Jesus called them unto him, saying, Suffer the little children to come unto me, and forbid them not: for of such is the kingdom of God. 17 Verily I say unto you, Whosoever shall not receive the kingdom of God as a little child, he shall in no wise enter therein

§ 124. THE RICH YOUNG RULER, THE PERILS OF RICHES, AND AMAZEMENT OF THE DISCIPLES. THE REWARDS OF FORSAKING ALL TO FOLLOW THE MESSIAH WILL BE GREAT, BUT WILL BE SOVEREIGN (PARABLE OF THE LABORERS IN THE VINEYARD)

In Perea

Mark 10:17-31	Matt. 19:16 to 20:16	Luke 18:18-30
17 And as he was going forth [8]into the way, there ran one to him, and kneeled to him, and asked him, Good [2]Master,	16 And behold, one came to him and said, [1]Master,[2] what good	18 And a certain ruler asked him, saying, Good [2]Master, what

* From this point Matthew, Mark and Luke will be parallel more frequently than they were even during the great ministry in Galilee.

Mark 10:17-31	Matt. 19:16 to 20:16	Luke 18:18-30
what shall I do that I may inherit eternal 18 life? And Jesus said unto him, Why callest thou me good? none is good save one, *even* God.	thing shall I do that I may have eternal 17 life? And he said unto him, ³Why askest thou me concerning that which is good? One there is who is good: but if thou wouldest enter into life, keep the 18 commandments. He saith unto him, Which? And Jesus said, Thou shalt not kill, Thou shalt not commit adultery,	shall I do to inherit 19 eternal life? And Jesus said unto him, Why callest thou me good? none is good save one, *even* God.
19 Thou knowest the commandments [*see Ex. 20:12-16; Deut. 5:16-20*], Do not kill, Do not commit adultery		20　　　Thou knowest the commandments, Do not commit adultery, Do not kill,
Do not steal, Do not bear false witness, Do not 19 defraud, Honour thy father and mother. 20　　And he said unto him, ²Master, all these things have I observed from 21 my youth. And Jesus looking upon him loved him, and said unto him, One thing thou lackest: go, sell whatsoever t h o u hast, and give to the poor, and thou shalt have treasure in heaven: and come, 22 follow me. But his countenance fell at the saying, and he went away sorrowful: for he was one that had great possessions. 23　　And Jesus looked round about, and saith unto his disciples, How hardly shall they that have riches enter into the kingdom of God!	Thou shalt not steal, Thou shalt not bear false witness, Honour thy father and thy mother: and, Thou 20 shalt love thy neighbour as thyself. The young man saith unto him, All these things have I observed: what lack I 21 yet? Jesus said unto him, If thou wouldest be perfect, go, sell that thou hast, and give to the poor, and thou shalt have treasure in heaven: and come, follow me. 22　　　　But when the young man heard the saying, he went away sorrowful: for he was one that had great possessions. 23　　And Jesus said unto his disciples, Verily I say unto you, It is hard for a rich man to enter into the kingdom of heaven.	Do not steal, Do not bear false witness, Honour thy father and mother. 21　　　And he said, All these things have I observed from my 22 youth up. And when Jesus heard it, he said unto him, One thing thou lackest yet: sell all that thou hast, and distribute unto the poor, and thou shalt have treasure in heaven: and come, follow me. 23 But when he heard these things, he became exceeding sorrowful; for he was very rich. 24　　　And Jesus seeing him said, How hardly shall they that have riches enter into the kingdom of God!

Mark 10:17-31	Matt. 19:16 to 20:16	Luke 18:18-30
24 And the disciples were amazed at his words. But Jesus answereth again, and saith unto them, Children, how hard is it [9]for them that trust in riches to enter into the kingdom 25 of God! It is easier for a camel to go through a needle's eye, than for a rich man to enter into the kingdom of God. 26 And they were astonished exceedingly, saying [10]unto him, Then who can be 27 saved? Jesus looking upon them saith, With men it is impossible, but not with God for all things are possible with God [*see Gen. 18:24;* 28 *Job, 42:2*]. Peter began to say unto him, Lo, we have left all, and followed thee. 29 Jesus said, Verily I say unto you,	24 And again I say unto you, It is easier for a camel to go through a needle's eye, than for a rich man to enter into the kingdom 25 of God. And when the disciples heard it, they were astonished exceedingly, saying, Who then can 26 be saved? And Jesus looking upon *them* said to them, With men this is impossible; but with God all things are 27 possible. Then answered Peter and said unto him, Lo, we have left all, and followed thee; what then shall 28 we have? And Jesus said unto them, Verily I say unto you, that ye which have followed me, in the regeneration when the Son of man shall sit on the throne of his glory, ye also shall sit upon twelve thrones, judging the twelve tribes of Isra- 29 el. And every one that hath left houses, or brethren, or sisters, or father, or mother, [4]or children, or lands, for my name's sake, shall	25 For it is easier for a camel to enter in through a needle's eye, than for a rich man to enter into the kingdom of God. 26 And they that heard it said, Then who can be saved? 27 But he said, The things that are impossible with men are possible with God. 28 And Peter said, Lo, we have left [12]our own, and followed thee. 29 And he said unto them, Verily I say unto you,
There is no man that hath left house, or brethren, or sisters, or mother, or father, or children, or lands, for my sake, and for 30 the gospel's sake, but he shall receive a hundredfold now in this time, houses, and		There is no man that hath left house, or wife, or brethren, or parents, or children, for the kingdom of God's sake.

Mark 10:17–31	Matt. 19:16 to 20:16	Luke 18:18–30
brethren, and sisters, and mothers, and children, and lands, with persecutions; and in the [11]world to come eternal life.	receive [5]a hundred fold,	30 who shall not receive manifold more in this time,
	and shall inherit eternal life.	and in the [11]world to come eternal life.
31 But many *that are* first shall be last; and the last first.	30 But many shall be last *that are* first; and first *that are* last.	

1 For the kingdom of heaven is like unto a man that is a householder,
2 which went out early in the morning to hire labourers into his vineyard. And when he had agreed with the labourers for a [6]penny a day,
3 he sent them into his vineyard. And he went out about the third hour
4 and saw others standing in the marketplace idle; and to them he said,
Go ye also into the vineyard, and whatsoever is right I will give you.
5 And they went their way. Again he went out about the sixth and the
6 ninth hour, and did likewise. And about the eleventh *hour* he went out,
7 and found others standing; and he saith unto them, Why stand ye here
all the day idle? They say unto him, Because no man hath hired us.
8 He saith unto them, Go ye also into the vineyard. And when even was
come, the lord of the vineyard saith unto his steward, Call the labourers,
9 and pay them their hire, beginning from the last unto the first. And when
they came that *were hired* about the eleventh hour, they received every
10 man a [6]penny. And when the first came, they supposed that they would
11 receive more; and they likewise received every man a [6]penny. And
when they received it, they murmured against the householder, saying,
12 These last have spent *but* one hour, and thou hast made them equal unto
us, which have borne the burden of the day and the [7]scorching heat.
13 But he answered and said to one of them, Friend, I do thee no wrong:
14 didst not thou agree with me for a [6]penny? Take up that which is thine,
and go thy way; it is my will to give unto this last, even as unto thee.
15 Is it not lawful for me to do what I will with mine own? or is thine eye
16 evil, because I am good? So the last shall be first, and the first last.

[1] Some ancient authorities read *Good Master.* See Mark 10:17; Luke 18:18. [2] Or, *Teacher.* [3] Some ancient authorities read *Why callest thou me good? None is good save one, even God.* See Mark 10:18; Luke 18:19. [4] Many ancient authorities add *or wife;* as in Luke 18:29. [5] Some ancient authorities read *manifold.* [6] The Roman denarius, about seventeen cents of our money. [7] Or, *hot wind.* [8] Or, *on his way.* [9] Some ancient authorities omit *for them that trust in riches.* [10] Many ancient authorities read *among themselves.* [11] Or, *age.* [12] Or, *our own homes.*

§ 125. JESUS AGAIN FORETELLS TO THE DISCIPLES HIS DEATH AND RESURRECTION (COMP. §§ 83, 85, 86, 88), AND REBUKES THE SELFISH AMBITION OF JAMES AND JOHN

Probably in Perea

Mark 10:32–45	Matt. 20:17–28
32 And they were in the way, going up	17 And as Jesus was going up to Jerusalem,

Mark 10:32-45	Matt. 20:17-28	Luke 18:31-34

to Jerusalem*; and Jesus was going before them: and they were amazed; ²and they that followed were afraid. And he took again the twelve, and began to tell them the things that were to happen unto him, *saying*,

33 Behold, we go up to Jerusalem; and the Son of man shall be delivered unto the chief priests and the scribes; and they shall condemn him to death, and shall deliver him unto the 34 Gentiles: and they shall mock him,
  and shall spit upon him, and shall scourge him, and shall kill him; and after three days he shall rise again.

35 And there come near unto him James and John, the sons of Zebedee, saying unto him, ⁴Master, we would that thou shouldest do for us whatsoever we shall ask of thee. And he 36 said unto them, What would ye that I should 37 do for you? And they said unto him, Grant

he took the twelve disciples apart, and in the way he said unto them,

18 Behold, we go up to Jerusalem; and the Son of man shall be delivered unto the chief priests and scribes; and they shall condemn him 19 to death, and shall deliver him unto the Gentiles to mock,

and to scourge, and to crucify; and the third day he shall be raised up.

20 Then came to him the mother of the sons of Zebedee with her sons, worshipping *him*, and asking a certain thing of him.

21 And he said unto her, What wouldest thou? She said unto him, Command that these my two sons may sit, one on thy right hand, and one on thy left hand, in thy kingdom.

31 And he took unto him the twelve, and said unto them, Behold, we go up to Jerusalem, and all the things that are written ⁵by the prophets shall be accomplished unto the Son of man.

32 For he shall be delivered up unto the Gentiles, and shall be mocked, and shamefully entreated, and spit upon: and 33 they shall scourge and kill him: and the third day he shall 34 rise again. And they understood none of these things; and this saying was hid from them, and they perceived not the things that were said.

* He left Galilee in § 122, crossing the Jordan into Perea, probably in company with many Jews from Galilee (who regularly went this way to Jerusalem), and will now soon cross the river again and reach Jericho (§ 126).

147

Mark 10:32–45	Matt. 20:17–28
unto us that we may sit, one on thy right hand, and one on 38 *thy* left hand, in thy glory. But Jesus said unto them, Ye know not what ye ask. Are ye able to drink the cup that I drink? or to be baptized with the baptism 39 that I am baptized with? And they said unto him, We are able. And Jesus said unto them, The cup that I drink ye shall drink; and with the baptism that I am baptized withal shall ye be baptized: 40 but to sit on my right hand or on *my* left hand is not mine to give: but *it is for them* for whom it hath 41 been prepared. And when the ten heard it, they began to be moved with indignation concerning 42 James and John. And Jesus called them to him, and saith unto them, Ye know that they which are accounted to rule over the Gentiles lord it over them: and their great ones exercise authority over them. 43 But it is not so among you: but whosoever would become great among you, shall be your ¹minister: 44 and whosoever would be first among you, shall be ²servant of 45 all. For verily the Son of man came not to be ministered unto, but to minister, and to give his life a ransom for many.	22 But Jesus answered and said, Ye know not what ye ask. Are ye able to drink the cup that I am about to drink?
	They say unto him, We are able.
	23 He saith unto them, My cup indeed ye shall drink:
	but to sit on my right hand, and on *my* left hand, is not mine to give, but *it is for them* for whom it hath been prepared of 24 my Father. And when the ten heard it, they were moved with indignation concerning the two 25 brethren. But Jesus called them unto him, and said, Ye know that the rulers of the Gentiles lord it over them, and their great ones 26 exercise authority over them. Not so shall it be among you; but whosoever would become great among 27 you shall be your ¹minister; and whosoever would be first among 28 you shall be your ²servant: even as the Son of man came not to be ministered unto, but to minister, and to give his life a ransom for many.

¹ Or, *servant.* ² Gr. *bond-servant.* ³ Or, *but some as they followed were afraid.* ⁴ Or, *Teacher.*
⁵ Or, *through.*

§ 126. BLIND BARTIMÆUS AND HIS COMPANION HEALED

At Jericho

Mark 10:46–52	Matt. 20:29–34	Luke 18:35–43
46 And they come to Jericho: and as he went out from Jericho, with his disciples and a great multitude, the son of Timæus, Bartimæus,	29 And as they went out from Jericho, a great multitude followed him. 30 And be-	35 And it came to pass, as he drew nigh unto Jericho, a cer-

Mark 10:46-52	Matt. 20:29-34	Luke 18:35-43
a blind beggar, was sitting by the way side.	hold, two *blind men sitting by the way side,	tain blind man sat by the way side begging: 36 and hearing a multitude going by, he inquired what this
47 And when he heard that it was Jesus of Nazareth, he began to cry out, and say, Jesus, thou son of David, have mercy 48 on me. And many rebuked him, that he should hold his peace: but he cried out the more a great deal, Thou son of David, have mercy on me. 49 And Jesus stood still, and said, Call ye him. And they call the blind man, saying unto him, Be of good cheer: rise, 50 he calleth thee. And he, casting away his garment, sprang up, and came to Jesus. 51 And Jesus answered him, and said, What wilt thou that I should do unto thee? And the blind man said unto him, ¹Rabboni, that I may re- 52 ceive my sight. And Jesus said unto him, Go thy way; thy faith hath ²made thee whole. And straightway he received his sight, and followed him in the way.	when they heard that Jesus was passing by, cried out, saying, Lord, have mercy on us, thou 31 Son of David. And the multitude rebuked them, that they should hold their peace: but they cried out the more, saying, Lord, have mercy on us, thou son of David. 32 And Jesus stood still, and called them,

and said, What will ye that I should do unto you? 33 They say unto him, Lord, that our eyes 34 may be opened. And Jesus being moved w i t h compassion, touched their eyes: and straightway they received their sight, and followed him. | 37 meant. And they told him, that Jesus of Nazareth passeth 38 by. And he cried, saying, Jesus, thou son of David, have 39 mercy on me. And they that went before rebuked him, that he should hold his peace: but he cried out the more a great deal, Thou son of David. have mercy on me. 40 And Jesus stood, and commanded him to be brought unto him:

and when he was come near, he 41 asked him, What wilt thou that I should do unto thee? And he said, Lord, that I may receive my sight. 42 And Jesus said unto him, Receive thy sight: thy faith hath ²made thee whole. 43 And immediately he received his sight, and followed him, glorifying God: and all the people, when they saw it, gave praise unto God. |

¹ See John 20:16.   ² Or, *saved thee.*

* Matthew mentions two blind men, while Mark and Luke describe one, probably the more conspicuous one.—The discrepancy as to place, "as he went out from Jericho," "as he drew nigh unto Jericho," is best explained by the recent suggestion that the healing occurred after he left the old Jericho, and as he was approaching the new Jericho which Herod the Great had built at some distance away. An older, and also possible explanation was that the blind men made application when he was approaching the city, but were not then healed, and only when he had left the city were they healed. (Comp. Matt. 15:23 ff., and Mark 8:22 f.)

§ 127. JESUS VISITS ZACCHÆUS, AND SPEAKS THE PARABLE OF THE POUNDS,* AND SETS OUT FOR JERUSALEM

Jericho

Luke 19:1-28

1, 2 And he entered and was passing through Jericho. And behold, a man called by name Zacchæus; and he was a chief publican, and he was
3 rich. And he sought to see Jesus who he was; and could not for the crowd,
4 because he was little of stature. And he ran on before, and climbed up
5 into a sycamore tree to see him: for he was to pass that way. And when Jesus came to the place, he looked up, and said unto him, Zacchæus, make
6 haste, and come down; for to-day I must abide at thy house. And he
7 made haste, and came down, and received him joyfully. And when they saw it, they all murmured, saying, He is gone in to lodge with a man that
8 is a sinner. And Zacchæus stood, and said unto the Lord, Behold, Lord, the half of my goods I give to the poor; and if I have wrongfully exacted
9 aught of any man, I restore fourfold [*see Ex. 22:1; Num. 5:6-7*]. And Jesus said unto him, To-day is salvation come to this house, forasmuch
10 as he also is a son of Abraham. For the Son of man came to seek and to save that which was lost [*Ezek. 34:16*].
11 And as they heard these things, he added and spake a parable, because he was nigh to Jerusalem, and *because* they supposed that the
12 kingdom of God was immediately to appear. He said therefore, A certain nobleman went into a far country, to receive for himself a king-
13 dom, and to return. And he called ten ¹servants of his, and gave them
14 ten ²pounds, and said unto them, Trade ye *herewith* till I come. But his citizens hated him, and sent an ambassage after him, saying, We will not
15 that this man reign over us. And it came to pass, when he was come back again, having received the kingdom, that he commanded these ¹servants, unto whom he had given the money, to be called to him, that he might
16 know what they had gained by trading. And the first came before him,
17 saying, Lord, thy pound hath made ten pounds more. And he said unto him, Well done, thou good ³servant: because thou wast found faithful in
18 a very little, have thou authority over ten cities. And the second came,
19 saying, Thy pound, Lord, hath made five pounds. And he said unto him
20 also, Be thou also over five cities. And ⁴another came, saying, Lord,
21 behold, *here is* thy pound, which I kept laid up in a napkin: for I feared thee, because thou art an austere man: thou takest up that thou layedst not
22 down, and reapest that thou didst not sow. He saith unto him, Out of thine own mouth will I judge thee, thou wicked ³servant. Thou knewest that I am an austere man, taking up that I laid not down, and reaping
23 that I did not sow; then wherefore gavest thou not my money into the bank, and ⁵I at my coming should have required it with interest?
24 And he said unto them that stood by, Take away from him the pound,
25 and give it unto him that hath the ten pounds. And they said unto

---

* The similar parable of the Talents was given several days later. See § 139. On this first occasion the illustration has a specific design (ver. 11 f.), which will not appear on the second, *viz.*, to check the wild enthusiasm of the multitude to make Jesus King in Jerusalem as they had once planned a year ago (John 6:15, § 73).

Luke 19:1-28

26 him, Lord, he hath ten pounds. I say unto you, that unto every one that hath shall be given; but from him that hath not, even that which he hath
27 shall be taken away from him. Howbeit these mine enemies, which would not that I should reign over them, bring hither, and slay them before me.
28 And when he had thus spoken, he went on before, going up to Jerusalem.

[1] Gr. *bond-servants.* [2] *Mina,* here translated a pound, is equal to one hundred drachmas. See 15:8. [3] Gr. *bond-servant.* [4] Gr. *the other.* [5] Or. *I should have gone and required.*

PART XI

THE LAST PUBLIC MINISTRY IN JERUSALEM

Friday before to Tuesday of Passion Week, Spring of A.␀. *30 (or* A.D. *29).* Just before Passover.* §§ *128a–138.*

§ 128 a. JESUS ARRIVES AT BETHANY,† NEAR JERUSALEM

Friday afternoon

John 11:55 to 12:1, 9–11

55 Now the passover of the Jews was at hand: and many went up to Jerusalem out of the country before the passover, to purify themselves.
56 They sought therefore for Jesus, and spake one with another, as they stood in the temple, What think ye? That he will not come to the
57 feast? Now the chief priests and the Pharisees had given commandment, that, if any man knew where he was, he should shew it, that they might take him.
1 Jesus therefore six days before the passover came to Bethany, where Lazarus was, whom Jesus raised from the dead.‡
9 The common people therefore of the Jews learned that he was there: and they came, not for Jesus' sake only, but that they might see Lazarus
10 also, whom he raised from the dead. But the chief priests took counsel
11 that they might put Lazarus also to death; because that by reason of him many of the Jews went away, and believed on Jesus.

In §§ *128b–138 we have the Saviour's movements and teachings on Sunday, Monday and Tuesday—the close of his public ministry, except the little that he said during the Jewish and Roman trial. All of his teaching thereafter will be given to his disciples.*

§ 128 b. HIS TRIUMPHAL ENTRY INTO JERUSALEM AS THE MESSIAH§

From Bethany to Jerusalem and back (*Sunday*). A Day of Messianic Demonstration

Mark 11:1–11	Matt. 21:1–11, 14–17	Luke 19:29–44
1 And when they draw nigh	1 And when they drew nigh	29 And it came to pass, when

---

* If the feast of John 5:1 was a Passover, and so his ministry lasted over three years, then his death was pretty certainly in A.D. 30; otherwise in A.D. 29.
† Compare former visits to this Bethany, §§ 104, 118, and see also below, § 141.
‡ John (12:2–8) gives the supper in the house of Simon the leper at this stage, probably because it is the last mention of Bethany in his Gospel. It seems better to follow the order of Mark here in the location of the anointing of Jesus by Mary of Bethany.
§ Jesus now makes a formal challenge to the Jerusalem leaders who have so long opposed his claims. This was a Day of Triumph that seemed to the excited crowds to mean the establishment of a political Messianic Kingdom.

Mark 11:1–11	Matt. 21:1–11, 14–17	Luke 19:29–44	John 12:12–19
unto Jerusalem, unto Bethphage and Bethany, at the mount of Olives,he sendeth two of his 2 disciples, and saith unto them, Go your way into the village that is over against you, and straightway as ye enter into it, ye shall find a colt tied, whereon no man ever yet sat; loose him, and bring him.	unto Jerusalem, and came unto Bethphage, unto the mount of Olives, then Jesus sent two 2 disciples, saying unto them, Go into the village that is over against you, and straightway ye shall find an ass tied, and a colt with her: loose *them*, and bring *them* unto me.	he drew nigh unto Bethphage and Bethany, at the mount that is called *the mount* of Olives, he sent two of the disciples, saying, 30 Go your way into the village over against *you;* in the which as ye enter ye shall find a colt tied, whereon no man ever yet sat: loose him, and bring him.	
3 And if any one say unto you, Why do ye this? say ye, The Lord hath need of him; and straightway ²he will send him ³back 4 hither. And they went away,and found a colt tied at the door without in the open street; and they loose 5 him. And certain of them that stood there said unto them, What do ye, loosing the 6 colt? And they said unto them even as Jesus had said: and	3 And if any one say aught unto you, ye shall say, The Lord hath need of them; and straightway he will send them. 6 And the disciples went, and did even as Jesus appointed them,	31 And if any one ask you, Why do ye loose him? thus shall ye say, The Lord hath need of him. 32 And they that were sent went away, and found even as he had said unto 33 to them. And as they were loosing the colt, the owners thereof said unto them, Why loose ye 34 the colt? And they said, The Lord hath need of him. 35 And they brought him	12 On the morrow ⁹a great multitude that had come to the feast, when they heard that Jesus was coming to Jerusalem, took 13 the branches of the palm trees, and went forth to meet

Mark 11:1–11	Matt. 21:1–11, 14 to 17	Luke 19:29–44	John 12:12–19
they let them 7 go. And they bring the colt unto Jesus, and cast on him their garments; and he sat upon him.	7 and brought the ass and the colt, and put on them their garments, and he sat thereon. 4 Now this is come to pass, that it might be fulfilled which was spoken ¹by the prophet [*see Isa. 62:11; Zech. 9:9*], saying: 5 Tell ye the daughter of Zion, Behold, thy K i n g, c o m e t h unto thee Meek, and riding upon an ass And upon a colt the foal of an ass.	to Jesus: and they threw their garments upon the colt, and set Jesus thereon.	him, and cried out, Hosanna: Blessed *is* he that cometh in the name of the Lord, even the King of 14 Israel. And Jesus, having found a young ass, sat thereon; as it is 15 written, Fear not, daughter of Zion: behold thy King cometh, sitting on an ass's colt. 16 These things understood not his disciples at the first: but when Jesus was glorified, then remembered they that these things were written of him, and that they had done these
8 And m a n y spread their garments upon the way; and others branches, which they had cut from 9 the fields. And they that went before, and they that followed, cried, Hosanna, Blessed *is* he that cometh in the name of the Lord [*see Ps. 118: 25–26*]:	8 And the most part of the m u l t i t u d e spread their garments in the way; and others c u t branches from the trees, and spread them in the way. 9 And the multitudes that went before him, and that followed, cried, saying, Hosanna to the	36 And as he went, they spread their garments in 37 the way. And as he was now drawing nigh, *even* at the descent of the m o u n t o f Olives t h e whole multitude of the disciples began to rejoice and praise God with a loud voice for all	things unto 17 him. The multitude therefore that was with him when he called Lazarus out of the tomb, a n d raised him from the dead bare witness. 18 For this cause also the multitude went and met him, for that they heard that he had done this sign.

154

Mark 11:1-11	Matt. 21:1-11, 14-17	Luke 19:29-44	John 12:12-19
10 Blessed *is* the kingdom that cometh, *the kingdom* of our father David: Hosanna in the highest.	son of David: Blessed *is* he that cometh in the name of the Lord; Hosanna in the highest.	the ⁵mighty works which they had seen; 38 saying, Blessed *is* the King that cometh in the name of the Lord: peace in heaven, and glory in the highest.	19 The Pharisees therefore said among themselves, ¹⁰Behold how ye prevail nothing: lo, the world is gone after him.

39 And some of the Pharisees from the multitude said unto him,

40 ⁶Master, rebuke thy disciples. And he answered and said, I tell you that, if these shall hold their peace, the stones will cry out.

41 And when he drew nigh, he saw the city and wept over it,

42 saying, ⁷If thou hadst known in this day, even thou, the things which belong unto peace! but now

43 they are hid from thine eyes. For the days shall come upon thee, when thine enemies shall cast up a ⁸bank about thee, and compass

44 thee round, and keep thee in on every side, and shall dash thee to the ground, and thy children within thee; and they shall not leave in thee one stone upon another; because thou knewest not the time of thy visitation [*see Ps. 139:9*].

Matt. 21:1-11, 14-17

11 And he entered into Jerusalem,

10 And when he was come into Jerusalem, all the city was stirred,

11 saying, Who is this? And, the multitudes said, This is the prophet, Jesus, from Nazareth

14 of Galilee. And the blind and the lame came to him in the temple: and he healed them.

into the temple;

15 But when the chief priests and the scribes saw the wonderful things that he did, and the children that were crying in the temple and saying, Hosanna to

Mark 11:1-11	Matt. 21:1-11,14-17
	the son of David; they were
	16 moved with indignation, and said unto him, Hearest thou what these are saying? And Jesus saith unto them, Yea: did ye never read [*see Ps.8:2*], Out of the
and when he had looked round about upon all things, it being now eventide, he went out unto Bethany with the twelve.	mouth of babes and sucklings thou 17 hast perfected praise? And he left them, and went forth out of the city to Bethany, and lodged there.

¹ Or, *through.* ² Gr. *sendeth.* ³ Or, *again.* ⁴ Gr. *layers of leaves.* ⁵ Gr. *powers.* ⁶ Or, *Teacher.*
⁷ Or, *O that thou hadst known.* ⁸ Gr. *palisade.* ⁹ Some ancient authorities read *the common people.*
¹⁰ Or, *Ye behold.*

§ 129. THE BARREN FIG TREE CURSED, AND THE SECOND * CLEANSING OF THE TEMPLE. (COMP. § 31)

Bethany and Jerusalem (*Monday*).   A Day of Messianic Power

Mark 11:12-18	Matt. 21:18, 19, 12, 13	Luke 19:45-48
12 And on the morrow, when they were come out from Bethany, he hungered.	18 Now in the morning as he returned to the city, he hungered.	
13 And seeing a fig tree afar off having leaves, he came, if haply he might find anything thereon: and when he came to it, he found nothing but leaves; for it was not the season of figs.	19 And seeing a ¹fig tree by the way side, he came to it and found nothing thereon, but leaves only;	
14 And he answered and said unto it, No man eat fruit from thee henceforward f o r ever. And his disciples heard it.	and he saith unto it, Let there be no fruit from thee henceforward f o r ever.	
15 And they come to Jerusalem: and he entered into the temple, and began to	12 And Jesus entered into the temple ²of God, and cast out all them that sold and	45 And he entered into the temple, and began to cast out them that sold,

* Once more at the close of the Ministry in Jerusalem, as at the beginning, Jesus asserts his authority over the Temple as the Messiah. In both instances his authority is sharply challenged by the Jewish rulers.

Mark 11:12–18	Matt. 21:18, 19, 12, 13	Luke 19:45–48
cast out them that sold and them that bought in the temple, and overthrew the tables of the money-changers, and the seats of them that 16 sold the doves; and he would not suffer that any man should carry a vessel through 17 the temple. And he taught, and said unto them, Is it not written, My house shall be called a house of prayer for all the nations? but ye have made it a den of 18 robbers. And the chief priests and the scribes heard it, and sought how they might destroy him: for they feared him, for all the multitude was astonished at his teaching.	bought in the temple, and overthrew the tables of the money-changers, and the seats of them that sold the doves; 13 and he saith unto them, It is written, My house shall be called a house of prayer: but ye make it a den of robbers.	46 say-ing unto them, It is written [see Isa. 56:7; Jer. 7:11], And my house shall be a house of prayer: but ye have made it a den of robbers. 47 And he was teach·ing daily in the temple. But the chief priests and the scribes and the principal men of the people sought to destroy 48 him: and they could not find what they might do; for the people all hung upon him, listening.

¹ Or, *a single.*   ² Some ancient authorities omit *of God.*

§ 130. THE DESIRE OF SOME GREEKS TO SEE JESUS PUZZLES THE DISCIPLES AND LEADS JESUS IN AGITATION OF SOUL TO INTERPRET LIFE AND DEATH AS SACRIFICE AND TO SHOW HOW BY BEING "LIFTED UP" HE WILL DRAW ALL MEN TO HIM

Jerusalem (*Monday*)

John 12:20–50

20 Now there were certain Greeks among those that went up to worship
21 at the feast: these therefore came to Philip, which was of Bethsaida of
22 Galilee, and asked him saying, Sir, we would see Jesus. Philip cometh
and telleth Andrew: Andrew cometh, and Philip, and they tell Jesus.

John 12:20–50

23 And Jesus answereth them, saying, The hour is come, that the Son of
24 man should be glorified.   Verily, verily, I say unto you, Except a grain
of wheat fall into the earth and die, it abideth by itself alone; but if it
25 die, it beareth much fruit.   He that loveth his ¹life loseth it; and he that
26 hateth his ¹life in this world shall keep it unto life eternal.   If any man
serve me, let him follow me; and where I am, there shall also my servant
27 be: if any man serve me, him will the Father honour.   Now is my soul
troubled; and what shall I say [see Ps. 42:6]?   Father, save me from this
²hour.   But for this cause came I unto this hour.   Father, glorify thy
28 name.   There came therefore a voice out of heaven, saying, I have both
29 glorified it, and will glorify it again.   The multitude therefore, that stood
by, and heard it, said that it had thundered: others said, An angel hath
30 spoken to him.   Jesus answered and said, This voice hath not come for
31 my sake, but for your sakes.   Now is ³the judgement of this world: now
32 shall the prince of this world be cast out.   And I, If I be lifted up´from
33 the earth, will draw all men unto myself.   But this he said, signifying by
34 what manner of death he should die.   The multitude therefore answered
him, We have heard out of the law that the Christ abideth for ever: and
how sayest thou, The Son of man must be lifted up? who is this Son of
35 man?   Jesus therefore said unto them, Yet a little while is the light
⁴among you.   Walk while ye have the light, that darkness overtake you
not: and he that walketh in the darkness knoweth not whither he goeth.
36 While ye have the light, believe on the light, that ye may become sons of
light.
These things spake Jesus, and he departed and ⁵hid himself from them.
37 But though he had done so many signs before them, yet they believed
38 not* on him: that the word of Isaiah the prophet might be fulfilled [see
Isa. 53:1], which he spake,
Lord, who hath believed our report?
And to whom hath the arm of the Lord been revealed?
39 For this cause they could not believe, for that Isaiah said again,
40 He hath blinded their eyes, and he hardened their heart;
Lest they should see with their eyes, and perceive with their heart,
And should turn,
And I should heal them.
41 These things said Isaiah [see Isa. 6: 1, 10], because he saw his glory: and he
42 spake of him.   Nevertheless even of the rulers many believed on him;
but because of the Pharisees they did not confess ⁷it, lest they should be
43 put out of the synagogue; for they loved the glory of men more than the
glory of God.
44 And Jesus cried and said, He that believeth on me, believeth not on
45 me, but on him that sent me.   And he that beholdeth me beholdeth
46 him that sent me.   I am come a light into the world, that whosoever
47 believeth on me may not abide in the darkness.   And if any man hear
my sayings, and keep them not, I judge him not: for I came not to judge
48 the world, but to save the world.   He that rejecteth me, and receiveth
not my sayings, hath one that judgeth him: the word that I spake, the
49 same shall judge him in the last day.   For I spake not from myself; but

---

* The rejection of Jesus by the Jews is clearly set forth by John's Gospel   The Pharisees made
many timid and afraid.

John 12:20–50

the Father which sent me, he hath given me a commandment, what I
50 should say, and what I should speak. And I know that his commandment is life eternal: the things therefore which I speak, even as the Father
hath said unto me, so I speak.

¹ Or, *soul.* ² Or, *hour?* ³ Or, *a judgement.* ⁴ Or, *out of.* ⁵ Or, *in.* ⁶ Or, *was hidden from them.*
⁷ Or, *him.*

§ 131. THE BARREN FIG TREE FOUND TO HAVE WITHERED

On the way from Bethany to Jerusalem. (*Tuesday**)

Mark 11:19–25	Matt. 21:19–22	Luke 21:37, 38
19 And ¹every evening ²he went forth 20 out of the city. And as they passed by in the morning, they saw the fig tree withered away from 21 the roots. And Peter calling to remembrance saith unto him, Rabbi, behold, the fig tree which thou cursedst is with22 ered away. And Jesus answering saith unto them, Have 23 faith in God. Verily I say unto you, Whosoever shall say unto this mountain, Be thou taken up and cast into the sea; and shall not doubt in his heart, but shall believe that what he saith cometh to pass; he shall have it. 24 Therefore I say unto you, All things whatsoever ye pray and	19 And immediately the fig tree withered 20 away. And when the disciples saw it, they marvelled, saying, How did the fig t r e e immediately 21 wither away? And Jesus answered and said unto them, Verily I say unto you, If ye have faith, and doubt not, ye shall not only do what is done to the fig tree, but even if ye shall say unto this mountain, Be thou taken up and cast into the sea, it shall be done. 22 And all things, whatsoever ye shall ask in prayer, believing, ye shall receive.	37 And every day he was teaching in the temple; and every night he went out, and lodged in the mount that is called *the mount* of Olives. 38 And all the people came early in the morning to him in the temple, to hear him.

ask for, believe that ye have received them, and ye shall have them.
25 And whensoever ye stand praying, forgive, if ye have aught against any
one; that your Father also which is in heaven may forgive you your
trespasses.³

¹ Gr. *whenever evening came.* ² Some ancient authorities read *they.* ³ Many ancient authorities
add ver. 26 *But if ye do not forgive, neither will your Father which is in heaven forgive your trespasses*

* The Synoptic Gospels give more details of the teaching of Jesus on this Tuesday in the Temple
and on the Mount of Olives than for any other single day. We had another Busy Day in Galilee
(§§ 61–66).

§ 132. THE RULERS (SANHEDRIN) FORMALLY CHALLENGE* THE AUTHORITY OF JESUS AS AN ACCREDITED TEACHER (RABBI)

Jesus bases His human authority on John the Baptist, His Forerunner who baptized him, and demands the Sanhedrin's opinion of the Baptism of John. This pertinent counter-question paralyzes the Jewish leaders and Jesus drives His argument home by three parables. (a) Parable of the Two Sons. (b) Parable of the Wicked Husbandmen. (c) Parable of the Marriage Feast of the King's Son.

In the court of the Temple.   (*Tuesday†*)   A Day of Controversy

Mark 11:27–12:12	Matt. 21:23–22:14	Luke 20:1–19
27 And they come again to Jerusalem: and as he was walking in the temple, there come to him the chief priests, and the scribes, and the 28 elders; and they said unto him,	23 And when he was come into the temple, the chief priests and the elders of the people came unto him as he was teaching, and said,	1 And it came to pass, on one of the days, as he was teaching the people in the temple, and preaching the gospel, there came upon him the chief priests and the scribes 2 with the elders; and they spake, saying unto him, Tell us: By
By what authority doest thou these things? or who gave thee this authority to do these things? 29 And Jesus said unto them, I will ask of you one ¹question, and answer me, and I will tell you by what authority I do 30 these things. The baptism of John, was it from heaven, or from men? answer me. 31 And they reasoned	By what authority doest thou these things? and who gave thee 24 this authority? And Jesus answered and said unto them, I also will ask you one ¹question, which if ye tell me, I likewise will tell you by what authority I do these 25 things. The baptism of John, whence was it? from heaven or from men? And they reasoned with them-	what authority doest thou these things? or who is he that gave thee this authority? 3 And he answered and said unto them, I also will ask you a ¹question; and tell me: 4 The baptism of John, was it from heaven, or from men? 5 And they reasoned with them-

---

* It was very common to test a Rabbi with hard questions. See this continued in the following sections. In like manner the Fourth Gospel gave us much animated dialogue between Jesus and the Jews at Jerusalem in chap. 5, and chap. 7–10. The Sanhedrin were within their rights in challenging the ecclesiastical and scholastic (scribal) standing of Jesus. He did not dodge in his answer.

† On this last day of Christ's public ministry the Sanhedrin seek to break the power of Jesus with the people whose hero he is since the Triumphal Entry. The first attempt fails miserably, but it is followed by a series of other efforts to entrap Jesus and so turn the crowd against him. The three parables leave the rulers exposed by Jesus and they keenly feel the denunciation of the reply of Jesus.

Mark 11:27–12:12	Matt. 21:23–22:14	Luke 20:1–19
with themselves, saying, If we shall say, From heaven; he will say, Why then did ye not believe him? 32 ⁷But should we say, From men—they feared the people: ⁸for all verily held John 33 to be a prophet. And they answered Jesus and said, We know not. And Jesus saith unto them, Neither tell I you by what authority I do these things.	selves, saying, If we shall say, From heaven; he will say unto us, Why then did ye 26 not believe him? But if we shall say, From men; we fear the multitude; for all hold John as a prophet. 27 And they answered Jesus, and said, We know not. He also said unto them, Neither tell I you by what authority I do these things. 28 But what think ye? A man had two sons; And he came to the first, and said, ²Son, go work to-day in the 29 vineyard. And he answered and said, I will not: but afterward he repented himself, and went. 30 And he came to the second, and said likewise. And he answered and said, I *go*, sir: and went not. 31 Whether of the twain did the will of his father? They say, The first. Jesus saith unto them, Verily I say unto you, that the publicans and the harlots go into the kingdom of God before you. For John 32 came unto you in the way of righteousness, and ye believed him not: but the publicans and the harlots believed him: and ye, when ye saw it, did not even repent your-	selves, saying, If we shall say, From heaven; he will say, Why did ye not be- 6 lieve him? But if we shall say, From men; all the people will stone us: for they be persuaded that John was a 7 prophet. And they answered, that they knew not whence *it* 8 *was*. And Jesus said unto them, Neither tell I you by what authority I do these things.

Mark 11:27–12:12	Matt. 21:23–22:14	Luke 20:1–19
	selves afterward, that ye might believe him.	
1 And he began to speak unto them in parables. A man planted a vineyard, and set a hedge about it, and digged a pit for the wine-press, and built a tower, and let it out to husbandmen, and went into another country.	33 Hear another parable: There was a man that was a householder, which planted a vineyard, and set a hedge about it, and digged a wine-press in it, and built a tower, and let it out to husbandmen, and went into another country.	9 And he began to speak unto the people this parable [*see Isa. 5:1–2*]: A man planted a vineyard,
2 And at the season he sent to the husbandmen a ²servant, that he might receive from the husbandmen of the fruits of the vine-3 yard. And they took him, and beat him, and sent him away 4 empty. And again he sent unto them another ²servant: and him they wounded in the head, and handled 5 shamefully. And he sent another; and him they killed: and many others; beating some, 6 and killing some. He had yet one, a beloved son: he sent him last unto them, saying, they will reverence 7 my son. But those husbandmen said a-mong themselves, This is the heir; come, let us kill him, and the inheritance shall be ours.	34 And when the season of the fruits drew near, he sent his ²servants to the husbandmen, to receive ⁴his fruits. 35 And the husbandmen took his ²servants, and beat one, and killed another, and stoned a n o t h e r. 36 Again, he sent other ²servants more than the first: and they did unto them in like manner.	and let it out to husbandmen, and went into another country for a long 10 time. And at the season he sent unto the husbandmen a ²servant, that they should give him of the fruit of the vineyard: but the husbandmen beat him, and sent him away empty. 11 And he sent yet another ²servant: and him also they beat, and handled him shamefully, and sent him away empty. 12 And he sent yet a third: and him also they wounded, and 13 cast him forth. And the Lord of the vine-yard said, What shall I do? I will send my beloved son: it may be they will reverence him.
8 And they took him, and killed him, and cast him forth out of the 9 vineyard. W h a t	37 But afterward he sent unto them his son, saying, They will reverence my son. 38 But the husbandmen, when they saw the son, said among themselves, This is the heir; come let us kill him and take his inheritance. 39 And they took him, and cast him forth out of the vineyard, and	14 But when the husbandmen saw him, they reasoned one with another, say-ing, This is the heir: let us kill him, that the inheritance may 15 be ours. And they cast him forth out of the vineyard, and killed him. What

Mark 11:27–12:12	Matt. 21:23–22:14	Luke 20:1–19
therefore will the lord of the vineyard do?	40 killed him. When therefore the lord of the vineyard shall come, what will he do unto those hus- 41 bandmen? They say	therefore will the lord of the vineyard do unto them?
he will come and destroy the hus- bandmen, and will give the vineyard unto others.	unto him, He will miserably destroy those miserable men, and will let out the vineyard unto other husbandmen, which shall render him the fruits in their sea- 42 sons. Jesus saith	16 He will come and de- stroy these husband- men, and will give the vineyard unto others. And when they heard it, they said, ¹⁰God forbid.
10 Have ye not read even this scripture; The stone which the builders re- jected, The same was made the head of the corner: 11 This was from the Lord, And it is marvellous in our eyes?	unto them, Did ye never read in the scriptures [*see Ps. 118: 22–23*], The stone which the builders re- jected, The same was made the head of the corner: This was from the Lord, And it is marvel- lous in our eyes?	17 But he looked upon them, and said, What then is this that is written [*see Ps. 118: 22*], The stone which the builders re- jected, The same was made the head of the corner?
	43 Therefore say I unto you, the kingdom of God shall be taken away from you, and shall be given to a nation bringing forth the fruits thereof.	
	44 ⁵And he that falleth on this stone shall be broken to pieces; but on whomsoever it shall fall, it will scat- 45 ter him as dust. And when the chief priests and the Pharisees heard his parables, they perceived that he spake of them.	18 Every one that falleth on that stone shall be broken to pieces; but on whomsoever it shall fall, it will scat- ter him as dust [*see Isa. 8:14–15*]. 19 And the scribes and the chief priests
12 And they sought to lay hold on him; and they feared the multi-	46 And when they sought to lay hold on him, they feared the	sought to lay hands on him in that very

Mark 11:27–12:12	Matt. 21:23–22:14	Luke 20:1–19
tude; for they perceived that he spake the parable against them: and they left him and went away.	multitudes, because they took him for a prophet.	hour; and they feared the people: for they perceived that he spake this parable against them.

1 And Jesus answered and spake again in parables unto them, saying,
2 The kingdom of heaven is likened unto a certain king, which made a
3 marriage feast for his son, and sent forth his ²servants to call them that
4 were bidden to the marriage feast: and they would not come. Again he
sent forth other ³servants, saying, tell them that are bidden, Behold, I
have made ready my dinner: my oxen and my fatlings are killed, and all
5 things are ready; come to the marriage feast. But they made light of it,
and went their ways, one to his own farm, another to his merchandise:
6 and the rest laid hold on his ³servants, and entreated them shamefully,
7 and killed them. But the king was wroth; and he sent his armies, and
8 destroyed those murderers, and burned their city. Then saith he to his
³servants, The wedding is ready, but they that were bidden were not
9 worthy. Go ye therefore unto the partings of the highways, and as many
10 as ye shall find, bid to the marriage feast. And those ³servants went out
into the highways, and gathered together all as many as they found, both
11 bad and good: and the wedding was filled with guests. But when the king
came in to behold the guests, he saw there a man which had not on a
12 wedding-garment; and he saith unto him, Friend, how camest thou in
hither not having a wedding-garment? And he was speechless. Then
13 the king said to the ⁴servants, Bind him hand and foot, and cast him out
into the outer darkness; there shall be the weeping and gnashing of teeth.
14 For many are called, but few chosen.

¹ Gr. *word.*   ² Gr. *Child.*   ³ Gr. *bond-servants.*   ⁴ Or, *the fruits of it.*   ⁵ Some ancient authorities omit ver. 44.   ⁶ Or, *ministers.*   ⁷ Or, *But shall we say, From men?*   ⁸ Or, *for all held John to be a prophet indeed.*   ⁹ Gr. *bond-servant.*   ¹⁰ Gr. *Be it not so.*

§ 133. THE PHARISEES AND THE HERODIANS TRY TO ENSNARE JESUS ABOUT PAYING TRIBUTE TO CÆSAR

Mark 12:13–17	Matt. 22:15–22	Luke 20:20-26
13 And they send unto him certain of the Pharisees and of the Herodians, that they might catch him in talk. 14 And when they were come, they say	15 Then went the Pharisees, and took counsel how they might ensnare him in *his* 16 talk. And they send to him their disciples*, with the Hero-	20 And they watched him, and sent forth spies, which feigned themselves to be righteous, that they might take hold of his speech, so as to deliver him up to the rule and to the au-

* The Pharisees send a group of their keenest students to go with the Herodians to catch Jesus with the dilemma about paying tribute to Cæsar, a live question in current politics and theology. They offered Jesus the alternative of popular disfavor or of disloyalty to the Roman government.

Mark 12:13-17	Matt. 22:15-22	Luke 20:20-26
unto him, ¹Master, we know that thou art true, and carest not for any one; for thou regardest not the person of men, but of a truth teachest the way of God: Is it lawful to give tribute unto Cæsar, or not? Shall we give, or shall we not 15 give? But he, knowing their hypocrisy, said unto them, Why tempt ye me? bring me a ²penny, that I 16 may see it. And they brought it. And he saith unto them,	dians, saying, ¹Master, we know that thou art true, and teachest the way of God in truth, and carest not for any one: for thou regardest not the person of 17 men. Tell us therefore, What thinkest thou? Is it lawful to give tribute unto 18 Cæsar, or not? But Jesus perceived their wickedness, and said, Why tempt ye me, 19 ye hypocrites? Shew me the tribute money. And they brought unto him a 20 ²penny. And he saith	thority of the governor. And they 21 asked him, saying, ¹Master, we know that thou sayest and teachest rightly, and acceptest not the person *of any*, but of a 22 truth teachest the way of God [*see John 3:2*]: Is it lawful for us to give tribute unto Cæsar, or not? 23 But he perceived their craftiness, and said unto 24 them, Shew me a ²penny.
Whose is this image and superscription? And they said unto 17 him, Cæsar's. And Jesus said unto them, Render unto Cæsar the things that are Cæsar's, and unto God the things that are God's.	unto them, Whose is this image and super- 21 scription? They say unto him, Cæsar's. Then saith he unto them, Render therefore unto Cæsar the things that are Cæsar's;and untoGod the things that are God's.	Whose image and superscription hath it? And they 25 said, Cæsar's. And he said unto them, Then render unto Cæsar the things that are Cæsar's, and unto God the things that 26 are God's. And they were not able to take
And they marvelled greatly at him.	22 And when they heard it, they marvelled, and left him, and went their way.	hold of the saying before the people: and they marvelled at his answer, and held their peace.

¹ Or. *Teacher.*   ² See marginal note on Matt. 18:28.

§ 134. THE SADDUCEES ASK HIM A PUZZLING QUES· TION* ABOUT THE RESURRECTION

In the Court of the Temple. (*Tuesday*)

Mark 12:18-27	Matt. 22:23-33	Luke 20:27-40
18 And there come unto him Sadducees, which say that there	23 On that day there came to him Sadducees, ¹which say that	27 And there came to him certain of the Sadducees, t h e y

* Probably a stock conundrum that the Sadducees had often propounded to the discomfort of the Pharisees.

Mark 12:18–27

is no resurrection;
and they asked him,
19 saying, ²Master,
Moses wrote unto us,
If a man's brother
die, and leave a wife
behind him, and
leave no child, that
his brother should
take his wife, and
raise up seed unto
20 his brother. There

were seven brethren:
and the first took a
wife, and dying left
21 no seed; and the sec-
ond took her, and
died, leaving no seed
behind him; and the
22 third likewise: and
the seven left no
seed. Last of all the
woman also died.
23 In the resurrection
whose wife shall she
be of them? for the
seven had her to
24 wife. Jesus said un-
to them, Is it not for
this cause that ye
err, that ye know
not the scriptures,
nor the power of
God?

25   For when they
shall rise from the
dead, they neither
marry, nor are given
in marriage; but are

as angels in heaven.

Matt. 22:23–33

there is no resurrec-
24 tion: and they asked
him, saying, ²Master,
Moses said, If a man
die, having no chil-
dren, his brother
³shall marry his wife,
and raise up seed un-
to his brother.

25   Now
there were with us
seven brethren: and
the first married and
deceased, and having
no seed left his wife
26 unto his brother: in
like manner the sec-
ond also, and the
third, unto the ⁴sev-
27 enth. And after them
all the woman died.
28 In the resurrection
therefore whose wife
shall she be of the
seven? for they all
29 had her. But Jesus
answered and said
unto them, Ye do
err, not knowing the
scriptures, nor the
power of God.

30 For in the resurrec-
tion they neither
marry, nor are given
in marriage, but are

as angels ⁵in heaven.

Luke 20:27–40

which say that there
is no resurrection;
and they asked him,
28 saying, ²Master,
Moses wrote unto us
[*see Gen. 38:8; Deut.
25:5–6*], that if a
man's brother die,
having a wife, and
he be childless, his
brother should take
the wife, and raise
up seed unto his
29 brother. There were
therefore seven breth-
ren; and the first
30 took a wife, and died
childless, and the
31 second; and the third
took her; and like-
wise the seven also
left no children; and
died.
32   Afterward
the woman also died.
33 In the resurrection
therefore whose wife
of them shall she be?
for the seven had her
34 to wife. And Jesus
said unto them,

The
sons of this ⁵world
marry, and are given
35 in marriage: but they
that are accounted
worthy to attain to
that ⁶world, and the
resurrection from the
dead, neither marry,
nor are given in mar-
36 riage: for neither can
they die any more:
for they are equal un-
to the angels; and
are sons of God, being
sons of the resurrec-

Mark 12:18-27	Matt. 22:23-33	Luke 20:27-40
26 But as touching the dead, that they are raised; have ye not read in the book of Moses, in *the place concerning* the Bush, how God spake unto him, saying, I *am* the God of Abraham, and the God of Isaac, and the God of Jacob?	31 But as touching the resurrection of the dead, have ye not read that which was spoken unto you by God, saying,	37 tion. But that the dead are raised,
	32 I am the God of Abraham, and the God of Isaac, and the God of Jacob? God is not *the God* of the dead, but of the	even Moses showed in *the place concerning* the Bush, when he calleth the Lord the God of Abraham, and the God of Isaac, and the
♂7 He is not the God of the dead, but of the living: ye do greatly err.	33 living. And when the multitudes heard it, they were astonished at his teaching.	38 God of Jacob [*see Ex. 3:6*]. Now he is not the God of the dead, but of the living: for all live unto him.
		39 And certain of the scribes answering said, ²Master, thou
		40 hast well said. For they durst not any more ask him any question.

¹ Gr. *saying.* ² Or, *Teacher.* ³ Gr. *shall perform the duty of a husband's brother to his wife.* Compare Deut. 25:5. ⁴ Gr. *seven.* ⁵ Many ancient authorities add *of God.* ⁶ Or, *age.*

§ 135. THE PHARISEES REJOICE OVER THE ROUT OF THE SADDUCEES AND A PHARISAIC LAWYER ASKS JESUS A LEGAL QUESTION

In the Court of the Temple. (*Tuesday*)

Mark 12:28-34	Matt. 22:34-40
28 And one of the scribes came, and heard them questioning together, and knowing that he had answered them well, asked him,	34 But the Pharisees, when they heard that he had put the Sadducees to silence, gathered themselves together. And one of them,
	35 selves together. And one of them, a lawyer, asked him a question,
What commandment is the first of all	36 tempting him, ¹Master, which is the great commandment in the
29 [*see Deut. 6:4*]? Jesus answered, The first is, Hear, O Israel; ³The Lord our God [*see Deut. 6:4*], the	law? And he said unto him,
30 Lord is one: and thou shalt love the Lord thy God ⁴with all thy heart, and ⁴with all thy soul, and ⁴with all thy mind, and ⁴with all	37 Thou shalt love the Lord thy God with all thy heart, and with all thy soul,
31 thy strength [*see Deut. 6:5*]. The second is this, Thou shalt love thy neighbour as thyself [*see Lev.*	38 and with all thy mind. This is the great and first commandment.
	39 ²And a second like *unto it* is this, Thou shalt love thy neighbour as

Mark 12:28–34	Matt. 22:34–40
19:18]. There is none other commandment greater than these. 32 And the scribe said unto him, Of a truth, ¹Master, thou hast well said that he is one; and there is none other but he: and to 33 love him with all the heart, and with all the understanding, and with all the strength, and to love his neighbour as himself, is much more than all whole burnt offerings and sacrifices [*see 1 Sam. 15:* 34 *22*]. And when Jesus saw that he answered discreetly, he said unto him, Thou art not far from the kingdom of God. And no man after that durst ask him any question.	40 thyself. On these two commandments hangeth the whole law, and the prophets.

¹ Or, *Teacher.* ² Or, *And a second is like unto it, Thou shalt love, etc.* ³ Or, *The Lord is our God: the Lord is one.* ⁴ Gr. *from.*

§ 136. JESUS, TO THE JOY OF THE MULTITUDE, SILENCES HIS ENEMIES BY THE PERTINENT QUESTION OF THE MESSIAH'S DESCENT FROM DAVID AND LORDSHIP OVER DAVID

In the Court of the Temple. (*Tuesday*)

Mark 12:35–37	Matt. 22:41–46	Luke 20:41–44
	41 Now while the Pharisees were gathered together, Jesus asked them a ques-	
35 And Jesus answered and said, as he taught in the temple, How say the scribes that the Christ is the son of David?	42 tion, saying, What think ye of the Christ? whose son is he? They say unto him, *The son* of David.	41 And he said unto them, How say they that the Christ is David's son?
	43 He saith unto them, How then doth David	
36 David himself said in the Holy Spirit, [*see Ps. 110:1*],	in the Spirit call him Lord, saying,	42 For David himself saith in the book of Psalms,
The Lord said unto my Lord, Sit thou on my right hand, Till I make thine enemies ¹the footstool of thy feet.	44 The Lord said unto my Lord, Sit thou on my right hand, Till I put thine enemies underneath thy feet?	The Lord said unto my Lord, Sit thou on my right hand, 43 Till I make thine enemies the footstool of thy feet.

Mark 12:35-37	Matt. 22:41-46	Luke 20:41-44
37 David himself calleth him Lord; and whence is he his son? And ²the common people heard him gladly.	45 If David then calleth him Lord, how is he 46 his son? And no one was able to answer him a word, neither durst any man from that day forth ask him any more questions.	44 David therefore calleth him Lord, and how is he his son?

¹ Some ancient authorities read, *underneath thy feet.*   ² Or, *the great multitude.*

§ 137. IN HIS LAST PUBLIC DISCOURSE, JESUS SOLEMNLY DENOUNCES* THE SCRIBES AND PHARISEES (COMP. § 107)

In the Court of the Temple.   (*Tuesday*)

Mark 12:38-40	Matt. 23:1-39	Luke 20:45-47
38 And in his teaching he said, Beware of the scribes,	1 Then spake Jesus to the multitudes and to his disciples, 2 saying, The scribes and the Pharisees sit on Moses' seat: all 3 things therefore whatsoever they bid you, *these* do and observe: but do not ye after their works; for they say, and do not. 4 Yea, they bind heavy burdens ¹and grievous to be borne, and lay them on men's shoulders; but they themselves will not move them with their finger. 5 But all their works they do for to be seen of men [*see Ex. 13: 9; Num. 13; 38-39; Deut. 6:8; 11:18*]: for they make broad their phylacteries, and enlarge the borders *of their garments*,	45 And in the hearing of all the people he said unto his disci-46 ples, Beware of the scribes,
which de-sire to walk in long		which desire to walk in long robes,

* Jesus has been criticized for lack of self-control in this exposure of the hypocrisy of the Pharisees. One must bear in mind the tremendous sins of which the Pharisees are guilty. The very teachers of righteousness are now in the act of rejecting and finally crucifying the Son of God. ꜱₑₑ my book, *The Pharisees and Jesus,* for full discussion.

Mark 12:38-40	Matt. 23:1-39	Luke 20:45-47
robes, and *to have* salutations in the 39 marketplaces, and chief seats in the synagogues, and chief places at feasts:	6 and love the chief place at feasts, and the chief seats in the 7 synagogues, and the salutations in the marketplaces, and to be called of men, 8 Rabbi. But be not ye called Rabbi: for one is your teacher, and all ye are breth- 9 ren. And call no man your father on the earth: for one is your Father, ²which 10 is in heaven. Neither be ye called masters: for one is your master, *even* the 11 Christ. But he that is ³greatest among you shall be your 12 ⁴servant. And who- soever shall exalt himself shall be hum- bled; and whosoever shall humble himself shall be exalted. 13 But woe unto you, scribes and Pharisees, hypocrites! because ye shut the king- dom of h e a v e n ⁵against men: for ye enter not in your- selves, neither suffer ye them that are en- tering in to enter.⁶	and love salutations in the marketplaces, and chief seats in the synagogues, and chief places at feasts;
40 they which devour widows' houses, ¹²and for a pretence make long prayers; these shall receive greater condemnation.		47 which de- vour widows' houses, and for a pretence make long prayers: these shall receive greater condemna- tion.
	15 Woe unto you, scribes and Pharisees, hypo- crites! for ye compass sea and land to make one proselyte; and when he is become so, ye make him twofold more a son of ⁷hell than yourselves.	

Matt. 23:1–39

16 Woe unto you, ye blind guides, which say, Whosoever shall swear by
the *temple, it is nothing; but whosoever shall swear by the gold of the
17 *temple he is *a debtor. Ye fools and blind: for whether is greater, the
18 gold, or the *temple that hath sanctified the gold? And, Whosoever
shall swear by the altar, it is nothing; but whosoever shall swear by the
19 gift that is upon it, he is *a debtor. Ye blind: for whether is greater, the
20 gift, or the altar that sanctified the gift? He therefore that sweareth
21 by the altar, sweareth by it, and by all things thereon. And he that
sweareth by the *temple, sweareth by it, and by him that dwelleth therein.
22 And he that sweareth by the heaven, sweareth by the throne of God, and
by him that sitteth thereon.

23 Woe unto you, scribes and Pharisees, hypocrites! for ye tithe mint and
¹⁰anise and cummin [*see Lev. 27:30; Mic. 6:8*], and have left undone the
weightier matters of the law, judgement, and mercy, and faith: but these
24 ye ought to have done, and not to have left the other undone. Ye blind
guides, which strain out the gnat, and swallow the camel.

25 Woe unto you, scribes and Pharisees, hypocrites! for ye cleanse the
outside of the cup and of the platter, but within they are full from ex-
26 tortion and excess. Thou blind Pharisee, cleanse first the inside of the
cup and of the platter, that the outside thereof may become clean also.

27 Woe unto you, scribes and Pharisees, hypocrites! for ye are like unto
whited sepulchres, which outwardly appear beautiful, but inwardly are
28 full of dead men's bones, and of all uncleanness. Even so ye also outwardly appear righteous unto men, but inwardly ye are full of hypocrisy
and iniquity.

29 Woe unto you, scribes and Pharisees, hypocrites! for ye build the
sepulchres of the prophets, and garnish the tombs of the righteous, and
30 say, If we had been in the days of our fathers, we should not have been
31 partakers with them in the blood of the prophets. Wherefore ye witness
32, 33 to yourselves, that ye are sons of them that slew the prophets. Fill ye
up then the measure of your fathers. Ye serpents, ye offspring of vipers,
34 how shall ye escape the judgement of ⁷hell? Therefore, behold, I send
unto you prophets, and wise men, and scribes: some of them shall ye kill
and crucify: and some of them shall ye scourge in your synagogues, and
35 persecute from city to city: that upon you may come all the righteous
blood shed on the earth, from the blood of Abel the righteous unto the
blood of Zachariah son of Barachiah, whom ye slew between the sanctuary
36 and the altar [*see Gen. 4:8; 2 Chron. 24: 20–21*]. Verily I say unto you, All
these things shall come upon this generation.

37 O Jerusalem, Jerusalem, which killeth the prophets, and stoneth them
that are sent unto her! how often would I have gathered thy children
together, even as a hen gathereth her chickens under her wings, and ye
38 would not! Behold, your house is left unto you ¹¹desolate [*see Jer. 12:7;
39 22:5*]. For I say unto you, Ye shall not see me henceforth, till ye shall
say, blessed *is* he that cometh in the name of the Lord [*see Ps. 118:26*].

¹ Many ancient authorities omit *and grievous to be borne.* ² Gr. *the heavenly.* ³ Gr. *greater.*
⁴ Or, *minister.* ⁵ Gr. *before.* ⁶ Some authorities insert here or after ver. 12, ver. 14, *Woe unto you,
scribes and Pharisees, hypocrites! for ye devour widows' houses, even while for a pretence ye make long
prayers; therefore ye shall receive greater condemnation.* See Mark 12:40: Luke 20:47, above. ⁷ Gr
Gehenna. ⁸ Or, *sanctuary;* as in ver. 35. ⁹ Or, *bound by his oath.* ¹⁰ Or, *dill.* ¹¹ Some ancient
authorities omit *desolate.* ¹² Or, *even while for a pretence they make.*

§ 138. JESUS CLOSELY OBSERVES* THE CONTRIBUTIONS IN THE TEMPLE, AND COMMENDS THE POOR WIDOW'S GIFT

(*Tuesday*)

Mark 12:41–44

41 And he sat down over against the treasury, and beheld how the multitude cast ¹money into the treasury: and many that were 42 rich cast in much. And there came ²a poor widow, and she cast in two mites, which make a 43 farthing. And he called unto him his disciples, and said unto them, Verily I say unto you, This poor widow cast in more than all they which are casting into the 44 treasury: for they all did cast in of their superfluity; but she of her want did cast in all that she had, *even* all her living.

Luke 21:1–4

1 And he looked up, ³and saw the rich men that were casting their 2 gifts into the treasury. And he saw a certain poor widow casting in thither two mites.

3 And he said, Of a truth I say unto you, This poor widow cast in more 4 than they all: for all these did of their superfluity cast in unto the gifts: but she of her want did cast in all the living that she had.

¹ Gr. *brass*.   ² Gr. *one*.   ³ Or, *and saw them that . . . treasury, and they were rich*.

* Notice that this was the last occurrence in the Saviour's public ministry, except the trial and the crucifixion. This is the last appearance of Jesus in the Temple. His public teaching is over save the words of defence in his trial and the seven sayings on the Cross. The Pharisees and Sadducees had withdrawn in terror at the explosion of the wrath of Jesus and even the disciples were at some distance as Jesus sat alone by the treasury. It is useless further to plead with his enemies. The task now remains to get the disciples prepared for the Master's death and the time is short and they as yet have completely failed to grasp the fact or the significance of his death and the promise of his resurrection on the third day.

PART XII

IN THE SHADOW WITH JESUS

Tuesday afternoon to Thursday night of Passion Week, A.D. *30 (or 29). Jerusalem.*

§§ *139–152. Jesus now seeks to prepare the disciples for the tragedy of His death and for carrying on His work after His departure.*

§ 139. SITTING ON THE MOUNT OF OLIVES, JESUS SPEAKS TO HIS DISCIPLES ABOUT THE DESTRUCTION OF JERUSALEM, AND HIS OWN SECOND COMING, IN APOCALYPTIC LANGUAGE. THE GREAT ESCHATOLOGICAL DISCOURSE*

(Tuesday Afternoon)

	Mark 13:1–37	Matt. 24 and 25	Luke 21:5–36
1 Occasion of the Prophecy about the Destruction of the Temple.	1 And as he went forth out of the temple, one of his disciples saith unto him, ¹⁸Master, behold, what manner of stones and what manner of buildings! 2 And Jesus said unto him, Seest thou these great build-	1 And Jesus went out from the temple, and was going on his way; and his disciples came to him to shew him the buildings of the temple. 2 But he answered and said unto them, See ye not all these things? verily	5 And as some spake of the temple, how it was adorned with goodly stones and offerings, 6 he said, As for these things which ye behold, the days will come, in which there shall not be

---

* This great discourse has as its background the death of Christ. Further on as part punishment for this crime lies the destruction of Jerusalem. This catastrophe is itself a symbol of the end of the world and in one sense a coming of Christ in power and judgment. But Christ boldly predicts his own personal return to earth, though the time is not revealed. But he does exhort an expectant attitude toward the promises of his coming and readiness for his return which will be at an unexpected hour. Jesus employs the common Jewish apocalyptic imagery to portray this most difficult subject. Some scholars insist that Jesus was himself merely a wild enthusiast who was carried away by the Messianic hopes of his people, but that is a one-sided and distorted view of Christ's life and ignores the great mass of his ethical teaching. It forgets also that Jesus has a world program of conquest and of power. The various aspects of the discourse are not kept distinct. Some think that the Gospels have misunderstood or misrepresented Jesus in this discourse. But we can catch the general drift of the teaching and leave alone minute details of time and place against which Jesus himself warned us.

173

Mark 13:1-37	Matt. 24 and 25	Luke 21:5-36

2 *Inquiry for Further Light from P e t e r and J a m e s and John and A n d r e w on Christ's Second Coming and the End of the World.*

Mark 13:1-37

ings? there shall not be left here one stone upon another, which shall not be thrown down. 3 And as he sat on the m o u n t o f Olives over against the temple, Peter and James and John and Andrew asked him privately, 4 Tell us, when shall these things be? and what *shall be* the sign when these things are all about to be accomplished? And 5 Jesus began to say unto them, Take heed that no man lead you astray. 6 Many shall come in my name, saying, I am *he;* and s h a l l l e a d many astray. 7 And when ye shall hear of wars and rumours of wars, be not troubled: *t h e s e things* must needs come to pass; but the end is not yet. 8 For nation shall r i s e against nation,

Matt. 24 and 25

I say unto you, There shall not be left here one stone upon another, that shall not be thrown down. 3 And as he sat on the mount of Olives, the disciples came unto him privately, saying, Tell us, when shall these things be? and what *shall be* the sign of thy ¹coming, and of ²the end of the world? 4 And Jesus answered and s a i d u n t o them, Take heed that no man lead you 5 astray. For many shall come in my name, saying, I am the Christ; and shall l e a d many astray. 6 And ye shall hear of wars and rumours of wars: see that ye be not troubled: for *these things* must needs come to pass; but the end is not yet. 7 For nation

Luke 21:5-36

left here one stone upon another, that shall not be **thrown down.**

7 And they asked him, saying, ¹⁸Master, when therefore shall these things be? and what *shall be* the sign when these things are about to come to pass? 8 And he said, Take heed that ye be not led astray: for many shall come in my name, saying, I am *he;* and, The time is at hand: go ye not after them. 9 And when ye shall hear of wars and tumults, be not terrified: for these things must needs come to pass first; but the end is not immediately. 10 Then said he unto them, Nation shall

174

Mark 13:1–37	Matt. 24 and 25	Luke 21:5–36
and kingdom against kingdom: there shall be earthquakes in divers places; there shall be famines:	shall rise against nation, and kingdom against kingdom: and there shall be famines and earthquakes in divers places.	rise against nation, and kingdom against kingdom: and there 11 shall be great earthquakes, and in divers places famines and pestilences; and there shall be terrors and great signs from heaven.
these things are the beginning of travail [*see Isa. 19:2*]. 9 But take ye heed to yourselves: for they shall deliver you up to councils; and in synagogues shall ye be beaten; and before governors and kings shall ye stand for my sake, for a testimony unto them. 10 And the gospel must first be preached unto all the nations. 11 And when they lead you *to judgement,* and deliver you up, be not anxious beforehand what ye shall speak: but whatsoever	8 But all these things are the beginning of travail. 9 Then shall they deliver you up unto tribulation, and shall kill you: and ye shall be hated of all the nations for my name's sake.	12 But before all these things, they shall lay their hands on you, and shall persecute you, delivering you up to the synagogues and prisons, ²²bringing you before kings and governors for my name's 13 sake. It shall turn unto you for a testimony. 14 Settle it therefore in your hearts, not to meditate beforehand how to 15 answer: for I

Mark 13:1–37	Matt. 24 and 25	Luke 21:5–36
shall be given you in that hour, t h a t speak ye: for it is not ye that speak, but the Holy 12 Ghost. And brother shall deliver u p brother t o death, and the father his child: and children shall rise up against parents, a n d 19cause them to be put to death [*see Micah 7:6*]. And 13 ye shall be hated of all men for my name's sake:	10 And then shall many stumble, and shall deliver up one another, a n d shall hate one another.	will give you a mouth and wisdom, which all your adversaries shall not be able to withstand or to gainsay. 16 But ye shall be delivered up even by parents, and brethren, and kinsfolk, and friends; and *some* of you 23shall they cause to be put 17 to death. And ye shall be hated of all men for my name's sake. 18 And not a hair of your head shall perish. 19 In your patience ye shall win y o u r 24souls.
	11 And many false prophets shall arise, and s h a l l l e a d many astray. 12 And because iniquity shall be multiplied, the love of the many shall wax	
but he that endureth to the end, the same shall be saved.	13 cold. But he that endureth to the end, the same shall be 14 saved. And ³this gospel of the kingdom s h a l l b e preached in t h e whole	

Mark 13:1-37	Matt. 24 and 25	Luke 21:5-36
	⁴world for a testimony unto to all the nations; and then shall the end come.	
3 *Sign of the Destruction of Jerusalem.* 14 But when ye see the abomination of desolation standing where he ought not	15 When therefore ye see the abomination of d e s o l a t i o n, which w a s spoken of ⁵by Daniel t h e prophet [*see Dan. 9:27; 11: 31; 12:11*], standing in ⁶the holy place	
(let him that readeth understand),	(let him that readeth understand),	
		20 But when ye see Jerusalem compassed with armies, t h e n know that her desolation is at
then let them that are in Judea flee unto the mountains: 15 and let him that is on the housetop not go down, nor enter in, to take anything out of his 16 house: and let him that is in the field return not back to take his cloke.	16 then let them that are in Judea flee unto the mountains: let him 17 tains: let him that is on the housetop not go down to take out the things that are in his 18 house: and let him that is in the field not return back to take his cloke.	hand. Then 21 let them that are in Judea flee unto the mountains; and let them that are in the midst of her departout;and let not them that are in the country enter therein.
		22 For these are days of v e n g e a n c e, that all things which are written may be

Mark 13:1–37	Matt. 24 and 25	Luke 21:5–36
17 But woe unto them that are with child and to them that give suck in those days!	19 But woe unto them that are with child and to them that give suck in those days! And	23 fulfilled. Woe unto them that are with child and to them that give suck in those days!
18 And pray ye that it be not in the winter.	20 pray ye that your flight be not in the winter, neither on a sabbath:	
19 For those days shall be tribulation, such as there hath not been the like from the beginning of the creation which God created until now, and never	21 for then shall be great tribulation, such as hath not been from the beginning of the world until now, no, nor ever shall be [*see Dan.12:1*].	
20 shall be. And except the Lord had shortened the days no flesh would have been saved: but for the elect's sake, whom he chose, he shortened the days.	22 And except those days had been shortened, no flesh would have been saved: but for the elect's sake those days shall be shortened.	
		for there shall be great distress upon the ²⁵land, and wrath unto this people.
		24 And they shall fall by the edge of the sword, and shall be led captive into all nations: and Jerusalem shall be trodden down of the Gentiles,

178

Mark 13:1-37	Matt. 24 and 25	Luke 21:5-36
		until the times of the Gentiles be fulfilled.

4 False Christs and the Second Coming.

Mark 13:1-37

21 And then if any man shall say unto you, Lo, here is the Christ; or, Lo, there; believe

22 *'it* not: for there shall arise false Christs and false prophets, and shall shew signs and wonders, that they may lead astray, if possible, the elect.

23 But take ye heed: behold, I have told you all things beforehand.

Matt. 24 and 25

23 Then if any man shall say unto you, Lo, here is the Christ, or, Here; believe

24 *'it* not. For there shall arise false Christs, and false prophets, and shall shew great signs and wonders; so as to lead astray, if possible, even the elect [*see Deut. 13:*

25 *1*]. Behold, I have told you

26 beforehand. If therefore they shall say unto you, Behold, he is in the wilderness; go not forth: Behold, he is in the inner chambers; believe *'it* not.

27 For as the lightning cometh forth from the east, and is seen even unto the west; so shall be the ¹coming of the Son of man.

28 Wheresoever the carcase is, there will the °eagles be gathered together.

24 But in those

29 But immedi-

Mark 13:1–37	Matt. 24 and 25	Luke 21:5–36
days, after that tribulation, the sun shall be darkened, and the moon shall not give her light, 25 and the stars shall be falling from heaven,	ately, after the tribulation of those days the sun shall be darkened, and the moon shall not give her light, and the stars shall fall from heaven	25 And there shall be signs in sun and moon and stars; and upon the earth distress of nations, in perplexity for the roaring of the sea and the 26 billows; men [26]fainting for fear, and for expectation of the things which are coming on [27]the world: for the
and the powers that are in the heavens shall be shaken.	and the powers of the heavens shall be shaken: 30 and then shall appear the sign of the Son of man in heaven [see Zech. 12:12]: and then shall all the tribes of the earth mourn, and	powers of the heavens shall be shaken [see Isa. 13:9–10; Ezek. 32:7–8; Joel 2:1–2, 10–11, 30–31; Amos 8:9; Zeph. 1:14–16].
26 And then shall they see the Son of man coming in clouds with great power 27 and glory. And then shall he send forth the angels, and shall gather together his elect from the four winds, from the uttermost part of the earth to the	they shall see the Son of man coming on the clouds of heaven with power and great glory. And he 31 shall send forth his angels [10]with [11]a great sound of a trumpet, and they shall gather together his elect from the four winds, from	27 And then shall they see the Son of man coming in a cloud with power and great glory [see Dan. 7:13–14 (Septuagint)].

	Mark 13:1–37	Matt. 24 and 25	Luke 21:5–36
	uttermost part of heaven.	one end of heaven to the other.	
			28 But when these things begin to come to pass, look up, and lift up your heads; because your redemption draweth nigh [*see Deut. 30:4 (Septuagint); Isa. 27: 12–13; Zech. 2: 6 (Septuagint).*
Parable of the Fig Tree.	28 Now from the fig tree learn her parable: when her branch is now become tender, and putteth forth its leaves, ye know that the sum-29 mer is nigh; even so ye also, when ye see these things coming to pass, know ye that ¹²he is nigh, *even* at 30 the doors. Verily I say unto you, This generation shall not pass away, until all these things be accomplished. 31 Heaven and earth shall pass away: but my words shall not pass away. 32 But of that day or that	32 Now from the fig tree learn her parable: when her branch is now become tender, and putteth forth its leaves, ye know that the summer is 33 nigh; even so ye also, when ye see all these things, know ye that ¹²he is nigh, *even* at 34 the doors. Verily I say unto you, This generation shall not pass away, till all these things be accomplished. 35 Heaven and earth shall pass away, but my words shall not pass away. 36 But of that day and hour knoweth no	29 And he spake to them a parable: Behold the fig tree, and all 30 trees: when they now shoot forth, ye see it and know of your own selves that the sum- mer is now 31 nigh. Even so ye also, when ye see these things coming to pass, know ye that the king- dom of God 32 is nigh. Ver- ily I say unto you, this gen- eration shall not pass away, till all things be accomplish- 33 ed. Heaven and earth shall pass away: but my words shall not pass away.

Mark 13:1-37	Matt. 24 and 25	Luke 21:5-36
hour knoweth no one, not even the angels in heaven, neither the Son, but the Father.	one, not even the angels of h e a v e n, [13]neither the Son, but the Father only. 37 And as *were* the days of Noah, so shall be the [1]coming of the Son of man [*see Gen. 6:11-13; 7:7,* 38 *21-23*]. For as in those days which were before the flood they were eating and drinking, marrying and giving in marriage, until the day that Noah entered into 39 the ark, and they knew not until the flood came, and took them all away; so shall be the [1]coming of the Son of man. 40 Then shall two men be in the field; one is taken, and one i s l e f t : 41 two women *shall be* grinding at the mill; one is taken, and one is left	
5 *R e a d i n e s s urged by Series of Parables.*	33 Take ye heed, watch [20]and pray: for ye know not when the time 34 is. *It is* as *when* a man,	34 But take heed to yourselves, lest haply your hearts be overcharged with surfeiting and

182

Mark 13:1–37	Matt. 24 and 25	Luke 21:5–36
sojourning in another country, having left his house, and given authority to his [21]servants, to each one his work, c o m m a n d - ed also the p o r t e r t o		drunkenness, and cares of this life, and that day come on you sud- denly as a 35 snare: for *so* shall it come upon all them that dwell on the face of all the earth.

Parable of the Porter

| 35 watch. Watch therefore: for ye know not when the lord of the house c o m e t h , whether at even, or at midnight, or at cockcrowing, or in the morn- 36 ing; lest com- ing suddenly he find you 37 sleeping. And what I say unto you I say unto all, Watch. | 42 Watch there- fore: for ye know not on what day your Lord cometh. | 36 But watch ye at every season, making sup- plication, that ye may prevail to escape all these things that shall come to pass, and to stand before the Son of man. |

Matt. 24 and 25

Parable of the Master of the House.

Parable of the Faithful Serv- ant and of the Evil Servant.

43 [14]But know this, that if the master of the house had known in what watch the thief was coming, he would have watched and would not have suffered his house
44 to be [15]broken through. Therefore be ye also ready.
45 for in an hour that ye think not the Son of man cometh. Who then is the faithful and wise [16]servant, whom his lord hath set over his household, to give
46 them their food in due season? Blessed is that [16]servant, whom his lord when he cometh shall find
47 so doing. Verily I say unto you, that he will set him
48 over all that he hath. But if that evil [16]servant shall say in his heart, My lord tarrieth; and shall begin to
49 beat his fellow-servants, and shall eat and drink with
50 the drunken; the lord of that [16]servant shall come in
51 a day when he expecteth not, and in an hour when he knoweth not, and shall [17]cut him asunder, and ap-

Matt. 24 and 25

point his portion with the hypocrites: there shall be the weeping and gnashing of teeth.

[1] Gr. *presence.* [2] Or, *the consummation of the age.* [3] Or, *these good tidings.* [4] Gr. *inhabited earth.* [5] Or, *through.* [6] Or, *a holy place.* [7] Or, *him.* [8] Or, *them.* [9] Or, *vultures.* [10] Many ancient authorities read *with a great trumpet, and they shall gather, &c.* [11] Or, *a trumpet of great sound.* [12] Or, *it.* [13] Many authorities, some ancient, omit *neither the Son.* [14] Or, *But this ye know.* [15] Gr. *digged through.* [16] Gr. *bond-servant.* [17] Or, *severely scourge him.* [18] Or, *Teacher.* [19] Or, *put them to death.* [20] Some ancient authorities omit *and pray.* [21] Gr. *bond-servants.* [22] Gr. *you being brought.* [23] Or, *shall they put to death.* [24] Or, *lives.* [25] Or, *earth.* [26] Or, *expiring.* [27] Gr. *the inhabited earth.*

Matt. chap. 25

Parable of the Ten Virgins.

1 Then shall the kingdom of heaven be likened unto ten virgins, which took their [1]lamps, and went forth
2 to meet the bridegroom. And five of them were
3 foolish, and five were wise. For the foolish, when
4 they took their [1]lamps, took no oil with them: but the
5 wise took oil in their vessels with their [1]lamps. Now while the bridegroom tarried, they all slumbered and
6 slept. But at midnight there is a cry, Behold, the
7 bridegroom! Come ye forth to meet him. Then all those virgins arose, and trimmed their [1]lamps.
8 And the foolish said unto the wise, Give us of your
9 oil; for our [1]lamps are going out. But the wise answered, saying, Peradventure there will not be enough
10 for us and you: go ye rather to them that sell, and buy for yourselves. And while they went away to buy, the bridegroom came; and they that were ready went in with him to the marriage feast: and the door was
11 shut. Afterward, come also the other virgins, saying,
12 Lord, Lord, open to us. But he answered and said,
13 Verily I say unto you, I know you not. Watch therefore, for ye know not the day nor the hour.

14   For *it is* as *when* a man, going into another country, called his own [2]servants, and delivered unto them his
15 goods. And unto one he gave five talents, to another two, to another one; to each according to his several
16 ability; and he went on his journey. Straightway he

Parable of the Talents

that received the five talents went and traded with
17 them, and made other five talents. In like manner
18 he also that *received* the two gained other two. But he that received the one went away and digged in the
19 earth, and hid his lord's money. Now after a long time the lord of those [2]servants cometh and maketh
20 a reckoning with them. And he that received the five talents came and brought other five talents, saying, Lord, thou deliveredst unto me five talents: lo,
21 I have gained other five talents. His lord said unto him, Well done, good and faithful [3]servant: thou hast been faithful over a few things, I will set thee over
22 many things; enter thou into the joy of thy lord. And he also that *received* the two talents came and said, Lord, thou deliveredst unto me two talents: lo, I have

Matt. chap. 25

23 gained other two talents. His lord said unto him, Well done, good and faithful ³servant; thou hast been faithful over a few things, I will set thee over many
24 things: enter thou into the joy of thy lord. And he also that had received the one talent came and said, Lord, I knew thee that thou art a hard man, reaping where thou didst not sow, and gathering where thou
25 didst not scatter: and I was afraid, and went away and hid thy talent in the earth: lo, thou hast thine
26 own. But his lord answered and said unto him, Thou wicked and slothful ³servant, thou knowest that I reap where I sowed not, and gather where I did not
27 scatter; thou oughtest therefore to have put my money to the bankers, and at my coming I should have re-
28 ceived back mine own with interest. Take ye away therefore the talent from him, and give it unto him
29 that hath the ten talents. For unto every one that hath shall be given, and he shall have abundance: but from him that hath not, even that which he hath
30 shall be taken away. And cast ye out the unprofit-able ³servant into the outer darkness: there shall be the weeping and gnashing of teeth.

6 Picture of the Judgment with Parable of the Sheep and the Goats.

31 But when the Son of man shall come in his glory, and all the angels with him [*see Zech. 14:5*], then
32 shall he sit on the throne of his glory: and before him shall be gathered all the nations: and he shall separate them one from another, as the shepherd separateth
33 the sheep from the ⁴goats; and he shall set the sheep
34 on his right hand, but the ⁴goats on the left. Then shall the King say unto them on his right hand, Come, ye blessed of my Father, inherit the kingdom pre-pared for you from the foundation of the world:
35 for I was an hungred, and ye gave me meat: I was thirsty, and ye gave me drink: I was a stranger, and
36 ye took me in; naked, and ye clothed me: I was sick, and ye visited me: I was in prison, and ye came unto
37 me. Then shall the righteous answer him, saying, Lord, when saw we thee an hungred, and fed thee?
38 or athirst, and gave thee drink? And when saw we thee a stranger, and took thee in? or naked, and
39 clothed thee? And when saw we thee sick, or in
40 prison, and came unto thee? And the King shall answer and say unto them, Verily I say unto you, Inasmuch as ye did it unto one of these my brethren,
41 *even* these least, ye did it unto me. Then shall he say also unto them on the left hand, ⁵Depart from me, ye cursed, into the eternal fire which is prepared for
42 the devil and his angels: for I was an hungred, and ye gave me no meat: I was thirsty, and ye gave me
43 no drink: I was a stranger, and ye took me not in:

185

Matt. chap. 25

44 naked, and ye clothed me not; sick, and in prison, and
   ye visited me not. Then shall they also answer,
   saying, Lord, when saw we thee an hungred, or athirst,
   or a stranger, or naked, or sick, or in prison, and did
45 not minister unto thee? Then shall he answer them,
   saying, Verily, I say unto you, Inasmuch as ye did
   it not unto one of these least, ye did it not unto me.
46 And these shall go away into eternal punishment:
   but the righteous into eternal life [see Dan. 12:2].

¹ Or, torches. ² Gr. bond-servants. ³ Gr. bond-servant. ⁴ Gr. kids. ⁵ Or, Depart from me under a curse.

§ 140. JESUS PREDICTS HIS CRUCIFIXION TWO DAYS HENCE (JEWISH FRIDAY)

Probably at Bethany on Tuesday evening (beginning of Jewish Wednesday). The Rulers in Jerusalem plot His death

Mark 14:1-2	Matt. 26:1-5	Luke 22:1-2
1 Now after two days was *the feast of* the passover and the unleavened bread:	1 And it came to pass, when Jesus had finished all these words, he said unto 2 his disciples, Ye know that after two days the passover cometh, and the Son of man is delivered up to be 3 crucified. Then were	1 Now the feast of unleavened bread drew nigh, which is called the Passover.
and the chief priests and the scribes	gathered together the chief priests, and the elders of the people, unto the court of the high priest, who was called Caiaphas: and	2 And the chief priests and the
sought how they might take him with subtilty, 2 and kill him: for they said, Not during the feast, lest haply there shall be a tumult of the people.	4 they took counsel together that they might take Jesus by subtilty, and kill him. 5 But they said, Not during the feast, lest a tumult arise among the people.	scribes sought how they might put him to death; for they feared the people.

§ 141. AT THE FEAST IN THE HOUSE OF SIMON THE LEPER MARY OF BETHANY ANOINTS JESUS FOR HIS BURIAL

At Bethany (Tuesday evening, Jewish Wednesday)

Mark 14:3–9	Matt. 26:6–13	John 12:2–8
3 And while he was in Bethany in the house of Simon the leper, as he sat at meat, there came a woman having ¹an alabaster cruse of ointment of ²spikenard very costly, *and* she brake the cruse, and poured it over 4 his head. But there were some that had indignation among themselves, *saying*, To what purpose hath this waste of the ointment been made? 5 For this ointment might have been sold for above three hundred ³pence, and given to the poor. And they murmured 6 against her. But Jesus said, Let her alone, why trouble ye her? she hath wrought a good work on me. 7 For ye have the poor always with you, and whensoever ye will ye can do them good: but me ye have not 8 always. She hath	6 Now when Jesus was in Bethany, in the house of Simon 7 the leper, there came unto him a woman having an alabaster cruse of exceeding precious ointment, and she poured it upon his head as he 8 sat at meat. But when the disciples saw it, they had indignation, saying, To what purpose is this waste? 9 For this ointment might have been sold for much, and given to the poor. 10 But Jesus perceiving it said unto them, Why trouble ye the woman? for she hath wrought a good work 11 upon me. For ye have the poor always with you; but me you have not always. 12 For in that she poured this ointment upon	2 So they made him a supper there: and Martha served; but Lazarus was one of them that sat at meat 3 with him. Mary* therefore took a pound of ointment of ²spikenard, very precious, and anointed the feet of Jesus, and wiped his feet with her hair: and the house was filled with the odour of the oint- 4 ment. But Judas Iscariot, one of his d i s c i p l e s, which should betray him, 5 saith, Why was not this ointment sold for three hundred ³pence, and given to the 6 poor? Now this he said, not because he cared for the poor; but because he was a thief, and having the ⁴bag ⁵took away what was put therein. 7 Jesus therefore said, ⁶Suffer her to keep it against the day of 8 my burying. For the poor ye have al-

* This anointing has nothing in common with that given by Luke (§ 59), except the fact of a woman anointing the Saviour's feet, and the name Simon, which was common. The former was in Galilee, this is at Bethany near Jerusalem. There the host despised the woman who anointed, here her brother is one of the guests, and her sister an active attendant. There the woman was "a sinner," a notoriously bad woman, here it is the devout Mary who "sat at the Lord's feet and heard his word" months before (§ 104). There the host thought strange that Jesus allowed her to touch him, here the disciples complain of the waste. There the Saviour gave assurance of forgiveness, here of perpetual and world-wide honor. Especially notice that here the woman who anoints is anticipating his speedy death and burial, of which at the former time he had never distinctly spoken. In view of all these differences it is absurd to represent the two anointings as the same, and outrageous on such slender ground to cast reproach on Mary of Bethany.

Mark 14:3–9	Matt. 26:6–13	John 12:2–8
done what she could: she hath anointed my body aforehand for 9 the burying. And verily I say unto you, Wheresoever the gospel shall be preached throughout the whole world, that also which this woman hath done shall be spoken of for a memorial of her.	my body, she did it to prepare me for burial. 13 Verily I say unto you, Wheresoever this gospel shall be preached in the whole world, that also which this woman hath done shall be spoken of for a memorial of her.	ways with you; but me ye have not always.

¹ Or, *a flask.* ² Gr. *pistic nard,* pistic being perhaps a local name. Some take it to mean *genuine*: others, *liquid.* ³ The word in the Greek denotes a coin worth about seventeen cents. ⁴ Or, *box.* ⁵ Or, *carried what was put therein.* ⁶ Or, *let her alone: it was that she might keep it.*

§ 142. JUDAS, STUNG BY THE REBUKE OF JESUS AT THE FEAST, BARGAINS WITH THE RULERS TO BETRAY JESUS

Tuesday Night in Jerusalem

Mark 14:10–11	Matt. 26:14–16	Luke 22:3–6
10 And Judas Iscariot, ¹he that was one of the twelve, went away unto the chief priests, that he might deliver him unto them.	14 Then one of the twelve, who was called Judas Iscariot, went unto the chief priests, and said, 15 What are ye willing to give me, and I will deliver him unto you?	3 And Satan entered into Judas who was called Iscariot, being of the number of the 4 twelve. And he went away, and communed with the chief priests and captains, how he might deliver him unto them.
11 And they, when they heard it, were glad, and promised to give him money. And he sought how he might conveniently deliver him *unto them.*	And they weighed unto him thirty pieces 16 of silver [*see Zech. 11:12*]. And from that time he sought opportunity to deliver him *unto them.*	5 And they were glad, and covenanted to give him 6 money. And he consented, and sought opportunity to deliver him unto them ²in the absence of the multitude.

¹ Gr., *the one of the twelve.* ² Or, *without tumult.*

§ 143. THE PREPARATION FOR THE PASCHAL MEAL AT THE HOME OF A FRIEND (POSSIBLY THAT OF JOHN MARK'S FATHER AND MOTHER)

Jerusalem, Thursday* afternoon.   (A Day of Preparation)

Mark 14:12–16	Matt. 26:17–19	Luke 22:7–13
12 And on the first day of unleavened bread, when they sacrificed the passover, his disciples say unto him, Where wilt thou that we go and make ready that thou mayest eat the passover [see Ex. 12:18–13 20]? And he sendeth two of his disciples, and saith unto them,	17 Now on the first *day* of unleavened bread the disciples came to Jesus, saying, Where wilt thou that we make ready for thee to eat the 18 passover? And he said,	7 And the day of unleavened bread came, on which the passover must be sacrificed.
		8 And he sent Peter and John, saying, Go and make ready for us the passover, that we may 9 eat. And they said unto him, Where wilt thou that we make 10 ready? And he said unto them, Behold, when ye are entered
Go into the city, and there shall meet you a man bearing a pitcher of water: follow him; 14 and wheresoever he shall enter in, say to the goodman of the house, The ¹Master saith, Where is my guest-chamber, where I shall eat the passover with my disciples? And he will himself shew you a large upper room furnished *and* ready: and there make ready for 16 us. And the disciples went forth, and came	Go into the city to such a man, and say unto him, The ¹Master saith, My time is at hand; I keep the passover at thy house with my disciples. And the disciples did as	into the city, there shall meet you a man bearing a pitcher of water; follow him into the house where 11 into he goeth. And ye shall say unto the goodman of the house, The ¹Master saith unto thee, Where is the guest-chamber, where I shall eat the passover with my disciples? 12 And he will shew you a large upper room furnished: there make ready. 13 And they went,

---

* Wednesday (A Day of Rest) was apparently spent with the disciples in retirement in Bethany. Thursday was spent wholly with the disciples till the arrest in Gethsemane after midnight.

Mark 14:12–16	Matt. 26:17–19	Luke 22:7–13
into the city, and found as he had said unto them: and they made ready the passover.	Jesus appointed them; and they made ready the passover.	and found as he had said unto them: and they made ready the passover.
	¹ Or, *Teacher.*	

§ 144. JESUS PARTAKES OF THE PASCHAL MEAL WITH THE TWELVE APOSTLES AND REBUKES THEIR JEALOUSY

Jerusalem, Thursday evening after sunset (beginning of Jewish Friday)

Mark 14:17	Matt. 26:20	Luke 22:14–16, 24–30
17 And when it was evening he cometh with the twelve.	20 Now when even was come he was sitting at meat with the twelve ¹disciples;	
		14 And when the hour was come, he sat down, and the apos-

15 tles with him. And he said unto them, With desire I have desired to eat
16 this passover* with you before I suffer: for I say unto you, I will not eat
   it, until it be fulfilled in the kingdom of God.
24   And there arose also a contention among them, which of them is ac-
25 counted to be ²greatest. And he said unto them, The kings of the Gentiles have lordship over them; and they that have authority over them
26 are called Benefactors. But ye *shall* not *be* so: but he that is the greater
   among you, let him become as the younger; and he that is chief, as he
27 that doth serve. For whether is greater, he that ³sitteth at meat, or he
   that serveth? is not he that ³sitteth at meat? but I am in the midst of you
28 as he that serveth. But ye are they which have continued with me in
29 my temptations; and ⁴I appoint unto you a kingdom, even as my Father
   appointed unto me, that ye may eat and drink at my table in my king-
30 dom; and ye shall sit on thrones judging the twelve tribes of Israel.

¹ Many authorities, some ancient, omit *disciples.* ² Gr. *greater.* ³ Gr. *reclineth.* ⁴ Or, *I appoint unto you, even as my Father appointed unto me a kingdom, that ye may eat and drink, etc.*

§ 145. DURING THE PASCHAL MEAL, JESUS WASHES THE FEET OF HIS DISCIPLES

Evening before the Crucifixion (our Thursday, Jewish Friday)

John 13:1–20

1   Now before† the feast of the passover, Jesus knowing that his hour
   was come that he should depart out of this world unto the Father, having

---

* Some regard certain expressions in the Gospel of John as showing that Jesus did not eat the Paschal meal, thus hopelessly contradicting the other Gospels. But no one of John's expressions shows what is supposed, and one of them really indicates the contrary. See note at end of volume. Matthew, Mark, and Luke clearly show that he did eat the regular Passover meal.

† It is needlessly inferred that John by this expression means that it was a full day before the passover meal. In fact, the words in verse 2 "during supper" rather imply that "before passover" was just before the meal began.

John 13:1-20

loved his own which were in the world, he loved them ¹unto the end.
2 And during supper, the devil having already put into the heart of Judas
3 Iscariot, Simon's *son*, to betray him, *Jesus*, knowing that the Father had
given all things into his hands, and that he came forth from God and
4 goeth unto God, riseth from supper, and layeth aside his garments; and
5 he took a towel and girded himself. Then he poured water into the
bason, and began to wash the disciples' feet, and to wipe them with the
6 towel wherewith he was girded. So he cometh to Simon Peter. He saith
7 unto him, Lord, dost thou wash my feet? Jesus answered and said unto
him, What I do thou knowest not now; but thou shalt understand here-
8 after. Peter saith unto him, Thou shalt never wash my feet. Jesus
9 answered him, If I wash thee not, thou hast no part with me. Simon
Peter saith unto him, Lord, not my feet only, but also my hands and my
10 head. Jesus saith to him, He that is bathed needeth not ²save to wash
11 his feet, but is clean every whit: and ye are clean, but not all. For he
knew him that should betray him; therefore said he, Ye are not all clean.
12 So when he had washed their feet, and taken his garments, and ³sat
13 down again, he said unto them, Know ye what I have done to you? Ye
14 call me, ⁴Master, and, Lord: and ye say well; for so I am. If I then, the
Lord and the ⁴Master, have washed your feet, ye also ought to wash one
15 another's feet. For I have given you an example, that ye also should
16 do as I have done to you. Verily, verily, I say unto you, A ⁵servant is
not greater than his lord; neither ⁶one that is sent greater than he that
17 sent him. If ye know these things, blessed are ye if ye do them. I
18 speak not of you all: I know whom I ⁷have chosen: but that the scripture
may be fulfilled, He that eateth ⁸my bread lifted up his heel against me
19 [*see Ps. 41:9*]. From henceforth I tell you before it come to pass, that,
20 when it is come to pass, ye may believe that ⁹I am *he*. Verily, verily, I
say unto you, He that receiveth whomsoever I send receiveth me; and
he that receiveth me receiveth him that sent me.

¹ Or, *to the uttermost.* ² Some ancient authorities omit *save,* and *his feet.* ³ Gr. *reclined.* ⁴ Or,
Teacher. ⁵ Gr. *bond-servant.* ⁶ Gr. *an apostle.* ⁷ Or, *chose.* ⁸ Many ancient authorities read *his
bread with me.* ⁹ Or, *I am.*

§ 146. AT THE PASCHAL MEAL JESUS POINTS OUT JUDAS AS THE BETRAYER

Thursday evening (Jewish Friday)

Mark 14:18-21	Matt. 26:21-25	Luke 22:21-23	John 13:21-30
18 And as they ¹sat and were eating, Jesus said, Verily I say unto you, One of you shall betray me, *even* he that eateth with me [*see Ps. 41:9*].	21 and as they were eating, he said, Verily I say unto you, that one of you shall betray me.	21 But behold, the hand of him that betrayeth me is with me on the table. 22 For the Son of man indeed goeth, as it hath been determined: but woe unto	21 When Jesus had thus said, he was troubled in the spirit and testified, and said, Verily, verily, I say unto you, that one of you shall betray me.

Mark 14:18–21	Matt. 26:21–25	Luke 22:21–23	John 13:21–30
		that man through whom he is betrayed!	
19 They began to be sorrowful, and to say unto him one by one, Is it I?	22 And they were exceeding sorrowful, and began to say unto him every one, Is it I, Lord?	23 And they began to question among themselves, which of them it was that should do this thing.	22 The disciples looked one on another, doubting of whom he spake.
20 And he said unto them, *It is* one of the twelve, he that dippeth with me in the dish.	23 And he answered and said, He that dipped his hand with me in the dish, the same shall betray me.		
21 For the Son of man goeth, even as it is written of him: but woe unto that man through whom the Son of man is betrayed! good were it for that man if he had not been born.	24 The Son of man goeth, even as it is written of him: but woe unto that man through whom the Son of man is betrayed! good were it for that man if he had not been born.		
			23 There was at the table reclining in Jesus' bosom one of his disciples, whom Jesus loved. Simon Peter therefore beckoneth to him, 24 and saith unto him, Tell *us* who it is of whom he speaketh. He leaning back, as he was, on 25 Jesus' breast saith unto him, Lord, who is it? Jesus therefore 26 answereth, He it is, for whom I shall dip the sop, and give it him. So when he had dipped the sop, he taketh and giveth it to Judas, *the son* of Simon Iscariot.
	25 And Judas, which betrayed him,		

Matt. 26:21–25	John 13:21–30
answered and said, Is it I, Rabbi? He saith unto him, Thou hast said.	

27 And after the sop, then entered Satan into him. Jesus therefore saith unto him, That thou doest,
28 do quickly. Now no man at the table knew for what intent he spake
29 this unto them. For some thought, because Judas had the [2]bag, that Jesus said unto him, Buy what things we have need of for the feast: or,
30 that he should give something to the poor. He then having received the sop went out straightway: and it was night.

[1] Gr. *him if that man.* [2] Or. *box.*

§ 147. AFTER THE DEPARTURE OF JUDAS JESUS WARNS THE DISCIPLES (PETER IN PARTICULAR) AGAINST DESERTION, WHILE ALL PROTEST THEIR LOYALTY

John 13:31–38

31 When therefore he was gone out, Jesus saith, Now [1]is the Son of man glorified, and God [1]is glorified in him;
32 and God shall glorify him in himself, and straightway shall he glorify
33 him.   Little children, yet a little while I am with you. Ye shall seek me: and as I said unto the Jews, Whither I go, ye cannot come; so now I say unto you
34 A new commandment

Mark 14:27-31	Matt. 26:31-35	Luke 22:31-38	John 13:31-38
			give unto you, that ye love one another ²even as I have loved you, that ye also love one another. By this shall all men know that ye are my disciples, if ye have love one to another.
			35

Mark 14:27-31	Matt. 26:31-35	Luke 22:31-38	John 13:31-38
27 And Jesus saith unto them, All ye shall be ³offended: for it is written [*see Zech. 13:7*], I will smite the shepherd, and the sheep shall be scattered 28 abroad. Howbeit, after I am raised up, I will go before you into Galilee.	31 Then saith Jesus unto them, All ye shall be ³offended in me this night: for it is written, I will smite the shepherd, and the sheep of the flock shall be scattered abroad. 32 But after I am raised up, I will go before you into Galilee. But Peter	31 Simon, Simon, behold, Satan ⁴asked to have you, that he might sift you as 32 wheat: but I made supplication for thee, that thy faith fail not: and do thou, when once thou hast turned again, stablish thy brethren.	36 Simon Peter saith unto him, Lord, whither goest thou? Jesus answered, Whither I go, thou canst not follow me now; but thou shalt follow afterwards.
29 But Peter said unto him, Although all shall be ³offended, yet will not I. 30 And Jesus saith unto him, Verily I say unto thee, that thou to-day, even this night, before the cock crow twice shalt deny me thrice. 31 But he spake exceeding vehemently, If I	33 answered and said unto him, If all shall be ³offended in thee, I will never be ³of-34 fended. Jesus said unto him, Verily I say unto thee, that this night, before the cock crow, thou shalt deny me 35 thrice. Peter saith unto him, Even if I must die with	33 And he said unto him, Lord, with thee I am ready to go both to prison and to 34 death. And he said, I tell thee, Peter, the cock shall not crow this day, until thou shalt thrice deny that thou knowest me.	37 Peter saith unto him, Lord, why cannot I follow thee even now? I will lay down my life for thee. 38 Jesus answereth, Wilt thou lay down thy life for me? Verily, verily, I say unto thee, The cock shall not crow, till thou hast denied me thrice.

Mark 14:27–31	Matt. 26:31–35	Luke 22:31–38
must die with thee, I will not deny thee. And in like manner also said they all.	thee, *yet* will I not deny thee. Likewise also said all the disciples.	

35 And he said unto them, When I sent you forth without purse, and wallet, and shoes, lacked ye anything? And they said, Noth-
36 ing. And he said unto them, But now, he that hath a purse, let him take it, and likewise a wallet: ⁴and he that hath none, let him sell his
37 cloke, and buy a sword. For I say unto you, that this which is written must be fulfilled in me [*see Isa. 53:12*], And he was reckoned with transgressors: for that which
38 concerneth me hath ⁶fulfilment. And they said, Lord, behold, here are two swords. And he said unto them, It is enough.

¹ Or, *was.* ² Or, *even as I loved you, that ye also may love one another.* ³ Or, *caused to stumble.*
⁴ Or, *obtained you by asking.* ⁵ Or, *and he that hath no sword, let him sell his cloak and buy one.*
⁶ Gr. *end.*

§148. JESUS INSTITUTES THE MEMORIAL OF EATING BREAD AND DRINKING WINE

Jerusalem. Evening before the Crucifixion

Luke* 22:17–20

17 And he received a cup, and when he had given thanks he said, Take this, and divide it a-
18 mong yourselves: for I say unto you, I will not drink from henceforth of

* Luke here (see § 144) departs from the order of Mark (and Matthew) and mentions the institution of the supper earlier in the evening. It seems best to follow the chronology of Mark, who places it after the departure of Judas.

Mark 14:22–25	Matt. 26:26–29	Luke 22:17–20	1 Cor.* 11–23:26
		the fruit of the vine until the kingdom of God shall come.	
22 And as they were eating, he took ¹bread, and when he had blessed, he brake it, and gave to them, and said, Take ye: this is my body.	26 And as they were eating, Jesus took ¹bread, and blessed, and brake it; and he gave to the disciples, and said, Take, eat; this is my body.	19 And he took ¹bread, and when he had given thanks, he brake it, and gave to them, saying, This is my body ⁵which is given for you: this do in remembrance of me. And the	23 For I received of the Lord that which also I delivered unto you, how that the Lord Jesus in the night in which he was betrayed took
23 And he took a cup, and when he had given thanks, he gave to them, and they all drank of it.	27 And he took ²a cup, and gave thanks, and gave to them, saying, Drink ye all of it;	20 cup in like manner after supper, saying,	24 bread; and when he had given thanks, he brake it, and said, This is my body, which ⁷is for you: this do in remembrance of me.
24 And he said unto them, This is my blood of ³the ⁴covenant which is shed for many [see Ex. 24:8; Lev. 4:18–20; Jer. 31:31; Zech. 9: 25 11]. Verily I say unto you, I will no more drink of the fruit of the vine, until that day when I drink it new in the kingdom of God.	28 for this is my blood of ³the ⁴covenant, which is shed for many unto remission of 29 sins. But I say unto you, I will not drink hence-forth of this fruit of the vine, until that day when I drink it new with you in my Father's king-dom.	This cup is the new ⁶covenant in my blood, even that which is poured out for you.	25 In like manner also the cup, after supper, saying, This cup is the new ⁶covenant in my blood: this do, as oft as ye drink it, in re-membrance of 26 me. For as often as ye eat this bread, and drink the cup, ye proclaim the Lord's death till he come.

¹ Or, *a loaf.* ² Some ancient authorities read *the cup.* ³ Or, *the testament.* ⁴ Many ancient authorities insert *new.* ⁵ Some ancient authorities omit *which is given for you...which is poured out for you.* ⁶ Or, *testament.* ⁷ Many ancient authorities read *is broken for you.*

---

* These are two parallel reports of the institution of the supper. Mark is followed by Matthew and 1 Corinthians (about A.D. 56) by Luke (not earlier than A.D. 58).

§ 149. THE FAREWELL DISCOURSE TO HIS DISCIPLES IN THE UPPER ROOM

Jerusalem

John 14*

1 Let not your heart be troubled: ¹ye believe in God, believe also in me.
2 In my Father's house are many ²mansions; if it were not so, I would have
3 told you; for I go to prepare a place for you. And if I go and prepare a
4 place for you, I come again, and will receive you unto myself; that where
5 I am *there* ye may be also. ³And whither I go, ye know the way. Thomas
saith unto him, Lord, we know not whither thou goest; how know we the
6 way? Jesus saith unto him, I am the way, and the truth, and the life:
7 no one cometh unto the Father, but ⁴by me. If ye had known me, ye would
have known my Father also: from henceforth ye know him, and have seen
8 him. Philip saith unto him, Lord, shew us the Father, and it sufficeth us.
9 Jesus saith unto him, Have I been so long time with you, and dost thou
not know me, Philip? he that hath seen me hath seen the Father; how sayest
10 thou, Shew us the Father? Believest thou not that I am in the Father, and
the Father in me? the words that I say unto you I speak not from myself:
11 but the Father abiding in me doeth his works. Believe me that I am in
the Father and the Father in me: or else believe me for the very works'
12 sake. Verily, verily, I say unto you, he that believeth on me, the works
that I do shall he do also; and greater *works* than these shall he do; because
13 I go unto the Father. And whatsoever ye shall ask in my name, that
14 will I do, that the Father may be glorified in the Son. If ye shall ask ⁵me
15 anything in my name, that will I do. If ye love me, ye will keep my com-
16 mandments. And I will ⁶pray the Father, and he shall give you another
⁷Comforter, that he may be with you for ever, *even* the Spirit of truth:
17 whom the world cannot receive; for it beholdeth him not, neither knoweth
18 him: ye know him; for he abideth with you, and shall be in you. I will
19 not leave you ⁸desolate: I come unto you. Yet a little while, and the
world beholdeth me no more; but ye behold me: because I live, ⁹ye shall
20 live also. In that day ye shall know that I am in my Father, and ye in
21 me, and I in you. He that hath my commandments, and keepeth them,
he it is that loveth me: and he that loveth me shall be loved of my Father,
22 and I will love him, and will manifest myself unto him. Judas (not Iscariot) saith unto him, Lord, what is come to pass that thou wilt manifest
23 thyself unto us, and not unto the world? And Jesus answered and said
unto him, If a man love me, he will keep my word: and my Father will
love him, and we will come unto him, and make our abode with him.
24 He that loveth me not keepeth not my words: and the word which ye
hear is not mine, but the Father's who sent me.
25 These things have I spoken unto you, while *yet* abiding with you.
26 But the ⁷Comforter, *even* the Holy Spirit, whom the Father will send in
my name, he shall teach you all things, and bring to your remembrance
27 all that I said unto you. Peace I leave with you; my peace I give unto

* Chapters 13 to 17 in John really belong together. There is first the effort of Jesus to stop
the bickerings of the Twelve, then his warning and their reply. Jesus continues to address them
with repeated interruption (dialogue), but finally they fear to ask him further (monologue). The
discourse concludes with the wonderful prayer (the real Lord's Prayer) in chapter 17.

John 14

you: not as the world giveth, give I unto you. Let not your heart be
28 troubled, neither let it be fearful. Ye heard how I said to you, I go away,
and I come unto you. If ye loved me, ye would have rejoiced, because
29 I go unto the Father: for the Father is greater than I. And now I have
told you before it come to pass, that, when it is come to pass, ye may
30 believe. I will no more speak much with you, for the prince of the world
31 cometh: and he hath nothing in me; but that the world may know that
I love the Father, and as the Father gave me commandment, even so I
do. Arise, let us go hence.*

[1] Or, *believe in God.* [2] Or, *abiding-places.* [3] Many ancient authorities read *And whither I go, ye know, and the way ye know.* [4] Or, *through.* [5] Many ancient authorities omit *me.* [6] Gr. *make request of.* [7] Or, *Advocate.* Or, *Helper.* Gr. *Paraclete.* [8] Or, *orphans.* [9] Or, *and ye shall live.*

§ 150. THE DISCOURSE ON THE WAY TO GETHSEMANE

Possibly on the Street

John 15 and 16†

1   I am the true vine, and my Father is the husbandman. Every branch
2 in me that beareth not fruit, he taketh it away: and every *branch* that
3 beareth fruit, he cleanseth it, that it may bear more fruit. Already ye
4 are clean because of the word which I have spoken unto you. Abide in
me, and I in you. As the branch cannot bear fruit of itself, except it
5 abide in the vine; so neither can ye, except ye abide in me. I am the vine,
ye are the branches: He that abideth in me, and I in him, the same beareth
6 much fruit: for apart from me ye can do nothing. If a man abide not in
me, he is cast forth as a branch, and is withered; and they gather them,
7 and cast them into the fire, and they are burned. If ye abide in me, and
my words abide in you, ask whatsoever ye will, and it shall be done unto
8 you. Herein [1]is my Father glorified, [2]that ye bear much fruit: and *so*
9 shall ye be my disciples. Even as the Father hath loved me, I also have
10 loved you: abide ye in my love. If ye keep my commandments, ye shall
abide in my love; even as I have kept my Father's commandments, and
11 abide in his love. These things have I spoken unto you, that my joy
12 may be in you, and *that* your joy may be fulfilled. This is my command-
13 ment, that ye love one another, even as I have loved you. Greater love
14 hath no man than this, that a man lay down his life for his friends. Ye
15 are my friends, if ye do the things which I command you. No longer do
I call you [3]servants; for the [4]servant knoweth not what his lord doeth:
but I have called you friends; for all things that I heard from my Father
16 I have made known unto you. Ye did not choose me, but I chose you,
and appointed you, that ye should go and bear fruit, and *that* your fruit
should abide: that whatsoever ye shall ask of the Father in my name,
17, 18 he may give it you. These things I command you, that ye may love
one another. If the world hateth you, [5]ye know that it hath hated me
19 before *it hated* you. If ye were of the world, the world would love its own;
but because ye are not of the world, but I chose you out of the world,

* Apparently they leave the Upper Room.
† Chapters 14–17 are called the Heart of Christ. Nowhere does the Master lay bare his very soul more completely than here in chapters 15 and 16, with the allegory of the Vine and the teaching concerning the Holy Spirit.

John 15 and 16

20 therefore the world hateth you. Remember the word that I said unto you, A ⁴servant is not greater than his lord. If they persecuted me, they will also persecute you; if they keep my word, they will keep yours also.
21 But all these things will they do unto you for my name's sake, because
22 they know not him that sent me. If I had not come and spoken unto them, they had not had sin: but now they have no excuse for their sin.
23, 24 He that hateth me hateth my Father also. If I had not done among them the works which none other did, they had not had sin: but now
25 have they both seen and hated both me and my Father. But *this cometh to pass*, that the word may be fulfilled that is written in their law, They
26 hated me without a cause [*see Ps. 35:19; 69:4*]. But when the ⁶Comforter is come, whom I will send unto you from the Father, *even* the Spirit of truth, which ⁷proceedeth from the Father, he shall bear witness of me:
27 ⁸and ye also bear witness, because ye have been with me from the beginning.

1 These things have I spoken unto you that ye should not be made to
2 stumble. They shall put you out of the synagogues: yea, the hour cometh, that whosoever killeth you shall think that he offereth service unto God.
3 And these things will they do, because they have not known the Father,
4 nor me. But these things have I spoken unto you, that when their hour is come, ye may remember them, how that I told you. And these things
5 I said not unto you from the beginning, because I was with you. But now I go unto him that sent me; and none of you asketh me, Whither goest
6 thou? But because I have spoken these things unto you, sorrow hath
7 filled your heart. Nevertheless I tell you the truth; It is expedient for you that I go away: for if I go not away, the ⁶Comforter will not come
8 unto you; but if I go, I will send him unto you. And he, when he is come,
9 will convict the world in respect of sin, and of righteousness, and of judge-
10 ment: of sin, because they believe not on me: of righteousness, because I
11 go to the Father, and ye behold me no more; of judgement, because the
12 prince of this world hath been judged. I have yet many things to say
13 unto you, but ye cannot bear them now. Howbeit when he, the Spirit of truth, is come, he shall guide you into all the truth: for he shall not speak from himself; but what things soever he shall hear, *these* shall he speak: and he shall declare unto you the things that are to come.
14 He shall glorify me: for he shall take of mine, and shall declare *it* unto
15 you. All things whatsoever the Father hath are mine: therefore said I,
16 that he taketh of mine, and shall declare *it* unto you. A little while, and ye behold me no more; and again a little while, and ye shall see me.
17 *Some* of his disciples therefore said one to another, What is this that he saith unto us, A little while, and ye behold me not; and again a little
18 while, and ye shall see me: and, Because I go to the Father? They said
19 therefore, What is this that he saith, A little while? We know not what he saith. Jesus perceived that they were desirous to ask him, and he said unto them, Do ye inquire among yourselves concerning this, that I said, A little while, and ye behold me not, and again a little while, and ye
20 shall see me? Verily, verily, I say unto you, that ye shall weep and lament, but the world shall rejoice: ye shall be sorrowful, but your sorrow
21 shall be turned into joy. A woman when she is in travail hath sorrow

John 15 and 16

because her hour is come: but when she is delivered of the child, she
remembereth no more the anguish, for the joy that a man is born into the
22 world. And ye therefore now have sorrow: but I will see you again,
and your heart shall rejoice, and your joy no one taketh away from you
23 [*see Isa. 66:14*]. And in that day ye shall ⁹ask me nothing. Verily,
verily, I say unto you, If ye shall ask anything of the Father, he will give
24 it you in my name. Hitherto have ye asked nothing in my name: ask
and ye shall receive, that your joy may be fulfilled.
25   These things have I spoken unto you in ¹⁰proverbs: the hour cometh,
when I shall no more speak unto you in ¹⁰proverbs, but shall tell you
26 plainly of the Father. In that day ye shall ask in my name: and I say
27 not unto you, that I will ¹¹pray the Father for you; for the Father himself loveth you, because ye have loved me, and have believed that I came
28 forth from the Father. I came out from the Father, and am come into
29 the world: again, I leave the world, and go unto the Father. His disciples
30 say, Lo, now speakest thou plainly, and speakest no ¹²proverb. Now know
we that thou knowest all things, and needest not that any man should
31, 32 ask thee: by this we believe that thou camest forth from God. Jesus
answered them, Do ye now believe? Behold, the hour cometh, yea, is
come, that ye shall be scattered, every man to his own, and shall leave
33 me alone: and *yet* I am not alone, because the Father is with me. These
things have I spoken unto you, that in me ye may have peace. In the
world ye have tribulation: but be of good cheer; I have overcome the world.

¹ Or, *was.* ² Many ancient authorities read *that ye bear much fruit, and be my disciples.* ³ Gr.
bond-servants. ⁴ Gr. *bond-servant.* ⁵ Or, *know ye.* ⁶ Or, *Advocate.* Or, *Helper.* Gr. *Paraclete.*
⁷Or, *goeth forth from.* ⁸ Or, *and bear ye also witness.* ⁹ Or, *ask me no question.* ¹⁰ Or, *parables.*
¹¹ Gr. *make request of.* ¹² Or, *parable.*

§ 151. CHRIST'S INTERCESSORY PRAYER

Possibly near Gethsemane

John 17

1   These things spake Jesus; and lifting up his eyes to heaven, he said,
2 Father, the hour is come; glorify thy Son, that the Son may glorify thee:
even as thou gavest him authority over all flesh, that whatsoever thou
3 hast given him, to them he should give eternal life. And this is life eternal,
that they should know thee the only true God, and him whom thou didst
4 send, *even* Jesus Christ. I glorified thee on the earth, having accomplished
5 the work which thou hast given me to do. And now, O Father, glorify
thou me with thine own self with the glory which I had with thee before
6 the world was. I manifested thy name unto the men whom thou gavest
me out of the world: thine they were, and thou gavest them to me; and
7 they have kept thy word. Now they know that all things whatsoever
8 thou hast given me are from thee: for the words which thou hast given me
I have given unto them; and they received *them*, and knew of a truth that
I came forth from thee, and they believed that thou didst send me.
9 I ¹pray for them: I ¹pray not for the world, but for those whom thou
10 hast given me; for they are thine: and all things that are mine are thine,
11 and I am glorified in them. And I am no more in the world, and these are

John 17

in the world, and I come to thee. Holy Father, keep them in thy name
12 which thou hast given me, that they may be one, even as we *are*. While
I was with them, I kept them in thy name which thou hast given me: and
I guarded them, and not one of them perished, but the son of perdition;
13 that the scripture might be fulfilled [*see Ps. 41:9*]. But now I come to thee:
and these things I speak in the world, that they may have my joy fulfilled
14 in themselves. I have given them thy word; and the world hated them,
15 because they are not of the world, even as I am not of the world. I ¹pray
not that thou shouldest take them ²from the world, but that thou shouldest
16 keep them ²from ³the evil *one*. They are not of the world, even as I am
17 not of the world. ⁴Sanctify them in the truth: thy word is truth. As
18 thou didst send me into the world, even so sent I them into the world.
19 And for their sakes I ⁴sanctify myself, that they themselves also may be
20 sanctified in truth. Neither for these only do I ¹pray, but for them also
21 that believe on me through their word; that they may all be one; even as
thou, Father, *art* in me, and I in thee, that they also may be in us: that
22 the world may believe that thou didst send me. And the glory which
thou hast given me I have given unto them; that they may be one, even
23 as we *are* one; I in them, and thou in me, that they may be perfected into
one; that the world may know that thou didst send me, and lovedst them,
24 even as thou lovedst me. Father, ⁵that which thou hast given me, I will
that, where I am, they also may be with me; that they may behold my
glory, which thou hast given me: for thou lovedst me before the foundation
25 of the world. O righteous Father, the world knew thee not, but I knew
26 thee; and these knew that thou didst send me; and I made known unto
them thy name, and will make it known; that the love wherewith thou
lovedst me may be in them, and I in them.

¹ Gr. *make request.* ² Gr. *out of.* ³ Or, *evil.* ⁴ Or, *Consecrate.* ⁵ Many ancient authorities read
those whom.

§ 152. GOING FORTH TO GETHSEMANE, JESUS SUFFERS LONG IN AGONY

IN AN OPEN GARDEN, BETWEEN THE BROOK KEDRON AND THE FOOT OF THE MOUNT OF OLIVES

Late in the night introducing Friday

Mark 14:26, 32–42	Matt. 26:30, 36–46	Luke 22:39–46	John 18:1
*26 And when they had sung a hymn, they went out unto the Mount of Olives.	30 And when they had sung a hymn, they went out unto the Mount of Olives.	39 And he came out, and went, as his custom was, unto the Mount of Olives; and the	1 When Jesus had spoken these words, he went forth with his disciples over the

* The Synoptic Gospels do not give the great discourse of Jesus in John 14 to 17. Hence they represent Jesus as going forth to Gethsemane after the institution of the supper (§ 148). The time was probably not long and they apparently sang the hymn (probably one of the Psalms) as they rose to leave the Upper Room (John 14:31). Hence the passage in John 15 to 17 comes in between singing the hymn and reaching Gethsemane.

Mark 14:26, 32–42	Matt. 26:30, 36–46	Luke 22:39–46	John 18:1
32 And they come unto ¹a place which was named Gethsemane: and he saith unto his disciples, Sit ye here, while I pray.	36 Then cometh Jesus with them unto ¹a place called Gethsemane, and saith unto his disciples, Sit ye here, while I go yonder and 37 pray. And he took with him Peter and the two sons of Zebedee, and began to be sorrowful and sore troubled.	disciples also followed him. 40 And when he was at the place, he said unto them,	⁴brook ⁵Kidron, where was a garden, into the which he entered, himself and his disciples.
33 And he taketh with him Peter and James and John, and began to be greatly amazed, and sore 34 troubled. And he saith unto them, My soul is exceeding sorrowful even unto death [*see Ps. 42:6*]: abide ye here, and watch.	38 Then saith he unto them, My soul is exceeding sorrowful, even unto death: abide ye here, and watch with 39 me. And he went forward a little, and fell on his face, and prayed,	Pray that ye enter not into temptation.	
35 And he went forward a little, and fell on the ground, and prayed that, if it were possible, the hour might pass away 36 from him. And he said, Abba, Father, all things are possible unto thee; remove this cup from me: howbeit not what I will, but what thou wilt.	saying, O my Father, if it be possible, let this cup pass away from me: nevertheless, not as I will, but as thou wilt.	41 And he was parted from them about a stone's cast: and he kneeled down and prayed, 42 saying, Father, if thou be willing, remove this cup from me: nevertheless not my will, but thine, be done. 43 ⁵And there appeared	

Mark 14:26, 32–42	Matt. 26:30, 36–46	Luke 22:39–46.
		unto him an angel from heaven strengthening him.
		44 And being in an agony he prayed more earnestly: and his sweat became as it were great drops of blood falling down upon the
		45 ground. And when he rose up from his
37 And he cometh, and findeth them sleeping, and saith unto Peter, Simon, sleepest thou? couldest thou not watch one hour?	40 And he cometh unto the disciples, and findeth them sleeping, and saith unto Peter, What, could ye not watch with me one hour?	prayer, he came unto the disciples, and found them sleeping for
38 ²Watch and pray, that ye enter not into temptation: the spirit indeed is willing, but the flesh is weak.	41 ²Watch and pray, that ye enter not into temptation: the spirit indeed is willing, but the flesh	46 sorrow, and said unto them, Why sleep ye? rise and pray, that ye enter not into temptation.
39 And again he went away, and prayed, saying the same words.	42 is weak. Again a second time he went away, and prayed, saying, O my Father, if this cannot pass away, except I drink it, thy will be done.	
40 And again he came, and found them sleeping, for their eyes were very	43 And he came again and found them sleeping, for their eyes were	

203

Mark 14:26, 32–42.	Matt. 26:30, 36–46.
heavy; and they wist not what to answer him.	44 heavy. And he left them again, and went away, and prayed a third time, saying again the same words.
41 And he cometh the third time, and saith unto them, Sleep on now, and take your rest: it is enough; the hour is come; behold, the Son of man is betrayed into the hands of	45 Then cometh he to the disciples, and saith unto them, Sleep on now, and take your rest: behold, the hour is at hand, and the Son of man is betrayed unto the hands of sinners.
42 sinners. Arise, let us be going: behold, h e that betrayeth me is at hand.	46 Arise, let us be going: behold, he is at hand that betrayeth me.

[1] Gr. *an enclosed piece of ground.* [2] Or, *Watch ye, and pray that ye enter not.* [3] **Many** ancient authorities omit verses 43, 44. [4] Or, *ravine.* Gr. *winter-torrent.* [5] Or, *of the Cedars.*

PART XIII

THE ARREST, TRIAL, CRUCIFIXION AND BURIAL OF JESUS

Thursday Night, Friday, and Saturday of Passion Week (Days of Darkness for the Kingdom of God*). §§ *153–168.*

§ 153. JESUS IS BETRAYED, ARRESTED AND FORSAKEN

Garden of Gethsemane.   Friday, long before dawn

Mark 14:43–52	Matt. 26:47–56	Luke 22:47–53	John 18:2–12
			2 Now Judas also, which betrayed him, knew the place: for Jesus ofttimes resorted thither with his dis-
43 And straightway, while he yet spake, cometh Judas, one of the twelve, and with him a multitude with swords and staves, from the chief priests and the scribes and the elders.	47 And while he yet spake, lo, Judas, one of the twelve, came, and with him a great multitude with swords and staves, from the chief priests and elders of the people.	47 While he yet spake, behold, a multitude, and he that was called Judas, one of the twelve, went before them;	3 ciples. Judas then, having received the *band of soldiers*, and officers from the chief priests and the Pharisees, cometh thither with lanterns and torches and weapons. 4 Jesus therefore, knowing all the things that were coming upon him, went forth, and saith unto them, Whom

---

* "Your hour and the power of darkness" (Luke 22:53).   Friday, the Day of Suffering, has become for Christians the Day of the Cross and of Glory.

205

Mark 14:43-52	Matt. 26:47-56		John 18:2-12
			5 seek ye? They answered him, Jesus of Nazareth. Jesus saith u n t o them, I am *he*. And Judas also, which betrayed him, was standing with them.
			6 When therefore he said unto them, I am *he*, they went backward, and fell to the ground.
			7 Again therefore he asked them, Whom seek ye? And they s a i d, Jesus of Naza-
			8 reth. Jesus answered, I told you that I am *he:* if therefore ye seek me, let these go their
			9 way: that the word might be fulfilled which he spake, Of those whom t h o u h a s t given me I lost not one.
44 Now he that betrayed him had given them a token, saying, Whomsoever I shall kiss, that is he: take him, and lead him away	48 Now he that betrayed him gave them a sign, saying, Whomsoever I shall kiss, that is he; take him.		
45 safely. And when he was come, straight-	49 And		

Mark 14:43-52	Matt. 26:47-56	Luke 22:47-53	John 18:2-12
way he came to him, and saith, Rabbi; and [1]kissed him.	straightway he came to Jesus, and said, Hail, Rabbi; and [1]kissed him.	and he drew near unto Jesus, to kiss 48 him. But Jesus said unto him, Judas, betrayest thou the Son of man with a kiss?	John 18:2-12
46 And they laid hands on him, and took him. 47 But a certain one of them t h a t stood by drew his sword, and smote the [2]servant of the high priest, and struck off his ear.	50 And Jesus said unto h i m, Friend, do that for which thou art come. Then they came and laid hands on Jesus, and took 51 him. And behold, one of them t h a t were w i t h Jesus stretched out his hand, and drew his sword, and smote the [2]servant of the high priest, and struck off 52 his ear. Then saith Jesus unto him, Put up again t h y sword into its place: for all they that take the sword shall perish w i t h 53 the sword. Or thinkest thou that I cannot beseech my Father, and he shall even now send me more than twelve legions of an- 54 gels? How then should the scriptures	49 And when they that were about him saw what would follow, they s a i d, Lord, shall we smite with the sword? 50 And a certain one of them smote the [2]servant of the high priest, and struck off his right ear. 51 But Jesus answered and said, Suffer ye thus far. And he touched his ear, and healed him.	10 Simon Peter therefore having a sword drew it, and struck t h e high priest's [2]servant, and cut off his right ear. Now the [2]servant's name was Malchus. 11 Jesus therefore said unto Peter, Put up the sword into the sheath: the cup which the Father hath given me, shall I not drink it? 12 So the [3]band and the [4]chief captain, and the officers of the Jews, seized Jesus and bound h i m.

207

Mark 14:43–52	Matt. 26:47–56	Luke 22:47–53
	b e fulfilled, that thus it	
48 And Jesus answered and said unto them,	55 must be? In that hour said Jesus to the multitudes,	52 And Jesus said unto the chief priests, and captains of the temple,
Are ye come out as against a rob-b e r , w i t h swords and staves to seize	Are ye come out as against a robber with swords and staves to seize	and elders, which were come against him, Are ye come out, as against a rob-be r , with swords and
49 me? I was daily with you in the temple teaching, and ye took me not: but *this is done* that the scriptures might be ful-	me? I sat daily in the temple teaching, and ye took me	53 staves? When I was daily with you in the temple, y e stretched not forth y o u r
50 filled. And they all left him, and fled.	56 not. But all this is come to pass, that the scriptures of the prophets might be ful-filled. Then all the disci-ples left him and fled.	hands against me: but this is your hour, and the power of darkness.
51 And a cer-tain young man followed with him, hav-ing a linen cloth c a s t a b o u t h i m , over *his* naked *body:* and they lay hold on		
52 him; but he left the linen cloth, and fled naked.		

[1] Gr. *kissed him much.*　　[2] Gr. *bond-servant*　　[3] Or, *cohort.*　　[4] Or, *military tribune.* Gr. *chiliarch.*

§ 154. JESUS FIRST* EXAMINED BY ANNAS, THE EX-HIGH-PRIEST

The Jewish Trial and related occurrences, §§ 154–162.

Friday before dawn

John 18:12–14, 19–23

12 So the ¹band and the ²chief captain, and the officers of the Jews, seized
13 Jesus and bound him, and led him to Annas first; for he was father in
14 law to Caiaphas, which was high priest that year. Now Caiaphas was
   he which gave counsel to the Jews, that it was expedient that one man
   should die for the people.
19 The high priest therefore asked Jesus of his disciples, and of his teach-
20 ing. Jesus answered him, I have spoken openly to the world; I ever taught
   in ³synagogues, and in the temple, where all the Jews come together;
21 and in secret spake I nothing. Why askest thou me? ask them that have
22 heard *me*, what I spake unto them: behold, these know the things which
   I said. And when he had said this one of the officers standing by struck
23 Jesus ⁴with his hand, saying, Answerest thou the high priest so? Jesus
   answered him, If I have spoken evil, bear witness of the evil; but if well,
   why smitest thou me?

¹ Or, *cohort.* ² Or, *military tribune.* Gr. *chiliarch.* ³ Gr. *synagogue.* ⁴ Or, *with a rod.*

§ 155. JESUS HURRIEDLY TRIED AND CONDEMNED BY CAIAPHAS AND THE SANHEDRIN, WHO MOCK AND BUFFET HIM

Residence of the High-priest Caiaphas. Before dawn on Friday

Mark 14:53,55–65	Matt.26:57,59–68	Luke 22:54, 63–65	John 18:24
53 And they led Jesus away to the high priest: and there come together with him all the chief priests and the elders and the scribes.	57 And they that had taken Jesus led him away to *the house of* Caiaphas the high priest, where the scribes and the elders were gathered together.	54 And they seized him, and led him away, and brought him into the high priest's house.	24 Annas therefore sent him bound unto Caiaphas the high priest.
55 Now the chief priests and the whole council sought	59 Now the chief priests and the whole council sought		

* The *Jewish trial* comprised three stages, the preliminary examination by Annas (§ 154), the informal trial by the Sanhedrin, probably before dawn, and the formal trial after dawn. With these are narrated two related matters, the denial by Peter and the suicide of Judas.

Mark 14:53, 55–65	Matt. 26:57, 59–68
witness against Jesus to put him to death; and found it	false witness against Jesus, that they might put him
56 not. For many bare false witness against him, and their witness agreed not together.	60 to death; and they found it not, though many false witnesses came.
57 And there stood up certain, and bare false witness against him,	61 But afterward came two, and said,
58 saying, We heard him say, I will destroy this ¹temple that is made with hands, and in three days I will build another made without	This man said, I am able to destroy the ¹temple of God, and to build it in three days [*see John 2:19*].
59 hands. And not even so did their witness agree together.	
60 er. And the high priest stood up in the midst, and asked Jesus, saying, Answerest thou nothing? what is it which these witness against thee?	62 And the high priest stood up, and said unto him, Answerest thou nothing? what is it which these witness against thee?
61 But he held his peace, and answered nothing. Again the high priest asked him, and saith unto him,	63 But Jesus held his peace.
	And the high priest said unto him, I adjure thee by the living God, that thou tell us whether

Mark 14:53, 55–65	Matt.26:57,59–68	Luke 22:54, 63–65
Art thou the Christ, the Son of the Blessed?	thou be the Christ, the Son of God.	
62 And Jesus said, I am: and ye shall see the Son of man sitting at the right hand of power, and coming with the clouds of 63 heaven [*see Ps. 110:1; Dan. 7: 13*]. And the high priest rent his clothes, and saith,	64 Jesus saith unto him, Thou hast said: nevertheless I say unto you, Henceforth ye shall see the Son of man sitting at the right hand of power, and coming on the clouds of heav- 65 en. Then the high priest rent his gar- ments, saying, He hath spok- en blasphemy:	
What further need have we of wit- 64 nesses? Ye have heard the blasphe- my [*see Lev. 24:16*]: what think ye? And they all con- demned him to be ²worthy 65 of death. And some began to spit on him, and to cover his face, and to buffet him, and to say un- to him, Proph- esy: and the officers receiv- ed him with ⁴blows of their hands.	what further need have we of witnesses? behold, now ye have heard the blasphe- 66 my:what think ye? They an- swered and said, He is ²worthy of death. 67 Then did they spit in his face and buffet him:and some smote him ³with the palms of their 68 hands, saying, Prophesy unto us,thou Christ, who is he that struck thee?	63 And the men that held ⁵*Je- sus* mocked him and beat 64 him. And they blindfolded him, and asked him, saying, Prophesy: who is he that struck thee? 65 And many other things spake they against him, reviling him.

¹ Or, *sanctuary*; as in Matt. 23:35; and chap. 27:5. ² Gr. *liable to*. ³ Or, *with rods*. ⁴ Or, *strokes of rods*. ⁵ Gr. *him*.

§ 156. PETER THRICE* DENIES HIS LORD

COURT OF THE HIGH-PRIEST'S RESIDENCE, DURING THE SERIES OF TRIALS

Friday before and about dawn

Mark 14:54, 66–72	Matt. 26:58, 69–75	Luke 22:54–62	John 18:15–18, 25–27
54 And Peter had followed him afar off,	58 But Peter followed him afar off,	54 But Peter followed afar off.	15 And Simon Peter followed Jesus, and *so did* another disciple. Now that disciple was known unto the high priest, and entered i n with Jesus into the court of the high priest;
even within, into the court of the high priest;	unto the court of the high priest, and entered in,		16 but Peter was standing at the door without. So the other disciple, which was known unto the high priest, went out and spake unto her that kept the door, and brought in Peter. 17 The maid therefore that kept the door saith unto Peter, Art thou also *one* of this man's disciples? H e saith, I am

* Each of the four Gospels records three denials; but the details differ considerably, as must always be the case where in each narrative a few facts are selected out of many sayings and doings. We have seen (footnote on § 154) that there were *three stages* of the Jewish trial, (1) before Annas (2) before Caiaphas and the Sanhedrin for informal examination, (3) before them in a formal trial. Now John gives only the first of the three stages, Luke only the last, Matthew and Mark give the second stage fully, and the third in brief mention. If Peter's denials ran through all three (and Luke says in ver. 59 that there was an hour between his second and third denials), then no one of the four Gospels could give each of the denials precisely at the time of its occurrence; and so each Gospel merely throws them together, as in another way we here bring them together in one section. There is no difficulty about the substantial fact of the denials; and we must be content with our inability to arrange all the circumstances into a complete programme.

Mark 14:54, 66–72	Matt. 26:58, 69–75	Luke 22:54–62	John 18:15–18, 25–27
			18 not. Now the [5]servants and the officers were standing *there*, having made [6]a fire of coals; for it was cold; and they were warming themselves: and Peter also was with them, standing and warming himself.
and he was sitting with the officers, and warming himself in the light *of the fire.*	and sat with the officers, to see the end.		
		55 And when they had kindled a fire in the midst of the court, and had sat down together, Peter sat in the midst of them.	
66 And as Peter was beneath in the court, there cometh one of the maids of the high priest;	69 Now Peter was sitting without in the court: and a maid came unto him, saying,		
67 and seeing Peter warming himself, she looked upon him, and saith, Thou also wast with the Nazarene, *even* Jesus.	Thou also wast with Jesus the Galilæan.	56 And a certain maid seing him as he sat in the light *of the fire*, and looking stedfastly upon him, said, This man also was with him.	25 Now Simon Peter was standing and warming himself. They said therefore unto him, Art thou also one of his disciples?
68 But he denied, saying, [1]I neither know, nor understand what thou sayest: and he went out into the [2]porch; [3]and the cock crew.	70 But he denied before them all, saying, I know not what thou sayest.	57 But he denied, saying, Woman, I know him not.	He denied and said, I am not.
	71 And when he was gone out into the proch, another *maid* saw him, and saith unto them that were there, This man also was with Jesus the		
69 And the maid saw him, and began again to say to them that stood by, This is *one* of them.		58 And after a little while another saw him, and said, Thou also art *one* of them. But Peter said, Man, I am not.	

213

Mark 14:54, 66–72	Matt. 26:58, 69–75	Luke 22:54–62	John 18:15–18, 25–27
70 But he again denied it.	Nazarene. 72 And again he denied with an oath, I know not the man.		
And after a little while again they that stood by said to Peter, Of a truth thou art one of them; for thou art a 71 Galilæan. But he began to curse, and to swear, I know not this man of whom ye 72 speak. And straightway the second time the cock crew.	73 And after a little while they that stood by came and said to Peter, Of a truth thou also art one of them; for thy speech bewrayeth thee. 74 Then began he to curse and to swear, I know not the man. And straightway the cock crew.	59 And after the space of about one hour another confidently affirmed, saying, Of a truth this man also was with him: for he is a Galilæan. 60 But Peter said, Man, I know not what thou sayest. And immediately, while he yet spake, the cock crew. 61 And the Lord turned, and looked upon Peter.	26 One of the 5servants of the high priest being a kinsman of him whose ear Peter cut off, saith, Did not I see thee in the garden 27 with him? Peter therefore denied again:
And Peter called to mind the word, how that Jesus said unto him, Before the cock crow twice, thou shalt deny me thrice. 4And when he thought thereon, he wept.	75 And Peter remembered the word which Jesus had said, Before the cock crow, thou shalt deny me thrice. And he went out, and wept bitterly.	And Peter remembered the word of the Lord, how that he said unto him, Before the cock crow this day, thou shalt deny me 62 thrice. And he went out, and wept bitterly.	and straightway the cock crew.

1 Or, *I neither know, nor understand: thou, what sayest thou?* 2 Gr. *forecourt.* 3 Many ancient authorities omit *and the cock crew.* 4 Or, *And he began to weep.* 5 Gr. *bond-servants.* 6 Gr. *a fire of charcoal.*

§ 157. AFTER DAWN, JESUS IS FORMALLY* CONDEMNED BY THE SANHEDRIN

Friday

Mark 15:1	Matt. 27:1	Luke 22:66-71
1 And straightway in the morning the chief priests with the elders and scribes, and the whole council, held a consultation,	1 Now when morning was come, all the chief priests and the elders of the people took counsel against Jesus to put him to death:	66 And as soon as it was day, the assembly of the elders of the people was gathered together, both chief priests and scribes, and they led him away into their council, saying, If 67 thou art the Christ, tell us. But he said unto them, If I tell you, ye will not believe: and if I ask *you*, ye will not answer. 68 But from henceforth shall the Son of man be seated on the right hand of the power of God [see Ps. 110:1; Dan. 7:13]. And they all said, Art thou then the Son of God? And he said unto them, ¹Ye say that I am. 71 And they said, What further need have we of witness? for we ourselves have heard from his own mouth.

¹ Or, *Ye say it, because I am.*

§ 158. REMORSE AND SUICIDE OF JUDAS THE BETRAYER

IN THE TEMPLE AND IN A PLACE WITHOUT THE WALLS OF JERUSALEM

Friday morning

Matt. 27:3-10	Acts 1:18, 19
3 Then Judas, which betrayed him, when he saw that he was con-	18 (Now this man obtained a field with the reward of his iniquity;

* This ratification of the condemnation after dawn was an effort to make the action legal. But no ratification of a wrong can make it right. Some modern Jewish writers admit the illegalities and argue the unhistorical character of the narrative. But the hate of the Sanhedrin for Jesus made them violate their own rules of legal procedure. See my book, *The Pharisees and Jesus.*

Matt. 27:3–10	Acts 1:18, 19
demned, repented himself, and brought back the thirty pieces of silver to the chief priests and 4 elders, saying, I have sinned in that I betrayed [1]innocent blood. 5 But they said, What is that to us? see thou *to it*. And he cast down the pieces of silver into the sanctuary, and departed; and he went 6 away and hanged himself. And the chief priests took the pieces of silver, and said, It is not lawful to put them into the [2]treasury, since it is the price of blood [*see Deut.* 7 *23:18*]. And they took counsel, and bought with them the potter's 8 field, to bury strangers in. Wherefore that field was called, The field of blood, unto this day. 9 Then was fulfilled that which was spoken [3]by Jeremiah the prophet, saying, And [4]they took the thirty pieces of silver, the price of him that was priced, [5]whom *certain* of 10 the children of Israel did price; and [6]they gave them for the potter's field, as the Lord appointed me [*see Zech. 11:13; Jer. 18:2; 19:2; 32:6–15*].	and falling headlong, he burst asunder in the midst, and all his 19 bowels gushed out. And it became known to all the dwellers at Jerusalem; insomuch that in their language that field was called Akeldama, **that is**, The field of blood.)

[1] Many ancient authorities read *righteous*. [2] Gr. *corbanas*, that is, *sacred treasury*. Comp Mark 7:11. [3] Or, *through*. [4] Or, *I took*. [5] Or, *whom they priced on the part of the sons of Israel*. [6] Some ancient authorities read *I gave*.

§ 159. JESUS BEFORE PILATE THE FIRST* TIME

Jerusalem. Friday, early morning

Mark 15:1–5	Matt. 27:2, 11–14	Luke 23:1–5	John 18:28–38
1 and bound Jesus, and carried him away, and delivered him up to Pilate.	2 and they bound him, and led him away, and delivered him up to Pilate the governor.	1 And the whole company of them rose up, and brought him before Pilate.	28 They lead Jesus therefore from Caiaphas into the [2]palace: and it was early; and t h e y themselves entered not into

* The Roman Trial also comprised three stages, (1) the first appearance before the Roman procurator Pilate (§ 159), (2) the appearance before Herod Antipas, the native ruler of Galilee appointed by the Romans (§ 160), and (3) the final appearance before Pilate (§ 161).

Mark 15:1-5	Matt. 27:2, 11-14	Luke 23:1-5	John 18:28-38
			the ²palace, that they might not be defiled, but might eat the
			29 passover. Pilate therefore went out unto them, and
		2 And they began to accuse him, saying, We found this man perverting our nation, and forbidding to give tribute to Cæsar, and saying that he himself is ¹Christ a king.	saith, What accusation bring ye against this
			30 man? They answered and said unto him, If this man were not an evil-doer we should not have delivered him up unto
			31 thee. Pilate therefore said unto them, Take him yourselves, and judge him according to your law. The Jews said unto him, It is not lawful for us to put any man to death:
			32 that the word of Jesus might be fulfilled, which he spake signifying by what manner of death he should die.
			33 Pilate therefore entered again into the ²palace, and called Jesus, and said unto him,
2 And Pilate asked him,	11 Now Jesus stood before the governor:	3 And Pilate asked him, saying,	

Mark 15:1–5	Matt. 27:2, 11–14	Luke 23:1–5	John 18:28–38
Art thou the King of the Jews? And he answering saith unto him, Thou sayest.	and the governor asked him, saying, Art thou the King of the Jews? And Jesus said unto him, Thou sayest.	Art thou the King of the Jews? And he answered him and said, Thou sayest.	Art thou the King of the 34 Jews? Jesus answered, Sayest thou this of thyself, or did others tell it thee concern- 35 ing me? Pilate answered, Am I a Jew? Thine own nation and the chief priests deliver- ed thee unto me: what hast thou done? 36 Jesus answer- ed, My king- dom is not of this world: if my kingdom were of this world, then would m y ³servants fight, that I should not be deliver- ed to the Jews: but now is my kingdom not from hence. 37 Pilate there- fore said unto him, Art thou a king then? Jesus answer- ed, ⁴Thou say- est that I am a king. To this end have I been born, and to this end am I come into the world, that I should bear witness unto

Mark 15:1-5	Matt. 27:2, 11-14	Luke 23:1-5	John 18:28-38
			the truth. Every one that is of the truth heareth my 38 voice. Pilate saith unto him, What is truth? And when he had said this, he went out again unto the Jews, and saith unto them, I find no crime in him.
		4 And Pilate said unto the chief priests and the multitudes, I find no fault in this man.	
3 And the chief priests accused him of many things.	12 And when he was accused by the chief priests and elders, he answered nothing.		
4 And Pilate again asked him, saying, Answerest thou nothing? behold how many things they accuse 5 thee of. But Jesus no more answered anything; insomuch that Pilate marvelled.	13 Then saith Pilate unto him, Hearest thou not how many things they witness against 14 thee? And he gave him no answer, not even to one word: insomuch that the governor marvelled greatly.		
		5 But they were the more urgent, saying, He stirreth up the people, teaching throughout all Judea, and beginning from Galilee even unto this place.	

[1] Or, *an anointed king.*   [2] Gr. *Prætorium.*   [3] Or, *officers;* as in verses 3, 12, 18, 22.   [4] Or, *Thou sayest it, because I am a king.*

§ 160. JESUS BEFORE HEROD ANTIPAS THE TETRARCH

Jerusalem. Friday, early morning

Luke 23:6-12

6   But when Pilate heard it, he asked whether the man were a Galilæan.
7 And when he knew that he was of Herod's jurisdiction, he sent him unto Herod, who himself also was at Jerusalem in these days.
8   Now when Herod saw Jesus, he was exceeding glad: for he was of a long time desirous to see him, because he had heard concerning him;*
9 and he hoped to see some [1]miracle done by him. And he questioned
10 him in many words; but he answered him nothing. And the chief priests
11 and the scribes stood, vehemently accusing him. And Herod with his soldiers set him at nought, and mocked him, and arraying him in gor-
12 geous apparel sent him back to Pilate. And Herod and Pilate became friends with each other that very day: for before they were at enmity between themselves.

[1] Gr. *sign.*

§ 161. JESUS THE SECOND TIME BEFORE PILATE

Pilate slowly and reluctantly and in fear surrenders to the demand of the Sanhedrin for the crucifixion of Christ.

Friday toward sunrise (John 19:14)

Mark 15:6-15	Matt. 27:15-26		
6 Now at [1]the feast he used to release unto them one pris-oner, whom they asked of 7 him. And there was one called Barab-b a s, *lying* bound with them that had made insurrec-tion, men who in the insurrec-tion had com-mitted mur-8 der. And the m u l t i t u d e went up and began to ask	15 Now at [1]the feast the gov-ernor was wont to release unto the multitude one prisoner, whom they 16 would. And they had then a notable pris-oner, called Barabbas.		

* See § 71.

Mark 15:6–15	Matt. 27:15–26	Luke 23:13–25	John 18:39–19:16
him *to do* as he was wont to do unto them.			
		13 And Pilate called together t h e c h i e f priests and the rulers and the	
		14 people, and s a i d u n t o t h e m , Y e brought unto me this man, as one that perverteth the people: and behold, I, having examined him before you, found no fault in this man touching those things whereof ye accuse him:	
		15 no, nor yet Herod: for he sent him back unto us; and behold, nothing worthy of death hath been done by him.	
			39 But ye have a custom, that I should release unto you one at the
9 And Pilate answered them, saying, Will ye that I release unto you the King of the Jews?	17 When therefore they were gathered together, Pilate said unto them, Whom will ye that I release unto you? Barabbas, or Jesus which is called	16 I will therefore chastise him, and release him.	passover: will ye therefore that I release unto you the King of the Jews?
10 For he perceived that for envy the chief priests	18 Christ? For he knew that for envy they had delivered		

221

Mark 15:6–15	Matt. 27:15–26	Luke 23:13–25	John 18:39–19:16
had delivered him up.	19 him up. And while he was sitting on the judgement seat, his wife sent unto him, saying, Have thou nothing to do with that righteous man: for I have suffered many things this day in a dream because of		
11 But the chief priests stirred up the multitude that he should rather release Barabbas unto them.	him. 20 Now the chief priests and the elders persuaded the multitudes that they should ask for Barabbas, and destroy Jesus. 21 But the governor answered and said unto them, Whether of the twain will ye that I release unto you? And they said, Barabbas.	18 But they cried out all together, saying, Away with this man, and release unto us 19 Barabbas: one who for a certain insurrection made in the city, and for murder, was cast into prison.	40 They cried out therefore again, saying, Not this man, but Barabbas. Now Barabbas was a robber.
			1 Then Pilate therefore took Jesus, and

Mark 15:6–15	Matt. 27:15–26	Luke 23:13–25	John 18:39–19:16
			scourged him.
			2 And the soldiers plaited a crown of thorns, and put it on his head, and arrayed him in a purple
			3 garment; and they came unto him, and said, Hail, King of the Jews! and they struck him •with their
			4 hands. And Pilate went out again, and saith unto them, Behold, I bring him out to you, that ye may know that I find no crime
			5 in him. Jesus therefore came out, wearing the crown of thorns and the purple garment. And *Pilate* saith unto them, Behold, the man!
₁2 And Pilate again answered and said unto them, What then shall I do unto him whom ye call the King of 13 the Jews? And they cried out again, Crucify 14 him. And Pilate said unto them, Why, what evil hath he done?	22 Pilate saith unto them, What then shall I do unto Jesus which is called Christ? They all say, Let him be crucified. 23 And he said, Why, what evil hath he done?	20 And Pilate spake unto them again, desiring to release Jesus; 21 but they shouted, saying, Crucify, crucify 22 him. And he said unto them the third time, Why, what evil hath this man done? I have found no cause	6 When therefore the chief priests and the officers saw him, they cried out, saying, Crucify *him*, crucify *him*. Pilate saith unto them, Take him yourselves, and crucify him, for I find

Mark 15:6–15	Matt. 27:15–26	Luke 23:13–25	John 18:39–19:16
		of death in him I will therefore chastise him and release him.	no crime in 7 him. The Jews answered him, We have a law, and by that law he ought to die, because he made himself the Son of 8 God. When Pilate therefore heard this
But they cried out exceedingly, Crucify him.	But they cried out exceedingly, saying, Let him be crucified.		

9 saying, he was the more afraid; and he entered into the ³palace again,
10 and saith unto Jesus, Whence art thou? But Jesus gave him no answer.
Pilate therefore saith unto him, Speakest thou not unto me? knowest
thou not that I have 'power to release thee, and have 'power to crucify
11 thee? Jesus answered him, Thou wouldest have no 'power against me,
except it were given thee from above: therefore he that delivered me unto
thee hath greater sin.
12 Upon this Pilate sought to release him: but the Jews cried out, saying,
If thou release this man, thou art not Cæsar's friend: every one that
13 maketh himself a king ˢspeaketh against Cæsar. When Pilate therefore
heard these words, he brought Jesus out, and sat down on the judgement
14 seat at a place called The Pavement, but in Hebrew, Gabbatha. Now it
was the Preparation of the passover: it was about the sixth hour.* And
he saith unto the Jews, Behold, your King!

		23 But they were instant with loud voices, asking that he might be crucified.	15 They therefore cried out, away with *him*, away with *him*, crucify him. Pilate saith unto them, Shall I crucify your King? The chief priests answered, We have no king but Cæsar.
	24 So when Pilate saw that		And their voices

---

* It appears that John, who wrote in Asia Minor, long after the destruction of Jerusalem, makes the day begin at midnight, as the Greeks and Romans did. We seem compelled so to understand him in 20:19 (comp. Luke 24:29–39); and in no passage of his Gospel is that view unsuitable. Here then we understand that Pilate passed the sentence about sunrise, which at the Passover, near the vernal equinox, would be 6 o'clock. The intervening three hours might be occupied in preparations, and the Crucifixion occurred at 9 o'clock, viz. the third hour as counted by the Jews (Mark 15:25).

Mark 15:6–15	Matt. 27:15–26	Luke 23:13–25	John 18:39–19:16
	he prevailed nothing, but rather that a tumult was arising, he took water, and washed his hands before the multitude [*see Deut. 21: 6–9*], saying, I am innocent ²of the blood of this righteous man: see 25 ye *to it.* And all the people answered and said, His blood *be* on us, and on our children.*	prevailed.	
15 And Pilate, wishing to content the multitude,		24 And Pilate gave sentence that what they asked for should 25 be done. And he released him that for insurrection and murder had been cast into prison, whom they asked for; but	
released unto them Barabbas,	26 Then released he unto them Barabbas:		
and delivered Jesus, when he had scourged him, to be crucified.	but Jesus he scourged and delivered to be crucified.	Jesus he delivered up to their will.	16 Then therefore he delivered him unto them to be crucified.

¹ Or, *a feast.* ² Some ancient authorities read *of this blood; see ye, etc.* ³ Gr. *Prætorium.* See Mark 15:16. ⁴ Or, *palace.* ⁵ Many ancient authorities insert ver. 17 *Now he must needs release unto them at the feast one prisoner.* Others add the same words after ver. 19. ⁶ Or, *with rods.* ⁷ Or, *authority.* ⁸ Or, *opposeth Cæsar.*

* Pilate, of course, could not escape full legal and moral responsibility for his cowardly surrender to the Sanhedrin to keep his own office. The guilt of the Sanhedrin (both Pharisees and Sadducees unite in the demand for the blood of Jesus) is beyond dispute. It is impossible to make a mere political issue out of it and to lay all the blame on the Sadducees, who feared a revolution. The Pharisees began the attacks against Jesus on theological and ecclesiastical grounds. The Sadducees later joined the conspiracy against Christ. Judas was a mere tool of the Sanhedrin, who had his resentments and grievances to avenge. There is guilt enough for all the plotters in the greatest wrong of the ages.

§ 162. THE ROMAN SOLDIERS MOCK* JESUS

Friday, between 6 and 9 A.M.

Mark 15:16–19	Matt. 27:27–30
16 And the soldiers led him away within the court, which is the ⁴Prætorium; and they call together 17 the whole ²band. And they clothe him with purple, and plaiting a crown of thorns, they put it on 18 him; and they began to salute him, Hail, King of the Jews! 19 And they smote his head with a reed, and did spit upon him, and bowing their knees worshipped him.	27 Then the soldiers of the governor took Jesus into the ¹palace, and gathered unto him the whole 28 ²band. And they ³stripped him, and put on him a scarlet robe. 29 And they plaited a crown of thorns and put it upon his head, and a reed in his right hand; and they kneeled down before him, and mocked him, saying, Hail, King 30 of the Jews! And they spat upon him, and took the reed and smote him on the head.

¹ Gr. *Prætorium*.   ² Or, *cohort*.   ³ Some ancient authorities read *clothed him*.   ⁴ Or, *palace*.

§ 163. JESUS ON THE WAY TO THE CROSS (*VIA DOLOROSA*) ON GOLGOTHA†

Before 9 A.M. Friday

Mark 15:20–23	Matt. 27:31–34	Luke 23:26–33	John 19:16–17
20 And when they had mocked him, they took off from him the purple, and put on him his garments. And they lead him out to crucify him.	31 And when they had mocked him, they took off from him the robe, and put on him his garments, and led him away to crucify him.		16 They took Jesus therefore; 17 and he went out bearing the cross for himself,
21 And they ²compel one passing by, Simon of Cyrene, coming from the country, the father of Alexander and Rufus, to go *with them*, that	32 And as they came out, they found a man of Cyrene, Simon by name: him they ¹compelled to go *with them*, that he might bear his cross.	26 And when they led him away, they laid hold upon one Simon of Cyrene, coming from the country, and laid on him the cross, to bear	

* The Sanhedrin likewise had mocked Jesus when they had condemned him to death (§ 155).
† Golgotha is the Aramaic word for "skull," and Calvary is the Latin word. The place cannot have been where the so-called "Church of the Holy Sepulchre" stands, far within the walls. There is of late a rapidly growing agreement that it was the northern end of the Temple hill, whose rounded summit (without the city wall), and southern face with holes in the rock, looks at a little distance much like a skull. This place fulfils all the conditions.

Mark 15:20–23		Luke 23:26–33
he might bear his cross.		it after Jesus.

Luke 23:26–33

27 And there followed him a great multitude of the people, and of women who bewailed and lamented him.

28 But Jesus turning unto them said, Daughters of Jerusalem, weep not for me, but weep for yourselves, and for your children.

29 For behold, the days are coming, in which they shall say, Blessed are the barren, and the wombs that never bare, and the breasts that never gave suck.

30 Then shall they begin to say to the moun-tains, Fall on us; and to the hills, Cover us

31 [see Hos. 10: 8]. For if they do these things in the green tree, what shall be done in the dry?

32 And there were also two others, male-factors, led with him to be put to death.

Mark 15:20–23	Matt. 27:31–34	Luke 23:26–33	John 19:16–17
22 And they bring him unto the place Golgotha, which is, being interpreted, The place of a 23 skull. And they offered him wine mingled with myrrh: but he received it not.	33 And when they were come unto a place called Golgotha, that is to say, The place of a 34 skull, they gave him wine to drink mingled with gall [see Ps. 69:21] and when he had tasted it, he would not drink	33 And when they came unto to the place which is called ³The skull,	unto the place called The place of a skull, which is called in Hebrew Golgotha:

¹ Gr. *impressed.* ² Gr. *impress.* ³ According to the Latin, *Calvary,* which has the same meaning.

§ 164. THE FIRST THREE HOURS ON THE CROSS

From nine A.M. till noon on Friday (three sayings of Jesus; the soldiers gambling for the garment of Jesus; the inscription on the Cross; the scoffing of Jesus by the multitude, the Sanhedrin, the soldiers, and even by the two robbers on each side of Christ)*

Mark 15:24–32	Matt. 27:35–44	Luke 23:33–43	John 19:18–27
24 And they crucify him, and part his garments among them, casting lots upon them, what each should take [see Ps. 22:18].	35 And when they had crucified him, they parted his garments among them, casting lots: 36 and they sat and watched him there.	33 there they crucified him, and the malefactors, one on the right hand and the other on 34 the left. ⁴And Jesus said, Father, forgive them: for they know not what they do. And parting his garments a-	18 where they crucified him, and with him two others, on either side one, and Jesus in the midst. 23 The soldiers therefore, when they had crucified Jesus, took his garments,

* It is not easy to tell the precise order of the events during this period of three hours, since the Gospels do not present them in the same detail or order. On the whole it has seemed best simply to follow Mark's arrangement as we have done uniformly in the Harmony. Thus the apparent order of the sayings is (1) The Prayer for Christ's enemies in Luke 23:34. (2) The Promise to the Repentant Robber in Luke 23:43. (3) The Charge to the Mother of Jesus and to the Beloved Disciple in John 19:26, 27. These three sayings are with reference to others.

Mark 15:24–32	Matt. 27:35–44	Luke 23:33–43	John 19:18–27
		mong them, they cast lots.	and made four parts, to every soldier a part; and also the ⁵coat: now the ⁵coat was without seam, woven from the top throughout. 24 They said therefore one to another, Let us not rend it, but cast lots for it, whose it shall be: that the scripture might be fulfilled, which saith, They parted my garments among them, And upon my vesture did they cast lots. [*Ps. 22:18*]. These things therefore the soldiers did.
25 And it was the third hour, and they crucified him. 26 And the superscription of his accusation was written over, THE KING OF THE JEWS.	37 And they set up over his head his accusation written, THIS IS JESUS THE KING OF THE JEWS.	38 And there was also a superscription over him, THIS IS THE KING OF THE JEWS.	19 And Pilate wrote a title also, and put it on the cross. And there was written, JESUS OF NAZARETH, THE KING OF 20 THE JEWS. This title therefore read many of the Jews: ⁷for the place where Jesus was crucified was nigh to the city: and it was written in Hebrew, *and*
27 And with him they crucify two robbers; one on his right hand, and one on his left³.	38 Then are there crucified with him two robbers, one on the right hand, and one on the left.		

Mark 15:24–32	Matt. 27:35–44	Luke 23:33–43	John 19:18–27
			in Latin, *and* in 21 Greek. The chief priests of the Jews therefore said to Pilate, Write not, The King of the Jews; but, that he said, I am King of 22 the Jews. Pilate answered, What I have written I have written.
29 And they that passed by railed on him, wagging their heads [*see Ps. 22:7*], and saying, Ha! thou that destroyest the ¹temple, and buildest it in three days 30 save thyself, and come down from the cross.	39 And they that passed by railed on him, wagging their 40 heads, and saying, Thou that destroyest the ¹temple, and buildest it in three days, save thyself: if thou art the Son of God come down from the cross.	35 And the people stood beholding.	
31 In like manner also the chief priests mocking *him* among themselves with the scribes said, He saved others; ²himself he cannot save. 32 Let the Christ, the King of Israel, now come down from the cross, that we may see and believe.	41 In like manner also the chief priests mocking *him*, with the scribes and 42 elders, said, He saved others; ²himself he cannot save. He is the King of Israel; let him now come down from the cross, and we will believe on 43 him. He trusteth on God [*see Ps. 22:8*]; let him deliver him now if he	And the rulers also scoffed at him, saying, He saved others: let him save himself, if this is the Christ of God, his 36 chosen. And the soldiers also mocked him, coming to him, offering 37 him vinegar, and saying, If thou art the King of the Jews, save thyself.	

Mark 15:24-32	Matt. 27:35-44	Luke 23:33-43	John 19:18-27
And they that were crucified with him reproached him.	desireth him: for he said, I am the Son of God. And the robbers also that were crucified with him cast upon him the same reproach.		

39   And one of the malefactors which were hanged railed on him, saying, Art not thou the Christ? save thyself and us.

40 But the other answered, and rebuking him said, Dost thou not even fear God, seeing thou art in the same condem-

41 nation? And we indeed justly; for we receive the due reward of our deeds: but this man hath done nothing amiss.

42 And he said, Jesus, remember me when thou comest⁶ in thy kingdom.

43 And he said unto him, Verily I say unto thee, To-day shalt thou be with me in Paradise.

25 But there were standing by the cross of Jesus

John 19:18-27

hismother, and his mother's sister, Mary the *wife* of Cleopas, and Mary Magda-
26 lene. When Jesus therefore saw his mother and the disciple standing by, whom he loved, he saith
27 unto his mother, Woman, behold, thy son! Then saith he to the disciple, Behold, thy mother! And from that hour the disciple took her unto his own *home.*

[1] Or, *sanctuary.* [2] Or, *can he not save himself?* [3] Many ancient authorities insert ver. 28 *And the scripture was fulfilled which saith, And he was reckoned with transgressors.* See Luke 22:37. [4] Some ancient authorities omit *And Jesus said, Father, forgive them: for they know not what they do.* [5] Or, *tunic.* [6] Some ancient authorities read *into thy kingdom.* [7] Or, *for the place of the city where Jesus was crucified was nigh at hand.*

§ 165. THE THREE HOURS OF DARKNESS FROM NOON TO THREE P.M.

(Four More Sayings* at the Close of the Darkness and the Death of Christ.)

Mark 15:33-37	Matt. 27:45-50	Luke 23:44-46
33 And when the sixth hour was come, there was darkness over the whole [1]land until the ninth hour. 34 And at the ninth hour Je-	45 Now from the sixth hour there was darkness over all the [1]land until the ninth hour. 46 And about the ninth hour Jesus	44 And it was now about the sixth hour, and a darkness came over the whole [1]land until the ninth 45 hour,[4] the sun's light failing.

* The probable order of these four sayings coming just before the death of Jesus in (1) The Cry of Desolation, Mark 15:34 = Matt. 27:46. (2) The Cry of Physical Anguish, John 19:28. (3) The Cry of Victory, John 19:30. (4) The Cry of Resignation, Luke 23:46. These four sayings of Jesus are with reference to himself.

Mark 15:33-37	Matt. 27:45-50	Luke 23:44-46	John 19:28-30
sus cried with a loud voice, Eloi, Eloi, lama sabachthani? which is, being interpreted, My God, my God, ²why hast thou forsaken me?	cried with a loud voice, saying Eli, Eli, lama, sabachthani? that is, My God, my God, ²why hast thou forsaken me[*Ps. 22:1*]?		
35 And some of them t h a t stood by, when they heard it, said, Behold, he calleth Elijah.	47 And some of them that stood there, when they heard it, said, This man calleth Elijah.		
36 And one ran, and filling a sponge full of vinegar, put it on a reed, and gave him to drink, saying, Let be; let us see whether Elijah cometh to take him down.	48 And straightway one of them ran, and took a sponge, and filled it with vinegar, and put it on a reed, and gave him to drink. 49 And the rest said, Let be; let us see whether Elijah cometh to save him.³		28 After this Jesus, knowing that all things are now finished, that the scripture might be accomplished, saith, I 29 thirst. There was set there a vessel full of vinegar: so they put a sponge full of the vinegar upon hyssop, and brought it to his mouth [*see Ps. 69:21*]. 30 When Jesus therefore had received the vinegar,
37 And Jesus uttered a loud voice,	50 And Jesus cried again with a loud voice,	46 ⁵And when Jesus had cried with a loud voice, he said, Father, into thy hands I commend my spirit [*see Ps. 31:5*]; and hav-	he said, It is finished:

Mark 15:33-37	Matt. 27:45-50	Luke 23:44-46	John 19:28-30
		ing said this,	and he bowed his head,
	and		and
and gave up the ghost.	yielded up his spirit.	he gave up the ghost.	gave up his spirit.

[1] Or, *earth.* [2] Or, *why didst thou forsake me?* [3] Many ancient authorities add *And another took a spear and pierced his side, and there came out water and blood.* See John 19:34. [4] Gr. *the sun failing.* [5] Or, *And Jesus, crying with a loud voice, said.*

§ 166. THE PHENOMENA ACCOMPANYING THE DEATH OF CHRIST

Mark 15:38-41

38 And the veil of the [2]temple was rent in twain from the top to the bottom.

39 And when the centurion, which stood by over against him, saw that he [1]so gave up the ghost, he said,

Truly this man was [3]the Son of
40 God. And there were also women beholding from afar: among

whom *were* both Mary Magdalene, and Mary the mother of James the [4]less and of

Matt. 27:51-56

51 And behold, the veil of the [2]temple was rent in twain from the top to the bottom; and the earth did quake; and the rocks were rent; and
52 the tombs were opened; and many bodies of the saints that had fallen asleep were
53 raised; and coming forth out of the tombs after his resurrection they entered into the holy city and appeared unto many.
54 Now the centurion, and they that were with him watching Jesus, when they saw the earthquake, and the things that were done, feared exceedingly, saying, Truly this was [3]the Son of
55 God. And many women were there beholding from afar, which had followed Jesus from Galilee, ministering unto him:
56 among whom was Mary Magdalene, and Mary the mother of James and Joses, and

Luke 23:45, 47-49

45 And the veil of the [2]temple was rent in the midst.

47 And when the centurion saw what was done,

he glorified God, saying, Certainly this was a righteous man.
48 And all the multitudes that came together to this sight, when they beheld the things that were done, returned smiting their breasts. And all his
49 acquaintance, and the women that followed with him from Gal-

234

Mark 15:38–41	Matt. 27:51–56	Luke 23:45, 47–49
Joses, and Salome; **41** who, when he was in Galilee, followed him, and ministered unto him: and many other women which came up with him unto Jerusalem.	the mother of the sons of Zebedee.	ilee, stood afar off, seeing these things.

¹ Many ancient authorities read, *so cried out and gave up the ghost.* ² Or, *sanctuary.* ³ Or, *a Son of God.* ⁴ Gr. *little.*

§ 167. THE BURIAL OF THE BODY OF JESUS IN THE TOMB OF JOSEPH OF ARIMATHEA AFTER PROOF OF HIS DEATH

Friday afternoon before 6 P.M.

Mark 15:42–46	Matt. 27:57–60	Luke 23:50–54	John 19:31–42
			31 The Jews, therefore, be- cause it was

the Preparation, that the bodies should not remain on the cross upon the sabbath (for the day of that sabbath was a high *day*), asked of Pilate that their legs might be broken, and *that* they might be taken away. **32** The soldiers therefore came, and brake the legs of the first, and of the **33** other which was crucified with him: but when they came to Jesus, and saw that he was dead already, they brake not his legs: howbeit one of **34** the soldiers with a spear pierced his side, and straightway there came out **35** blood and water. And he that hath seen hath borne witness, and his witness is true: and he knoweth that he saith true, that ye also may **36** believe. For these things came to pass, that the scripture might be fulfilled [*see Ex. 12:46; Num. 9:12; Ps. 34:20*], A bone of him shall not **37** be ³broken. And again another scripture saith [*see Zech. 12:10. Deut. 21:22–23; Ex. 34:24*], They shall look on him whom they pierced.

Mark 15:42–46	Matt. 27:57–60	Luke 23:50–54	John 19:31–42
42 And when even was now come, because it was the Pre- paration, that is, the day be- fore the sab- **43** bath, there came Joseph of Arimathæa, a councillor of honourable es- tate,	**57** And when even was come, there came a rich man from A r i m a t h æ a, named Joseph,	**50** And behold, a man named Joseph, who was a councillor, a good man and a **51** righteous (he	**38** And after these things Joseph of Ari- mathæa,

Mark 15:42-46	Matt. 27:57-60	Luke 23:50-54	John 19:31-42
		had not consented to their counsel and deed), *a man* of Arimathæa, a city of the Jews, who was	
who also himself was looking for the kingdom of God;	who also himself was Jesus' disciple:	looking for the kingdom of God:	being a disciple of Jesus, but secretly for fear of the Jews, asked of
and he boldly went in unto Pilate, and asked for the body of Jesus. 44 And Pilate marvelled if he were already dead: and calling unto him the centurion, he asked him whether he ¹had been any while dead.	58 this man went to Pilate, and asked for the body of Jesus.	52 this man went to Pilate, and asked for the body of Jesus.	Pilate that he might take away the body of Jesus: and
45 And when he learned it of the centurion, he granted the corpse to Joseph.	Then Pilate commanded it to be given up.		Pilate gave *him* leave. He came therefore, and took away 39 his body. And there came also Nicodemus, he who at the first came to him by night, bringing a ⁴mixture of myrrh and aloes, about a hundred pound
46 And he bought a linen cloth, and taking him down, wound him in the linen cloth,	59 And Joseph took the body, and wrapped it in a clean linen cloth,	53 And he took it down, and wrapped it in a linen cloth,	40 *weight.* So they took the body of Jesus, and bound it in linen cloths with

Mark 15:42-46	Matt. 27:57-60	Luke 23:50-54	John 19:31-42
			the spices, as the custom of the Jews is to 41 bury. Now in the place where he was crucified there was a garden; and
and laid him in a tomb which had been hewn out of a rock; and he rolled a stone against the door of the tomb.	60 and laid it in his own new tomb, which he had hewn out in the rock: and he rolled a great stone to the door of the tomb and departed.	and laid him in a tomb that was hewn in stone, where never man had 54 yet lain. And it was the day of the Preparation, and the sabbath ²drew on.	in the garden a new tomb wherein was never man yet 42 laid [see Deut. 21:22-23]. There then because of the Jews' Preparation (for the tomb was nigh at hand) they laid Jesus.

¹ Many ancient authorities read, *were already dead.* ² Gr. *began to dawn.* ³ Or, *crushed.* ⁴ Some ancient authorities read *roll.*

§ 168. THE WATCH OF THE WOMEN BY THE TOMB OF JESUS

The women maintain their watch and rest on the Sabbath (beginning 6 P.M.) while the Pharisees have a guard of Roman soldiers to keep watch over the Roman seal on the tomb.

Friday afternoon till Saturday afternoon

Mark 15:47	Matt. 27:61-66	Luke 23:55-56
47 And Mary Magdalene and Mary the *mother* of Joses beheld where he was laid.	61 And Mary Magdalene was there, and the other Mary, sitting over against the sepulchre.	55 And the women, which had come with him out of Galilee, followed after, and beheld the tomb, and how his body was laid. 56 And they returned, and prepared spices and ointments. And on the sabbath* they rested

* Luke (23:54) notes that "the Sabbath drew on" after the burial on Friday afternoon. The Sabbath began at 6 P.M. Then Luke notes that the women rested during the Sabbath (our Friday night and Saturday).

Matt. 27:61-66

Luke 23:55-56

according to the com-
mandment [*see Ex.
12:16; 20:8-11; Deut.
5:12-15*].

62   Now on the mor-
row, which is *the day*
after the Preparation,
the chief priests and the Pharisees were gathered
together unto Pilate, saying, Sir, we remem-
63 ber that that deceiver said, while he was yet
alive, After three days I rise again. Com-
64 mand therefore that the sepulchre be made
sure until the third day, lest haply his disciples
come and steal him away, and say unto the
people, He is risen from the dead: and the last
65 error will be worse than the first. Pilate said
unto them, [1]Ye have a guard: go your way,
66 [2]make it *as* sure as ye can. So they went, and
made the sepulchre sure, sealing the stone, the
guard being with them.

[1] Or, *take a guard.*   [2] Gr. *make it sure, as ye know.*

PART XIV

THE RESURRECTION, APPEARANCES, AND ASCENSION OF CHRIST

During forty days beginning with Sunday after the death of Christ. Spring of A.D. *30 (or 29). Judea and Galilee*.* §§ *169–184.*

§ 169. THE VISIT OF THE WOMEN TO THE TOMB OF JESUS

They watch the tomb late on the Sabbath (our Saturday afternoon); and the purchase of spices by them after the Sabbath (after 6 P.M. Saturday) on the first day of the week.

GOLGOTHA AND BETHANY

Our late Saturday afternoon and early evening

Mark 16:1	Matt. 28:1
	1 Now late †on the sabbath day, as it began to dawn toward the first *day* of the week, came Mary Magdalene and the other Mary to see the sepulchre.
1 And when the sabbath was past, Mary Magdalene, and Mary the *mother* of James, and Salome, bought spices, that they might come and anoint him.	

---

* Of this period we see that he remained at or near Jerusalem for a week. Then he probably left at once for Galilee (Matt. 28:7; Mark 16:7). In the month that followed we cannot fix the exact time of the events that occurred in Galilee, but just at the end of the forty days we find him again in Jerusalem.

† This phrase once gave much trouble, but the usage of the vernacular *Koiné* Greek amply justifies the translation. The visit of the women to inspect the tomb was thus made before the sabbath was over (before 6 P.M. on Saturday). But the same Greek idiom was occasionally used in the sense of "after." See Robertson, Grammar of the Greek New Testament in the Light of Historical Research, p. 645. The distance from Bethany to Golgotha was not more than a sabbath day's journey. The spices could be purchased after sundown either in Bethany or Jerusalem. It must be borne in mind that the Jewish First Day of the Week began at 6 P.M. on our Saturday.

§ 170. THE EARTHQUAKE, THE ROLLING AWAY OF THE STONE BY AN ANGEL, AND THE FRIGHT OF THE ROMAN WATCHERS

Sunday before sunrise

Matt. 28:2–4

2   And behold, there was a great earthquake; for an angel of the Lord descended from heaven, and came and rolled away the stone, and sat upon
3   it.   His appearance was as lightning, and his raiment white as snow:
4   and for fear of him the watchers did quake, and became as dead men.

§ 171. THE VISIT OF THE WOMEN TO THE TOMB OF JESUS ABOUT SUNRISE SUNDAY MORNING AND THE MESSAGE OF THE ANGELS ABOUT THE EMPTY TOMB

Golgotha.   Early Sunday morning

Mark 16:2–8		Luke 24:1–8	John 20:1
2 And very early on the first day of the week t h e y come to the tomb when the sun was risen. 3 And they were saying among t h e m s elves, Who shall roll us away the stone from the door of the 4 tomb? and looking up		1 But on the first day of the week, at early dawn,* they came unto the tomb, bringing t h e s p i c e s which they had prepared. 2 And they found the stone roll- ed away from 3 the tomb. And they entered in, and found not the body	1 Now on the first *day* of the week cometh Mary Magda- lene early while it was yet dark unto the tomb, and seeth the stone taken away from the tomb.

* So he had already risen at early dawn on the first day of the week.   He was buried (§ 167) shortly before sunset on Friday, and at sunset the sabbath began.   So he lay in the tomb a small part of Friday, all of Saturday, and 10 or 11 hours of Sunday.   This corresponds exactly with the seven times repeated statement that he would or did rise "on the third day," which *could not possibly* mean after 72 hours.   The phrase two or three times given, "after three days," naturally denoted for Jews, as for Greeks and Romans, a whole central day and any part of a first and third, thus agreeing with "on the third day."   Even the "three days and three nights" of Matt. 12:40 need not, according to known Jewish usage, mean more than we have described.   So these expressions *can* be reconciled with "on the third day," and with the facts as recorded, while "on the third day" *cannot* mean after 72 hours.   See Note 13 at end of the Harmony for full discussion of the ques- tion.   There is no real appeal from the testimony of Luke, who gives the whole period.   Luke states that Jesus was buried just before the sabbath "drew on" (our Friday evening); that the women rested during the sabbath (our Saturday), and that Jesus was already risen early Sunday morning when the women came to the tomb.

Mark 16:2–8	Matt. 28:5–8	Luke 24:1–8
they see that the stone is rolled back:for it was exceeding great. And 5 entering into the tomb, they saw a young man sitting on the right side, arrayed in a white robe; and they were 6 amazed. And he saith unto them, Be not amazed: ye seek Jesus the N a z a r e n e, which hath been crucified: he is risen; he is not here: behold, the place where they 7 laid him! But go, tell his disciples and Peter, He goeth before you into Galilee: there shall ye see him, as he said unto you. 8 And they went out, and fled from the tomb; for trembling and astonishment had come upon them;and they said nothing to any one; for they were afraid.	5 And the angel answered and said unto the women, Fear not ye: for I know that ye seek Jesus, which hath been crucified. 6 He is not here; for he is risen, even as he said. Come, see the place ¹where the 7 Lord lay. And go quickly, and tell his disciples, He is risen from the dead; and lo, he goeth before you into Galilee; there shall ye see him: lo, I have 8 told you. And they departed quickly from the tomb with fear and great joy, and ran to bring his disciples word.	²of the Lord Jesus. 4 And it came to pass, while they were perplexed thereabout, behold, two men stood by them in dazzling apparel: 5 and as they were affrighted, and bowed down their faces to the earth, they said unto them, Why seek ye ³the living among 6 the dead? ⁴He is not here, but is risen: remember how he spake unto you when he was yet in Galilee, saying 7 that the Son of man must b e delivered up into the hands of sinful men, and be crucified, and the third day 8 rise again. And they remembered h i s words.

¹ Many ancient authorities read *where he lay.*   ² Some ancient authorities omit *of the Lord Jesus*
³ Gr. *him that liveth.*   ⁴ Some ancient authorities omit *He is not here, but is risen.*

241

§ 172. MARY MAGDALENE AND THE OTHER WOMEN REPORT TO THE APOSTLES AND PETER AND JOHN VISIT THE EMPTY TOMB

Luke 24:9–12	John 20:2–10
9 and returned [1]from the tomb, and told all these things to the eleven,	2 She runneth therefore, and cometh to Simon Peter, and to the other disciple, whom Jesus loved, and saith unto them, They have taken away the Lord out of the tomb, and we know not where
10 and to all the rest. Now they were Mary Magdalene, and Joanna, and Mary the *mother* of James: and the other women with them told these things unto the apostles.	3 they have laid him. Peter therefore went forth, and the other disciple, and they went toward the
11 And these words appeared in their sight as idle talk; and they disbelieved them.	4 tomb. And they ran both together; and the other disciple outran Peter, and came first to the tomb;
12 [2]But Peter arose, and ran into the tomb; and stooping and looking in, he seeth the linen clothes by themselves; and he [3]departed to his home, wondering at that which was come to pass.	5 and stooping and looking in, he seeth the linen cloths lying; yet
	6 entered he not in. Simon Peter therefore also cometh, following him, and entered into the tomb; and he beholdeth the linen cloths
	7 lying, and the napkin, that was upon his head, not lying with the linen cloths, but rolled up in a
	8 place by itself. Then entered in therefore the other disciple also, which came first to the tomb, and
	9 he saw, and believed. For as yet they knew not the scripture, that he must rise again from the dead.
	10 So the disciples went away again unto their own home.

[1] Some ancient authorities omit *from the tomb.*   [2] Some ancient authorities omit verse 12.   [3] Or, *departed, wondering with himself.*

Five appearances are given as occurring on the day of his resurrection, and five subsequently during the forty days. The five appearances on this day were (1) to Mary Magdalene (John and Mark); (2) to other women (Matthew); (3) to the two going to Emmaus; (4) to Simon Peter (Luke 24:34); (5) to ten apostles and others.

§ 173. THE APPEARANCE OF JESUS TO MARY MAGDALENE AND THE MESSAGE TO THE DISCIPLES

Jerusalem. The first day of the week (Sunday)

John 20:11–18

11 But Mary was standing without at the tomb weeping: so, as she

Mark 16:9-11 | John 20:11-18

wept, she stooped and looked into
12 the tomb; and she beholdeth two
angels in white sitting, one at the
head, and one at the feet, where
13 the body of Jesus had lain. And
they say unto her, Woman, why
weepest thou? She saith unto
them, Because they have taken
away my Lord, and I know not

9   ¹Now when he was risen early
on the first day of the week, he appeared first to Mary Magdalene,
from whom he had cast out seven
²devils.

14 where they have laid him. When
she had thus said, she turned herself back, and beholdeth Jesus
standing, and knew not that it
15 was Jesus. Jesus saith unto her,
Woman, why weepest thou? whom
seekest thou? She, supposing him
to be the gardener, saith unto him,
Sir, if thou hast borne him hence,
tell me where thou hast laid him,
16 and I will take him away. Jesus
saith unto her, Mary. She turneth
herself, and saith unto him in Hebrew, Rabboni; which is to say,
17 ³Master. Jesus saith to her, ⁴Touch
me not; for I am not yet ascended
unto the Father: but go unto my
brethren, and say to them, I ascend
unto my Father and your Father,

10   She went and told them that
had been with him, as they
mourned and wept.

18 and my God and your God. Mary
Magdalene cometh and telleth the
disciples, I have seen the Lord;
and *how that* he had said these
things unto her.

11   And
they, when they heard that he
was alive, and had been seen of
her, disbelieved.

¹ The two oldest manuscripts, and some other authorities, omit from ver. 9 to the end. Some other authorities have a different ending to the Gospel. ² Gr. *demons.* ³ Or, *Teacher.* ⁴ Or, *Take hold not on me.*

§ 174. THE APPEARANCE OF JESUS TO THE OTHER WOMEN

Jerusalem.   Sunday the first day of the week

Matt. 28:9-10

9   And behold, Jesus met them, saying, All hail. And they came and
10 took hold of his feet, and worshipped him. Then saith Jesus unto them,
Fear not: go tell my brethren that they depart into Galilee, and there
shall they see me.

§ 175. SOME OF THE GUARD REPORT TO THE JEWISH RULERS

Matt 28:11–15

11 Now while they were going, behold, some of the guard came into the
city, and told unto the chief priests all the things that were come to pass.
12 And when they were assembled with the elders, and had taken counsel,
13 they gave large money unto the soldiers, saying, Say ye, His disciples
14 came by night, and stole him away while we slept. And if this ¹come to
15 the governor's ears, we will persuade him, and rid you of care. So they
took the money, and did as they were taught: and this saying was spread
abroad among the Jews, *and continueth* until this day.

¹ Or, *come to a hearing before the governor.*

§ 176. THE APPEARANCE TO TWO DISCIPLES (CLEOPAS AND ANOTHER) ON THE WAY TO EMMAUS

Sunday afternoon

Mark 16:12, 13	Luke 24:13–32
12 And after these things he was manifested in another form unto two of them, as they walked on 13 their way into the country. And they went away and told it unto the rest: neither believed they them.	13 And behold, two of them were going that very day to a village named Emmaus, which was threescore furlongs from Jerusalem. 14 And they communed with each other of all these things which 15 had happened. And it came to pass, while they communed and questioned together,

16 that Jesus himself drew near, and went with them. But their eyes
17 were holden that they should not know him. And he said unto them,
¹What communications are these that ye have one with another, as
18 ye walk? And they stood still, looking sad. And one of them, named
Cleopas, answering said unto him, ²Dost thou alone sojourn in Jerusalem and not know the things which are come to pass there in
19 these days? And he said unto them, What things? And they said
unto him, The things concerning Jesus of Nazareth, which was a
prophet mighty in deed and word before God and all the people: and
20 how the chief priests and our rulers delivered him up to be condemned to
21 death, and crucified him. But we hoped that it was he which should
redeem Israel. Yea and beside all this, it is now the third day since
22 these things came to pass. Moreover certain women of our company
23 amazed us, having been early at the tomb; and when they found not his
body, they came, saying, that they had also seen a vision of angels, which
24 said that he was alive. And certain of them that were with us went to
the tomb, and found it even so as the women had said: but him they saw
25 not. And he said unto them, O foolish men, and slow of heart to believe
26 ³in all that the prophets have spoken! Behoved it not the Christ to suffer
27 these things, and to enter into his glory? And beginning from Moses
and from all the prophets, he interpreted to them in all the scriptures

Luke 24:13-32

28 the things concerning himself. And they drew nigh unto the village, whither they were going: and he made as though he would go further.
29 And they constrained him, saying, Abide with us: for it is toward evening, and the day is now far spent. And he went in to abide with them.
30 And it came to pass, when he had sat down with them to meat, he took
31 the ⁴bread, and blessed it, and brake, and gave to them. And their eyes were opened, and they knew him; and he vanished out of their sight.
32 And they said one to another, Was not our heart burning within us, while he spake to us in the way, while he opened to us the scriptures?

¹ Gr. *What words are these that ye exchange one with another?* ² Or, *Dost thou sojourn alone in Jerusalem, and knowest thou not the things.* ³ Or, *after.* ⁴ Or, *loaf.*

§ 177. THE REPORT OF THE TWO DISCIPLES AND THE NEWS OF THE APPEARANCE TO SIMON PETER

Jerusalem. Sunday evening

Luke 24:33-35	1 Cor. 15:5
33 And they rose up that very hour, and returned to Jerusalem, and found the eleven gathered together, and them that were with them, 34 saying, The Lord is risen indeed, and hath appeared to Simon. 35 And they rehearsed the things *that happened* in the way, and how he was known of them in the breaking of the bread.	5 and that he appeared to Cephas.

§ 178. THE APPEARANCE TO THE ASTONISHED DISCIPLES (THOMAS ABSENT) WITH A COMMISSION AND THEIR FAILURE TO CONVINCE THOMAS

Jerusalem. Sunday evening

Mark 16:14	Luke 24:36-43	John 20:19-25
14 And afterward he was manifested unto the eleven themselves as they sat at meat;	36 And as they spake these things, he himself stood in the midst of them, ¹and saith unto them, Peace *be* unto you. 37 But they were terrified and affrighted, and supposed that they beheld a spirit.	19 When therefore it was evening, on that day, the first *day* of the week, and when the doors were shut where the disciples were, for fear of the Jews, Jesus came and stood in the midst, and saith unto them, Peace *be* unto you.

245

Mark 16:14	Luke 24:36–43	John 20:19–25
and he up-braided them with their unbelief and hardness of heart, because they believed not them which had seen him after he was risen.		

38 And he said unto them, Why are ye troubled? and wherefore do reasonings arise in your heart?

39 See my hands and my feet, that it is I myself; handle me, and see; for a spirit hath not flesh and bones, as ye behold me having. ¹And when he had said this, he shewed them his hands and his feet.

41 And while they still disbelieved for joy, and wondered, he said unto them, Have ye here anything to eat?

42 And they gave him a piece of a broiled fish².

43 And he took it, and did eat before them.

20 And when he had said this, he shewed unto them his hands and his side.

The disciples therefore were glad, when they saw

21 the Lord. Jesus therefore said to them again, Peace *be* unto you: as
22 the Father hath sent me, even so send I you. And when he had said this, he breathed on them, and saith unto them, Receive ye the ⁴Holy
23 Ghost: whosoever sins ye forgive, they are forgiven unto them; whosoever *sins* ye retain, they are retained.*

24 But Thomas, one of the twelve, called ⁵Didymus, was not with them
25 when Jesus came. The other disciples therefore said unto him, We have seen the Lord. But he said unto them, Except I shall see in his hands the print of the nails, and put my finger into the print of the nails and put my hand into his side, I will not believe.

¹ Some ancient authorities omit *and saith unto them, Peace be unto you.* ² Some ancient authorities omit ver. 40. ³ Many ancient authorities add *and a honeycomb.* ⁴ Or, *Holy Spirit.* ⁵ That is, *Twin.*

* Of our Lord's final commissions to the apostles and others (Luke 24:33), this is the first. See a second in § 181, and a third in § 183.

§ 179. THE APPEARANCE TO THE DISCIPLES THE NEXT SUNDAY NIGHT AND THE CONVINCING OF THOMAS

Jerusalem

John 20:26–31	1 Cor. 15:5.
26 And after eight days again his disciples were within, and Thomas with them. Jesus cometh, the doors being shut, and stood in the midst, and said, Peace *be* unto you. 27 Then saith he to Thomas, Reach hither thy finger, and see my hands; and reach *hither* thy hand, and put it into my side: and be not 28 faithless, but believing. Thomas answered and said unto him, My 29 Lord and my God. Jesus saith unto him, Because thou hast seen me, [1]thou hast believed: blessed *are* they that have not seen, and *yet* have believed. 30 Many other signs therefore did Jesus in the presence of the disciples, which are not written in 31 this book: but these are written, that ye may believe that Jesus is the Christ, the Son of God; and 'that believing ye may have life in his name.	5 [and that he appeared to Cephas;] then to the twelve;

[1] Or, *hast thou believed?*

§ 180. THE APPEARANCE TO SEVEN DISCIPLES BESIDE THE SEA OF GALILEE.* THE MIRACULOUS DRAUGHT OF FISHES

John 21

1 After these things Jesus manifested himself again to the disciples at the
2 sea of Tiberias; and he manifested *himself* on this wise. There were together Simon Peter, and Thomas called [1]Didymus, and Nathanael of Cana in Galilee, and the *sons* of Zebedee, and two other of his disciples.
3 Simon Peter saith unto them, I go a fishing. They say unto him, We also come with thee. They went forth, and entered into the boat; and that
4 night they took nothing. But when day was now breaking, Jesus stood
5 on the beach; howbeit the disciples knew not that it was Jesus. Jesus

* The precise date of this seventh appearance is not known except that it was after that on the Resurrection Day and before the Ascension.

John 21

6 therefore said unto them, Children, have ye aught to eat? They answered
 him, No.   And he said unto them, Cast the net on the right side of the
 boat, and ye shall find.   They cast therefore, and now they were not
7 able to draw it for the multitude of fishes.   That disciple therefore whom
 Jesus loved saith unto Peter, It is the Lord.   So when Simon Peter heard
 that it was the Lord, he girt his coat about him (for he was naked), and
8 cast himself into the sea.   But the other disciples came in the little boat
 (for they were not far from the land, but about two hundred cubits off),
9 dragging the net *full* of fishes.   So when they got out upon the land, they
10 see ²a fire of coals there, and ³fish laid thereon, and ⁴bread.   Jesus saith
11 unto them, Bring of the fish which ye have now taken.   Simon Peter
 therefore went ⁵up, and drew the net to land, full of great fishes, a hundred
 and fifty and three: and for all there were so many, the net was not rent.
12 Jesus saith unto them, Come *and* break your fast.   And none of the disciples durst inquire of him, Who art thou? knowing that it was the Lord.
13 Jesus cometh, and taketh the ⁶bread, and giveth them, and the fish like-
14 wise.   This is now the third time that Jesus was manifested to the disciples, after he was risen from the dead.
15   So when they had broken their fast, Jesus saith to Simon Peter, Simon,
 son of ⁷John, ⁸lovest thou me more than these?   He saith unto him,
 Yea, Lord; thou knowest that I ⁹love thee.   He saith unto him, Feed my
16 lambs.   He saith to him again a second time, Simon, *son* of ⁷John, ⁸lovest
 thou me?   He saith unto him, Yea, Lord; thou knowest that I ⁹love thee.
17 He saith unto him, Tend my sheep.   He saith unto him the third time,
 Simon, *son* of ⁷John, ⁹lovest thou me?   Peter was grieved because he said
 unto him the third time, ⁹Lovest thou me?   And he said unto him, Lord,
 thou knowest all things; thou ¹⁰knowest that I ⁹love thee.   Jesus saith
18 unto him, Feed my sheep.   Verily, verily, I say unto thee, When thou
 wast young, thou girdedst thyself, and walkedst whither thou wouldest:
 but when thou shalt be old, thou shalt stretch forth thy hands, and another
19 shall gird thee, and carry thee whither thou wouldest not.   Now this he
 spake, signifying by what manner of death he should glorify God.   And
20 when he had spoken this, he saith unto him, Follow me.   Peter, turning
 about, seeth the disciple whom Jesus loved following; which also leaned
 back on his breast at the supper, and said, Lord, who is he that betrayeth
21 thee?   Peter therefore seeing him saith to Jesus, Lord, ¹¹and what shall
22 this man do?   Jesus saith unto him, If I will that he tarry till I come,
23 what *is that* to thee? follow thou me.   This saying therefore went forth
 among the brethren, that that disciple should not die: yet Jesus said not
 unto him, that he should not die; but, If I will that he tarry till I come,
 what *is that* to thee?
24   This is the disciple which beareth witness of these things, and wrote
 these things: and we know that his witness is true.
25   And there are also many other things which Jesus did, the which if
 they should be written every one, I suppose that even the world itself
 would not contain the books that should be written.

¹ That is, *Twin*.   ² Gr. *a fire of charcoal*.   ³ Or, *a fish*.   ⁴ Or, *a loaf*.   ⁵ Or, *aboard*.   ⁶ Or, *loaf*.
⁷ Gr. *Joanes*.   See ch. 1:42.   ⁸, ⁹ *Love* in these places represents two different Greek words.   ¹⁰ Or,
perceivest.   ¹¹ Gr. *and this man, what?*

§ 181. THE APPEARANCE TO ABOVE FIVE HUNDRED* ON AN APPOINTED MOUNTAIN IN GALILEE, AND A COMMISSION GIVEN

Mark 16:15–18	Matt. 28:16–20	1 Cor. 15:6
	16 But the eleven disciples went into Galilee, unto the mountain, where Jesus had appointed them. And	
	17 when they saw him, they worshipped *him:* but some doubted.	6 then he appeared to above five hundred brethren at once, of whom the greater part remain until now, but some are fallen asleep:
	18 And Jesus came to them and spake unto them, saying, All authority hath been given unto me in heaven and on earth.	
15 And he said unto them, Go ye into all the world, and preach the gospel to the whole creation.	19 Go ye therefore, and make disciples of all the nations, baptizing them into the name of the Father and of the Son and of the Holy Ghost: teaching	
	20 them to observe all things whatsoever I commanded you:	
16 He that believeth and is baptized shall be saved: but he that disbelieveth shall be con-		
17 demned. And these signs shall follow them that believe: in my name shall they cast out ²devils; they shall speak with		
18 ⁴new tongues; they shall take up serpents, and if they drink any deadly thing, it shall in no		

* The meeting attended by so large a number as stated by Paul was most probably that which Jesus had appointed (Matt. 28:16), and it could be held on an appointed mountain without attracting the attention of unbelievers. — The Commission in Mark may perhaps be reckoned the same as Matthew's here. A third Commission is given by Luke in § 183. This is what is called by many the Great Commission.

Mark 16:15–18	Matt. 28:16–20
wise hurt them; they shall lay hands on the sick, and they shall recover.	
	and lo, I am with you ¹alway, even unto ²the end of the world.

¹ Gr. *all the days.*   ² Or, *the consummation of the age.*   ³ Gr. *demons.*   ⁴ Some ancient authorities omit *new.*

§ 182. THE APPEARANCE TO JAMES THE BROTHER OF JESUS

1 Cor. 15:7

7   Then he appeared to James; then to all the apostles.

§ 183. THE APPEARANCE TO THE DISCIPLES WITH ANOTHER COMMISSION

Jerusalem

Luke 24:44–49	Acts 1:3–8
44 And he said unto them, These are my words which I spake unto you, while I was yet with you, how that all things must needs be fulfilled, which are written in the law of Moses, and the prophets, and the psalms, concerning me. 45 Then opened he their mind, that they might understand the scrip- 46 tures; and he said unto them, Thus it is written [*see Hos. 6:2*], that the Christ should suffer, and rise again from the dead the third 47 day; and that repentance ¹and re- mission of sins should be preached in his name unto all ²nations, be- 48 ginning from Jerusalem. Ye are 49 witnesses of these things. And behold, I send forth the promise of my Father upon you: but tarry ye in the city, until ye be clothed with power from on high.	3 to whom he also ³shewed himself alive after his passion by many proofs, appearing unto them by the space of forty days, and speak- ing the things concerning the 4 kingdom of God: and ⁴being as- sembled together with them he charged them not to depart from Jerusalem, but to wait for the promise of the Father, which, *said he*, ye heard from me: for 5 John indeed baptized with water; but ye shall be baptized ⁵with the Holy Ghost not many days hence. 6 They therefore, when they were come together, asked him, saying, Lord, dost thou at this time re- store the kingdom to Israel? 7 And he said unto them, It is not for you to know times or seasons, which the Father hath ⁶set within 8 his own authority. But ye shall receive power, when the Holy

Acts 1:3–8

Ghost is come upon you: and ye shall be my witnesses both in Jerusalem, and in all Judea and Samaria, and unto the uttermost part of the earth.

¹ Some ancient authorities read *unto.* ² Or, *nations. Beginning from Jerusalem, ye are witnesses.* ³ Gr. *presented.* ⁴ Or, *eating with them.* ⁵ Or, *in.* ⁶ Or, *appointed by.*

§ 184. THE LAST APPEARANCE AND THE ASCENSION

On Olivet between Jerusalem and Bethany

Mark 16:19, 20	Luke 24:50–53	Acts 1:9–12
	50 And he led them out until *they were* over against Bethany, and he lifted up his hands, and blessed	
19 So then the Lord Jesus, after he had spoken unto them, was received up into heaven,	51 them. And it came to pass, while he blessed them, he parted from them, ¹and was carried up into heaven.	9 And when he had said these things, as they were looking, he was taken up; and a cloud received him out of their sight.
and sat down at the right hand of God.		10 And while they were looking stedfastly into heaven as he went, behold two men stood by them in
		11 white apparel; which also said, Ye men of Galilee, why stand ye looking into heaven? this Jesus, which was received up from you into heaven, shall so come in like manner as ye beheld him going into heaven.
	52 And they ²worshipped him, and returned to Jerusalem with great joy: and 53 were continually in	12 Then returned they unto Jerusalem.

251

Mark 16:19–20	Luke 24:50–53
20 And they went forth, and preached everywhere, the Lord working with them, and confirming the word by the signs that followed. Amen.	the temple, blessing God.

[1] Some ancient authorities omit *and was carried up into heaven.*   [2] Some ancient authorities omit *worshipped him, and.*

EXPLANATORY NOTES ON POINTS OF SPECIAL DIFFICULTY IN THE HARMONY

1. About Harmonies of the Gospels

We do not know how soon an effort was made to combine in one book the several portrayals of the life of Jesus. Luke in his Gospel (1:1-4) makes a selection of the material and incorporates data from different sources, but with the stamp of his own arrangement and style. He followed, in the main, the order of Mark's Gospel, as is easily seen. But this method is not what is meant by a harmony of the Gospels, for the result is a selection from all sorts of material (oral and written), monographs and longer treatises.

The first known harmony is Tatian's Diatessaron (*dia tessaron*, by four) in the second century (about 160 A.D.) in the Syriac tongue. It was long lost, but an Arabic translation has been found and an English rendering appeared in 1894 by J. Hamlyn Hill. It is plain that Tatian has blended into one narrative our Four Gospels with a certain amount of freedom as is shown by Hobson's *The Diatessaron of Tatian and the Synoptic Problem* (1904). There have been modern attempts also to combine into one story the records of the Four Gospels. There is a superficial advantage in such an effort in the freedom from variations in the accounts, but the loss is too great for such an arbitrary gain. The word harmony calls for such an arrangement, but it is not the method of the best modern harmonies which preserve the differences in material and style just as they are in the Four Gospels.

In the third century Ammonius arranged the Gospels in four parallel columns (the *Sections* of Ammonius). This was an attempt to give a conspectus of the material in the Gospels side by side. In the fourth century Eusebius with his *Canons* and *Sections* enabled the reader to see at a glance the parallel passages in the Gospels. The ancients took a keen interest in this form of study of the Gospels, as Augustine shows.

Of modern harmonies that by Edward Robinson has had the most influence. The edition in English appeared in 1845, that in Greek in 1846. Riddle revised Robinson's Harmony in 1889. There were many others that employed the Authorized Version, like Clark's, and that divided the life of Christ according to the feasts.

Broadus (June, 1893) followed Waddy (1887) in the use of the Canterbury Revision, but was the first to break away from the division by feasts and to show the historical development in the life of Jesus. Stevens and Burton followed (December, 1893) Broadus within six months and, like him, used the Canterbury Revision and had an independent division of the life of Christ to show the historical unfolding of the events. These two harmonies have held the field for nearly thirty years for students of the English Gospels. In 1903 Kerr issued one in the American Standard Version and James one in the Canterbury Revision (1901).

Harmonies of the Gospels in the Greek continued to appear, like Tischendorf's (1851, new edition 1891), Wright's *A Synopsis of the Gospels in Greek* (1903), Huck's *Synopse der drei ersten Evangelien* (1892, English translation in 1907), Campbell's *First Three Gospels in Greek* (1899), *A Harmony of the Synoptic Gospels in Greek* by Burton and Goodspeed (1920).

The progress in synoptic criticism emphasized the difference in subject matter and style between the Synoptic Gospels and the Fourth Gospel as appears in the works of Huck, Campbell, and Burton and Goodspeed that give only the Synoptic Gospels. Burton and Goodspeed have also an English work, *A Harmony of the Synoptic Gospels for Historical and Critical Study* (1917). In 1917 Sharman (*Records of the Life of Jesus*) gives first a harmony of the Synoptic Gospels with references to the Fourth Gospel and then an outline of the Fourth Gospel with references to the Synoptic Gospels.

Once more in 1919 Van Kirk produced *The Source Book of the Life of Christ* which is only a partial harmony, for the parables and speeches of Jesus are only referred to, not quoted. But he endeavored to show the results of Gospel criticism in the text of the book. There is much useful material here for a harmony, but it is not a real harmony that can be used for the full story of the life of Jesus. Van Kirk, however, is the first writer to place Mark in the first column instead of Matthew. I had already done it in my outline before I saw Van Kirk's book, but his was published first. It is an immense improvement to put Mark first. The student thus sees that the arrangement of the material is not arbitrary and whimsical, but orderly and natural. Both Matthew and Luke follow Mark's order except in the first part of Matthew where he is topical in the main. John supplements the Synoptic Gospels, particularly in the Judean (Jerusalem) Ministry.

Slowly, therefore, progress has been made in the harmonies of the Gospels. But the modern student is able to reproduce the life and words of Jesus as has not been possible since the first century. It is a fourfold portrait of Christ that we get, but the whole is infinitely richer than the picture given by any one of the Four Gospels. The present Harmony aims to put the student in touch with the results of modern scholarly research and to focus attention on the actual story in the Gospels themselves. One may have his own opinion of the Fourth Gospel, but it is needed in a harmony for completeness.

2. *Synoptic Criticism*

The criticism of the synoptic gospels has been able to reach a broad general conclusion that is likely to stand the test of time. The reason for this happy solution lies in the fact that the processes and results can be tested. It is not mere subjective speculation. Any one who knows how to weigh evidence can compare Mark, Matthew, and Luke in the English, and still better in the Greek. The pages of the present harmony offer proof enough. It is plain as a pikestaff that both our Matthew and Luke used practically all of Mark and followed his general order of events. For this reason Mark has been placed first on the pages where this Gospel appears at all. But another thing is equally clear and that is that both Matthew and Luke had another source in common because they each give practically identical matter for much that is not in Mark at all. This second common source for Matthew and Luke has been called Logia because it is chiefly discourses. It is sometimes referred to as "Q", the first letter of the German word *Quelle* (source). Unfortunately we do not have the whole of the Logia (Q) before us as in the case of Mark, though we probably do not possess the original ending of Mark in 16:9–20. But we can at least reproduce what is preserved. Still, just as sometimes either Matthew or Luke made use of Mark, so in the case of the Logia that is probably true. Hence we cannot tell the precise limits of the Logia. Besides, a small part of Mark is not employed by either Matthew or Luke and that may be true of the Logia. But the fact of these two sources for Matthew and Luke seems to be proven.

But there are various other points to be observed. One is that both Matthew and Luke may have had various other sources. Luke tells us (Luke 1:1–4) that he made use of "many" such sources, both oral and written. And a large part of Luke does not appear in the other gospels or at least similar events and sayings occur in different environments and times. Hence our solid conclusion must allow freedom and flexibility to the writers in various ways. We can see for ourselves how Matthew and Luke handled both Mark and the Logia, each in his own way and with individual touches of style and purpose.

One other matter calls for attention. Papias is quoted by Eusebius as saying that Matthew wrote in Hebrew (or Aramaic) whereas our present Matthew is in Greek. It is now commonly held that the real Matthew (Levi) wrote the Logia first in Aramaic and that either he or some one else used that with Mark and other sources for our present Gospel of Matthew.

It should be added also that there is a considerable body of evidence for the view that Mark wrote under the influence of Simon Peter and preserves the vividness and freshness of Peter's own style as an eyewitness.

One other result has come. It is increasingly admitted that the Logia was very early, before 50 A.D., and Mark likewise if Luke wrote the Acts while Paul was still alive. Luke's Gospel comes (Acts 1:1) before the Acts. The date of Acts is still in dispute, but the early date (about A.D. 63) is gaining support constantly. The upshot of these centuries of synoptic criticism has brought into sharp outline the facts that now stand out with reasonable clearness. There are many points in dispute still, but we at least know how the synoptic gospels were written, and are reasonably certain of the dates and the authors.

There are many good books on the subject, like Hawkin's *Horae Synopticae* (second edition), Sanday's *Oxford Studies in the Synoptic Problem*, Harnack's *Sayings of Jesus* and his *Date of the Synoptic Gospels and Acts*. My own views appear in my *Commentary on Matthew* (Bible for Home and School), *Studies in Mark's Gospel*, and *Luke the Historian in the Light of Research*.

3. The Authorship of the Fourth Gospel

It has come to pass that one has to defend the use of the Fourth Gospel on a par with the Synoptic Gospels. The Johannine problem is an old one and a difficult one. It cannot be said that modern scholarship has come to a clear result here, as is true of the Synoptic Gospels. As a matter of fact, the battle still rages vigorously. There are powerful arguments on both sides. A mere sketch of the real situation is all that can be attempted here.

The Gospel and the Epistles are in the same style and can be confidently affirmed to be by the same author. The Apocalypse has some striking peculiarities of its own. There are likenesses in vocabulary and idiom beyond a doubt of a subtle nature, but the grammatical irregularities in the Book of Revelation have long been a puzzle to those who hold to the Johannine authorship. A full discussion of these grammatical details can be found in the leading commentaries on the Apocalypse. A brief survey is given in my *Grammar of the Greek New Testament in the Light of Historical Research*. The facts are undisputed and have a most interesting parallel in the papyri fragments of some of the less educated writers of the *Koiné* as one can see for himself in Milligan's *Greek Papyri* or in any other collection.

There are two solutions of the problem with two alternatives in each instance. There are those who roundly assert that the same man could not have written both the Gospel and the Apocalypse. Some of these affirm that the Apostle John wrote the Apocalypse but not the Gospel. Certainly a "John" wrote the Revelation or claimed it at any rate. Others of this group hold that an inferential Presbyter John (not "the elder" in 2 and 3 John) supposed to be meant by Papias wrote the Apocalypse while some one else wrote the Gospel whether the Apostle John or not.

But a considerable body of scholars still hold that the same man wrote both the Gospel and the Apocalypse, but a different explanation is offered by two groups. One class of writers affirm that John wrote the Apocalypse first before he had come to be at home in the Greek idiom as we see it in the Gospel and the Epistles. We know that John and Peter were fishermen and were not considered men of literary training by the Sanhedrin (Acts 4:14). This explanation is sufficient but for the further fact that the early date of the Apocalypse (about 70 A.D.) is not now so generally held to be true. The later or Domitianic date as given by Irenæus seems pretty clearly to be correct. So the other group suggest that the books may belong substantially to the same period (the Domitianic date) and that the explanation of the grammatical infelicities in the Apocalypse may be due to the fact that John being on the Isle of Patmos when he wrote did not have the benefit of friends in Ephesus who apparently read the Gospel (John 21:24–25). Besides, the excited state of John's mind because of the visions may have added to the number of the solecisms in the Apocalypse. This view I personally hold as probable. The unity of both Gospel and Apocalypse is denied by some.

So the matter stands as between the Gospel and the Apocalypse. But the Fourth Gospel has difficulties of its own. These relate in part to the book in itself. It is true there is a great similarity in language and style between the narrative parts of the book and the discourses of Jesus. It is affirmed that the writer has colored the speeches of Jesus with his own style or even made up the dialogues so that they are without historical value or at least on a much lower plane than the Synoptic Gospels as objective history. There is something in this point, but one must remember that the Synoptic Gospels vary in their manner of reporting the speeches of Jesus and aim to give the substance rather than the precise words of the Master in all instances. It is at most a matter of degree. There is a Johannine type of thought and phrase beyond a doubt, but curiously enough we have a paragraph in Matthew 11:24–31 and Luke 10:21–23 that is precisely like the Johannine specimens, written long before the Fourth Gospel. One must remember the versatility of Jesus, who could not be retained in any one style or mold. But there are those who admit the Johannine authorship of the Gospel and yet who refuse to put it on the same plane as the Synoptic Gospels. Every one must decide for himself on this point. For myself I see too much of Christ in the Fourth Gospel in the most realistic and dramatic form to be mere invention. We can enlarge our conception of Christ to make room for the Fourth Gospel.

But even so it is urged that the Beloved Disciple cannot be the Apostle John. If not, then the Fourth Gospel ignores the Apostle John,—a very curious situation. It is a long story for which one must go to the able books in defense of the Johannine authorship by Ezra Abbott, James Drummond, W. Sanday, Luthardt, Watkins and many others. The ablest modern attacks are made by Bacon and Wendt and Schmiedel. My own view is given in my *The Divinity of Christ in the Gospel of John.*

4. *The Jesus of History*

It is not long since the cry of "Back to Christ" was raised and away from Paul and John. Soon this cry was changed to an appeal to the Jesus of History in opposition to the Christ of Theology. So we had the "Jesus or Christ" controversy (see the Hibbert Journal Supplement for 1909). It was gravely affirmed by some that Paul had created the Christ of Christianity and had permanently altered the simple program of Jesus for a social Kingdom and had turned it into a great ecclesiastical system with speculative Christological interpretations quite beyond the range of the vision of the Jesus of the Synoptic Gospels. It was admitted that the Fourth Gospel, the Apocalypse, and the Epistles all gave the Pauline view.

To the Synoptic Gospels, therefore, we all went. But the Christ of Paul and of John is in the Synoptic Gospels. In all essentials the picture is the same in Luke as in John and Paul. The shading is different, but Jesus in Luke is the Son of God as well as the Son of Man (see my *Luke the Historian in the Light of Research*). It was admitted that Matthew gives the picture of Jesus as the Jewish Messiah. Mark reflects Peter's conception of Jesus and gives Jesus as Lord and Christ (see my *Studies in Mark's Gospel*). And Q (the Logia), the earliest document that we have for the life of Christ and almost contemporary with the time of Christ, gives the same essential features of Jesus as the Son of Man and Son of God (see my article *The Christ of the Logia* in the Contemporary Review for August, 1919). The sober results of modern critical research show the same figure in the very earliest documents that we possess (Q and Mark's Gospel). The Christ of Paul and of John walks as the Jesus of History in the Synoptic Gospels. We do know the earthly life of Jesus much more distinctly and the research of centuries has had a blessed outcome in the enrichment of our knowledge. Matthew and Luke are the first critics of the sources for the life of Jesus. We see how they made use of Mark, the Logia, and other documents. The Fourth Gospel comes last with knowledge of the Synoptic Gospels.

There are, to be sure, a few men who even deny that Jesus ever lived at all. That was the next step; but this absurdity has met complete refutation. The Christ of faith is the Christ of fact. There is no getting away from the fact of Christ, the chief fact of all the ages, the centre of all history, the hope of the ages. Jesus Christ we can still call him, our Lord and Saviour, and he never made such an appeal to men as he does today in the full blaze of modern historical research. Men are just beginning to take his words to heart in all the spheres of human life. The one hope of a new world of righteousness lies precisely in the program of Jesus Christ for the life of the individual in his private affairs, in his family relations, in his business and social dealings, in his political ideals and conduct. And nations must also follow the leadership of Jesus the supreme Teacher of the race.

The purpose of a harmony is not to teach theology, but to make available for men of any faith the facts in the Gospels concerning Jesus of Nazareth. Each interprets these facts and teachings as he sees the light. We can all acknowledge our debt to modern scholarship for the tremendous contributions made to a richer understanding of the environment into which Jesus came and to a juster appreciation of the real significance of his person and his message. The Gospels are still the most fascinating books in the world for sheer simplicity and beauty. One can first trace the picture of Jesus in the Logia, then in Mark, in Matthew, in Luke, in John. To these he can add the pictures of Christ in the Acts, the Epistles, the Apocalypse.

5. *The Two Genealogies of Christ*

Sceptics of all ages, from Porphyry and Celsus to Strauss, have urged the impossibility of reconciling the difficulties in the two accounts of the descent of Jesus. Even Alford says it is impossible to reconcile them. But certainly several possible explanations have been suggested. The chief difficulties will be discussed.

1. In Matthew's list several discrepancies are pointed out.

(a) It is objected that Matthew is mistaken in making three sets of fourteen each. There are only forty-one names, and this would leave one set with only thirteen. But does Matthew say he has mentioned forty-two names? He does say (1:17) that there are three sets of fourteen and divides them for us himself: "So all the generations from Abraham unto David are fourteen generations; and from David unto the carrying away to Babylon fourteen generations; and from the carrying away to Babylon unto the Christ fourteen generations." The points of division are David and the captivity; in the one case a man, in the other an event. He counts David in each of the first two sets, although Jechoniah is counted only once. David was the connecting link between the patriarchal line and the royal line. But he does not say "from David to Jechoniah," but "from David to the carrying away unto Babylon," and Josiah is the last name he counts before that event. And so the first name after this same event is Jechoniah. Thus Matthew deliberately counts David in two places to give symmetry to the division, which made an easy help to the memory.

(b) The omissions in Matthew's list have occasioned some trouble. These omissions are after Joram, the names of Ahaziah, Joash, Amaziah, and after Josiah, these of Jehoiakim and Eliakim (2 Kings 8:24; 1 Chron. 3:11; 2 Chron. 22:1, 11; 24:27; 2 Kings 23:34; 24:6). But such omissions were very common in the Old Testament genealogies. See 2 Chron. 22:9. Here "son of Jehoshaphat" means "grandson of Jehoshaphat." So in Matt. 1:1 Jesus is called the son of David, the son of Abraham. A direct line of descent is all that it is designed to express. This is all that the term "begat" necessarily means here. It is a real descent. Whatever omissions were made for various reasons, would not invalidate the line. The fact that Ahaziah, Joash, and Amaziah were the sons of Ahab and Jezebel would be sufficient ground for omitting them.

(c) Matthew mentions four women in his list, which is contrary to Jewish custom, viz. Tamar, Rahab, Ruth, and the wife of Uriah. But neither one is counted in the lists of fourteen, and each one has something remarkable in her case (Broadus, Comm. on Matt. *in loco*). Three were guilty of gross sin, and one, Ruth, was of Gentile origin and deserved mention for that reason. This circumstance would seem to indicate that Matthew did not simply copy the genealogical history of Joseph. He did this, omitting what suited his purpose and adding likewise remarks of his own. His record is thus reliable and yet made a part of his own story.

2. A comparison of the lists of Matthew and Luke.

If no list had been given by Luke, no further explanations would be necessary. But Luke not only gives a list, but one radically different from Matthew's, and in inverse order. Matthew begins with Abraham and comes to Jesus; Luke begins with Jesus and concludes with Adam [the son of God]. Several explanations are offered to remove the apparent contradiction.

(a) As early as Julius Africanus it was suggested that the two lines had united in accordance with the law of Levirate marriage. By this theory, Heli and Jacob being stepbrothers, Jacob married Heli's widow and was the real father of Joseph. Thus both genealogies would be the descent of Joseph, one the real, the other the legal. This theory is ably advocated by McClellan, pp. 416 ff., and Waddy, p. xvii. It is argued that Jechoniah's children were born in captivity and so, being slaves, lost both his royal dignity and his legal status. Stress is laid upon the word "begat" to show that Matthew's descent must be the natural pedigree of Joseph, and upon the use of the expression "son (as was supposed) of Joseph." Hence both Joseph's real and legal standing are shown, for by Luke's account he had an undisputed legal title to descend from David. This is certainly possible, although it rests on the hypothesis of the Levirate marriage.

(b) Lord Arthur Hervey, in his volume on the Genealogies of Our Lord, and in Smith's Dictionary, argues that Matthew gives Joseph's legal descent as successor to the throne of David. According to this theory Solomon's line failed in Jechoniah (Jer. 22:30) and Shealtiel of Matthew's line took his place. Luke's account, on the other hand, gives Joseph's real parentage. Matthew's Matthan and Luke's Mattathias are identified as one, and the law of Levirate marriage comes into service with Jacob and Heli. This explanation has received favor with such writers as Mill, Alford, Wordsworth, Ellicott, Westcott, Fairbairn. McNeile (on Matthew) considers this the "only possible" view. The chief objection seems to be the most natural meaning of "begat," implying direct descent, and the necessity for two suppositions, one about Shealtiel and another about Jacob and Heli. It is even fairly probable that the Shealtiel and Zerubbabel of Matthew and Luke are different persons.

(c) The third and most plausible solution yet suggested makes Matthew give the real descent of Joseph, and Luke the real descent of Mary. Several arguments of more or less weight can be adduced for this hypothesis.

(1) The most natural meaning of "begat" in Matthew is preserved. Jesus goes through David's royal line and so fulfils prophecy. It is not elsewhere stated that Mary was of Davidic descent, although presumptive evidence exists in the language of the angel (Luke 1:32) and the enrollment of Mary (Luke 2:5). So Robinson (Revised edition).

(2) The use of Joseph without the article, while it is used with every other name in the list. "The absence of the article puts the name outside of the genealogical series properly so-called."—Godet. This would seem to indicate that Joseph belonged to the parenthesis, "as was supposed." It would read thus, "being son (as was supposed of Joseph) of Heli." Luke had already clearly stated the manner of Christ's birth, so that no one would think he was the son of Joseph. Jesus would thus be Heli's grandson, an allowable meaning of "son." See Andrews' (new edition) *Life of Our Lord*, p. 63.

(3) It would seem proper that Matthew should give the *legal* descent of Jesus, since he wrote chiefly for Jews. This, of course, could only be through Joseph.

(4) And it would seem equally fitting that Luke should give the *real* genealogy of Jesus, since he was writing for all. And this could come only through Mary. If it is objected that a woman's genealogy is never given, it may be replied that women are mentioned for special reasons in Matthew's list, though not counted, and that Mary's name is not mentioned in this list. The genealogy goes back to her father either by skipping her as suggested above and making son mean the grandson of Heli, or by allowing Joseph to stand in her place in the list, as he would have to do anyhow. On the whole, then, this theory seems the most plausible and pleasing. So practically Luther, Bengel, Olshausen, Lightfoot, Wieseler, Robinson, Alexander, Godet, Weiss, Andrews (new edition, p. 65), Broadus, and many recent writers.

But Bacon (Genealogy of Jesus Christ, Hastings D. B. and Am. J. of Theol. Jan., 1911) says that nearly all writers of authority abandon any effort to reconcile the two pedigrees of Jesus save as the effort of Christians to give "His Davidic sonship rather than His actual descent." See Machen's survey of negative criticism, on the subject in Princeton Theol. Review (Jan., 1906). Barnard (Hastings D.C.G.) admits two independent accounts, but sees no solution, but Sweet (Int. St. Bible Encyl.) accepts the view that Matthew gives the real genealogy of Joseph and Luke that of Mary. Plummer

(Comm. on Luke) thinks it incredible that Mary's genealogy should be given by Luke.

6. The Probable Time of the Saviour's Birth

Every one now understands that the accepted date of our Lord's birth is wrong by several years. The estimates of the true date vary all the way from one to seven years B.C. There are various data that fix the year with more or less certainty, but none of them with absolute precision. They do, however, agree in marking pretty clearly a narrow limit for this notable occurrence, B.C. 6 or 5.

1. The death of Herod the Great is relied on with most certainty to fix the year of Christ's birth. The rule of Archelaus and Antipas demands B.C. 4. Josephus mentions an eclipse of the moon which occurred shortly before he died. Ant. XVII, 6, 4. This eclipse is the only one alluded to by Josephus, and fixes with absolute certainty the time after which the birth of Jesus could not have occurred, since, according to Matt. 2:1-6, Jesus was born while Herod was still living. The question to be determined would be the year of this eclipse. Astronomical calculations name an eclipse of the moon March 12 and 13, in the year of Rome 750, and no eclipse occurred the following year that was visible in Palestine. Josephus (Ant. XVII, 8, 1), says that Herod died thirty-seven years after he was declared king by the Romans. In 714 he was proclaimed king, and this would bring his death counting from Nisan to Nisan, as Josephus usually does, "in the year from 1st Nisan 750 to 1st Nisan 751, according to Jewish computation, at the age of seventy" (Andrews). Herod died shortly before the Passover of 750, then, according to the eclipse and the length of his reign. Caspari contends for January 24, 753, as the date of Herod's death, because there was a total eclipse of the moon January 10. So he puts his death fourteen days later. Mr. Page (*New Light from Old Eclipses*) argues for the eclipse that occurred July 17, 752, as the one preceding Herod's death. He thinks that this makes unnecessary the subtraction of two years from the reign of Tiberius on the theory that Tiberius was contemporary ruler with Augustus for two years. But he finds difficulty in lengthening Herod's reign so long, and his theory has gained no great acceptance as yet. Our present era makes the birth of Christ in the year of Rome 754, and is due to the Abbot Dionysius Exiguus in the Sixth Century. Hence it is clear that if Herod died in the early spring of 750, Jesus must have been born *at least* four years before 754, the common era, and likely in the year 749.

2. It has been inferred by some that Jesus was at least two or three years old when Herod slaughtered the infants in Bethlehem, Matt. 2:16. Thus the year would be put two years further back to the end of 747 or beginning of 748. But this is not demanded by the "two years" of Matthew, for Herod

would naturally extend the limit so as to be sure to include the child in the number slain, and a child just entering the second year would be called "two years" old by Jewish custom. No more definite note of time comes from this circumstance, save that the massacre probably took place some months before Herod's death, which fact would bring the Saviour's birth back some time into the year 749.

3. The appearance of the "star in the east" (Matt. 2:2). This, of course, was before Herod's death, and would agree in time with the slaughter of the children, if the star be looked upon as a supernatural phenomenon, and not the wise men's interpretation of a natural conjunction of planets. Kepler first suggested that, as there was a conjunction of Jupiter and Saturn in 747, to which Mars was added in 748, this conjunction might have been the bright star that led on the wise men. See Wieseler, *Synopsis*, p. 57. Kepler had also suggested that a periodical star or a comet might have joined the constellation. The Chinese records preserve the account of the appearance of a comet in the spring of 749. Either of these theories is fascinating in itself, especially to those minds that prefer a natural explanation of anything that looks miraculous. Both phenomena are possible in themselves, but they hardly meet the requirements of the record in Matthew. (1) The word used is *aster*, star, and not *astron*, a group of stars. (2) Rev. C. Pritchard, whose calculations have been verified at Greenwich (Smith's Dic.), has shown that those "planets could never have appeared as one star, for they never approached each other within double the apparent diameter of the moon." So Ideler's hypothesis that the wise men all had weak eyes seems rather feeble. (3) The year 747 would conflict slightly with other evidence for Christ's birth that favors 749, although Wieseler, p. 53, note 4, contends that the star first appeared to the wise men two years before their visit, and a second time on their visit to Bethlehem. (4) Besides, the star is said to have stood over "where the young child was," v. 9. If it were a natural star it would have kept going as they went, and would not have stopped till they stopped. Even then it would appear as far away as ever from Bethlehem. It seems best, therefore, to admit the existence of a miracle here, and hence gain nothing from the visit of the Magi to establish the date of the Saviour's birth, save that it was not long before the slaughter of the infants, and would at least agree with the date 749. See Broadus, Comm. *in loco.*

4. The language of the heavenly host in Luke 2:14 is urged by some as fixing the birth at a time when there was universal peace throughout the world. The closing of the temple of Janus in the time of Augustus is also adduced, but it is not certainly known when it was closed apart from 725 and 729. It was intended to be closed at the end of 744, but was delayed on account of trouble among the Daci and Dalmatæ. See Greswell i. 469. Nothing specific can be obtained from this fact, save that there was a time

of comparative quiet in the Roman world from 746 to 752. There was a hush in the clangor of war when Jesus was born.

5. The entrance of John the Baptist upon his ministry gives us another note of time. See Luke 3:1 f. John emerged from the wilderness seclusion in the fifteenth year of the reign of Tiberius. Augustus died August 29, 767. Adding fifteen years to this, the fifteenth year of Tiberius would begin August 29, 781. John was of a priestly family and so could naturally enter upon his work when thirty years of age. Thirty years subtracted from this gives 751, as the date of John's birth. But that is too late by two years to agree with the other date. Here, however, the Roman histories come to our help. Tacitus, Ann. 1, 3: "Tiberius is adopted by Augustus as his son, and *colleague in empire*." Vell. Pat. 2, 121; "At the request of Augustus, Tiberius was invested with equal authority in all the provinces." So Suetonius Aug. 97 and Tib. 21. It is clear, then, that Tiberius reigned jointly with Augustus about two years before he assumed full control of the empire at the death of Augustus. Luke could have used either date, but Tiberius' power was already equal to that of Augustus in the provinces two years before his death. Luke would naturally use the provincial point of view. Taking off the two years from the joint reign of Augustus, we again come to the year 749, as John was born six months before Jesus. So if John was born in the early part of the spring, Jesus would have been born in the summer or fall of 749.

6. The age of Jesus at his entrance upon his ministry, Luke 3:23. "And Jesus himself, when he began to teach, was about thirty years of age." So most modern scholars, taking the language in the obvious sense. Origen refers it to the beginning of a new life, by the second birth of baptism, after his spiritualizing fashion. The Authorized Version has it: "And Jesus himself began to be about thirty years of age," applying the "beginning" to the period of thirty years. McClellan argues that it means "about thirty years, beginning"; that is, a little the rise of thirty years. The Revised Version seems to be preferable and the only doubt would be as to what is included in the phrase "about thirty years." It has been variously argued that Jesus was from one to three years younger or older than thirty. It seems more reasonable to give the words the meaning that he was just about thirty, a few months under or over. Apparently this fact explains the idiom. The argument that Jesus had to be exactly thirty years old because the priest had to be so, when he entered upon his work, has no great force. For Jesus was not a priest save in a spiritual sense. John had been preaching no great while when Jesus was baptized by him and so entered upon his public ministry. If John began his ministry when he was thirty years old in the fifteenth year of Tiberius, then Jesus's ministry would begin about six months later. His birth would then come in the latter part of 749,

unless John was born in the latter part of 748, when it would be earlier in the year.

7. The building of the temple of Herod gives a further clue to the date of Christ's birth. In John 2:20, the Jews say, "Forty and six years was this temple in building." Josephus tells us in one place that Herod began rebuilding the temple in the fifteenth year of his reign, War. I, 21, 1, and in another that he did so in the eighteenth year of his reign, Ant. XV, 11, 1. In the account of Herod's death, Ant. XVII, 8, 1, he used two dates for his reign, according as he counted from his declaration as king by the Romans 714, or the death of Antigonus 717. Eighteen and fifteen would both be correct, according as he reckoned from the one date or the other. Eighteen added to forty-six and both to 714 would make 778. It was at the first Passover in his ministry that this expression is used. It has been probably six months since his baptism. If thirty and a half years be taken from 778, his birth would be thrown back to the year 747, unless the forty-six years be taken as completed, when it would be 748. So Robinson. But this does not quite agree with the other notes of time we have. Many modern harmonists count the eighteen years from 717, and so bring the whole number, adding forty-six, down to 780, or, if the years are complete, 781. Thirty and a half from this would give the autumn of 749 or 750. This is done because Josephus usually reckons Herod's reign from the death of Antigonus, 717. On the whole it seems clear that Josephus is wrong in the War. It is common enough to find Josephus in one passage contradicting what he has said elsewhere. The temple was begun the year that the Emperor came to Syria, as is plain from Josephus. According to Dio Cassius, LIV, 7, this visit was made in B.C. 20 or 19. Correcting Josephus by himself and by Dio Cassius we thus again get B.C. 5 as the probable year of the birth of Christ. See Schuerer, *History of the Jewish People in the Time of Jesus Christ*, Div. I., Vol. I., p. 410.

8. The census of Augustus Cæsar mentioned in Luke 2:1 f., furnishes the last note of time for this event. This subject is involved in a great many difficulties, and for a full discussion, the reader is referred to Ramsay's *Was Christ Born at Bethlehem*, and his *Bearing of Recent Discovery on the Trustworthiness of the New Testament* (Chap. XX) and to my *Luke the Historian in the Light of Research*. Every statement made by Luke in 2:1-7 was once challenged. Every one is now shown to be correct.

(1) It used to be said that no census was ever taken by Augustus, but heathen writers mention three, in 726, 746, 767. One of these, 746, may be the one here mentioned, which was delayed for various reasons, or which was executed slowly in the distant provinces. But it is not necessary that the phrase "all the world" should be pressed to its literal meaning, though this is more natural. Nor does the argument from silence prove that no

other general census was taken by Augustus. But Ramsay has triumphantly vindicated Luke and the general census under Augustus by proof from the papyri that Augustus inaugurated a periodical census every fourteen years from B.C. 8 on. The second occurred A.D. 6 (Acts 5:37). See Ramsay's *Was Christ Born at Bethlehem*, and *Bearing of Recent Discovery on Trustworthiness of the New Testament* (Chap. XX) and my *Luke the Historian* (Chap. XX). We have only to think that there was delay in the carrying out of the census in Palestine to bring this date down to B.C. 6 (or even 5).

(2) It is not a "taxing," but an "enrollment" (Rev. Ver.) that was taken. There was a taxing later (Acts 5:37). And if it were done while Herod was king, Augustus could not have taxed Judea without Herod's consent. But Herod was not now in good form with Augustus.

(3) This helps to explain another objection that the enrollment would not have included Judea anyhow, because it was not yet a province, but a kingdom. But it is not likely that Herod would have displeased Augustus by refusing such information if it was desired. Tacitus asserts that the *regna*, the dependent kingdoms, were included in the census taken by Augustus.

(4) Hence, also, it is natural that the enrollment should have taken place according to the Jewish and not according to the usual Roman method, because Herod would wish it to be in accordance with the customs of his kingdom. So every one went to his own city. We now know from numerous papyri that in Egypt the family went to the home city. The Jews were used to enrollment by tribes and that was allowed. See Deissmann's *Light from the Ancient East*, p. 268, and Ramsay's *Was Christ Born at Bethlehem*, p. 108.

(5) We now have to meet the objection that Quirinius was not governor till ten years later, A.D. 6, when a taxing did occur. (See Acts 5:37.)

It is now possible to give a real solution of this problem. Luke is now shown to be wholly correct in his statement that Quirinius was twice governor, and that the first census took place during the first period. A series of inscriptions in Asia Minor show that Quirinius was governor of Syria B.C. 10–7 and so twice governor of Syria (second time A.D. 6; Josephus, Ant. XVIII, 1:1). See Ramsay, *Bearing of Recent Discovery*, pp. 273–300, and my *Luke the Historian*, pp. 127–9. Tertullian (*adv. marc.* iv, 19) says that Sentius Saturninus was governor of Syria B.C. 9–6. But we now know that Varus was controlling the internal affairs of Syria while Quirinius was leader of the army. Luke is therefore quite accurate in his statement about Quirinius being twice governor of Syria. The *Lapis Tiburtinus* has *iterum Syriam* about Quirinius. Ramsay has cleared up this famous historical puzzle and has completely vindicated Luke.

Few subjects have excited as much interest, even needless curiosity, as the date of the birth of the Saviour. But it is noticeable that by the masses of Christians more interest is taken in the day of Christ's birth than in the year. The Christmas festivities and the natural desire to make that the birthday of Jesus cause this widespread interest in December 25. Not only is it impossible to determine with any degree of certainty the day of the month, but the time of the year also is equally uncertain. The chief thing that appears proved is that December 25 is not the time, since the shepherds would hardly be in the fields at night with the flocks, which were usually taken into the folds in November and kept in till March. The nights of December would scarcely allow watching in the mountain fields even as far south as Bethlehem. And besides, the long journey from Nazareth to Bethlehem would hardly be made by Joseph and Mary in winter, the rainy season. McClellan argues for December 25, but his arguments are not convincing. The ancients had various days for Christ's birth: May 20 (Clement of Alexandria), April 20, December 25, January 5. Tertullian and others even say that the day of his birth (December 25) was kept in the register at Rome. But chronologists attach little weight to this testimony, since the same tradition puts the birth of John, June 24; the annunciation of Mary, March 25, and Elizabeth's conception, September 25—the four cardinal points of the year. If one might hazard an opinion, it would be that the birth of Jesus occurred in the summer or early in the fall of 749 or of 748, that is b.c. 6 or 5. Turner (Chronology, Hastings D B) reaches b.c. 6 as the probable year of the birth of Jesus though he did not have the new light on the census and on Quirinius which confirms it. Hitchcock (Hastings D C G) saw the bearing of the periodical census that called for b.c. 7–5, but did not yet know the discovery about Quirinius. Armstrong (Chronology New Testament, Int. St. Bible Encycl.) is less certain about the precise year.

7. The Feast of John 5:1, and the Duration of Our Lord's Ministry

It seems almost impossible to decide with certainty what feast is alluded to in John 5:1. One can only speak with moderation where everything is so doubtful. Various feasts have been suggested as solving the problem.

1. The Feast of Dedication has been proposed by Kepler and Petavius. But this view has met with no great amount of favor, for there is too short an interval between the first Passover and December, when it occurred. It might be a later Feast of Dedication, but this feast was not one of the great feasts and would hardly have drawn Jesus all the way from Galilee to attend it. He did attend this feast once (John 10:22), but he was already in Judea at this time, having come up to attend the Feast of Tabernacles (John 7:2, 14). So Robinson, Clark, etc. So this feast seems to be ruled out of the question.

2. The Feast of Tabernacles is advocated by Ebrard, Ewald, Patritius.

It is very unlikely that the Feast of Tabernacles after the first Passover could be meant, as the Saviour did not return to Galilee for some time afterwards. He could hardly have come back so soon to Jerusalem. But the Feast of Tabernacles after the Passover of John 6:4 is mentioned later, John 7:2 f., which Jesus attended, it seems, because he was hindered from going up to the previous Passover by the murderous designs of the Jews. It is possible that the feast of John 5:1 may have been the Feast of Tabernacles after a Passover not mentioned, and so would come after the second Passover of his public ministry. But we do not know that Jesus attended any other Feast of Tabernacles save the one in John 7:2, which he may have done because he missed the preceding Passover.

3. The Feast of Purim, first suggested by Kepler, has had great favor with modern harmonists, but apparently more on sentimental than on scholarly grounds. Meyer says, "Without doubt it was Purim." But it is by no means so certain as Meyer would have us believe. (*a*) Meyer relies on John 4:35 and 6:4 to show that this was the Feast of Purim just before John 6:4. But the expression, "Say not ye, There are yet four months and then cometh the harvest?" may be, and probably is a proverbial saying indicating the usual length of time between sowing and reaping, which, as a matter of fact, was about four months. Hence nothing can be determined by this note of time. And, besides, the four months could precede the Passover just as well as Purim, because the sowing lasted a month or so. (*b*) The Feast of Purim occurred a month before the Passover. Is it at all likely that two circuits of all Galilee were made in the meantime, besides much work of other kinds? See Luke 8:1 and Matt. 9:25–38. The three general circuits throughout Galilee, besides the mission of the twelve and a large part of their training, the general statements about the Master's work of preaching and healing, require an expansion rather than a contraction of the time for this period of his ministry. It seems then quite unreasonable, when once the mind takes in this enlarged conception of the missionary work of Jesus, as recorded by the Synoptic Gospels, to limit it to the amount of work mentioned by John, since he omits much of the early ministry, because, it would seem, the others are so full just here. (*c*) The Feast of Purim, moreover, was observed at home in the synagogues, and not by going to Jerusalem. See Esther 9:22 and Jos. Ant. xi. 6, 13. But "the multitude" (John 5:13) seems to imply (Robinson) a concourse of strangers at one of the great festivals. (*d*) It seems hardly probable, besides, that Jesus would go to any feast just a month before the Passover and come back to Galilee and not go to the Passover itself (John 6:4). Least of all would he do this in the case of Purim. (*e*) The man who was healed at this feast was healed on the Sabbath (John 5:9), and this occasioned the outburst among the people. But the Feast of Purim was never celebrated on the

Sabbath, and when it came on a Sabbath it was postponed. See Reland, Antiq. Sacr. 4, 9.

4. Pentecost is held to be the feast here alluded to by many early and some later writers, such as Chrysostom, Cyril of Alexandria, Erasmus, Calvin, Bengel, etc. Norris makes it the Pentecost after the first Passover, but to do this, has to crowd into this short interval Christ's first Judean ministry, the journey through Samaria together with the first part of his Galilean ministry. So this idea has little weight. McClellan argues that the allusions of Jesus in John 5:17–47, "infallibly point to Pentecost," meaning the Pentecost after a second Passover that is not mentioned. He further contends that this best suits the chronological arrangement and the term "a feast of the Jews." This view is certainly possible and cannot be positively disproved, although it is not so "infallibly" clear as McClellan imagines.

5. The Passover has always met with many adherents, being the second Passover in the Saviour's ministry and making four in all (John 2:13; 5:1; 6:4; 12:1). An unnamed Passover may exist in the ministry even if not referred to here. The arguments in favor of this interpretation are the most satisfactory. We cannot consider them as absolutely conclusive, yet the Passover meets all sides of the case better than any of the other feasts. (a) The plucking of ears from standing grain by the disciples (Luke 6:1) would indicate a time after the Passover and before Pentecost. This incident appears to have happened after the feast mentioned in John 5:1. (b) It is fairly implied (John 5:1) that the feast took Jesus to Jerusalem. The Passover would more likely be the one to lead him there. It is expressly stated that he attended two Passovers and a special reason is given for his not attending a third. If there was another Passover in his ministry, this would naturally be the one. (c) This suits best the hostility manifested at this feast, which would have time to become acute (Broadus' Comm. on Matt.) and break out with increased vigor in Galilee and prevent his attending the next Passover (John 6:4; 7:1). (d) If this Passover be a second Passover of the ministry, sufficient time is afforded for the great Galilean ministry without artificial crowding. His ministry would be long enough to allow the great work recorded as done by him. Only two serious objections can be urged to this idea. (1) It is objected that the article would be used with "feast," if the Passover were thus mentioned as *the* feast. But to this we can reply: (a) The article is sometimes omitted when the Passover is meant (Matt. 27:15; Mark 15:6). (b) The absence of the article proves nothing whatever one way or the other. No conclusion can be drawn for or against the idea of the Passover. (c) The article does occur in many manuscripts, including the Sinaitic, and is put in the margin of the Revised Version. So nothing can be gained against this theory here. (2) The chief

269

objection is that Jesus would not have remained so long away from Jerusalem, a year and six months, from the Second Passover till the Feast of Tabernacles after the Third Passover. But (a) we do not know that he did not attend any other feast in that time, for silence proves nothing; and (b) a good reason is given for his failure to attend the Third Passover, which may have applied to the others, if he did not go, *viz.*, the desire of the Jews to kill him (John 7:1).

Hence it is natural that there should be a variety of opinions as to the length of the Saviour's ministry, varying all the way from one to four years, leaving out mere guesses based on five and more Passovers. McKnight argues that the ministry may have lasted five or more full years, since all the Passovers of Christ's ministry may not be mentioned.

(1) The *Bi-paschal* theory makes the time of the public life of Jesus one year, allowing only two Passovers to the Gospel of John. Browne in his *Ordo Saeclorum* advocates this view. But the words, "the Passover," in John 6:4 must be omitted, and for this there is not enough documentary evidence. If this could be done, Westcott thinks Browne would make out a good case. But with the present text, his view cannot be entertained.

(2) The *Tri-paschal* theory finds only three Passovers in the life of Christ. Hence the public work of Jesus would be from two to two and a half years in length. This view is quite possible, as is shown in the Harmony. These writers usually make the feast of John 5:1 Purim before the Passover of John 6:4, or Pentecost after it.

(3) The *Quadri-paschal* theory contends for four Passovers and a ministry of from three to three and a half years. This theory follows from making John 5:1 a Passover or Purim before or Pentecost or Tabernacles after an unnamed Passover. This seems to be the more probable length of the Saviour's public work on earth. How short a space was even this to compass such a marvellous work. The ministry of Jesus seems crowded beyond our comprehension. It would be certain that the Saviour's public life lasted about three years and a half, if it was admitted that John 5:1 referred to a Passover. Various writers seek to find an allusion to the three years of the Saviour's ministry in the Parable of the Barren Fig Tree (Luke 13:6), but this application of the parable is by no means certain, since three might naturally be used as a round number. But there can very well have been a passover not mentioned. All we can say is that we know that the ministry of Jesus was two and a half years in length with the probability of three and a half.

8. The Four Lists of the Twelve Apostles

It is interesting to compare the four lists of Jesus' chosen apostles as given by Matthew, Mark, Luke, and Acts.

	Mark 3:16 f.	Matthew 10:2 f.	Luke 6:14 f.	Acts 1:13 f.
1.	Simon Peter	Simon Peter	Simon Peter	Simon Peter
2.	James	Andrew	Andrew	James
3.	John	James	James	John
4.	Andrew	John	John	Andrew
5.	Philip	Philip	Philip	Philip
6.	Bartholomew	Bartholomew	Bartholomew	Thomas
7.	Matthew	Thomas	Matthew	Bartholomew
8.	Thomas	Matthew	Thomas	Matthew
9.	James the son of Alpheus	James the son of Alpheus	James the son of Alpheus	James the son of Alpheus
10.	Thaddeus	Thaddeus	Simon the Zealot	Simon the Zealot
11.	Simon the Cananæan	Simon the Cananæan	Judas the brother of James	Judas the brother of James
12.	Judas Iscariot	Judas Iscariot	Judas Iscariot	

Let us examine the names here given.

(1) The lists are given some time after the selection was made, and hence represent a later grouping according to later developments in this inner circle. The primacy of Peter in these lists does not mean necessarily that he was the acknowledged leader at first. See discussion under (4) below. The point to note here is that we are not to think of Peter as the formal leader of the Twelve before the death of Christ. Jesus was himself that leader.

(2) One mark of an apostle was that he should have been with the Lord from the baptism of John until the day that he was received up (Acts 1:21 f.). Perhaps no great stress is to be laid on any exact time here, provided it began in the time of John. An apostle must know the Lord. Hence Paul received the vision of Christ. We have some knowledge of seven of these apostles before this time. If we infer from John 1:41 that John followed the example of Andrew in finding his own brother, it was not long till James was a disciple as well as John, Andrew, and Peter. Philip and Nathanael are soon added to the list (John 1:43 f.). Later Matthew hears the call of the Saviour, too (Matt. 9:9; Mark 2:13 f.). Of the other five we have no knowledge previous to this occasion. Jesus had "found" them by the same insight that led to his other selections. He chose Judas, though knowing that he was a devil.

(3) Observe the three groups of four, headed by Simon Peter, Philip, and James the son of Alpheus, respectively. The great variety in the arrangement of the other names makes this uniformity significant. It seems

clear that there are three recognized groups among the apostles (Bengel, Broadus, Clark). Each group has the same persons in every list, although there is such a variety in the order. In the first group Matthew and Luke have the same order, while Mark and Acts agree. In the second group Mark and Luke have a like order, while Matthew and Acts agree in putting Matthew at the end of this group. In the third group Matthew and Mark agree exactly, while Luke and Acts are identical save the dropping out of Judas Iscariot from the list in Acts because of his apostasy and death. No great importance can be attached to the precise order within the groups since Luke, in the Gospel and Acts, gives a different arrangement in the first and second groups.

(4) Observe also that Simon Peter not only stands at the head of his group, but at the head of all the groups, while Judas Iscariot is always at the bottom till he drops out entirely. Simon finally occupied a position of precedence of some sort. He was one of the inner circle of three that was so close to the Saviour's heart. Perhaps it was this, rather than any notion of primacy in authority or power. He was the spokesman because of his natural impetuosity. The question as to who should be greatest among the apostles illustrates the spirit of rivalry about precedence that existed among them. In the October, 1916, Journal of Theol. Studies, Dr. A. Wright argues that the critical text in Mark 14:10 means "Judas Iscariot the first of the Twelve." The *Koiné* did sometimes use *heis* as an ordinal (see Moulton, *Prolegomena*, p. 96, and my *Grammar of the Greek New Testament*, pp. 671 f.). But the disputes among the Twelve show that they themselves considered Jesus only as leader till his death. See my article on "The Primacy of Judas Iscariot," the Expositor (London) for April, 1917, and one by Rendel Harris in the June, 1917, issue, and Wright's reply in the November, 1917, number.

(5) There are among the Twelve three pairs of brothers—Simon and Andrew, James and John, James the son of Alpheus and Judas the brother of James. The first two pairs form the first group of the Twelve. It is, however, uncertain whether Judas is the brother or the son of James. The Greek is ambiguous, James's Judas. The Revised Version translated it "Judas son of James," but the Epistle of Jude begins "Judas a servant of Jesus Christ and brother of James." But the Jude of the Epistle and the Judas of the Twelve were hardly the same. Cf. Broadus, Comm. on Matt., p. 216.

(6) There are some apparent discrepancies in the names in the various lists. Bartholomew occurs in every list, but is generally understood to be another name for Nathanael. Thaddeus is also called Judas the brother of James. Matthew and Mark give Thaddeus, and Luke in Gospel and Acts gives Judas the brother of James. It was a very common circumstance

for one to have two names. Lebbeus, given in some MSS. in Matthew and Mark, is only a marginal explanation of Thaddeus. Both are terms of endearment. Matthew and Mark again call Simon the Cananæan, while Luke in the Gospel and Acts speaks of him as Simon the Zealot. But "Zealot" is simply a translation into Greek of the Aramaic "Cananæan." Jesus gave the other Simon the name "Cephas," which was translated into the Greek "Peter," meaning rock. He is called by all three names in the New Testament. Matthew likewise had another name, Levi, and Thomas was also called Didymus, which was a Greek translation of Thomas, meaning "twin."

9. The Sermon on the Mount

Do Matthew and Luke record the same discourse? Let us consider the several theories on this subject. My own view will be stated last.

1. Some hold that the two discourses are entirely distinct in time, place, circumstances and audience. The arguments for this theory usually presented are these.

(a) The time of delivery of the two sermons appears to be different. Matthew gives the sermon before his call (Matt. 9:9), while Luke precedes his sermon by the call of the twelve. Hence Matthew's discourse comes quite a while before Luke's in the early Galilean ministry. But it may be well replied that, inasmuch as Matthew's arrangement in ch. 8–13 is not chronological, but topical, it is entirely possible, even likely, that the same arrangement should prevail in ch. 5–7. It is perfectly natural that Matthew, writing for Jewish readers and about the Messianic reign, should give at the beginning of his account of that reign the formal principles that rule in this new state of affairs, as proclaimed by Jesus on a later occasion. In the early part of the ministry of Jesus, besides, the hearers would hardly be prepared for so advanced and radical ideas. Besides, Matthew makes no note of time whatever for this discourse.

(b) The place appears to be different. One is on a mountain (Matt. 5:1), while the other is on a plain (Luke 6:17). Hence the one is called by Clark the Sermon on the Mount, and the other the Sermon on the Plain. Miller (Int. Stand. Bible Encyclopædia) is uncertain whether Matthew and Luke report the same discourse and so discusses also Luke's "Sermon on the Plain." But his argument is not convincing. If it is necessary that "plain" here shall mean a place away from a mountain, down in a valley, this would seem to refer to a different place. McClellan seeks to show that Luke uses "and" in 6:17–20 by way of anticipation. He presents for effective grouping events that happened after Jesus came down out of the mountain before he gives the sermon delivered to the whole body of disciples up in the mountain. This is possible, but another interpretation is much more likely. The plain here is really simply "a level place" (Rev. Ver.). So then the two accounts of Matthew and Luke will harmonize quite well. Jesus first went up into the mountain to pray (Luke 6:12) and selected and instructed the Twelve. Afterwards he came down to a level place on the mountain side whither the crowds had gathered, and stood there and wrought miracles (Luke 6:17). He then went up a little higher into the mountain where he could sit down and see and teach the multitudes (Matt. 5:1). Matthew gives the multitudes as the reason for his going up into the mountain. By this arrangement any discrepancy between "sat" in Matthew and "stood" in Luke disappears. Waddy has given an admirable arrangement of the material at this point in Note C, p. xix. Many writers affirm that the tradition mentioned by Jerome, making the Horns of Hattin the place where the Sermon on the Mount was delivered, suits this explanation exactly. There is a level place on it where the crowds could have assembled. It is not necessary to insist that this mountain is the Mount of Beatitudes, nor need we contend, as Robinson does, that the mountain must be very close to Capernaum.

(c) The audience is different. Matthew (4:25) states that his audience was composed of "great multitudes from Galilee and Decapolis and Jerusalem and Judea and from beyond Jordan," while Luke (6:17) says that there was "a great multitude of his disciples, and a great number of the people from all Judea and Jerusalem, and the sea coast of Tyre and Sidon." Matthew says (5:1) also that "his disciples came unto him." Hence both assemblages were composed of great multitudes from many regions besides many of his disciples, but in neither case is Jesus said to address himself to any save his disciples, his followers (Matt. 5:1 and Luke 6:20). So in both accounts the Saviour seems to withdraw a little from the great outside crowd of curiosity seekers. But the multitudes also must have heard something of what he said, for they were astonished at his teaching (Matt. 7:28). Andrews well shows that the audience in Matthew were not mostly Jews (according to Kraft), and the audience in Luke mostly heathen. Matthew omits Tyre and Sidon, but he had already mentioned Syria (4:24), which includes Tyre and Sidon. Neither list may be complete. Hence nothing can be made out of Luke's omission of Galilee, Decapolis, and beyond Jordan. Great multitudes from the same general regions are alluded to as being present.

(d) The contents are radically different. It is objected by Alford, Greswell, etc., that Luke omits large portions of what Matthew has so that Luke has only thirty verses, while Matthew has one hundred and seven. But this leaves out of consideration the several large portions of the same matter which Luke has placed elsewhere, or which Jesus repeated on other occasions (cf. Matt. 6:9–13 and Luke 11:2–4; Matt. 6:25–34 and Luke 12:22–31). Jesus often repeated his sayings on other occasions as all teachers do and ought to do. Neither evangelist gives a complete report of this wonderful discourse. So Matthew omits some things which Luke records (cf. Matt. 5:12 with Luke 6:23–6; Matt. 7:12 with Luke 6:31–40). Nor need we be surprised that Luke, writing generally for all Christians, omits large portions towards the beginning of the sermon that were designed especially for Jews (see Matt. 5:17–27; 6:1–18). These Matthew would be sure to record. Luke adds four woes to the beatitudes. It is unnecessary to remark upon minor variations of language, since the gospels manifestly aim to give the sense of what the Saviour said and not the *verbatim* words. The variations in the Synoptic reports of the sayings of Jesus add much to the interest of the narratives. Moreover, to offset these variations, which admit of explanation, it ought to be remembered that the two discourses begin alike and end alike, that they have a general similarity in the order of the different parts, and that they show a general likeness and often absolute identity of expression.

So these differences all melt away on careful comparison, and it is not proved that there are two distinct sermons.

2. Another theory holds that the two sermons are distinct, but spoken on the same day, and near together. So Augustine, who is followed by Lange. The further points of this theory are two. (*a*) The one (Matt.) was spoken before the choice of the Apostles, to the disciples alone, and while Jesus was sitting on the mountain. (*b*) The other (Luke) was spoken after the choice of the Apostles, to the multitudes, and standing upon the plain. It is not hard to see that these points do not solve the question. In Matt. 7:28 we are told that the multitudes were astonished at his teaching and in Luke 6:20 that "he lifted up his eyes on his disciples, and said." So this distinction vanishes. The question of the mountain and the plain has been already discussed, and another more probable explanation suggested. It is only a conjecture that the discourse of Matthew was before the appointment of the Twelve. This theory has had no great following.

3. Wieseler holds that Matthew has simply brought together detached sayings of Jesus on different occasions and does not mean to present the whole as one discourse; Luke's account being only one of the discourses used by Matthew. But this violates the evident notes of place and audience and surroundings by which Matthew gives local color and cast to the entire discourse. See Matt. 5:1 and 8:1. The case of the grouping of the miracles in chapters 8 and 9 is not parallel, since there Matthew does not state that they occurred on one occasion. The fact that various portions of this discourse are repeated elsewhere by Matthew is immaterial, because this was a common habit of Jesus in his discourses. Votaw in his exhaustive and able discussion of the Sermon on the Mount in the extra volume in the Hastings D B admits the possibility of this hypothesis, but considers it far less probable

than the historical reality of the Sermon as recorded by both Matthew and Luke. Moffatt (Encycl. Biblica) considers it "a composition rather than an actual address," while Bacon (Sermon on the Mount) admits only what is also in Luke. Adeney (Hastings' D C G) holds to the essential integrity of the address in Matthew.

4. Both Matthew and Luke give substantially similar accounts of the same discourse. In that case we have a good illustration of the use of the Logia in Matthew and Luke. Most of the arguments for this interpretation have been mentioned in rebuttal of the previously mentioned theories. (a) This is the most natural explanation in view of the large volume of similar matter in both, in the beginning, progress, and close of the discourse. It is always best to give the Scripture the most natural and manifest setting, when possible. (b) This theory is the most probable one, since it is hardly likely that Jesus would again make the same sermon to the same audience, and under the same circumstances. (c) There are no objections to this theory that do not admit of a probable explanation. See the discussion above. The omissions and additions in each case suit the specific purpose of the writer. The apparent contradictions, when studied carefully, blend into a harmonious whole. Hence we seem to be justified in maintaining the identity of the discourses recorded by Matthew and Luke. For a careful outline of this matchless discourse see Broadus on Matthew. Stalker, *The Ethics of Jesus*, has a very able exposition of the teaching.

10. The Combination of Luke and John

We now have to deal with the most perplexing question in harmonistic study, the proper disposal of the mass of material furnished by Luke in 9:51–18:14. McClellan discusses ten schemes, pushes them all aside, and then suggests another which is no more convincing and equally complicated. Nothing can be attempted here but a presentation of the chief points in this endless discussion. All the principal plans for arranging this part of Luke proceed on one or the other of the following ideas:

1. Some hold that this portion of Luke is neither orderly nor chronological. Hence many of the incidents, here recorded as apparently belonging to the last six months of the Saviour's ministry, in reality are to be placed earlier. They are put here as a sort of summing up of things not mentioned elsewhere. So Robinson and others. In favor of this theory it is urged that Luke here speaks of some things that Matthew and Mark put before the third Passover, such as the healing of a demoniac (Luke 11:14–36) and the blasphemy following. But it may be well replied.

(a) It is not at all clear that we have here the same events that are recorded in Matthew and Mark. Similar miracles were often wrought in the Master's work and similar sayings were frequently repeated on similar or different occasions. This was a common habit with him, as we have heretofore seen.

(b) This portion of Luke is his distinctive contribution to the ministry of Christ in addition to his account of the nativity. He has condensed his account of the withdrawals from Galilee, apparently to make room for the description of another part of Christ's work. Matthew and Mark almost confine themselves to the ministry in Galilee, while Luke thus devotes the bulk of his narrative to what seems to be a later ministry, after Jesus has left Galilee. It is hardly likely that this account should be a mere jumble of scattered details.

(c) Especially is this unlikely in view of Luke's express statement (1:3) that he was going to write an orderly narrative. In no real sense could this be true, if this large section is dislocated in time and order of events.

2. Others refer the entire narrative (Luke 9:51–18:14) to the last journey of the Saviour to Jerusalem to the Passover and see a triple reference to the same journey arguing for triplications in Luke. Others prefer to understand it as meaning the journey to the Feast of the Tabernacles or Dedication. Some would combine this idea with the unchronological plan noticed above. In favor of this journey being continuous and the last one to Jerusalem, the following arguments are adduced:

(a) The language of Luke 9:51, "when the days were being completed that he should be received up," implies that the end was drawing near, and that he was setting his face towards Jerusalem to meet it. This is true without doubt, for Wieseler's interpretation of "received up" as meaning Christ's reception by man is entirely too forced. The expression points to the end of Christ's earthly career. But what does the vague expression, "the days were being completed," mean? Does it have to mean only a few weeks? May it not include as much as six months? For we know that Jesus had been instructing his disciples on this very subject expressly and pointedly, and at the Transfiguration he had spoken of his "decease." Henceforward this was the uppermost subject in his mind. So the interpretation is correct, but the inference is not necessary. This journey in Luke 9:51 need not be either just before the Passover or the Dedication. It could be as early as Tabernacles and be thus described.

(b) It is insisted that this is Jesus' final departure from Galilee, the one described by Matthew and Mark. No place is allowed for a return to Galilee after the departure in Luke 9:51. Robinson urges that Luke 9:51 naturally means a final departure from Galilee. But it may simply mean that he left it as a sphere of activity, not that he never entered Galilee again. And then Luke 17:11 expressly says that Jesus went "through the midst of Samaria and Galilee." This means more than going on the border between the two countries, as McClellan argues. He went through some portions of

Samaria and Galilee. In order for McClellan to carry out his scheme he has to resort to the artificial device of referring part of John 10:40 to the departure from Galilee, and the other half to the Perean ministry after a diversion of considerable length into Samaria and back into Galilee. So the effort is not convincing to place all the material in this large section of Luke in one last journey to Jerusalem.

3. The combination of Luke's narrative with that of John. Wieseler was the first to point out a possible parallel between Luke and John. John gives us three journeys,—the Feast of Tabernacles (John 7:2 ff.), the journey to Bethany at the raising of Lazarus (John 11:17 f.), the final Passover (John 12:1). Luke likewise three times in this section speaks of Jesus going to Jerusalem, 9:51; 13:22; 17:11. Hence it would seem possible, even probable, that their journeys corresponded. If so, John 7:2–11:54 is to be taken as parallel to Luke 9:51–18:14. This plan is followed by various modern scholars.

According to John's chronology, Jesus was in Jerusalem at the Feast of Tabernacles (7:2), at the Feast of Dedication (10:22), and at the Passover (12:1). Just after the Feast of the Dedication we find him abiding beyond Jordan, where John had baptized (John 10:40). From this point he comes to Bethany near Jerusalem at the raising of Lazarus (John 11:17), whence he withdraws to a little town called Ephraim in the hills north of Jerusalem (John 11:54). Here he abides awhile with his disciples away from his enemies till he goes to the Passover. Such is John's outline of these last six months of the Saviour's life.

(a) But how is all this to be reconciled with the statement of Luke (17:11) that Jesus went through Samaria and Galilee? If Jesus went back to Galilee, John would have mentioned it, we are told. Not necessarily, not unless it fell in with his plan to do so. Hence no conflict need exist between Luke and John. Luke says he went through Galilee and John permits it by the break in his narrative at 11:54. Various points in the six months have been suggested as the point when the return to Galilee was made. The most natural point is from Ephraim, whither he had withdrawn (John 11:54). It was not far to go up through Samaria and join in Galilee (Luke 17:11) the pilgrims from his own country who were in the habit of going to the Passover through Perea, to avoid passing through Samaria. This supposition is not improbable, as Robinson and McClellan urge, but very natural; it makes Luke and John both agree, and allows Luke 9:51 to mean that Jesus then left Galilee as a field of operations. Various other theories are suggested for this return to Galilee, but none of them appear as fitting as this one. It was just before the Passover, when such a journey from Galilee to Jerusalem would be made.

(b) One other point needs to be considered. The theory we hold makes the journey in Luke 9:51 identical with the one in John 7:2–10, *viz.*, to Taber-

278

nacles. Many hold such identity to be impossible because of apparent contradictions in the narratives. Andrews makes three objections against this identity: (1) That the Lord refused to go with his brethren (John 7:6). But it was his brothers who were not favorable to him that he refused to go with. He simply wished to avoid publicity. His face was set (Luke 9:51) all the time, but he was not going with them. (2) That the manner of the going is unlike; the one in John is secret, while the one in Luke is public. But the secrecy in John may merely mean the avoidance of the caravan routes and so through Samaria (Luke). The messengers sent before were not to herald his coming to gather crowds simply, but to make ready for him. It was needed, since the Samaritans saw that his face was as if he were going to Jerusalem. (3) That he went rapidly according to John and slowly according to Luke. He does, according to John, appear in Jerusalem before the feast is over, but Luke does not make him move slowly. Nor is it necessary to connect the sending of the seventy (Luke 10:1 ff.) with this journey. It belongs rather to the interval between Tabernacles and Dedication. So the secret going of John and the going through Samaria of Luke agree. John explains, 7:10, that Jesus rejected the advice of his brothers. This theory is held irrespective of this being the final departure from Galilee. It is not necessary to fill out every detail in this programme and show where Jesus was between Tabernacles and Dedication. The main outlines remain clear and harmonious and are fairly satisfactory. This combination of Luke and John preserves the integrity of both narratives and fills up a large blank that would otherwise exist in these closing months of the Saviour's life. Upon the whole, therefore, this view seems decidedly preferable, though nothing like absolute certainty can be claimed in regard to the question.

We do not know what special source Luke had for 9:51–18:14. Some of it may have come from the Logia (Q). Hawkins (*Oxford Studies*, pp. 55 ff.) calls it "the Travel Document." Burton (*Some Principles of Literary Criticism and Their Application to the Synoptic Problem*) suggests "The Peræan Document" and thinks that Luke may have drafted it early out of oral material. But at any rate it is a great and characteristic portion of his Gospel and adds greatly to our knowledge of Christ.

11. Did Christ Eat the Passover?

To put this question in another form, it would be, On what day of the month was Jesus crucified? For the crucifixion occurred on the same Jewish day as the eating of the meal recorded by all four Evangelists. Nearly all agree that the crucifixion occurred on Friday and the meal was eaten the evening before, our Thursday, but the beginning of the Jewish day, counting from sunset to sunset. But what day of the month was it? The Passover feast began on the 15th Nisan, the lamb being slain in the afternoon of the 14th. But the day of the week would vary with the new moon. If Jesus ate the regular Passover supper, he was crucified on the 15th Nisan. If he ate an anticipatory meal a day in advance and was himself slain at the hour of killing the paschal lamb, he was crucified on the 14th Nisan. In that case he did not really eat the Passover supper at all. So then we must seek to determine the truth about this matter, because express statements are made about it in the Gospels.

1. Some sentimental views of the question need to be disposed of first. A great controversy once raged in the early churches about the Passover.

(a) In the latter part of the second century some of the churches of Asia Minor, largely composed of Jewish Christians, kept up the Passover on the ground that Jesus had eaten it the night before his crucifixion. Polycarp, the disciple of John, expresses the persuasion that Jesus ate the Passover.

(b) But some of the churches were afraid of this example and its application to the discussion about the relation of the Mosaic laws to Christianity. So they took the position that Jesus did not eat the Passover himself, but as the Paschal Lamb, was crucified at the time the lamb was slain. He was our Passover. The Greek churches now hold this position, while the Latin churches hold that Jesus ate the Passover. But those arguments are purely subjective and do not affect the question of fact. Hence we waive this old-time controversy and come to the testimony of the Gospels themselves.

2. The testimony of the Synoptists, Mark, Matthew, and Luke. The evidence they give is abundant and explicit to the effect that Jesus ate the regular Paschal Supper on the evening after the 14th Nisan.

(a) Jesus predicted that his death would occur during the Feast of the Passover. See Matthew 26:2, "Ye know that after two days the Passover cometh, and the Son of Man is delivered up to be crucified." See also Mark 14:1 and Luke 22:1, where the fact is alluded to. Passover is used in the general sense of the feast of unleavened bread, as Luke explains. The feast of unleavened bread followed the Passover meal, beginning the next morning and lasting a week. But the one term was used to include the other. The Passover was expanded to mean the entire feast that followed, and *vice versa*.

(b) It is true that the Jewish authorities decided not to put Jesus to death during the feast (Matthew 26:5; Mark 14:2). But this decision was reached not because of any compunctions of conscience in the matter, but because they were afraid of a tumult among the people, owing to the great crowds, many of whom were friendly to Christ. But so soon as Judas offered his services, their fears vanished and they proceeded with their murderous designs (Matthew 26:14; Mark 14:11). The rulers did expedite matters at the crucifixion that the bodies might not be exposed on the Sabbath.

But they had often tried to slay Jesus on the Sabbath heretofore. Public executions did take place during the feasts (Deut. 17:12 f.).

(c) The Synoptists flatly say (Matthew 26:17, 20; Mark 14:12, 17; Luke 22:7, 14) that on the first day of unleavened bread Jesus sent Peter and John from Bethany into the city to make preparations for eating the Passover, and that on the evening of the same day he ate it with his disciples. Luke calls it "the hour." Now, the first day of unleavened bread was the 14th Nisan. There is no question about this. Josephus speaks of the feast lasting eight days. The lamb of the supper being slain on the afternoon of this day, it was regarded as the beginning of the feast. Besides, Mark and Luke end the whole matter by saying that on this day they sacrificed the Passover. Jesus himself calls it the Passover (Luke 22:15). It is useless to say that Jesus ate the Passover a day in advance. This could not be done, especially by one to whom the temple authorities were hostile. Equally useless is it to say that the Jews ate the Passover a day too late. If a mistake was made about the new moon, they would hardly keep the Passover on two different days, nor would Jesus be apt to make a point about the matter.

3. The testimony of John. If we had only the evidence of the Synoptists, no serious trouble would ever arise on this question. Strauss has strenuously urged that John is on this point in hopeless conflict with the other Evangelists, since he makes Jesus eat the Passover on the evening after the 13th Nisan (Wednesday), and not the evening after the 14th (Thursday). This idea has gained a foothold among many able modern writers who see a clear contradiction between the Synoptics and the Fourth Gospel. Some of these evidently do so because they hold that the Paschal controversy in Asia Minor arose from this supposed conflict of John with the Synoptists, and that this shows John's Gospel to have been in existence when that controversy began. It is not worth while to maintain that John in chapter 13 alludes to a different meal on a different occasion. The points of contact with the Synoptists are too sharp and clear, such as the sop given to Judas. But five passages in John are produced as being in direct opposition to the statements of the Synoptic Gospels. A careful examination of each of these five passages in the Fourth Gospel will show that John does not say that Jesus ate the Passover meal a day in advance of the regular time, but quite the contrary.

(a) John 13:1 f., "Now before the feast of the Passover, Jesus knowing, etc." Here, it is alleged, a distinct statement is made that this supper was before the Passover, and consequently twenty-four hours before. But several things are taken for granted in this inference. One is that the phrase "feast of the Passover" is to be confined to this particular meal, and is not to include the entire festival of unleavened bread (*cf*. Luke 22:1). Often by a metonymy of speech the name of a part is given to the whole. Besides, it is not certain that verse 1 is to be connected with verse 2. The best exegetes agree that a complete idea may be presented therein, either a general statement that Jesus loved his own before the Passover and until the end, or that he came into special consciousness of this love just before the Passover. And if the more natural interpretation be taken and the application of this love be made in verse 2, it is not necessary that the "before" be as much as twenty-four hours. Observe also the text adopted in the Revised Version in verse 2, not "supper being ended," but "during supper." With this reading agree the other references in 13:4, "riseth from supper," 13:12, "sat down again," 13:23, "there was at the table reclining in Jesus' bosom." So the natural meaning is that just before the meal began, Jesus purposed to show his love for his own by a practical illustration. So, after they had all reclined at the table according to custom, Jesus arose and passed around the tables, washing their feet; then he reclined again and proceeded with the meal. So nothing at all can be made out of this passage against the view that this was the regular Passover; but, on the other hand, the most natural meaning is that John is here describing what took place at this Passover meal. Else, why should he mention the Passover at all?

(*b*) John 13:27, "That thou doest, do quickly." The objection is made that the disciples would not have thought that Jesus referred to the feast (13:29), if the Passover meal was already going on or was over. So, it is urged, this remark must have been made a day before the Passover was celebrated. But if that were the case, where would be the necessity for hurry, as there would be plenty of time on the morrow? The word "feast" here need not be confined to the paschal supper, but more naturally refers to the whole of the feast, of which the supper was a part. So this haste was needed to provide for the feast of unleavened bread which began on the next morning. No real force lies in the fact that this day was a holy day, being the first day of the Passover festival. The Mishna expressly allows the procuring, even on a Sabbath, what was needed for the Passover. If this could be done on a Sabbath, much more could it be done on a feast day which was not a Sabbath. Hence not only was it possible for the disciples to have misunderstood the remark of Jesus on the Passover evening, but it was far more natural that such misapprehensions should arise then than a day before. So this passage, like the preceding, when rightly understood, really confirms the Synoptists.

(*c*) John 18:28, "They themselves entered not into the palace, that they might not be defiled, but might eat the Passover." At first sight this does look like a contradiction. For this was certainly after the feast of John 13:2, and if they had not eaten the Passover meal, why here is a clear case of conflict of authorities. But it is by no means certain that the phrase "eat the Passover" means simply the paschal supper. This phrase occurs five times in the New Testament besides this, but all in Matthew, Mark, and Luke (Matt. 26:17; Mark 14:12, 14; Luke 22:11, 15). In all of these the reference is to the paschal supper. But the word "passover" is used in three senses in the New Testament, the paschal supper, the paschal lamb, or the paschal festival. The word is used eight times in John besides this instance, and in every case the Passover festival is meant. So we may fairly infer that the usage of John must determine his own meaning rather than that of the Synoptists. This becomes more probable when we remember that John wrote much later than they, after the destruction of Jerusalem, when these terms were not used so strictly. He always speaks of "the Jews" as separate from Christians. And this very expression is used in 2 Chronicles 30:22, "And they did eat the festival seven days." The Septuagint translates it, "And they fulfilled (kept) the festival of unleavened bread seven days." See Robinson. So it is entirely possible for the phrase, "eat the Passover," to mean in this instance also the celebration of the Passover festival. Some have urged that the Sanhedrin had not eaten the Passover at the regular hour because of the excitement of the trial. But this is hardly tenable. And, moreover, since this remark was made early in the morning, how could that affect the eating of the supper in the evening? For whatever impurities one had during the day passed away at evening. Hence this uncleanness must belong to the same day on which it was incurred. If the Passover festival had begun, this would be true, for they would wish to participate in the offerings of that day. So this passage likewise becomes an argument in favor of agreement with the Synoptists.

(d) John 19:14, "Now it was the Preparation of the Passover." This is claimed to mean the day preceding the Passover festival. Hence Christ was crucified on the 14th Nisan, in opposition to the Synoptists. The afternoon before the Passover was used as a preparation, but it was not technically so called. This phrase "Preparation" was really the name of a day in the week, the day before the Sabbath, our Friday. We are not left to conjecture about this question. The Evangelists all use it in this sense alone. Matthew uses it for Friday (27:62), Mark expressly says that the Preparation was the day before the Sabbath (15:42), Luke says that it was the day of the Preparation and the Sabbath drew on (23:54), and John himself so uses the word in two other passages (19:31, 42), in both of which haste is exercised on the Preparation, because the Sabbath was at hand. The New Testament usage is conclusive, therefore, on this point. This, then, was the Friday of Passover week. And this agrees with the Synoptists. Besides, the term "Preparation" has long been the regular name for Friday in the Greek language, caused by the New Testament usage. It is so in the Modern Greek to-day. It was the Sabbath eve, just as the Germans have Sonnabend for Sunday eve, *i.e.*, Saturday afternoon. So this passage also becomes a positive argument for the agreement between John and the Synoptists.

(e) John 19:31, "For the day of that Sabbath was a high day." From this passage it has been argued that at this Passover the first day of the Passover festival coincided with the weekly Sabbath. But that is an entirely gratuitous inference. This coincidence would, of course, be a "high day," but so would the first day of the feast, the last day, or the Sabbath of the feast. In John 7:37 the last day is called "the great day of the feast." The Sabbath occurring during the festival would be a high day likewise. Robinson's arguments on this point are quite conclusive. Nothing can be made out of the expression against the position of the Synoptists.

McClellan discusses various other passages in John which show that the crucifixion occurred on Friday, and that this was the first day of the feast (John 18:39, 40; 19:31, 42; 20:1, 19, etc.). We conclude then that a fair interpretation of the passages alleged not only removes all contradiction between John and the Synoptists, but rather decidedly favors the view that they have the same date for the Passover meal, and that Jesus ate the Passover at the regular hour and was crucified on Friday, 15th Nisan.

It is reassuring to note that David Smith (*The Days of His Flesh*, Appendix VIII) reaches the same conclusion as that just stated. He makes it out that Jesus ate the regular Passover meal and was crucified on Friday 15th of Nisan and that the passages in John really agree with the Synoptic account.

12. The Hour of the Crucifixion

In John 19:14 it is stated that the time when Pilate sentenced Jesus to be crucified, or rather when he began the last trial in which he sentenced him, was about the sixth hour. We read, however, in Mark 15:25 that it was the third hour when Christ was crucified. The Synoptists all unite in saying that the darkness began at the sixth hour. The Jewish way of counting the hours was to divide the night and day into twelve divisions each, beginning at sunrise and sunset. The hours would thus vary in length with the time of year. Just after the vernal equinox the third hour of Mark would be about 9 A.M., and the sixth hour of the Synoptists would be about noon. The ninth hour, when Jesus gave his piteous cry to God (Mark 15:34), would be about 3 P.M. But how can the sixth hour of John, the time when Jesus was sentenced by Pilate, be reconciled to this schedule? A real difficulty is here presented, but by no means an insuperable one, as Alford and Meyer hold. Let us discuss some of the more usual explanations. Andrews and McClellan give quite a variety of suggested solutions.

1. Some hold that "sixth" in John is a textual error for "third." This could easily happen, since the gamma and the digamma of the Greek are

very similar. Eusebius said that the accurate copies had it "third" in John. But the textual evidence is overwhelmingly against it, and, besides, the difficulty would not be removed. John is evidently speaking of the time at the last trial and Mark of the time after Jesus has been led out to the crucifixion. So nothing is gained by this hypothesis. We should still be confronted with the same difficulty. The change to *third* in John was a mere stupid scribal correction.

2. Others would change the punctuation in John 19:14 so as to make "of the Passover" belong to "sixth hour," beginning from midnight. But there is no evidence that the Passover began with midnight. So Hofmann. This is very forced and unnatural.

3. Views that hinge on the word "preparation." Some would hold that John simply says that about noon the preparation time of the Passover begins. But Preparation here means Friday, and noon is not the hour needed to harmonize with Mark. Equally arbitrary is it to count six hours backward from noon so as to reach six o'clock.

Augustine suggested that the six hours are to be counted from 3 A.M. This would make 9 A.M., and would concur with the hour of Mark. But this is wholly arbitrary and unsatisfactory, and would not relieve the trouble.

4. Equally arbitrary is the solution that makes Mark refer to the hour of the sentence and John to the crucifixion, just the reverse of the Scripture account. Augustine also proposed that Jesus was crucified at the third hour by the tongues of the Jews, and at the sixth by the hands of the soldiers.

5. Others hold that Mark and John both speak in general terms. Hence the crucifixion may have taken place between 9 and 12 in the morning. Mark looks in one direction and John in the other without aiming at definiteness. The Jews, it is true, were not as exact in the use of expressions of time as we are to-day, but this solution hardly meets the requirements of the case. Mark puts his *third* hour at the beginning of the crucifixion, and John his *sixth* hour at the beginning of the last trial. This reconciliation does not reconcile.

6. The most satisfactory solution of the difficulty is to be found in the idea that John here uses the Roman computation of time, from midnight to noon and noon to midnight, just as we do now. Hence the sixth hour would be our six o'clock in the morning. If this hour was the beginning of the last trial of Jesus, we then have enough, but not too much, time for the completion of the trial, the carrying away of Jesus outside the city walls, together with the procuring of the crosses, etc. All the events, moreover, narrated by the Evangelists, could have occurred between dawn (John 18:27) and six or seven.

For a long time it was doubted whether the Romans ever used this method of computing time for civil days. Farrar vehemently opposes this idea.

But Plutarch, Pliny, Aulus Gellius, and Macrobius expressly say that the Roman civil day was reckoned from midnight to midnight. So the question of fact may be considered as settled. The only remaining question is whether John used this mode of reckoning. Of course, the Romans had also the natural day and the natural night just as we do now. In favor of the idea that John uses the Roman way of counting the hours in the civil day, several things may be said.

(a) He wrote the Gospel late in the century, probably in Asia Minor, long after the destruction of Jerusalem, when the Jewish method would not likely be preserved. Roman ideas were prevalent in Asia Minor. John evidently is not writing for the Jews primarily, since he constantly speaks of "the Jews" as outsiders. John is writing to be understood by the people, and this is the way it would be understood in Asia Minor.

(b) All the passages in John, where the hour is mentioned, allow this computation. John 1:39 would be 10 A.M.; 4:6 f. would be 6 P.M., counting from noon also (as we do). This hour suits best the circumstances. In the evening the women would come to get water, Jesus would have time for his journey thither, and would be tired and hungry. In John 4:52 the hour would be 7 P.M. This hour likewise suits the circumstances better. John 11:9, Are there not twelve hours in the day? is not against this idea, since here obviously the natural day, as opposed to night, is meant. The Romans used both methods and so do we.

(c) Moreover, one passage in John (20:19), when compared with Luke 24:29, 36, makes it necessary to understand that John used the Roman method in this instance. It was toward evening, and the day had declined, according to Luke, when Jesus and the disciples drew near to Emmaus. Here he ate supper and, "rising up that very hour," the disciples returned seven miles to Jerusalem and told these things to the eleven who were together. But while they were narrating these things Jesus appeared to them. Now John, in mentioning this very appearance of Jesus (20:19), says that it "was evening on *that day*, the first day of the week," i.e., evening of the day when Mary Magdalene had seen the Lord. But with the Jews the evening began the day. Hence John, here at least, is *bound* to mean the Roman day. It was the evening of the same day in the morning of which Mary had seen Jesus. This appears conclusive. John did use the Roman method here, may have done so always, almost certainly did so in 19:14. Besides, as McClellan shows, the natural meaning of John's phrase is that it was the sixth hour of the Friday (Preparation) of the Passover. But we have just seen that John in 20:19 counts according to the Roman day. Hence the sixth hour of Friday would be six o'clock in the morning.

This is the only solution that really harmonizes John and Mark. The rest make the hours agree, but the hours bring together different events.

This method harmonizes the whole narrative, and seems entirely probable, if we can assume that the Romans or Greeks employed hours in this sense, a point denied by Ramsay.

Sir W. M. Ramsay (*The Expositor* for March, 1893, and Extra Volume, Hastings D B) contends that Mark and John are at variance, but that it is of small moment, since the ancients had little notion about hours. He seeks to show that the martyrdom of Polycarp and Pronius, usually relied on to prove that in Asia Minor the hours were counted from midnight, took place in the afternoon, instead of the morning, the usual time. Hence the eighth and tenth hours respectively would be 2 P.M. and 4 P.M. Ramsay argues that, when hours were counted, they were always counted from sunrise. He holds that John is more accurate about hours than Mark and that hence Mark is in error. He agrees that John "stood on the Roman plane" in the use of time, but denies that the sixth hour can be our 6 A.M. But the evidence is too uncertain for such a dogmatic position.

13. The Time of the Resurrection of Christ

1. Mark, Luke, and John say that the resurrection had taken place early on the first day of the week, *i.e.* early Sunday morning. Mark (16:9) says that Jesus, "having risen early, on the first day of the week, appeared, etc." The position of "early" is ambiguous in the Greek and the passage is disputed. Mark (16:2) states that it was very early on the first day of the week, the sun having risen, when the women came to the sepulchre. Luke (24:1) says that the women came to the tomb at early dawn on the first day of the week. John (20:1) says that Mary Magdalene came to the tomb in the morning on the first day of the week. So then, there is no doubt that these three Evangelists mean to say that Jesus rose very early on Sunday morning, and that shortly after that event came the two Marys and some other women to anoint his body with spices.

Much objection is made to some of the details in the accounts of Mark and John especially as being inconsistent. John (20:1) says that Mary comes while it is yet dark, while Mark says (16:2) that the sun was risen. But Mark also says in the same verse that it was very early, which would agree with John's statement that it was yet dark. Hence' Mark's other statement, that the sun was risen, must be interpreted in the light of his own words. Two solutions can be offered.

(a) We may suppose, as McClellan and others, that John's note of time refers to the starting from Bethany, while it was yet dark or very early (Mark). In a few minutes it would be early dawn (Luke), and by the time the women come to the tomb, the sun would be up. All this is entirely possible and looks even probable, for in the twilight of early dawn, the border line is very narrow between darkness and sunrise. A stiff morning walk would pass through all the stages. It all depends on where you take your stand in this fleeting interim. Mark covers both sides and so includes it all from the first glimmering light till the full light of day.

(*b*) Or the expression, "the sun was risen" (aorist participle), may simply be a general expression applicable to the phenomena of sunrise. The first gleam of daylight comes from the rising sun, though not yet completely risen. Robinson gives several examples from the Septuagint, where the same phrase is used in the aorist tense in a general way for the dawning light of day (Judges 9:33; 2 Kings 3:22; Ps. 104:22). Either of these explanations is entirely possible and removes the difficulty.

2. But Matthew seems to put the resurrection on the evening after the Sabbath, our Saturday evening. He says (28:1), "But late on the Sabbath day, as it was dawning into the first day of the week, came Mary Magdalene and the other Mary to view the sepulchre." If this passage means that the visit was made at the end of the Sabbath day (evening) and after the resurrection of Jesus, then Matthew is in plain contradiction to the other Evangelists. Some have taken the position that Jesus rose at sunset on the Sabbath day, forgetting that Mark (16:9) says that he rose early in the morning. There are several ways of reconciling Matthew with the other gospels.

(*a*) Greswell, Alford and others would translate "late on the Sabbath day" by "late in the week." The Greek word is the same in this verse for Sabbath and week. In both cases, therefore, the translation could be the same. But little sense would result from this translation. "Late in the week" and "dawning into the first day of the week" hardly fit well. By this explanation the latter expression is used for the first part of Sunday and the visit occurred in this dawning part of the day.

(*b*) Others would translate "late on the Sabbath day" by "after the Sabbath day." Godet, Grimm and others contend that the Greek idiom could mean this, and the *Koine* allows it (Robertson, *Grammar of the Greek New Testament*, pp. 645 f.). This rendering is possible, though the papyri have instances of "late on" for this preposition (*opse*), and it is so translated by several English translators. Thus the Greek idiom allows either "late on" or "after."

(*c*) Matthew does not clearly say that this visit was made after the resurrection of the Saviour although his words may mean that. Hence the words may have their natural meaning as sustained by the papyri. Late on the Sabbath day, about sundown say, the two Marys go to view the sepulchre (Matt. 28:1), having rested through the day (Luke 23:56). The women who had come with Jesus from Galilee had gone thither on Friday, after his burial, to see where he was laid and had prepared spices. If they went at nightfall at the close of the Sabbath (Matt. 28:1) "to see the sepulchre," they could have bought spices after sundown (Mark 16:1). Then (Mark 16:2) in the early morning, they rose and took the spices and went to anoint his body. It was then that they saw the angel (Matt. 28:5). Matthew does not say that in the visit of 28:1 the angel appeared to them. He speaks of the earthquake having come, and the resurrection, and then resumes. This view gains some support from the use of the same Greek word in Luke 23:54, "And it was the day of the Preparation (Friday) and the Sabbath drew on (was dawning)." Here the meaning seems to be that the Sabbath *dawned* at the close of the day. So Westcott, McClellan and others. However it may be about the visit of the women in Matt. 28:1, Matthew certainly does not mean to say that Jesus rose at sunset on the Sabbath. The whole course of his narrative in the rest of the chapter shows that it was the morning of Sunday when the angel appeared. While (Matt. 28:11) the women went to the disciples, the soldiers ran to the chief priests (Matt. 28:13) and said that the disciples came by *night* and stole him while they slept, clearly implying that it was now day. Hence Matthew does not teach that Jesus rose at sunset, but the reverse. Besides, Matthew expressly says that Jesus rose on the third day, which would not be true, if he rose on the Sabbath.

(d) Sabbath day may be used of the day followed by the night, according to a possible understanding of the language. The Jews originally counted from evening to evening, but this custom did not prevail universally. Jonah (1:17) and Matthew (12:40) speak of three days and three nights, following the day by the night. Meyer, Morison, Clark and others hold this view, and it is possible, but certainly not so satisfactory as the view given under (c). At any rate, it remains clear that Matthew agrees with the other Evangelists in putting the resurrection of Jesus Sunday morning. The chief point of difficulty is Matthew's visit of the women in 28:1, whether this was in the evening before simply "to view the sepulchre," or in the morning to anoint the body of the Saviour. The condensed account of Matthew leaves this question unsettled, and there we too shall have to leave it. And this last matter does not affect the question as to the time of the Lord's resurrection, but only the number of the visits made by the women.

14. The Length of Our Lord's Stay in the Tomb

Quite an effort is made in some quarters to show that Jesus remained in the tomb seventy-two hours, three full days and nights. The effort seems due to a desire to give full value to the expression "three days" and to vindicate scripture. But a minutely literal interpretation of this phrase makes "on the third day" flatly erroneous. A good deal of labor has been expended in the impossible attempt to make three and four equal to each other. There are three sets of expressions used about the matter, besides the express statements of the Gospels about the days of the crucifixion and resurrection. Let us examine these lines of evidence.

1. Luke settles the matter pointedly by mentioning all the time between the crucifixion and the resurrection (Luke 23:50–24:3). The burial took place Friday afternoon just before the Sabbath drew on (Luke 23:54). The women rested on the Sabbath (Saturday) (Luke 23:56), and went to the sepulchre early Sunday morning, the first day of the week (Luke 24:1). There is no escaping this piece of chronology. This is all the time there was between the two events. Jesus then lay in the tomb from late in the afternoon of Friday till early Sunday morning. The other Gospels agree with this reckoning of the time, as we have already seen.

2. But how about the prediction of Jesus, repeatedly made, and once illustrated by the case of Jonah, that he would rise after three days? Are two nights and a day and two pieces of days three days? Let us see.

(a) The well-known custom of the Jews was to count a part of a day as a whole day of twenty-four hours. Hence a part of a day or night would be counted as a whole day, the term day obviously having two senses, as night and day, or day contrasted with night. So then the part of Friday would count as one day, Saturday another, and the part of Sunday the third day. This method of reckoning gives no trouble to a Jew or to modern men, for that matter. In free vernacular we speak the same way today.

(b) Besides, the phrase "on the third day" is obliged to mean that the resurrection took place on that day, for, if it occurred after the third day, it would be on the fourth day and not on the third. Now it so happens that this term "third day" is applied *seven* times to the resurrection of Christ (Matt. 16:21; Matt. 17:23; Matt. 20:19; Luke 27:7, 21, 46; 1 Cor. 15:4). These numerous passages of Scripture, both prophecy and statement of history, agree with the record of the fact that Jesus did rise on the third day. (Luke 24:7.)

(c) Moreover, the phrase "after three days" is used by the same writers (Matthew and Luke) in connection with the former one, "the third day," as meaning the same thing. Hence the definite and clear expressions must explain the one that is less so. The chief priests and Pharisees remember (Matt. 27:63) that Jesus said, after three days I rise again. Hence they urge Pilate to keep a guard over the tomb until the *third day* (Matt. 27:64). This is their own interpretation of the Saviour's words. Besides, in parallel passages in the different Gospels, one will have one expression and another the other, naturally suggesting that they regarded them as equivalent. (Cf. Mark 8:31 with Matt. 16:21, Luke 9:22 with Mark 10:34.) On the third day cannot mean on the fourth day, while after three days can be used as meaning on the third day.

(d) Matthew 12:40 is urged as conclusive the other way. But the "three days and three nights" may be nothing more than a longer way of saying three days, using day in its long sense. And we have already seen that the Jews counted any part of this full day (day and night) as a whole day (day and night). Hence this passage may mean nothing more than the common "after three days" above mentioned, and, like that expression, must be interpreted in accordance with the definite term "on the third day" and with the clear chronological data given by Luke and the rest. They seemed to be conscious of no discrepancy in these various expressions. Most likely they understood them as well as we do at any rate.

A LIST OF THE PARABLES OF JESUS

The Sign of the Temple, § 31.
The Physician, § 39 (cf. § 47).
The Three Parables about the New Dispensation, § 48.
The Blind Guiding the Blind, The Mote and the Beam, § 54.
The Wise and Foolish Builders, § 54.
The Children in the Market Place, § 57.
The Two Debtors, § 59.
Parables about Satan's Kingdom, § 61.
The Unclean Spirit that Returned, § 62.
The Sower, § 64.
The Seed Growing of Itself, § 64.
The Tares, § 64.
The Mustard Seed, §§ 64 and 110.
The Leaven, §§ 64 and 110.
The Hid Treasure, § 64.
The Pearl of Great Price, § 64.
The Net, § 64.
The Scribe, § 64.
The Parable of Corban, § 77.
The Unmerciful Servant, § 92.
The Good Shepherd, § 101.
The Good Samaritan, § 103.
The Importunate Friend, § 105.
The Rich Fool, § 108.
The Waiting Servants, § 108.
The Wise Steward, § 108.
The Fig Tree, § 109.
Seats at Feasts, § 114.
Feast for the Poor, § 114.
The Great Supper, § 114.
The Tower and the King, § 115.
The Lost Sheep, § 116 (cf. § 91).
The Lost Coin, § 116.
The Lost Son, § 116.
The Unrighteous Steward, § 117

The Rich Man and Lazarus, § 117.
Unprofitable Servants, § 117.
The Importunate Widow, § 121.
The Pharisee and the Publican, § 121.
The Laborers in the Vineyard, § 124.
The Pounds, § 127.
The Two Sons, § 132.
The Wicked Husbandmen, § 132.
The Rejected Stone, § 132.
The Marriage Feast and the Wedding Garment, § 132.
The Fig Tree, § 139.
The Porter, § 139.
The Master and the Thief, § 139.
The Wise Servant, § 139.
The Ten Virgins, § 139.
The Talents, § 139.
The Sheep and the Goats, § 139.

A LIST OF THE MIRACLES OF JESUS

The Water Made Wine, § 29.

The Courtier's Son, § 38.

The First Draught of Fishes, § 41.

The Capernaum Demoniac, § 42.

Simon's Mother-in-law, § 43.

A Leper, § 45

The Paralytic, § 46.

The Impotent Man, § 49.

The Man with a Withered Hand, § 51.

The Centurion's Servant, § 55.

The Widow's Son, § 56.

A Blind and Dumb Man, § 61.

The Stilling of the Storm, § 65.

The Gadarene Demoniacs, § 66.

The Woman with an Issue of Blood, § 67.

Jairus' Daughter, § 67.

Two Blind Men, § 68.

A Dumb Demoniac, § 68.

The Five Thousand Fed, § 72.

Jesus Walking on the Water, § 74.

The Phœnician Woman's Daughter, § 78.

The Deaf and Dumb Man, § 79.

The Four Thousand Fed, § 79.

A Blind Man Healed, § 81.

The Demoniac Boy, § 87.

The Shekel in the Fish's Mouth, § 89.

The Man Born Blind, § 100.

The Woman with an Infirmity, § 110.

The Man with the Dropsy, § 114.

The Raising of Lazarus, § 118.

The Ten Lepers, § 120.

Blind Bartimæus and His Companion, § 126.

The Fig Tree Cursed, § 129.

Malchus' Ear, § 153.

The Second Draught of Fishes, § 180.

Besides these particular miracles numerous general groups must be
added, as Mark 6:56; Matt. 4:23 f.; 9:35 f.; Luke 4:40 f.; 5:15 f.;
6:17-19; 7:21 f.; John 2:23; 3:2; 4:45; 20:30; 21:25.

LIST OF OLD TESTAMENT QUOTATIONS IN THE GOSPELS

Mark 1: 2, from Mal. 3:1; Isa. 40:3.
"   1: 3,   "   Isa. 40:3.
"   1:11,   "   Ps. 2:7; Isa. 42:1.
"   1:24,   "   Ps. 16:10.
"   1:44,   "   Lev. 13:49; 14:2–32.
"   2:24,   "   Ex. 20:10; Deut. 5:14; 23:25
"   2:25,   "   Lev. 24:9; 1 Sam. 21:1–6.
"   4:12,   "   Isa. 6:9, 10.
"   4:29,   "   Joel 3:13.
"   4:32,   "   Dan. 4:9.
"   6:18,   "   Lev. 18:16; 20:21.
"   7:6, 7, "   Isa. 29:13.
"   7:10,   "   Ex. 20:12; 21:17; Lev. 20:9; Deut. 5:16.
"   8:18,   "   Isa. 6:9, 10; Jer. 5:21; Ezek. 12:2.
"   8:38,   "   Ps. 62:12; Prov. 24:12.
"   9: 7,   "   Deut. 18:15; Isa. 42:1; Ps. 2:7.
"   9:12,   "   Mal. 4:5.
"   9:13,   "   1 Kings 10:2, 10.
"   9:48,   "   Isa. 66:24.
"   9:49,   "   Lev. 2:13.
"   10: 4,   "   Deut. 24:1.
"   10: 6,   "   Gen. 1:27; 5:2.
"   10:7, 8, "   Gen. 2:24.
"   10:19,   "   Ex. 20:12–17; Deut. 5:16–21.
"   10:27,   "   Gen. 18:14; Job 42:2.
"   11: 9,   "   Ps. 118:26.
"   11:17,   "   Isa. 5:17; Jer. 7:11.
"   12: 2,   "   Isa. 5:1 f.
"   12:10, 11, " Ps. 118:22 f.
"   12:19,   "   Gen. 38:8; Deut. 25:5, 6.
"   12:26,   "   Ex. 3:6.
"   12:29,   "   Deut. 6:4, 6.
"   12:31,   "   Lev. 19:18.
"   12:33,   "   1 Sam 15:22.

Mark 12:36, from Ps. 8:7; 110:1.
"   13:12,   "   Mic. 7:6.
"   13:14,   "   Dan. 9:27.
"   13:19,   "   Dan. 12:1.
"   13:24,   "   Dan. 8:10; Eccl. 12:2; Joel 4:16.
"   13:26,   "   Dan. 7:13.
"   14:12,   "   Ex. 12:18–20.
"   14:18,   "   Ps. 41:9.
"   14:24,   "   Ex. 24:8; Lev. 4:18–20; Jer. 31:31.
"   14:27,   "   Zech. 13:7.
"   14:34,   "   Ps. 42:6.
"   14:62,   "   Ps. 110:1; Dan. 7:13.
"   14:64,   "   Lev. 24:16.
"   15:24,   "   Ps. 22:18.
"   15:34,   "   Ps. 22:1.
Matt. 1: 1–17,   "   1 Chron. 1:34; 2:1–15; 3:1–19.
"   1:23,   "   Isa. 7:14.
"   2: 2,   "   Num. 24:17.
"   2: 6,   "   Mic. 5:1 f.
"   2:15,   "   Hos. 11:1.
"   2:18,   "   Jer. 31:15.
"   3: 3,   "   Isa. 40:3.
"   3:17,   "   Ps. 2:7; Isa. 42:1.
"   4: 4,   "   Deut. 8:3.
"   4: 6,   "   Ps. 91:11.
"   4: 7,   "   Deut. 6:16.
"   4:10,   "   Deut. 6:13.
"   4:15 f.,   "   Isa. 8:23; 9:1 f
"   5: 4,   "   Isa. 61:2.
"   5: 5,   "   Ps. 37:11.
"   5: 6,   "   Ps. 55.
"   5: 7,   "   Ps. 18:25; Prov. 11:17.
"   5: 8,   "   Ps. 24:3–5.
"   5:21 f.,   "   Ex. 20:13; Deut. 5:17.
"   5:27,   "   Ex. 20:14; Deut. 5:18.
"   5:31,   "   Deut. 24:1.
"   5:33 ff.,   "   Ex. 20:7; Num. 30:2; Lev. 19:12; Deut. 5:11; 23:21; Isa. 66:1; Ps. 48:2.
"   5:38,   "   Ex. 21:24; Lev. 24:20; Deut. 19:21.
"   5:43,   "   Lev. 19:18; Deut. 23:6; 25:19.
"   8:11,   "   Isa. 49:12.
"   8:17,   "   Isa. 53:4.

Matt.	9:13,	from	Hos. 6:6.
"	9:36,	"	Num. 27:17; Ezek. 24:5.
"	10:35,	"	Mic. 7:6.
"	11: 5,	"	Isa. 2:18–19; 35:5–6; 61:1.
"	11:10,	"	Mal. 3:1.
"	11:15,	"	Mal. 4:5.
"	11:23,	"	Isa. 14:13–15.
"	11:24,	"	Gen. 19:24.
"	11:29 f.,	"	Jer. 6:16.
"	12: 2,	"	Ex. 20:10; Deut. 5:14; 23:25.
"	12: 3,	"	Lev. 24:9; 1 Sam. 21:1–6.
"	12: 5,	"	Num. 28:9–10
"	12: 7,	"	Hos. 6:6.
"	12:18–21,	"	Isa. 42:1–4.
"	12:40,	"	Jonah 1:17; 2:1–2; 3:5; 4:3; 1 Kings 10:1–10.
"	13:14, 15,	"	Isa. 6:9, 10.
"	13:32,	"	Dan. 4:9–21.
"	13:35,	"	Ps. 78:2.
"	13:43,	"	Dan. 12:3.
"	15: 4,	"	Ex. 20:12; 21:17; Lev. 20:9.
"	15:8, 9,	"	Isa. 29:13.
"	16: 4,	"	Jonah 3:4.
"	16:18,	"	Ps. 89:4, 26, 38, 48.
"	16:27,	"	Ps. 62:12; Prov. 24:12.
"	17: 5,	"	Isa. 42:1; Deut. 18:5; Ps. 2:7.
"	17:11–12,	"	1 Kings 19:2, 10; Mal. 4:5–6.
"	18:16,	"	Deut. 19:15.
"	19: 4,	"	Gen. 1:27; 5:2.
"	19: 5,	"	Gen. 2:24.
"	19: 7,	"	Deut. 24:1.
"	19:18,	"	Ex. 20:12, 13, 14; 21:17; Deut. 5:19, 20.
"	19:19,	"	Lev. 19:18; Ex. 20:12.
"	19:26,	"	Gen. 18:14.
"	21: 5,	"	Isa. 62:11; Zech. 9:9.
"	21: 9,	"	Ps. 118:26.
"	21:13,	"	Isa. 56:7; Jer. 7:11.
"	21:16,	"	Ps. 82.
"	21:33,	"	Isa. 5:1 f.
"	21:42,	"	Ps. 118:22.
"	21:44,	"	Isa. 8:14.
"	22:24,	"	Deut. 25:5.
"	22:32,	"	Ex. 3:6, 15.

Matt. 22:37,   from Deut. 6:5.
  "   22:39,   "   Lev. 19:18.
  "   22:44,   "   Ps. 110:1.
  "   23:5–6,   "   Ex. 13:9; Num. 13:38–39; Deut. 6:8; 11:18.
  "   23:23,   "   Lev. 27:30; Mic. 6:8.
  "   23:35,   "   Gen. 4:8; 2 Chron. 24:20–21.
  "   23:38 f., "   Ps. 118:26; Jer. 12:7; 22:5.
  "   24:15,   "   Dan. 9:27; 11:31; 12:11.
  "   24:21,   "   Dan. 12:1.
  "   24:24,   "   Deut. 13:1.
  "   24:29,   "   Dan. 8:10; Joel 4:16.
  "   24:30,   "   Dan. 7:13; Isa. 13:9–10; Ezek. 32:7–8; Amos
                    8:9; Zeph. 1:14–16.
  "   24:37,   "   Gen. 6:11–13; 7:7, 21–23.
  "   25:31,   "   Zech. 14:5.
  "   25:46,   "   Dan. 12:2.
  "   26:28,   "   Ex. 24:8; Lev. 4:18–20; Jer. 31:31; Zech. 9:11.
  "   26:31,   "   Zech. 13:7.
  "   26:64,   "   Ps. 110:1; Dan. 7:13.
  "   26:65,   "   Lev. 24:16.
  "   27: 6,   "   Deut. 23:18.
  "   27:9, 10, "   Jer. 18:2; 19:2; 32:6; Zech. 11:13.
  "   27:24,   "   Deut. 21, 6–9.
  "   27:34,   "   Ps. 69:21.
  "   27:35,   "   Ps. 22:19.
  "   27:46,   "   Ps. 22:1.
Luke 1:15,   "   Num. 6:3; Judg. 13:4–5; 1 Sam. 1:11.
  "   1:17,   "   Mal. 3:1; 4:5–6.
  "   1:19,   "   Dan. 8:16; 9:21.
  "   1:31,   "   Isa. 7:14.
  "   1:32,   "   2 Sam. 7:12–17.
  "   1:35,   "   Ex. 13:12.
  "   1:38,   "   Gen. 18:14.
  "   1:46 f., "   1 Sam. 2:1–10.
  "   1:48,   "   1 Sam. 1:11.
  "   1:49,   "   1 Sam. 2:2.
  "   1:50,   "   Ps. 103:17.
  "   1:51,   "   1 Sam. 2:4; Ps. 89:10.
  "   1:52,   "   1 Sam. 2:7; Job. 5:11; 12:19.
  "   1:53,   "   1 Sam. 2:5; Ps. 107:9.
  "   1:54,   "   Isa. 41:8–9; Gen. 17:7; Mic. 7:20.
  "   1:59,   "   Lev. 12:3.

Luke	1:68,	from	Ps. 72:18; 111:9.
"	1:69,	"	1 Sam. 2:10; Ps. 18:3.
"	1:71,	"	Ps. 18:4; 106:10.
"	1:72 f.,	"	Gen. 17:7; Lev. 26:42; Ps. 105:8; Mic. 7:20.
"	1:76,	"	Mal. 3:1.
"	1:78,	"	Mal. 4:2.
"	1:79,	"	Isa. 8:22; 9:2.
"	2:21,	"	Gen. 17:12; Lev. 12:3.
"	2:23 f.,	"	Ex. 13:2, 12; Lev. 12:1–8.
"	2:30,	"	Isa. 52:10.
"	2:32,	"	Isa. 42:6; 49:6.
"	2:41,	"	Ex. 23:14–17; Deut. 16:1–8.
"	2:52,	"	1 Sam. 2:26.
"	3:4–6,	"	Isa. 40:3–5.
"	3:22,	"	Ps. 2:7; Isa. 42:1.
"	3:23–38,	"	1 Chron. 1:1–4, 24–28; 2:1–15; 3:17; Ruth 4:18–22.
"	4: 4,	"	Deut. 8:3.
"	4: 8,	"	Deut. 6:13.
"	4:10 f.,	"	Ps. 91:11.
"	4:12,	"	Deut. 6:16.
"	4:18 f.,	"	Isa. 58:6; 61:1 f.
"	4:25–27,	"	1 Kings 17:1; 17:8–9; 18:1–2; 2 Kings 5:1, 14.
"	4:34,	"	Ps. 16:10.
"	5:14,	"	Lev. 13:49; 14:2–32.
"	6: 2,	"	Ex. 20:10; Deut. 5:14; 23:25.
"	6: 3,	"	Lev. 24:9; 1 Sam. 21:1–6.
"	6:21,	"	Isa. 61:2.
"	7:22,	"	Isa. 2:18–19; 35:5–6; 61:1.
"	7:27,	"	Mal. 3:1.
"	8:10,	"	Isa. 6:9 f.
"	10:12,	"	Gen. 19:24.
"	10:15,	"	Isa. 14:13–15.
"	10:27,	"	Lev. 18:5; 19:18; Deut. 6:4 f.
"	11:29,	"	Jonah 3:1–4.
"	11:31,	"	1 Kings 10:1–3.
"	11:32,	"	Jonah 3:5–10.
"	11:42, 51,	"	Lev. 27:30; Gen. 4:8; 2 Chron. 24:20 f.; Mic. 6:8.
"	12:53,	"	Mic. 7:6.
"	13:14, 19,	"	Ex. 20:8–11; Deut. 5:12–15; Dan. 4:10–12, 20 f.
"	13:27, 29,	"	Ps. 6:8; 13:29; 107:3; Isa. 49:12.
"	17:12,	"	Lev. 13:45–46.
"	17:13 f.,	"	Lev. 13:49; 14:1–3.

Luke 17:26,   from Gen. 6:11–13; 7:7, 21–23.
"   17:28, 33,   "   Gen. 18:20–22; 19:24–25; Gen. 19:26.
"   18:20,   "   Ex. 20:12–17; Deut. 5:16–21.
"   19:8, 10,   "   Ex. 22:1; Num. 5:6–7; Ezek. 34:16.
"   19:38,   "   Ps. 118:26.
"   19:46,   "   Isa. 56:7; Jer. 7:11.
"   20:9,   "   Isa. 5:1 f.
"   20:17,   "   Ps. 118:22 f.
"   20:18,   "   Isa. 8:14.
"   20:28, 38,   "   Gen. 38:8; Deut. 25:5 f.; Ex. 3:6.
"   20:42 f.,   "   Ps. 8:7; 110:1.
"   21:20,   "   Dan. 9:27.
"   21:22,   "   Dan. 12:1.
"   21:25 f.,   "   Dan. 8:10; Joel 4:16; Isa. 13:9 f.; Ezek. 32:7 f.;
                         Amos. 8:9; Zeph. 1:14 f.
"   21:27, 28,   "   Dan. 7:13; Deut. 30:4 (LXX); Isa. 27:12 f.;
                         Zech. 2:6 (LXX).
"   22:37,   "   Isa. 53:12.
"   22:46,   "   Ps. 31:5.
"   22:69,   "   Ps. 110:1; Dan. 7:13.
"   23:30,   "   Hos. 10:8.
"   23:46,   "   Ps. 31:6.
"   23:56,   "   Ex. 12:16; 20:8–11; Deut. 5:12–15.
"   24:46,   "   Hos. 6:2.
John 1:23,   "   Isa. 40:3.
"   1:29, 36,   "   Isa. 53:7.
"   1:49,   "   2 Sam. 7:14; Ps. 2:7.
"   1:51,   "   Gen. 28:12.
"   2:18,   "   Ex. 16:4, 15; Neh. 9:15; Ps. 69:9.
"   3:14,   "   Num. 21:8–9.
"   4: 5,   "   Josh. 24:32.
"   5:10,   "   Ex. 20:10; Deut. 5:14.
"   6:14,   "   Deut. 18:15.
"   6:31,   "   Ex. 16:4; Neh. 9:15; Ps. 78:24.
"   6:45,   "   Isa. 54:13.
"   7:22,   "   Gen. 17:9–14; Lev. 12:1–3.
"   7:38,   "   Prov. 18:4.
"   7:42,   "   2 Sam. 7:12; Isa. 11:1; Mic. 5:2.
"   8: 5,   "   Lev. 20:10; Deut. 22:22–24.
"   8:17,   "   Deut. 77:6; 19:15.
"   8:39,   "   Isa. 6:9 f.
"   10:16,   "   Ezek. 35: 23; 37:24.

John 10:34,   from Ps. 82:6.
" 12:13,   " Ps. 118:26.
" 12:14 f.,   " Zech. 9:9.
" 12:27,   " Ps. 42:6.
" 12:38,   " Isa. 53:1.
" 12:40,   " Isa. 6:9 f.,
" 13:18,   " Ps. 41:9.
" 15:25,   " Ps. 35:19; 69:5.
" 16:22,   " Isa. 66:14.
" 17:12,   " Ps. 41:9.
" 19:24,   " Ps. 22:18.
" 19:29,   " Ps. 69:21.
" 19:36,   " Ex. 12:46; Num. 9:12; Ps. 34:21.
" 19:37,   " Zech. 12:10.
" 19:42,   " Deut. 21:22.

A LIST OF SOME UNCANONICAL SAYINGS OF JESUS

Some of the more important reported sayings of Christ are given which are not found in the Gospels or Acts; whether true words of the Master or not, it is not known. Some certainly are not like the Spirit of Christ, but it will be of service to the student to compare them with the genuine Words of Jesus in our Gospels. The Apocryphal Gospels are passed by as not worth using in this list.

1. The Logia of Jesus (Grenfell and Hunt):

Jesus saith: Except ye fast to the world, ye shall in no wise find the Kingdom of God; and except ye keep the Sabbath, ye shall not see the Father.

Jesus saith: I stood in the midst of the world, and in the flesh was I seen of them, and I found all men drunken, and none found I athirst among them, and my soul grieveth over the sons of men because they are blind in their heart.

Jesus saith: Wherever there are . . . and there is one . . . alone, I am with him. Raise the stone and there thou shalt find me, cleave the wood and there am I.

Jesus saith: A prophet is not acceptable in his own country, neither doth a physician work cures upon them that know him.

Jesus saith: A city built upon the top of a high hill and stablished, can neither fall nor be hid.

2. Readings found in Codex D.

One is concerning a man found working on the Sabbath, and comes after Luke 6:4: O man, if indeed thou knowest what thou doest, thou art blessed; but if thou knowest not, thou art cursed and art a transgressor of the law.

Likewise Codex D has, after Matt. 20:28: But you seek to increase from little, and from greater to be less.

3. Quotations found in various early Fathers.

From Barnabas: Let us resist all iniquity, and hold it in hatred. They who wish to see me and lay hold on my kingdom must receive me by affliction and suffering.

From Origen and others: Show yourselves tried money changers.

Ask great things, and the small shall be added to you; and ask heavenly things, and the earthly shall be added unto you.

He who is near me is near the fire: he who is far from me, is far from the kingdom.

For those that are sick I was sick, and for those that hunger, I suffered hunger, and for those that thirst, I suffered thirst.

From Clement of Rome (Ep. II.): Keep the flesh pure, and the seal unspotted.

When the two shall be one, and that which is without as that which is within, and the male with the female neither male nor female.

If ye kept not that which is small, who will give you that which is great? For I say unto you, that he that is faithful in very little is faithful also in much.

From Justin Martyr: In whatsoever I may find you, in this will I also judge you. Such as I may find thee, I will judge thee.

From Ignatius: Take hold, handle me, and see that I am not an incorporeal spirit.

From Clement of Alexandria: He that wonders shall reign, and he that reigns shall rest. Look with wonder at that which is before you. My mystery is for me and for the sons of my house.

From Papias: The days will come in which vines shall spring up, each having ten thousand stocks, and on each stock ten thousand branches, and on each branch ten thousand shoots, and on each shoot ten thousand bunches and on each bunch ten thousand grapes, and each grape when pressed shall give five and twenty measures of wine. And when any saint shall have seized one bunch, another shall cry: I am a better bunch; take me; through me bless the Lord.

SIMILAR INCIDENTS AND CHIEF REPEATED SAYINGS

Calling Disciples: §§ 28, 41, and 53.

Cleansing the Temple: §§ 31 and 129.

Owning Jesus as Messiah: §§ 28, 35, 41, 76, 82, 118.

Rejection at Nazareth: §§ 39 and 69.

Miraculous Draught of Fishes: §§ 41 and 180.

Parables of Mustard Seed and Leaven: §§ 64 (d) and 110.

The Tours of Galilee: §§ 44, 60, and 70.

Healings on the Sabbath: §§ 42, 43, 49–51, 100, 110, 114.

The Lists of the Twelve: §§ 53 and 70.

Courtier's Son and Centurion's Servant: §§ 38 and 55.

The Model Prayer: §§ 54 and 105.

The Anointing of Christ: §§ 59 and 141.

The Blasphemous Accusation: §§ 61, 68, and 106.

Groups of Parables: §§ 64, 91–92, 108, 114–117, 121, 124, 132, 139.

Sending the Twelve and Sending the Seventy: §§ 70 and 102.

Feeding the Five Thousand and the Four Thousand: §§ 72 and 79.

Tests of Discipleship: §§ 76, 83 and 115.

Jesus Foretelling His Death: §§ 31, 83, 85, 86, 88, 125, 139–152.

The Twelve Contending for Supremacy: §§ 90, 125, 144.

Attacking Jesus in Jerusalem: §§ 31, 49, 96–101, 111, 119, 124–135, 153–167.

Foretelling the Second Coming: §§ 84, 120, 127, 139, 148–151.

Divorce: §§ 54 and 122.

Like Children: §§ 90 and 123.

Rewards of Service: §§ 93 and 124.

Worldly Anxieties: §§ 54 and 108.

The Ninety and Nine: §§ 91 and 116.

Baptism of Death: §§ 108 and 125.

The Pounds and the Talents: §§ 127 and 139.

The Agony of Christ: §§ 130 and 152.

Denouncing the Scribes and Pharisees: §§ 61 and 137.

Lament Over Jerusalem: §§ 113, 128, and 137.

About a Sword: §§ 70, 147, 153.

The Three Commissions: §§ 178, 181, and 183.

In general the Later Judean Ministry and the Perean Ministry, chiefly Luke's contribution to the Life of Christ, furnish many events and discourses similar to those described in the Galilean Ministry. Sections 102 to 127 furnish most of the so-called "doublets" or repeated sayings of Jesus or similar miracles. This is just what we should expect in a popular teacher who journeyed in different parts of the country. Some of these were real doublets, spoken by Jesus more than once. Others may be grouped by Luke in a different place. We have no way to decide the problem.